THE
BOOM
&
THE
BOOM

WORLD SCIENCE FICTION STUDIES

VOL. 3

SERIES EDITORS

Professor Sonja Fritzsche, Michigan State University
Professor Gerry Canavan, Marquette University

PETR LANG
Oxford - Berlin - Bruxelles - Chennai - Lausanne - New York

THE BOOM & THE BOOM

HISTORICAL RUPTURE AND POLITICAL ECONOMY IN CONTEMPORARY BRITISH AND CHINESE SCIENCE FICTION

Lyu Guangzhao

PETR LANG
Oxford - Berlin - Bruxelles - Chennai - Lausanne - New York

Bibliographic information published by Die Deutsche Nationalbibliothek
Die Deutsche Nationalbibliothek lists this publication in the Deutsche Nationalbibliografie; detailed bibliographic data is available on the Internet at http://dnb.d-nb.de.

A catalogue record for this book is available from the British Library.

Library of Congress Cataloging-in-Publication Data

Names: Lyu, Guangzhao, 1993- author.
Title: The boom & the boom : historical rupture and political economy in contemporary British and Chinese science fiction / Guangzhao Lyu.
Description: Oxford ; New York : Peter Lang, 2024. | Series: World science fiction studies, 2296-8814 ; volume no. 3 | Originally presented as the author's thesis (doctoral) - University College London, 2022. | Includes bibliographical references and index.
Identifiers: LCCN 2024018088 (print) | LCCN 2024018089 (ebook) | ISBN 9781803742328 (paperback) | ISBN 9781803742335 (ebook) | ISBN 9781803742342 (epub)
Subjects: LCSH: Science fiction, English—History and criticism. | Science fiction, Chinese—History and criticism. | Politics in literature. | Society in literature. | Literature and society—Great Britain. | Literature and society—China. | LCGFT: Literary criticism.
Classification: LCC PR830.S35 L98 2024 (print) | LCC PR830.S35 (ebook) | DDC 823/.0930876209—dc23/eng/20240525
LC record available at https://lccn.loc.gov/2024018088
LC ebook record available at https://lccn.loc.gov/2024018089

This book is sponsored by Shanghai Pujiang Programme (23PJC009).

Cover image: Yisan.
Cover design by Peter Lang Group AG

ISSN 2296-8814
ISBN 978-1-80374-232-8 (print)
ISBN 978-1-80374-233-5 (ePDF)
ISBN 978-1-80374-234-2 (ePub)
DOI 10.3726/b20901

Published by Peter Lang Ltd, Oxford, United Kingdom
info@peterlang.com - www.peterlang.com

This publication has been peer reviewed.

For Yifan, and my parents

Contents

A Note on the Text

All names spelled in Mandarin (pinyin) in this book follow the convention of placing the family name first, followed by the given name.

Acknowledgements

"Beginning a PhD is a significant undertaking." This quote, from the very first email I received in January 2018 from my supervisor at UCL, James Kneale, has been a constant source of courage and confidence throughout the years. It has guided me through all the difficulties, accidents, stresses and the challenges posed by the COVID lockdown, ultimately allowing me to complete my PhD thesis, which becomes the basis of this book. Without his steadfast support and guidance, both academically and emotionally, both in-person and online, this book – along with several journal publications and conference presentations stemming from it – would have been an impossible task. Meanwhile, I extend my heartfelt gratitude to my second supervisor, Lu Xiaoning from SOAS, who has been willing to overcome all the administrative obstacles and joins this cross-university supervision team. Over the years, she has provided insightful perspectives on contemporary Chinese society and culture, ensuring that this project stays on track.

I feel extremely grateful to my PhD examiners, Mark Bould and Song Mingwei, for their kind words and constructive suggestions during my viva in September 2022. Their encouraging comments and remarks in their examination report continue to inspire me, and I wish I can ever live up to the praise they offered. Special thanks are owed to Gerry Canavan and Sonja Fritzsche, editors of Peter Lang's *World Science Fiction Studies* series, for placing their trust in this project, reaching out to me even before the manuscript was completed. I express my thanks to Laurel Plapp, senior acquisitions editor at Peter Lang, for her efforts in coordinating the revision and publication of this book. Additionally, my sincere appreciation goes to the two anonymous reviewers whose detailed reports have significantly contributed to making this a better book.

As I worked on this project, I had the privilege of engaging with diverse academic communities, allowing for the exchange of ideas with colleagues and comrades in comparative literature and science fiction studies – especially Centre for Multidisciplinary and Intercultural Inquiry at University College London, where I earned my degree, and College of Foreign Languages and Literature at Fudan University in Shanghai, my current academic home. I express my profound gratitude to Angela Chan, with whom I co-convened the London Chinese Science Fiction Group (LCSFG) in April 2019. Under her watch, the group has gradually gained recognition for our efforts in introducing Chinese science fiction to English-speaking readers. I also had the pleasure of working with a fantastic team at the London Science Fiction Research Community (LSFRC), where I co-organized reading groups and conferences alongside Francis Gene-Rowe, Tom Dillon, Rachel Hill, Katie Stone, Sasha Myerson, Ibtisam Ahmed, Josie Taylor, Avery Delany, Cristina Diamant and Ma Chen (Mia). Both experiences at LCSFG and LSFRC have been invaluable to this book. Special mention should go to the Science Fiction Research Association for acknowledging my previous achievements and awarding me their "Support a New Scholar" grant (2021–2). Also, I could not have survived my PhD without peer support at UCL, including He Sui, Liang Meng, Byron Byrne-Taylor, Tom Kelly, Lydia Hayes, Firdevs Bulut, Mathis Jonathan Olafson, Izabella Wódzka, Viktoria Herold and many others.

I often joked that my accommodation rents over the years in London were truly worth it because I barely went outside my room due to the COVID lockdown, staying there twenty-four hours a day, seven days a week. I feel very fortunate to have met a group of wonderful friends at Goodenough College during such a difficult time, most notably Feng Kaiyun and Han Xiao, who made my life in London beyond good enough. Thank you for always being there in every possible way and for showing me that pursuing a doctoral degree does not have to be a one-person quest.

I wish to extend my appreciation to people who believe in me and entrusted me with various opportunities for academic collaboration and cooperation: Wu Yan, Song Mingwei, Li Guangyi, Zhang Feng, Cheng Lin, Chen Ling, Yao Lifen, Xi Kun, Veronica Hollinger, Paul March-Russell, Andrew M. Butler, Nick Hubble, Polina Levontin, Jo Lindsay Walton, Yen Ooi, Regina Kanyu Wang, Angus Stewart, July Blalack, Tasnim Qutait,

Frances Weightman, Sarah Dodd, Giuseppe Porcaro, Stewart Baker and Phoenix Alexander.

Apart from James's email I've mentioned at the start, the other phrase I have remembered for these years is from my parents: "We are always on your side." Beginning a PhD is a significant undertaking not only because it is a hard and dangerous safari (although it is rewarding) where many have gone astray in the wilderness of ideas, but also because of mental damage. I cannot even think of this book without my parents' emotional support and sacrifices. Also standing on my side is my partner, Xu Yifan, who not only tolerates my complaints when having difficulties starting a new paragraph (even a new sentence! Apologies) but also actively engages in discussions about my research (she's the first reader of everything I write). Her unwavering support, understanding and encouragement have been my pillars of strength throughout this journey. Despite the distance between China and the UK, she has consistently shown care and love, making this academic pursuit a more enriching and emotionally fulfilling experience. I am immensely grateful for her presence in my life.

Some portions of this books have been originally published in the following journals, and I thank the editors for permission to reuse the following materials as part of this book:

- "A Nostalgic Return to the Future: The Utopian Dialectic in Hao Jingfang's *Vagabonds*." *Utopian Studies* 32, no. 3 (2021): 636–51.
- "Demise of False Utopia: China's Post-socialist Transition in Han Song's *Red Star over America*." *Science Fiction Studies* 49, no. 1 (2022): 100–19.
- "From a Pin to an Elephant: Politics of Consumption and the Debordian Spectacle in James Lovegrove's *Days*." *Critique: Studies in Contemporary Fiction*, online first (2023).
- "Past the Point of No Return: Deleuzian Deterritorialization in M. John Harrison's *Kefahuchi Tract* Trilogy." *Science Fiction Studies* 50, no. 2 (2023): 197–215.
- "The Dark Forest: An Economized Hunting Ground for Human Capital in *Three Body Trilogy*." *Comparative Critical Studies* 19, no. 3 (2022): 361–79.

- "The Money Fetish and the Politics of Prosumption in Long Yi's *Earth Province*." *Foundation* #145 (2023): 34–46.
- "Waste People and the Vampiric Society: Heterotopia of Migrant Workers in Chen Qiufan's *Waste Tide*." *Extrapolation* 62, no. 3 (2021): 309–29.

Abbreviations

ANR	Army of the New Republic
BBC	British Broadcasting Corporation
BNOC	British National Oil Corporation
BRI	Belt and Road Initiative
BwO	body without organs
CASS	Chinese Academy of Social Sciences
CAST	China Association for Science and Technology
CCPPD	Publicity Department of the Communist Party of China
CINIC	China Internet Network Information Center
CWA	China Writers Association
DCMS	Department for Culture, Media and Sport
DNH	Department of National Heritage
GDP	Gross Domestic Product
GLC	Greater London Council
IPO	Initial Public Offering
LCSFG	London Chinese Science Fiction Group
LSE	London School of Economics and Political Science
LSFRC	London Science Fiction Research Community
MAD	Mutual Assured Destruction
NCB	National Coal Board
NHS	National Health Service

NUM	National Union of Miners
PFI	Private Finance Initiative
PVC	Polyvinyl chloride
QE	Quantitative Easing
SASAC	State-owned Assets Supervision and Administration Commission
SFRA	Science Fiction Research Association
SFS	*Science Fiction Studies*
SFW	*Science Fiction World*
SOAS	School of Oriental and African Studies, University of London
SOE	state-owned enterprises
USS	Universities Superannuation Scheme Limited
UUK	Universities UK
WSFS	World Science Fiction Society
WTO	World Trade Organization

INTRODUCTION

Mapping the Field : The Boom and the Boom

> There certainly seems to be something of a boom.
>
> – China Miéville, in an interview with Andrew M. Butler

Back in the fall of 2018, when I just arrived in London as a newly enrolled doctoral student embarking on a project on science fiction (sf), I was told there was one place I simply cannot afford to miss – the sf megastore Forbidden Planet in Holborn, which was a wise idea. I ventured to the store and, not long after, my attention was captured by a book bearing an intriguing title: *The City & The City*, authored by China Miéville. Published in 2009, this novel introduces an unusual duality of two cities Besźel and Ul Qoma. They share pretty much the same geographical space but remain invisible to each other. This invisibility is the result of a long-term socialization, where citizens of each city are disciplined from childhood to *unsee* their neighbours from the other city, even when walking the same streets. Any contact or interaction, unless officially authorized, is considered a serious felony.

This setting feels extraordinary to me. Out of curiosity, I set out on a quest to learn more about its author Miéville. I noticed that long before *The City & The City*, he had already gained reputation for his earlier works, regarded as one of the pioneers whose writings are well known for the "liquefaction of generic frontiers" between sf, fantasy, detective fiction and others (Edwards and Venezia, "Unintroduction" 6). These achievements have made him unique in the latest resurgence of British sf – "something of a *boom*" in his own words as he spoke to Andrew M. Butler during an interview in 2002 (Butler, "Beyond" 7; emphasis added). At that moment, Miéville found himself unable to pinpoint the exact nature of the "boomness" or "boomtitude" he alluded to, leaving his discussion suspended with a rather ambiguous declaration: "[T]he fact that everyone's talking about it is to a certain extent definitional of the fact that something's going on"

(Butler, "Beyond" 7). One year later, Istvan Csicsery-Ronay, Jr. offered a gentle reminder that whatever the boom refers to, it is "not a writer's or critic's term" ("Editorial" 353). Instead, it is borrowed from the domain of economics, representing a surge in the cultural marketplace of intellectual capital, which not only brings commercial gains but also sparks a burst of creativity in British sf.

This "boom" that had come into spotlight at the turn of the twenty-first century is now termed the British SF Boom, though there are several dates suggested for the Boom's first ignition. It could be the time when *Interzone* came into being in spring 1982, a quality magazine where British sf writers could "present their new works unhindered by the too often myopic demands of sf magazines in the US" (Carr 37), "one that contributed significantly to the culture of science fiction in Britain" with the support of a new generation of British authors (Ashley 133). It could also be the publication of Iain M. Banks's *Consider Phlebas* in 1987 which drew "non-traditional readers into the genre" (Bould, "Bould" 308). Apart from those early hints of the Boom, Mark Bould claims that the Boom began in 1990, "the richest year in terms of symbolic events" (Bould, "Bould" 308). Among these events was the release of the steampunk novel *The Difference Machine* by William Gibson and Bruce Sterling, which not only takes place in a British setting but also has a British first edition and a pre-publication excerpt featured in *Interzone* (Bould, "Bould" 308). Another noteworthy event in that same year was the publication of Colin Greenland's *Take Back Plenty*, marking the first British novel to secure the Arthur C. Clarke Award. Meanwhile, *Interzone*, already solidifying its status as an essential platform for British sf and being held in high regard alongside its prestigious American counterparts such as *Asimov's*, *F&SF* and *Analog* in terms of both quality and influence (Ashley 134), changed to a monthly publishing schedule. For Andrew M. Butler, the pivotal year of the British Boom was 1995, highlighting Jeff Noon's victory in the John W. Campbell Award for best new sf writer and the release of Ken MacLeod's *The Star Fraction* (qtd. in Bould, "Bould" 309). This intricacy in defining the Boom provides a unique space to investigate the historical transition in the UK during the long 1990s – or, to use terms with *political savvy*, during the Thatcherite and post-Thatcherite eras.

Nevertheless, just like Besźel and Ul Qoma in Miéville's *The City & The City*, the British SF Boom did not see its neighbour – another boom of sf emerging rather simultaneously in China in the 1990s. This "Chinese SF Boom" is initially known as the "Chinese SF New Wave" (Song M., "After 1989" 8), shaped by the tremendous and continuous contributions of "New-born Generation" sf writers during the past three decades (Wu Y. et al. 52). Though the term "Chinese New Wave" is not coined to relate to the Anglo-American new wave in the mid-1960s and the 1970s when Song Mingwei first proposed it, he contends in his 2023 monograph *Fear of Seeing* that these two distinct "new waves" converge in their capacity to unveil the "invisible" realms of reality. The notion of the "invisible" persists as a symbolic motif, signifying domains that transcend our conventional perception, providing a vehicle to portray our fears and aspirations, and also challenging established ethical norms and political ideologies.

While I essentially agree with "Chinese New Wave," I wish to propose an alternative name: Chinese SF Boom. This choice of term holds a two-fold intention. Firstly, it mirrors the nomenclature of the British SF Boom, enabling a comparative reading of the two sf booms that were previously ignorant of each other. Secondly, analogous to the British SF Boom that signifies the rise of British sf over its American counterpart in the global sf market, the term "Chinese SF Boom" also resounds with the remarkable success of Chinese sf in the commercial field since the 1990s. This not only emphasizes on its market prowess but also invites scholarly inquiry to explore the socio-political context behind its burgeoning popularity.

This popularity has even transcended boundaries and borders, with Chinese sf attracting worldwide attention. A watershed moment arrived in 2015 when Liu Cixin's *The Three-Body Problem*, translated into English by Ken Liu, won the Hugo Award for Best Novel – a historic milestone as the first non-English work to receive such acclaim. Subsequently, stories of the Chinese SF Boom, old and new alike, have been translated one after another for non-Chinese-speaking readers, collected in anthologies and magazines, introduced in sf conventions and conferences and discussed in academic journals.[1] Despite its unprecedented popularity both among

1 Here, I am aware of a longstanding critique within postcolonial studies which highlights that a significant portion of what has been translated and/or published

and beyond Chinese readership in very recent years, the Chinese Boom, whether dating from 1989 or 1991 from different perspectives to be discussed later, is in fact deeply rooted in, and even nurtured by, the fundamental social and cultural shifts during the 1990s in China. It is a historical transition away from the discourse of new enlightenment and elitism of the 1980s to a post-socialist condition where "the constant noise of commercialization in the background and the ever-evolving institutional and conceptual changes that have accompanied economic reforms" (Kong 3) can never be neglected.

Although the two sf booms in China and the UK were cultivated in an epoch of transition and rupture, of breaking with the past and travelling to the new (if the "newness" can ever be reached), their unawareness of each other is not surprising – especially given the preference of Chinese readers for American sf works. An exception might be Arthur C. Clarke, who is perhaps the most well-known British sf writer familiar to Chinese fandom (alongside Isaac Asimov, Robert Heinlein, Philip K. Dick and William Gibson, among others). His influence in China goes even higher nowadays as the "mentor" of the Hugo-winning Liu Cixin. But still, Clarke is usually viewed as "the British writer who comes closest to the *American* model of sf promoted by Campbell" (Luckhurst, *Science Fiction* 133; emphasis added) and his stories are best accepted with features echoing the American Golden Age. Therefore, during the 1990s, China was celebrated for a wide-spreading interest in the American sf, which accounts for "at least one third of all titles in translation" (Jiang 123), whereas writers of the British Boom remained voiceless in the Chinese market.

as "postcolonial literature" in the global north is often limited to material that aligns with Anglo-American perceptions and concepts of the global south. In other words, writers from the global south might feel compelled to tailor their work to suit a global north audience in order to secure publication or translation opportunities. This is also evident in the translation of Chinese sf. The distinctive "Chineseness" of Chinese sf is frequently invoked as a marketing label, even though this approach often leads to skewed receptions and misinterpretations. With this label, according to Virginia L. Conn, the production of Chinese sf "attempts to describe a 'China' that is recognizably legible as a single entity while also being understandable by a non-Chinese audience" (84), which, however, often yields a simplistic and biased outcome.

In the meantime, Chinese sf also encountered an equal invisibility in the UK. Back then, Chinese sf works were largely marginalized by the mainstream Chinese literature, "never given recognition as 'serious' writing" (Pohl viii), and rarely translated into English at all. Even in the few occasions where they did appear in translation, "they seldom reached a wide audience" (vii). According to Fei Dao, one of the Chinese Boom authors, Chinese sf was like "a hidden lonely army [...] laid low in the wilderness where nobody really cared to look at it" (see Song M., "Introduction" xi), but this, of course, is now changing. Signed copies of the latest translations of Liu Cixin, Chen Qiufan, Hao Jingfang and Han Song found themselves side by side with those written by Adrian Tchaikovsky, Ian McDonald, Neal Asher, Tade Thompson and others. And concurrently, classical works of the British SF Boom that have also been translated into Chinese – including those of Iain M. Banks, China Miéville, Alastair Reynolds and Charles Stross – have also managed to create a favourable readership in China, though still a long way from their American counterparts.

Of course, the simultaneous emergence of these two sf booms is not merely a historical coincidence. They were both conceived and nurtured amidst profound socio-cultural transformations within the two countries, brought about by a myriad of reforms in political economy orchestrated by Margaret Thatcher and Deng Xiaoping. Since the Thatcher decade, the increasing tension at the heart of British culture indicates "a break with the past and the apparent shininess of all things new, on the one hand, and an aching acknowledgement of the still powerful and destructive effects of the past on the other" (Tew et al. 16). Similarly, over the same time, China made every endeavour to adapt to a different economic structure and a cultural narrative shaped by epochal shifts. These years of change for both the UK and China, spanning from the late twentieth century onwards, have not only borne witness to but also propelled the rejuvenation of sf in the two countries – an era defined by a succession of robust economic reforms geared towards privatization and commodification.

This process has effectively fostered self-reliance, intensified social competition and heightened efficiency. As a result, it is shrouded in the shadow of Francis Fukuyama's contentious proclamation about the end of history – a claim that heralded the triumph of free-market capitalism.

Mark Fisher, influenced by Fredric Jameson and Slavoj Žižek, reiterates the term "capitalist realism" in a tone of irony and criticism, elaborating on a discourse in which "it is easier to imagine the end of the world than it is to imagine the end of capitalism" (Fisher, *Capitalist Realism* 2). In this case, how do the two sf booms reflect on and respond to such dramatic transformations concerning cultural politics? How do they function in repositioning Britain and China in the post-Thatcher and post-Deng eras? Can they provide or imagine approachable alternatives to the ostensibly inescapable capitalist realism?

Before delving into particular texts to address these intriguing queries directly, the following section of this chapter will serve to introduce the historical trajectories of market-oriented reforms in both Britain and China. This aims to map out the intellectual field since the late 1980s where the drive for privatization, by which responsibilities are transferred from the state to individuals, have fundamentally reshaped the two societies. I will look back into the politico-economic and literary histories, arguing that the dawning of the two sf booms both in China and Britain are deeply rooted in the social change of the two countries in the 1980s and 1990s, when the state retreated from social provision and left individuals to bear the costs of market competition. The British SF Boom steadfastly upholds a critical standpoint against right-wing politics. Over time, it has evolved into an organic form of rebellion that specifically targets the cultural governance framework propagated during and after the Thatcher era – a framework that incorporates cultural production within the domain of political discipline.

In comparison, however, the Chinese SF Boom has developed a much more ambiguous relation with China's market boom engineered by Deng Xiaoping in the 1990s. The rise of the market fostered a "bottom-up" discourse that amplified the voice of the mass public, which took the place of the "top-down" elitism of the 1980s that almost killed Chinese sf during the political campaign against "spiritual pollution" (1983–4). And it is because of this bottom-up discourse that Chinese sf has gained a new dynamism. However, the Chinese Boom offers a more complicated response to its historical context than its British counterpart. Apart from its critiques of the consequence of China's market turn, such as regional or urban-rural unevenness, social stratification, economic deprivation and the widening gap between the rich and the poor, Chinese sf sometimes also conveys a sense of hesitance, confusion and nostalgia. The pursuit of a socialist utopia and people's endeavours to achieve modernization are still an important part of the contemporary Chinese dream.

In such an era of change, writers of the British and the Chinese SF Booms find themselves immediately confronting a moment of historical rupture. The past is gone, but what to come is not always what people have expected. Therefore, the Boom writers resort to a theme with a centuries-long history, one that writes about hope, alternative, possibility and difference, something needed most urgently to undermine capitalist realism where the wellspring of imagination appears to have run dry. That is utopia. In Chapter 1, I will examine two of the most influential utopias in contemporary British and Chinese sf: the Amanduo society in Han Song's *Red Star Over America* (2000) and the Culture created by Iain M. Banks. With the sense of "eeriness" in his writings, Han Song usually blends the imageries of utopia and dystopia, blurring the boundaries between "good" and "bad" places and creating a new form of utopianism that accounts for the rapid social transition in China since the 1990s. Drawing on Tom Moylan's "critical utopia" and Mikhail Bakhtin's "chronotope," I will argue that the collapse of Amanduo – the almighty AI network governing a socialist utopia – reflects the decline of top-down elitist discourse in China during the 1980s, and the protagonist's journey in the post-Amanduo world represents China's ideological transition during the post-socialist era.

Compared to Amanduo, Banks's intergalactic Culture has a much stronger and clearer message to deliver. Out of his dissatisfaction and distrust of Thatcherism, Banks envisions a post-scarcity, post-hierarchical, and post-capitalist leftist utopia called the Culture, prefiguring the possibility of an alternative world beyond late capitalism. At the same time, however, the Culture appears less utopian once perceived from its opponent's perspective. During the Idiran-Culture war in *Consider Phlebas* (1987) and the Azad Game in *The Player of Games* (1988), the Culture's triumph indicates a historical shift from imperial empires (like the Idirans and the Azadians) to the rhizomic Empire conceptualized by Michael Hardt and Antonio Negri.

Chapter 2 provides a different way of reading and building utopias. They are depicted not merely as specific locations with defined social or ideological frameworks, but rather as an ongoing dialectical *process*. Within this context, nothing remains rigidly fixed, as the landscape remains open to continuous experimentation and scrutiny. In *Vagabonds* (2011–12), Hao Jingfang sets up not one single but two opposing worlds: the libertarian Earth that welcomes market competition and individualistic pursuit for capital and the egalitarian Martian Republic built upon scarcity and under the supervision of a central archive system that provides social welfare and protection. However, neither of the two societies is perfect enough to be called a true utopia. People in both societies see the other world as the negation of their own, though this, again, simply invites them to an unending cycle of "negating the negation."[2] This, I believe, represents another stage of China's post-socialist transition, invoking a utopian hope for a post-post-socialist alternative.

Similarly, Ken MacLeod also delves deep into the concept of the simultaneous existence of various utopian visions, taking his exploration even further than Hao Jingfang. In his *Fall Revolution* quartet (1995–9), MacLeod resorts to a Nozickian idea of meta-utopianism and creates a space that literally welcomes all kinds of possible societies – ranging from libertarian anarchy to religious fundamentalism – among which everyone would be able to find a niche they prefer. Usually considered "left-wing struggles against neoliberal consensus" (Winter, *Science Fiction* 91), this quartet, based on meta-utopianism, is written against the sense of historical exhaustion in the 1990s, a time when "revivalism replaced radicalism, and an ersatz nostalgia displaced both anticipation and expectation" (Tew et al. 18).

On top of "historical rupture," another pivotal keyword in this book is "political economy." With this, I will explore the critical response of the British and Chinese SF Booms to the economic context characterized by capitalist realism and biopolitics, where social subjects are systematically

2 The process of "negating the negation" is a key component of the Hegelian dialectical method, where a negation (a contradiction or opposition) is itself negated, leading to a higher level of understanding or synthesis. It suggests that contradictions and conflicts within a particular system or idea can lead to its transformation and the emergence of something new, often at a higher level of development.

reshaped to conform to the dictates of market competition. Chapter 3, centred on Chen Qiufan's *Waste Tide* (2013), will shed light on the plight of migrant workers in China, vividly portrayed as "waste people." These migrant labourers find themselves ensnared in the dichotomy of "economic acceptance" and "social rejection," forming an autonomous community that can be conceptualized through Michel Foucault's notion of heterotopia. Out of the humiliation inflicted upon them by the Silicon Isle natives and the resulting mentality of failure and trauma, the waste people cultivate a fervent desire for change and transgression. Yet, their efforts and sacrifices for self-liberation ultimately prove futile, as they unwittingly become victims of the vampiric logic inherent in the relentless forces of market competition.

Drawing a parallel between *Waste Tide* and China Miéville's New Weird novel *Perdido Street Station* (2000), which ingeniously melds the realistic elements of contemporary London to craft the fictional city of New Crobuzon, I will also employ Foucault's heterotopia to examine the social marginality experienced by non-human communities in the shadow of human-dominated mainstream discourse. This ongoing struggle between the centre and the periphery is further underscored by a greater peril embodied by the capitalist monstrosities known as "slake-moths," insatiable predators that feed on the sentience of individuals, regardless of their ethnic origins. This can be further perceived as the materialization of the capitalist logic per se and its exploitive nature.

Chapter 4 starts with a historical account of the general decline of class consciousness in the UK throughout the 1980s when the vision of personal affluence was increasingly connected to people's choice in the marketplace, rather than their class identity at the sites of mass production. Personal desires are recognized by the Thatcher government and taken as the motivation to pursue a unique style of life – a marker of Thatcherite individualism – through consumption. Therefore, in this chapter, I will read one of James Lovegrove's early novels, *Days* (1997), as an example of the consumer dreamland in which a different political identity can be formed. This consumption-based identity, however, is established upon the production not of material commodities but of Debordian spectacles. These politicized consumers, as I will argue, never attain the status of liberated agents within the intricate web of social production. They are, instead, spectators in the Debordian sense, who are granted not a political subjectivity but a collective unconscious.

From such a politics of consumption, I will then move to Long Yi's *Earth Province* (2018), a narrative that paints a portrait of a society deeply entrenched in the fetishism of money. Within this dystopian landscape, individuals are compelled to pay taxes for virtually every aspect of their lives, including the basic acts of breathing and having sex, while human bodies are commodified and marketed as consumable meat exported to extra-terrestrial beings. I will read this novel as a representation of China's market-oriented discourse after the post-socialist transition, especially the rise of a prosumer economy (George Ritzer) that allows for a "double exploitation" – where people are exploited both as labourers and consumers, where there emerges a synergic implosion of both production and consumption.

Such a sense of capitalist exploitation in *Earth Province* is also represented in Liu Cixin's famous thought experiment: the Dark Forest. In the final chapter, I will argue that his *Three-Body* trilogy (2006–10) has become more than a work of sf. It has reached beyond the domain of literature, becoming a broader social and cultural phenomenon during China's historical transformation since the 1990s. A metaphor of post-socialist modernity in China, the Dark Forest proposes a new politico-economic discourse where the subject is remade into human capital and where competitive market principles penetrate every social sphere. Through investigating the impulse of dehumanization, I will also argue that this process of turning people into "non-people" is a literary representation of the process of "economization" in China's current reality. And in this way, the *Three-Body* trilogy introduces an irreconcilable dichotomy between the Self and the Other, indicating an alienated humanism that sacrifices morality and humanity for the sake of survival.

It should be noted that this is also a "root-tree" structure that Gilles Deleuze and Félix Guattari wish to challenge, where the Multiple always originates from the One – a structure that nourishes all kinds of exploitation. Searching for a path of escape, or a line of flight in the Deleuzo-Guattarian terminology, I am introduced to M. John Harrison's *Kefahuchi Tract* trilogy

(2002–12), which guides us towards our eventual deterritorialization and liberates us from the capitalist realism and the self-centredness with competition and calculation in nature. Under the mysterious halo of the Kefahuchi Tract, all binary structures are deformed. This interrogates real-world capitalist realism where history has shifted its direction towards the market – something of a historical rupture to which both the Chinese and British SF Boom attempt to respond.

A Journey to the Right: The Rise of Thatcherism

When Roger Luckhurst writes about Ken MacLeod's *Fall Revolution* series[3] – comprised of *The Star Fraction* (1995), *The Stone Canal* (1996), *The Cassini Division* (1998) and *The Sky Road* (1999) – in his 2003 article on the British SF Boom and cultural governance in the UK (as part of the ground-breaking special issue on the British SF Boom of *Science Fiction Studies*), one single character is highlighted repetitively: David Reid.

In the novels, Reid is first known as a computer science student at the University of Glasgow in the mid-1970s, and a passionate Trotskyist who often mocks the libertarian and anarchist thoughts of his friend and later archenemy Jonathan Wilde. But as we follow Reid into the late 1980s and the 1990s, we see him slide into disenchantment from his once-fervent belief in socialism and the Fourth International, pursuing a personal agenda that gradually leads him rightward. Reid feels beaten when he speaks to Wilde in the 1995 setting of *The Stone Canal* (about the time when MacLeod wrote the novels): "I haven't changed my ideas, long-term, but I know a defeat when I see one […] The last time I hung out with the left was during the Gulf War. The kids don't know shit, and the older guys […] that is, the ones older than us, *they look like men who've been told they have cancer*" (114; emphasis added).

3 A more comprehensive and in-depth analysis of the *Fall Revolution* series will be presented in Chapter 2.

Eventually, these observations lead him to establish another society on New Mars; a new world accessed through a wormhole, founded upon nothing else but free market and commercial contracts – the purest wonderland for anarcho-capitalism. Luckhurst takes seriously Reid's conversion from Trotskyism to a radical anti-statist position. He argues that Reid embodies "a historically accurate trajectory of the Left in late twentieth-century Britain," and his mental shift represents "how elements of the 'hard left' in the 1970s flipped over into a libertarian embrace of the subversive possibilities of the capitalism in the 1990s" (Luckhurst, "Cultural" 430).

This, of course, is not an overstatement. Propelled by the intellectual contributions of cultural materialists like Raymond Williams and E. P. Thompson, among others, the British left rose to prominence during the 1960s. It played a pivotal role in shaping a radical political discourse deeply intertwined with a multitude of interconnected cultural movements led by a cadre of far-left intellectuals and activists. This ascent of the British left unfolded against the backdrop of the post-war "Consensus Period" of the welfare state, characterized by a steadfast commitment to policies designed to diminish social inequalities, establish a safety net for the vulnerable and ensure access to essential services such as healthcare, education and social security. Significantly, this era also witnessed a substantial expansion of trade unions, the practice of collective bargaining and a prevailing belief in the government's role in addressing pressing social and economic challenges.

For the political activist Tariq Ali, editor of the radical newspaper *Black Dwarf* and leading figure in the International Marxist Group (IMG, with which the young Reid also identifies himself in the *Fall Revolution* series), such a surge in cultural radicalism and industrial militancy that we can see from the British left provides something revolutionary – a vision of change, hope or in his own words: "[T]he only real alternative to capitalist policies [...] the only way forward" (Ali 10). Despite Ali's enthusiasm and optimism, however, from the mid-1970s the British left began to fall as sharply as it had ascended, in line with the decline of the Consensus Period. In MacLeod's series, this is the moment in history when Reid began his study in Glasgow. Due to the lingering impact of the oil crisis, the UK economy was suffering from a persistent "stagflation." The simultaneous high-level inflation and unemployment, as the symptoms of a continuous economic stagnation and an overloaded public expenditure on social welfare during the 1970s, had arguably created an unprecedented dilemma for the Keynesian practices that were usually adopted by the social democratic government. To increase money supply – a conventional Keynesian tactic to stimulate economic growth and create jobs – would only drive prices and the inflation rate even higher.

Therefore, the tenure of Prime Minister James Callaghan, who sought to consolidate the social democratic strategy inherited from his predecessors and aimed at constructing a "cohesive society" (Callaghan 398) through sustained cooperation between trade unions and the government, was abruptly disrupted by a series of industrial conflicts and mounting tensions. These challenges arose as a direct consequence of his ill-fated endeavour to enforce a stringent 5 per cent wage increase cap as a measure to combat inflation, which not only failed to address the economic issues at hand but also exacerbated social discontent. In the face of "the general tide of disillusionment and dislike" against the Labour government (Callaghan 540) culminating at the Winter of Discontent that ate up 30 million working days, three times as many as in 1978 (Beckett 464–5), Margaret Thatcher, Callaghan's successor, was required to propose an alternative mechanism that could bring the UK out of economic recession and restore its international competitiveness.[4] This aspiration was evident in the Conservative Party's campaign and *General Election Manifesto 1979* which demonstrated that Britain was "a once great nation that has somehow fallen behind."

Recognizing the inability of Keynesianism to deal with the stagflation, the Thatcher government pointed out that the constellation of crises trapping the UK "stemmed from the tendency of successive governments to hand power to the State, which had eroded the ground left for the exercise of individual responsibility, undermined private enterprise and

4 It is noteworthy that certain neoliberal policies were already being implemented by the Labour government before Margaret Thatcher's Conservative administration assumed power in 1979. James Callaghan made efforts to enact a policy of wage restraint and austerity as measures to address mounting inflation and stabilize the economy. However, it is crucial to emphasize that these endeavours were conducted on a considerably smaller scale and with far less ideological fervour than the policies later championed by Thatcher.

provoked rising interest rates and prices" (Newton 147). Thus, they called for denationalization. In contrast to the ineffective expansionary monetary policies adopted in the 1970s to stimulate consumption, Thatcher launched an array of radical new policies that strived for profound supply-side reforms "with control of the money supply [that] led to a greater emphasis on interest rate policy" (Collins 508).

During the first Thatcher administration, there was a strong push for market-driven solutions to address Britain's economic challenges, often referred to as the "sick-man" syndromes (K. Morgan 647). This included a significant financial restructuring shaking out obsolete industries, especially in manufacturing. Additionally, the government embarked on the privatization of state-owned assets, such as British Petroleum in 1979, Cable and Wireless in 1980 (though not fully completed until 1987), and the British National Oil Corporation (BNOC) in 1981. There was also a notable reduction in income tax, intended to incentivize aspirational workers and small private businesses.

Meanwhile, complying with the declaration in the 1979 Election Manifesto that we "cannot go on, year after year, tearing ourselves apart in increasingly bitter and calamitous industrial disputes" which were at least partially due to "the extension of trade union power and privileges," Thatcher sought to impose much more serious restrictions on industrial actions and tried to establish a so-called "fair" and "responsible" bargaining with organized labour. Not surprisingly, these efforts encountered significant resistance, leading to confrontations with industry opponents, whom she famously referred to as "the enemy within" during her speech to the 1922 Committee in July 1984.

Disappointed by a substantial reduction in state subsidies for the mining industry, as declared by the National Coal Board (NCB) in 1981, and disheartened by the government's subsequent decision to pivot away from economic dependence on mining due to the lower cost of imported coal (Newton and Porter 197), the National Union of Mineworkers (NUM), under the leadership of Arthur Scargill, emerged as a formidable force opposing Margaret Thatcher's neoliberal approaches In direct response to the NCB's announcement of plans to close twenty collieries in 1984, the NUM called for the "Miners' Strike." This strike represented a decisive and vehement expression of resistance against what Scargill perceived as the abandonment of the public sector and the stifling of trade union autonomy by the Thatcher government.

Scargill accused the NCB of intending to shut seventy-five pits by the end of 1985, "cutting 64,000 jobs and shrinking the workforce from 202,000 to 138,000" (Newton 156), which was proven true according to cabinet papers released in 2014 (Higham n.p.). Margaret Thatcher, however, was determined not to compromise any further and considered this conflict crucial to demonstrate the credibility of her government's commitment to conduct supply-side reforms and complete the transformation towards a market-based Britain. Taken aback by Margaret Thatcher's unwavering resolve and stringent policies, the NUM and the striking miners discovered themselves "facing the concentrated power of the state in an unprecedented form," including but not limited to massive arrests, the deployment of roadblocks and the large-scale use of police forces, which greatly disrupted the NUM's picketing movements (Milne 24). Under myriad pressures imposed by the Thatcher government, the strike came to an end in March 1985, witnessing the demolition, led by foreign competition, of traditional British industry in the 1980s. "[The] steel industry (Sheffield) and shipbuilding (Glasgow)," as David Harvey observes, "more or less totally disappeared within a few years, and with them a good deal of trade union power" (*A Brief History* 59).

The government's triumph over trade unions was significant, and therefore considered the watershed of the UK's transition to a neoliberal state as Thatcher planned:

> From 1972 to 1985 the conventional wisdom was that Britain could only be governed with the consent of the trade unions [...] Even as we were reforming trade union law and overcoming lesser disputes [...] many on the left and outside it continued to believe that the miners had the ultimate veto and would one day use it. *That day had now come and gone.* (Thatcher, *Downing* 377–78; emphasis added)

The power of the trade unions, consequentially, was seized and legislated away by the consolidation of the 1984 Trade Union Act and the 1986 Wages Act. The "enemies within" standing against Thatcher's reforms of privatization and marketization therefore collapsed, especially after the Miners' Strike as well as other rear-guard actions and resistance mounted in "Sheffield, the Greater London Council (which Thatcher had to abolish in order to achieve her broader goals in the 1980s), and Liverpool (where half the local councillors had to be gaoled)" (Harvey, *A Brief History* 59–60). All were crushed in the mid-1980s.

Cleansing everyone against them, the Conservative government continued their neoliberal transformation on an even larger scale, proceeding with further schemes of privatization even in core utilities – an act deemed as "a major feature of Thatcherism," including selling off British Aerospace (1985), the National Bus Company (1985), and Associated British Ports (1985). These moves were "politically advantageous in many ways: [...] it relieved the taxpayers of costly subsidies [...] it forced the unions to deal with private employers (who might downsize or go out of business if costs became too high) rather than engage in political strikes" (Reitan 56–7). In this way, the decline of manufacturing industries and the shrinking trade unions coincided with the ascendancy of the UK's financial sector. The City of London reaped benefits from the reforms to the London Stock Exchange in 1986, known as the "Big Bang," and, more significantly, from the Thatcher government's consistent efforts throughout the 1980s of deregulation – which aimed at enabling free-market capital to serve in a more effective and efficient manner in the (re)distribution of resources.

With her relentless agenda to dismantle national ownership of enterprises, establish strong state power over the unions force supply-side reforms in favour of "financializaton" and weed out economically uncompetitive businesses in manufacturing, Margaret Thatcher fundamentally shifted Britain away from its social democratic roots towards a neoliberal paradigm. "The retreat from planning and corporatism, the transfer of property, in the form of shares and houses, from the collective (namely the State and the local authorities) to the individual, the reduction of taxation and of spending on public sector programmes" (Newton 150) – these approaches have effectively made the UK a different nation moving to the right, creating an encouraging environment for free-market competition. These principles, against which opposition was largely neutralized – sometimes even wholly eradicated – during Thatcher's reign, have since become firmly embedded in both the political and social landscapes of Britain.

Their enduring influence has cast a long shadow over subsequent administrations, well into the 1990s and the early years of the twenty-first century.

In this way, while the "sick man" syndromes of the UK, at least in the economic sphere, were addressed to a certain extent during Thatcher's leadership, the remedy employed led to the emergence of a new set of issues that were as pervasive as the problems that were initially tackled. Different from the post-war Britain seeking to ensure "greater social justice, less extreme economic inequality and a continued economic growth compatible with these social purposes" (Thompson 288), the Thatcherite Britain was going directly the other way. Poverty was escalating after 1979. In that year 13.4 per cent of the population lived beneath median incomes (before housing costs), which, in 1992, rose to 22.2 per cent. The Gini index – an indicator of inequality – ascended from 0.253 to 0.339. This coefficient, which spans the spectrum from 0 (signifying perfect equality) to 1 (indicating extreme inequality), underscored a widening chasm in both income and wealth distribution (see Newton 174).

This economic disparity had a corresponding impact in the political domain. During the 1980s, the Conservative Party consistently secured significant parliamentary majorities in England but faced declining support in Wales and Scotland. The 1987 elections illustrated this pattern, with a marginal 1.2 per cent shift towards the Labour Party across the entire UK, while Scotland and Wales exhibited a substantial 7 per cent swing in favour of Labour (see Newton 174). These regions, steeped in the principles of social democracy, upheld their commitment to these values by electing a notable contingent of Labour MPs to Westminster.

The Iron Lady stepped down as Prime Minister in November 1990, as a result of eroding support from both her cabinet and the public due to her radical poll tax proposal and internal Conservative conflicts over European integration. Yet the ideological framework known as "Thatcherism," characterized by her market-centric reforms that facilitated Britain's neoliberal metamorphosis, continued to wield significant influence within the corridors of Downing Street. While her immediate successor, John Major, did manage to replace poll tax with council tax, which proved more acceptable, and even increased governmental spending and borrowing in certain instances (see Tomlinson 432) – actions reminiscent of "One Nation

Toryism" (Haigron 179) – these moves were more tactical than strategical. Aimed at mending internal party rifts and reclaiming lost electoral favour from Labour, they did not constitute a meaningful or effective critique of the foundational principles that undergirded Thatcher's enduring legacy.

Indeed, as outlined in the 1992 Conservative Party General Election Manifesto, the assertion that "competition and private ownership are the most potent drivers of economic efficiency, innovation, and choice" (n.p.) takes centre stage. This was a clear statement confirming the Conservative intention towards the process of denationalization that was to be carried out on a further stage. The privatized UK Coal was formed in 1994 after a further wave of pit closures. The state ownership of the British Railway was gradually split up into franchises and run by the private sector from 1994 to 1997. Schools were allowed to opt out of the control of local authority and a limited internal market (quasi-market) was introduced into the National Health Service (NHS) (Gifford 104). Consequently, under the Major administration spanning from 1990 to 1997, which exhibited a certain alignment with the principles of the "social market" reminiscent of the German Christian Democrats (Riddell 427), the trajectory of the "neoliberal revolution" persisted (Newton 195), albeit with a more subdued and less confrontational momentum compared to the Thatcher era.

Such a transformation or "re-invention" of contemporary Britain marked by large-scale neoliberal and non-interventionist reforms was "so successful that even Labour had bought into the project" (Newton 233).[5] Instead of bringing back Wilson and Callaghan's social democratic economic approaches, Tony Blair, after his landslide victory in 1997 that ended Conservative's eighteen-year administration, complied with his election manifesto calling for a "New Labour, New Life for Britain" and distanced the new government from the "old" Labour conventions. Most

5 The transformation of the Labour Party, which was initially set in motion by James Callaghan's endeavours to quell the Winter of Discontent, continued to evolve throughout the 1980s, which was overshadowed by the prominence of Thatcher's leadership. During Neil Kinnock's tenure as the Party leader (1983–92), as Anthony Seldon argues, the Labour had already embarked on a substantial shift "towards the right" (512) evident in their stances on defence policies and their willingness to embrace privatization.

influentially and remarkably, Clause IV of Labour's constitution, which originally appealed to the "common ownership of the means of production, distribution and exchange" (Adams 144) since 1918, was altered to allow for a society encouraging the realization of "our true potential" by which "power, wealth and opportunity are in the hands of the many, not the few, where the rights we enjoy reflect the duties we owe, and where we live together, freely, in a spirit of solidarity, tolerance, and respect" (see Labour's *Rule Book*). The liberal ideal of "equality of opportunity" now replaced the social democratic aspiration to greater social and economic equality of outcome.

The prudence of New Labour in creating a "dynamic economy" can be identified in the statement that "the enterprise of the market and the rigour of competition are joined with the forces of partnership and co-operation" between a "thriving private sector" and "high-quality public services" (Clause IV). But this "co-operation," not surprisingly, was later proven a further endorsement of market drives and the "modernization" programme in various social spheres much in line with Thatcherism – which can be considered "a continuing capitulation to the Thatcherite legacy" (Finlayson, "Tony" 12) – through the expanded involvement of the Private Finance Initiative (PFI).[6] Under the PFI, private companies are entrusted with the responsibility of executing and managing public projects. The emphasis on their presumed "efficiency" and their need to be "accountable to shareholders," a rationale championed by the Blair government as it introduced market forces into the public sector (Newton 213), has inadvertently resulted in the erosion of workers' future security – especially the undermining of formerly state-provided pension schemes (O. Morgan and Mathiason n.p.). The National Health Service (Private Finance) Act 1997 and the Learning and Skills Act 2000 signify pivotal legislative shifts that pledged to expand the realm for market competition and the infusion of private investments. These changes specifically impact the spheres of health

6 "I always thought," said Tony Blair to the BBC in 2013 in memory of Margaret Thatcher, on the event of her death "my job was to build on some of the things she had done rather than reverse them" (BBC News n.p.).

and education, thereby amplifying the influence of market dynamics in domains that traditionally operated within the public realm.

Meanwhile, apart from the PFI-related policy changes, the independence of the Bank of England in 1998 over setting interest rates indicated further steps of deregulation and financializaton to guarantee the City of London's position as a favourable destination of international mobile capital. The process of de-industrialization went on during the first two administrations of Blair from 1997 to 2005 when "services have grown considerably faster, implying that the long-term decline of employment in goods production has continued" (Coutts, Glynn and Rowthorne 846) – as 30 per cent of jobs in manufacturing and mining/quarrying were lost before Blair left office in June 2007.[7] In short, the free-market revolution and supply-side reforms, the neoliberal transformation of Britain started by Margaret Thatcher and followed by John Major, as well as the consequential regional and social ruptures between Producer's (Southern Wales, Northern England, Southern Scotland) and Consumer's Britain (the South East and the Home Counties) (Newton 25, 246), were not slowed down but even accelerated and intensified under Blair's New Labour government. For the first time in history, "the public was to the left of a Labour government" (Benn xi).

In response to the onset of the Financial Crisis in 2007, marked by its disruptive repercussions, the Brown administration temporarily reverted to interventionist and Keynesian macro-economic strategies. This approach harked back to the "Old" Labour tradition, creating a surge in public spending and the implementation of expansionary monetary policies. These measures, whose concern "was recapitalization of the broken banks with State support" (Newton 231), were soon abandoned in 2010 by the Cameron Coalition government composed of the Conservative Party and the Liberal Democrat (led by Nick Clegg). It was then replaced by the continuation of neoliberalism in diverse manifestations. The staggering state budget deficit, triggered by the Financial Crisis, necessitated remedies that involved great reductions in government investments in public services and social welfare according to the austerity programme announced

7 Data was accessed via the Nomis database for official labour market statistics.

in 2010. The marathon of NHS reforms saw another substantial change towards the market legislated by the Health and Social Care Act 2012, in which qualified private providers are allowed to take part in "competitive tendering for the provision of services" (Section 75), therefore establishing "a more vigorous competitive market" and paving "the way for further NHS privatisation" (Ruane 175).

Market competition, having been brought into secondary education by Tony Blair, was extended to the realm of higher education. Marked by a significant reduction in public funding for universities, this transition beginning in 2012 was complemented by the rise of tuition fees from £3,375 to £9,000 per year (Brown and Carasso 1). This shift effectively transferred the burden of education costs from the state to individual students, resulting in a redefinition of the students' role. Their identity changed from that of "clients or partners in an educational project" to that of "consumers with needs" (Brown and Carasso 149). Likewise, university staff have also found themselves drawn into the momentum of the market-oriented reforms, whose "defined benefit pension" promised by the Universities Superannuation Scheme (USS) will be replaced by a "defined contribution scheme" – linking the personal pension to the investment of USS and the market performance in general. The change of USS was proposed by Universities UK (UUK), therefore not a direct involvement of Theresa May's administration, but still it was indeed an apparent representation of marketization and the retreat of state protection over individuals that could date all the way back to the Thatcher age.

Over the past four decades, Britain has been undergoing a dramatic yet relatively consistent transformation away from its post-war welfare state foundations, navigating treacherous waters towards an increasingly entrenched neoliberal landscape. The policies of privatization and marketization, introduced by Margaret Thatcher, have left an indelible mark, surviving subsequent governments with only minor adjustments. It was during such a transformation that the UK was fracturing – huge gaps are evident and widening between the rich and the poor, between the affluent Greater London and other regions of destitution because of an array of supply-side reforms, and between different social classes or ethnic groups.

As the nation hurtles down this perilous path, the scars of inequality and division are etched ever more deeply into its identity.

As we move well into the 2020s, the looming spectre of another worrying period of stagflation appears on the horizon. This time, the threat arises from a fresh wave of economic recession, precipitated by the Covid pandemic, as the repercussions of the Quantitative Easing (QE) measures employed to alleviate the Financial Crisis of 2007–8 continue to linger without effective resolution. In this unfolding scenario, Scott Newton's closing question in his monograph on British political and economic history until before Brexit is even more pertinent for this occasion: "[I]t was arguable that Britain was overdue for another reinvention; but would there be a Britain left to reinvent?" (248).

Challenging the Normative: British SF Boom as Left-Wing Responses

Thatcher's triumph over the striking miners during the mid-1980s was certainly more than just a landmark of the economic restructuring in the UK that facilitated the coal industry's integration into market competition. It was in fact an early harbinger of a profound shift within the realms of ideology and culture. The values rooted in self-reliance and individualism, or Thatcherism, extended their influence beyond mere fiscal and economic considerations, assuming a crucial role in the shaping of the Thatcherite or neoliberal subjects. In other words, this Thatcherite turn should be interpreted as a strategic political manoeuvre, one directed at fortifying the centralized power of the state (despite her avowals of advocating for its diminishment), which strengthened persistent government intervention within the framework of neoliberalism, aimed at safeguarding privatization and an unfettered market ethos. With the fading influence of trade unions, the phrase "enemy within," metaphorically harnessed to rationalize the contentious closures of coal pits, resurfaced to confront left-leaning local authorities, academic departments in humanities and social sciences, and even the Anglican Church. This marked a broader ideological confrontation that sought to challenge those aligned with progressive agendas.

Labour-led authorities such as the Greater London Council (GLC) and Sheffield City Council, which strived to run "varieties of municipal socialism," including "support for local enterprise, council house building, job creation schemes, subsidized public transport and the promotion of the arts," found themselves labelled as "loony lefties" (Newton 143–84). They were then attacked by the pro-Conservative press and eventually "saw their functions stripped away, with councils obliged to put services out to competitive tendering on the part of private providers" (Newtown 159–60). The 1985 report entitled "Faith in the City" coordinated by the Archbishop of Canterbury Robert Runcie, which "called for more support for disadvantaged groups and, in essence, argued for higher social welfare spending," was notoriously considered "pure Marxist theology" produced by "a load of Communist clerics" (Campbell 390) that indicated a split between the Church and the Conservative government. Meanwhile, higher education was directed by the government, through funding re-distribution, to shift its teaching and research "away from the arts and social sciences towards 'enterprise,' business and vocational studies" (Newton 160), mostly including science and engineering. The newly established Universities Funding Council announced that their funding schemes would be determined not by student or research demand, "but by the needs of the competitive economy that the Thatcher ministry was building" (Reitan 105).

These approaches on top of Thatcher's market-oriented and enterprise-favoured reforms managed to promote "a new political, economic and cultural hegemony" built upon the values of neoliberalism (Newton 161). Such values, in a further case, found their way into the public culture in which the void caused by the retreat of state, social protection and welfare were to be compensated by a system preferring individual responsibility and personal aspiration. "Who is society? There is no such thing," said the Iron Lady in 1987 to *Women's Own*:

> There are individual men and women and there are families and no government can do anything except through people and people look to themselves first and then also to help look after our neighbour and life is a *reciprocal* business [...] if you can earn your own living then really you have a duty to do it [...] the quality of our lives will

> depend upon how much each of us is prepared to take responsibility for ourselves. (Thatcher, "Interview" n.p.; emphasis added)

In line with her determination to maximize personal responsibility and incentivize neoliberal competition among individuals, Margaret Thatcher also endeavoured to revive those values of the Victorian good old days – even if "more a matter of style than of substance" (Samuel 10) – when hard work, she was convinced, was a means of self-fulfilment and jobs crucial for an individual's prosperity and thrift. Portraying herself as a grocer's daughter from Grantham, she told *Evening Standard* in 1983 in a nostalgic tone that "we were taught to work jolly hard. We were taught to prove yourself; we were taught self-reliance [...] All of these things are Victorian values. They are also perennial values" (qtd. in Samuel 14). Those who were less able and less fortunate in making their own way of life, however, were to be supported by their neighbours as a "reciprocal" requirement instead of the larger society as a general entity to which everyone was a member.

These Victorian values and "the Puritan work ethic" (Samuel 12) Thatcher advocated fervently were promoted more as a political campaign for her economic reforms that led to austerity government in spending, privatization of publicly owned assets and the retreat of the state in welfare provision. Her governments built a society where the subjects are expected to take responsibility for their own lives despite the sense of precariousness and uncertainty and where personal aspirations are increasingly directed to the marketplace. "All forms of social solidarity," in David Harvey's words, "were to be dissolved in favour of individualism, private property, personal responsibility, and family values" (*A Brief History* 23).

As Stuart Hall aptly observes, the cultural landscape that unfolds from these dynamics hinges upon a discourse that can be truly comprehended only when perceived "from the imaginary position of knowledge of the self-reliant, self-interested, self-sufficient taxpayer" (Hall, *Hard Road* 49). These "imaginary positions" of the subjects are certainly not isolated from each other, since "the liberty-loving citizen is *also* the worried parent, the respectable housewife, the careful manager of the household budget, the solid English citizen 'proud to be British ...' " (Hall, *Hard Road* 49; emphasis in original). Social lives are therefore reconstructed based on "a distinctively neoliberal, free-market, possessive individualist" framework, as well as the Thatcherite, biased Victorian values of "tradition, Englishness, respectability, patriarchalism, family and nation" (Hall, *Hard Road* 39). This, interestingly enough, jibes with another policy implemented during Thatcher's reign – the British Nationality Act of 1981, terminating the longstanding "jus soli" (birthright citizenship) that had previously underwritten British identity. The stricter immigration controls guaranteed by the new law led us to a right-wing ideology dependent on cultural cohesion in the name of Britishness, which also effectively alleviated the state's welfare provision.

In tandem with this historical transition, the cultural politics of Thatcherism can be understood as part of a larger picture, a hyperobject,[8] whose tentacles have also reached the United States and other parts of the world. This larger picture is known by multiple labels, each addressing a particular yet interconnected aspect, such as post-Fordism, post-industrialism and – more of a celebration of "the penetration of aesthetics into everyday life and the ascendancy of popular culture over the High Arts" (Hall, "Meaning" 121) – postmodernism, as the cultural logic of late capitalism.

This last point on postmodernism, of course, deserves some more elaboration. Often characterized as "authoritarian populism" (Hall, "Great" 15), Thatcherism's underlying ideology resonates with the voice of the "corner shop" and people's politics as Thatcher "was confident that she spoke for an influential section of the working-class and she challenged the stereotypes of the old class system" (P. Clarke 380). Although such a rhetoric later appeared dubious or even ironic in light of her actions of tearing

8 The term "hyperobject" is apparently borrowed from Timothy Morton. Identifying himself with the Object-Oriented Ontology, he describes the hyperobjects as entities or phenomena that exist on a vast scale, extending across time and space far beyond the human scale of perception and understanding (See his 2013 book *Hyperobject: Philosophy and Ecology after the End of the World*). These entities, such as climate change and ecosystems, are *nonlocal* and *viscous*, exerting pervasive effects, challenging conventional perceptions and call for new ways of comprehending their intricate interconnectedness and vast nature. In this context, the emergence of Thatcherism is never a standalone phenomenon, but one of the many potential events – originating from a larger being such as the Capitalocene (Haraway 99–103) – that reveals itself to us.

down working-class safety nets, a lot of people were still fascinated by her *anti-elitist* posture that was particularly appealing to "the entrepreneurial/ consumerist sentiment of the working-class demographic" (Horton 26). Emerging from the lower middle-class fraction, Margaret Thatcher was forthright in her scepticism towards the pretentious "high culture" and advocated for "middle-brow" cultural facets such as the "anti-Modernism" of Rudyard Kipling and Philip Larkin's poetry, the music of Edward Elgar or better still Andrew Lloyd-Webber, and "the unadventurous realism" of Anthony Trollope's interminable *Barchester* novels (see Luckhurst, "Cultural" 417).

I am not suggesting that the postmodern or late-capitalist social conditions in the UK in the 1980s were a direct outcome of Thatcherite cultural politics. Instead, it is crucial to recognize that the reception of Thatcherism by specific social segments (sufficiently so to secure her electoral victories three times) should be perceived as part of the public response against various established manifestations of high modernism, which had "conquered the university, the museum, the art gallery network, and the foundations" (Jameson, "Postmodernism" 125). According to Fredric Jameson, these manifestations were deemed "lifeless, stifling, canonical, the ossified monuments that must be dismantled to create anything new" (125). In response to the modernist sense of totality, sameness and rationalism, social subjects in a neoliberal discourse, empowered by the politics of consumption and post-Fordism, resorted to individuality, multiplicity and heterogeneity, alongside the decline of grand narrative. All these elements back in the 1980s were exactly what was promised in Thatcher's Conservative scheme. It strove to promote a politico-economic structure of diversity and differentiation, where everyone was granted the individualistic freedom to choose their own lifestyles in the marketplace, thriving in the "rhymes" of these emerging postmodern cultural phenomena (Campsie 174) and eventually realizing their individual aspirations.

As argued in the previous section, it was apparent that Thatcher's regime was a difficult time for the leftists. Left-wing local authorities had their powers increasingly contained. University departments considered non-helpful for economic and financial competitions were starved of limited funding. The parliamentary Labour Party was facing internal splits. Trade unions were seriously weakened after the failed Miners' Strike. During this time, culture was known for its rising centrality in providing a different voice against the seemingly invincible momentum towards an increasingly neoliberal discourse. Since the 1980s, the cultural industries "have become the mediating element in every other process" especially for issues "around social regulation, morality and the governance of social conduct in late-modern societies" (Hall, "Centrality" 209, 227). They were seen "as the place from which *change* could be generated," the only place where "true opposition to Thatcherism could come from" (S. Moore 17; emphasis added). Therefore, the 1980s British fiction (not only *science* fiction) is characterized not solely by its publication timeline, but crucially by its overtly leftist and dissenting political orientation. Such writers as Martin Amis, Salman Rushdie, Ian McEwan, Graham Swift, Kazuo Ishiguro and Jeanette Winterson have all contributed to envisioning anti-Thatcherite campaigns in their writings, indicating an intellectual field in which "liberal left thinking has become the new literary orthodoxy" (Horton 22).[9]

The British SF Boom, in a way, started to take shape in line with this new orthodoxy, although sf's tradition of envisaging post-capitalist alternatives date back to long before the 1980s and can be traced far beyond the UK. Since the mid-1960s, sf was connected to postmodernism so closely during the New Wave that Jean Baudrillard claims that "science fiction [...] is no longer anywhere, and it is everywhere, in the circulation of models, here and now, in the very principle of the surrounding simulation" (126). It was also seen as a representation of the effacement of "the older (essentially high modernist) frontier between high culture and so-called mass

9 In the meantime, however, it should be noted that many among these writers started to turn rightward since the 1990s, most notably including Martin Amis, Salman Rushdie and Ian McEwan who have been identified by Ziauddin Sardar as the vanguard of the "Blitcons" (British literary neoconservatives) in a 2006 article published in the left-leaning weekly *New Statesman*. Sardar criticized these writers for publicly advocating anti-Muslim sentiments, anti-immigration viewpoints, and endorsing the Iraq invasion (see Sardar 153–63). This transition, in some way, can be perceived as one of the "tentacles" of the same hyperobject that led to the subsumption of oppositional culture into the domain of cultural commodities during the New Labour era – an aspect that will be explored further later in this chapter.

or commercial culture" (Jameson, *Postmodernism* 2). Therefore, sf writers of and before this time such as Brian Aldiss, Philip K. Dick, Ursula K. Le Guin, J. G. Ballard, Thomas Pynchon, Samuel R. Delany, William Gibson, Bruce Sterling, among others, have all occupied significant positions within the framework of postmodern theorists.

One of the sub-genres of sf informed by postmodernism is apparently cyberpunk, renowned for its distinct departure from technocratic optimism. It offers a critical aesthetic and cultural counterpoint to what can be referred to as "Hobbesian lawlessness" (Ross 146), as well as a reaction to the technologically mediated discourse associated with neoliberalism. This perspective is often traced back to William Gibson's *Neuromancer* (1984), which is regarded as "the supreme literary expression if not of postmodernism, then of late capitalism itself" (Jameson, *Postmodernism* 419). At the same time, notions such as posthumanism, embodiment, sexuality and the cyborg were subjects of scrutiny by Donna Haraway. Her exploration drew upon a range of sf writers, among them Joanna Russ, James Tiptree, Jr, Anne McCaffrey and Octavia E. Butler.

However, all these writers I just mentioned, apart from a few exceptions (Aldiss and Ballard), are Americans. One of the multiple reasons for the American dominance, according to Paul Kincaid, is that the previous British New Wave had "made British writers look with a certain distrust upon what were considered the hackneyed dead-end ideas of traditional sf [...] many turned towards the mainstream or towards fantasy during the immediate post-New Wave period" (Bould and Butler 486). But still, hints of change within British sf specifically responding to Thatcherism have never been far from reach, reflecting on sf's cultural significance of perceiving late capitalism and Thatcherite neoliberalism.[10] And this change may have started with a new magazine: *Interzone*.

10 Gwyneth Jones's remarkable series of novels from the 1980s, including *Divine Endurance* (1984), *Escape Plans* (1986), and *Kairos* (1988), stand out as some of the most compelling science fiction works that directly engage with the era of Thatcherism. This distinction sets them apart from many of the acclaimed British Boom works in the 1990s and the early 2000s, which often focus on the aftermath of Thatcherism rather than its immediate impact.

Interzone was initially launched in 1982 on a quarterly basis, providing a reliable platform for sf publication which was later regarded as the definitive magazine that cradled the British SF Boom (Butler, "Thirteen" 376). The following year saw the release of Terry Pratchett's *The Colour of Magic*, when the author's reputation established by his non-sf writings assured the popularity of fantastic genres among the bestsellers, as well as Colin Greenland's *The Entropy Exhibition: Michael Moorcock and the British "New Wave" in Science Fiction* – "constituting a farewell of sorts to the New Wave" (Bould, "Bould" 308). In 1987, Iain M. Banks published *Consider Phlebas*, the first of the Culture series, drawing "non-traditional readers to the genre" (Bould, "Bould" 308) and promoting a reinvention of space opera or space baroque. These dates and events mentioned above, as noted by Mark Bould, although to some extent covered by the popular presence of cyberpunk, can all be understood as the potential start points of the British SF Boom ("Bould" 307–10).

As the 1990s and the new millennium approached, Thatcher's legacies did not fade away along with her standing down from the Downing Street. They were, despite certain modifications, succeeded by the Major and Blair administrations, still very much alive and governing the British society and culture. With the collapse of the Soviet Union, the fall of the Berlin Wall, China's rapid shift towards marketization and privatization, and the implementation of economic and political reforms in previously socialist countries, an ideological void emerged where genuine alternatives to late-capitalist or neoliberal practices were largely absent. Consequently, neoliberalism underwent a new phase, as these global developments reshaped its trajectory.

The inherent logic of neoliberalism – "a normative mode of reason" as initially put forward by Michel Foucault in his 1979 lectures – has eventually become the predominant guiding philosophy across numerous domains, succinctly labelled by William Davis as "normative neoliberalism" (127). In this way, culture, which used to be a site from which to challenge the Thatcherite discourse, is now under siege. It is now being assimilated into the calculations of neoliberal economics, wherein its values are harnessed to perpetuate and facilitate the mechanisms of the knowledge economy, expected to "sustain and grease the wheels of the knowledge economy, so part of economic policy must be engineering that culture" (Finlayson, *Making* 155). Such an engineering process, or "cultural governance" according to Roger Luckhurst, was conducted through the management of the Department of National Heritage (DNH) established in 1992 and renamed as the Department of Culture, Media and Sport (DCMS) in 1997.

From then on, the government is able to devolve its budget on public spending to "some forty-five separate bodies" in the cultural sphere, including the Arts Council, museums, libraries, galleries and others. This strategy is aligned with "a mode of governance built on a small central core that was to 'steer' a complex set of apparently autonomous institutions" – which reflects the economized significance given to the "financial and symbolic capital of sport, tourism, heritage, media and the arts" (Luckhurst, "Cultural" 419). Under the DNH's supervision, the anti-Thatcherism *Zeitgeist* of the 1980s was chained for the purpose of social cohesion, which facilitated by the professionalization of art and literature, involving cultural management initiatives such as awards, marketing and more. Following his examination of popular music and fine art that were increasingly corporatized and measured based on their success "only in financial terms" (420), Luckhurst goes further in pointing out that "cultural change," when rendered as the object of cultural governance, "might be harnessed to produce subjects that would happily skip and jump around the Edenic post-political garden of Cool Britannia" (421).

"Cool Britannia" was a cultural movement initially in youth culture associated with Britpop and later articulated to the New Labour's political campaign. It was also a programme of cultural rebranding and subject remaking, from the "Rule Britannia" deeply connected to Britain's imperial and colonial past to the "Cool Britannia" rooted in the rise of mass culture, the age of cultural commodity and normative neoliberalism, and in the postmodern detachment of images or signs from their meanings. It generated the Foucauldian forms "of consumer-based identity to which we are subjected, and by which – often willingly – we are disciplined" (Finlayson, *Making* 148). In this way, those images or signs of Cool Britannia managed to develop "an autonomous force," an "imposition of market mechanisms" of late capitalism in the cultural sphere (Fisher, *Capitalist* 44), eroding its foundation for critically analysing the current neoliberal socio-political discourse and for imagining possible alternatives.

Powerful control from the government was therefore exerted through funding, budget assessments, policy reviews, managerial audits and selection for prizes and titles. "The unpredictability of cultural production," as noted by Luckhurst ("Cultural" 419–23), can be managed into cultural *industries* where musicians, artists, writers and so on will be encouraged to "produce profit and import/export balance sheets" and "praised for adding to the economic vibrancy of the nation," before leading to a "frenzy" for prizes (English 18). In line with Perri 6's suggestion (then research director of the New Labour think tank) that "government is essentially in the business of changing the cultures of its own staff, the organisations that cluster around it [...] and the wider public" (Perri 6 262), the steering wheel of cultural governance has managed to incorporate culture as part of an economic calculation where some cultural products will be rewarded with funding while others starve.

This, in essence, was a process of "mainstreaming" oppositional culture or, in other words, the inoculation of culture into "an inoffensive populist mainstream" (Luckhurst, "Cultural" 423). Meanwhile, the lost ability to imagine alternatives, the seeming triumph of the market and the normalized calculative logics of human capital spreading globally, and the schizophrenic understanding of history have all contributed to the "end of history" mentality celebrated by Francis Fukuyama and others, creating a sense of temporal stasis or historical exhaustion. As late capitalism reached its perceived "terminal zone," signalling its own culmination, the concept of "time" lost its significance. Our expectation of future is then "construed solely in terms of a further domination of space: more road networks, business parks, retirement pueblos, shopping malls" (Gąsiorek 48), whereas the commodified and neoliberalized world of the present remained unchallenged.

Taking shape in such an environment, the British SF Boom developed, quietly but surely, "below the radar" of cultural governance and therefore "could still find spaces outside [its] de-differentiation or 'mainstreaming' effect" (Luckhurst, "Cultural" 423). Although it emerged in a discourse where contesting neoliberalism was considered an orthodoxy for British literature (as discussed above), British sf sustained its left-wing stance during the historical rupture that embraced commodified cultural products. Sf, largely deemed as a lowly popular genre that was hardly accepted by highbrow culture endorsed by elitism, separated itself from "serious" art and literature, so as to maintain an underground, subversive quality that major postmodern British authors (like the Blitcons) have largely lost. It provided a space where the potential for envisioning alternatives and, more significantly, offering critical responses to the prevailing rightward transition in society could take place. This space was seen as intricately linked to a distinct cultural and political momentum, simultaneously defying "the staid literary and political culture of Britain in the 1990s" (O'Connell, "British" 2).

Similarly, Istvan Csicsery-Ronay, Jr. claims in his *Editorial Introduction* of the British SF Boom special issue of *Science Fiction Studies* in 2003: "[the Boom] comes out of a particular historical moment when British culture navigated between powerful opposing tides" ("Editorial" 354), namely the dynamic between the conservatism of literary culture and the rich mix of immigrant cultures, between techno-scientific imperialism and anti-hegemonism. In this way, Iain M. Banks's *Culture* series (1987–2012), Gwyneth Jones's *Aleutian* trilogy (1994–9), Ken MacLeod's *Fall Revolution* (1995–9), China Miéville's *Bas-Lag* (2000–4), Stephen Baxter's *Xeelee* sequence (since 1991), as well as many others during the Boom, can all be seen in various ways as left-wing responses to Thatcherite legacies and the ongoing social transformation of Britain.

But still, when compared to the Chinese Boom that boasts an explicit manifesto (to be explored later), the Anglo-American New Wave that had its day in the 1970s, and the cyberpunk movement of the 1980s led by American writers, the emergence of the British SF Boom seems to be more serendipitous and less deliberate in nature. As noticed by Andrew M. Butler, the Boom "has no resident polemicist (although M. John Harrison, China Miéville, and others have found spaces to talk about it), no key writer (although some would suggest Miéville), and no defining anthology or magazine (although *Interzone* could take some of the credit)" (Butler, "Thirteen" 275–6). It did not witness a group of leading writers and editors setting out a clear manifesto like the New Wave's declaration that "science fiction must jettison its present narrative forms and plots [...] It is inner space, not out, that needs to be explored" (Ballard 117), nor cyberpunk's endeavours to rebuild the very core of sf by creating a hybrid of the (cyber) rationality and (punk-ish) dystopian societies. The Boom appeared, it seems, accidentally.

However, the accidental emergence of the British SF Boom does not compromise its complexity and sophistication. Based on his arguments on cultural governance, Luckhurst specifically points out two representative narrative formulae in the Boom: (1) the disaster and post-apocalyptic narratives structured around moments of imperial anxiety and an increasingly voiceless British national identity (taking Gwyneth Jones's *Bold as Love* [2001], *Castles Made of Sand* [2002] and James Lovegrove's *Untied Kingdom* [2003] as examples), and (2) "the hacker/cyberjock subversion of surveilled totalities" such as Ken MacLeod's *The Stone Canal* (1996) and Justina Robson's *Silver Screen* (1999), calling for a resistance of being routinized within a totality aided by a "mainstreaming of culture" (Luckhurst "Cultural" 429).

Meanwhile, another defining feature of the Boom is believed to be a blurring boundary between various literary sub-genres, especially sf, gothic and fantasy. Mark Bould reiterates Mark Rose's sf-fantasy distinction: "[the] changed worlds of fantasy are presented as literary substitutions for reality, [...] related to the empirical worlds paradigmatically or metaphorically," whereas the "changed worlds of science fiction are presented as logical extensions of reality, [...] related to the empirical world syntagmatically or metonymically" (Rose 21–2). Bould continues to claim that the Boom is very likely able to shift the genre's centre away from the metonymic pole and transform sf into what Carl Malmgren initially described as science fantasy – a "hybrid form combining features" of sf and fantasy that can be recognized by their different obligation "to be faithful to scientific epistemology" (Malmgren, "Towards" 260). However, in contrast to Malmgren's idea, Bould believes that "it might make more sense [...] to think of science fantasy as the parent genre" (Bould, "What" 407) and the British SF Boom has in fact witnessed a returning to the umbrella genre that had been artificially divided into sf and fantasy.

Therefore, as the boundaries between various literary genres continue to blur, the British SF Boom has seen the rise of the New Weird, exemplified by the works of authors like China Miéville and M. John Harrison. The term "New Weird" was coined by Harrison in 2003, which he believes stands for "a fusion of SF, horror, and surrealism [...] which similarly emphasised the need to model its fictional world on complex, real-world problems" (Vint, "From" 200). By immersing itself in a "metaphorical or allegorical confrontation with the uncanny aspects of the post-normal future" (Canavan 217), the New Weird has crafted a distinct and thought-provoking response – nurtured within a context of specific domestic social changes set in motion by Margaret Thatcher – to the prevailing discourse grounded in the competitive interplay between calculative agencies and "market imperatives." This discourse, as Mark Fisher suggests, embodies a vision of "capitalist realism," denying all alternative forms of modernity other than late capitalism in the contemporary global landscape (*Postmodernism* 2, 23).

Meanwhile, apart from the New Weird, the blurring boundary that underpins the British SF Boom also manages to bring forward new possibilities for the remixing of previous canonical sf works: "[W]here British science fiction has become most systematically parodic and revisionary is in its revival of the subgenre of space opera" (Butler, "Thirteen" 383). The result of this revival is the New Space Opera. While challenging and introspecting on its American, Campbellian and Golden-Age traditions and shying away from "its military and imperialist underpinnings" (Vint, "From" 198), the New Space Opera has established a British sf vision where "it is no longer possible to identify heroes and villains with any certainty" (Butler, "Thirteen" 384). This transition resonates with the differentiation proposed by Richard Mathews between "vertical" and "horizontal" heroes: the former pertains to individuals who ascend or descend as they are driven towards or away from absolute good or evil, while the latter grapple on a level where values must be discerned without the guidance of divine intervention (Mathews 92). The apparent heroes of the Boom space operas, Butler argues, have become the flawed leader mutually elected and acknowledged among individuals who see each other as brothers, and very often, it would be trickier to tell the heroes from the villains.

In this case, with these literary and narrative characteristics that distinguish the British SF Boom from previous sf trends, it has become the focus of a relatively large number of academic studies. The first corpus of academic engagement could be dated back to the 2003 issue of *SFS* edited by Mark Bould, Andrew M. Butler and Istvan Csicsery-Ronay, Jr. featuring the British SF Boom. It provides a systematic discussion about the definition, representative writers and narrative styles, socio-political background and cultural implications, setting the tone for further studies on the Boom. Ten years later, in 2013, another journal *CR: The New Centennial Review* continues this topic by collecting new literary materials and extending them to demonstrate the interaction between the Boom and globalization, where the special issue editor Hugh Charles O'Connell claims that the British SF Boom is a literary and cultural attempt to imagine a coherent alternative future and "wrest a utopian impulse from the ravages of such historical exhaustion" (O'Connell, "Boom's" 68–9).

When the British SF Boom finally received broader attention from academics in 2003 (the *SFS* special issue), more than ten years had passed since Istvan Csicsery-Ronay, Jr.'s 1991 observation that sf had become "an aspect of the quotidian consciousness of people living in the post-industrial world, daily witnesses to the transformations of their values and material conditions in the wake of technological acceleration beyond their conceptual threshold" (Csicsery-Ronay, Jr., "SF" 389). In the editorial introduction to the 2003 special issue, he wrote again that "the 1990s generation has responded to the respect the Boom has brought with it, and doubtless new talents have begun to emerge in the midst of it all" ("Editorial" 354). In the following years, besides the special issue of *CR* in 2013, there are also monographs and essay collections dedicated to specific authors, including Iain M. Banks (Colebrook and Cox; Kincaid *Iain*; Hubble et al.; Norman), China Miéville (Edwards and Venezia; Freedman *Art*), Ken MacLeod (Butler and Mendlesohn), M. John Harrison (Bould and Reid; Williams and Bould) and Adam Roberts (Callow Jr and McFarlane).

Although by now the British Boom has largely retreated from its historical stage – sometime around the mid-2000s – giving way to works featuring gender/racial politics and ecocriticism because of the changes in intellectual field in the most recent decade, it should still be properly remembered. For a long time, the British Boom remained outside the scope of academic attention, only gradually gaining widespread recognition and establishing its rightful place in the cultural history of sf in the early twenty-first century. Originating from the left-wing melancholy of British intellectuals in the 1980s, the British Boom is aligned with the anti-Thatcherism sentiments prevailing in the mainstream literary field at the time. It remained hidden beneath the spotlight of the latter, quietly exploring the political potential of popular sf works. It is precisely due to this silence that British sf managed to resist the "mainstreaming" process in the 1990s British cultural landscape, maintaining its own independence and political criticality not co-opted by the Majorite and Blairite cultural governance like Cool Britannia. It stood as one of the most direct and critical responses to Thatcherism, its left-wing political messages serving as a resounding echo – providing utopian insights into a landscape from which we have yet to find an escape.

Before the Chinese SF Boom: Spiritual Pollution and "Top-down" Elitism

On the other side of the Boom-Boom duality, the Chinese SF Boom also emerges as a reaction to China's historical rupture and transition at the end of the twentieth century, intricately intertwined with the advent of neoliberalism. In David Harvey's *A Brief History of Neoliberalism*, Deng Xiaoping was joined by Margaret Thatcher, Ronald Reagan and Paul Volcker (then chair of the US Federal Reserve) as one of the four "epicentres" of "a revolutionary turning-point in the world's social and economic history" during the years 1978–80 (*A Brief History* 1).[11] Despite the inherent differences distinguishing China's market-oriented reforms "with Chinese characteristics" from those carried out by the Thatcher administration that were usually categorized as typical neoliberal approaches, the reinvention of China in economic, political, social and cultural domains, kindled by "the Deng Xiaoping Theory" or "Dengism,"

11 On the cover of Harvey's book, however, it was Augusto Pinochet, former president of Chile from 1974 to 1990, rather than Paul Volcker, who was placed among the other three heads of state.

appeared even more dramatic than the Thatcherite transitions in Britain. Such a reinvention was considered "a conjunctural accident" happening to coincide "with the turn to neoliberal solutions in Britain and the United States" (Harvey, *A Brief History* 120) where individual initiatives were unleashed for competition in a freer market that encourages self-entrepreneurship and self-responsibility.

Compared to its left-leaning British counterpart, however, the Chinese SF Boom, emerging in the 1990s, has developed a more complicated and ambiguous relation with the shifting social discourse. On the one hand, it has indeed provided critical responses to the unpopular by-products of China's transition such as class stratification, regional unevenness, and personal confusion and uncertainty of the future caused by the retreat of state protection. On the other hand, Chinese sf also benefits from the process of marketization and privatization, as well as the flourishing popular culture developed upon the relics of elitist high modernism in the 1980s. This leaves lots of room for academic interpretation, which, in this chapter, will begin with a discussion on the mixed fortune of Chinese sf during the 1980s – an age in China known for the movement of New Enlightenment and elitism – before moving to the Chinese Boom.

After the Cultural Revolution (1966–76), Chinese intellectual elites experienced a notably more open and dynamic political and cultural environment. This shift permitted a collective contemplation or reflection on the decade of darkness, during which literature and various artistic endeavours had predominantly served as propaganda tools to promote Maoist ideals of Class Struggle. The revolutionary discourse, where people's subjectivities were moulded towards a quest for a socialist totality, has been scrutinized and challenged by those liberal-minded intellectuals who "formed a common enlightenment camp around their 'unity of attitude' with regard to views on culture and reform" (Xu J. 197). Informed by an intellectual movement termed "the New Enlightenment," which is usually compared to the one interrupted in the 1930s, literary production since the late 1970s was detached from its pragmatic service for political or ideological imperatives and therefore developed a literary "autonomy" (Zhang H. 30). With this autonomy, literary works can be reviewed based on their own aesthetic values rather than their connection to a grand narrative.

For the genres emerging in the 1980s – especially the "Scar Literature" directly interrogating the national trauma during the Cultural Revolution, the "Root-seeking Literature" endeavouring to restore a national identity constructed upon local traditions, as well as the avant-garde fictions deeply influenced by modernist and post-modernist theories from European and American critics – it was *human beings* that were considered the narrative focuses of literature, instead of a centralized socio-political context. Through this movement of cultural liberation promoted by a number of academic and literary elites aiming at amplifying humanist voices, Chinese intellectuals have occupied a pivotal position guiding the production and propagation of the elite culture and thus bringing forward "a universalistic high culture of humanism and modernism" and a "philosophical discourse of modernity" (Zhang X. 103).

In fact, the blossoming of the New Enlightenment was not limited to "high literature" attempting to shape a "universalistic" discourse of "top-down" elite culture, guided by a group of high-profile intellectuals. Chinese sf also witnessed a remarkable but short prosperity in its own name. Following his brave publication of "Petroleum Protein" (*Shiyou danbai*) in the early days of 1976, which is likely one of the earliest identified Chinese sf stories from the closing phase of the Cultural Revolution, Ye Yonglie rose from the ashes. He further fuelled a renaissance of sf in China by crafting a ground-breaking novel in 1978,[12] titled *Little Know-It-All Travels to the Future* (*Xiaolingtong manyou weilai*), captivating a widespread readership across the country.

In this story, the protagonist Mr Little Know-It-All boards a hovercraft terminating at a futuristic utopian city. There he is impressed and even enchanted by various scientific gadgets and by people's much-improved living and medical conditions in this parallel world, including flying cars, artificial organs and foods, and fluorescent paints, among others. Fitting into this "outsider" narrative usually adopted in the enlightenment literature around

12 "*Shiyou danbai*" was also translated as "Strange Cakes" in the anthology of Chinese sf, i.e., *Science Fiction from China*, edited by Wu Dingbo and Patrick D. Murphy and published in 1989.

the late-Qing and the May Fourth periods,[13] Mr Little Know-It-All, upon his return to his home world, faithfully records what he has witnessed in this utopian wonderland established on scientific and moral advancement. His observations of the futuristic social and familial structures, however, do not lead to "the diagnosis of social and institutional illness" (Isaacson 125) – a common thematic focus in early Chinese sf stories that have revealed the confrontation between the introduction of foreign ideas and hydra-headed local traditions.[14] Instead, it suggests a dedicated attempt, during the New Enlightenment after the Cultural Revolution, to look for a socialist modernity emerging in the elite cultural discourse.

Encouraged by the sensational success of *Mr. Little Know-It-All* and more liberal environment for literary and sf creation during the New Enlightenment, "new magazines were launched, writers experimented with new genres and techniques, and a group of new authors gained the limelight" (Wu D. xxi). Apart from Ye Yonglie and his remarkable contributions to Chinese sf circles, various stories from sf-dedicated writers like Tong Enzheng's "Death Ray on a Coral Island" (*Shanhudaoshang de siguang*, 1978), Zheng Wenguang's "Flying Toward the Constellation of Sagittarius" (*Feixiang renmazuo*, 1979) and Wei Yahua's "Dear Illusion" (*Wenrou zhixiang de meng*, 1981) have earned reputations not only from their increasing readership but also in the domain of mainstream literature and high culture.[15]

13 The narrative of "outsiders" can be commonly identified in modern Chinese literature depicting the visit of an *intruder* to a comparatively enclosed environment, whose interaction with those locals could lead to a dramatic encounter connecting the old and the new, the traditional and the modern, and the past and present.

14 Works of this type include Xu Nianci's "New Tales of Mr. Braggadocio" (*Xin faluo xiansheng Tan*, 1904), Wu Jianren's "The New Story of the Stone" (*Xin shitou ji*, 1905), Lao She's *Cat Country* (*Mao cheng ji*, 1932–3), as well as various other non-sf stories in the same period.

15 Among them, Tong's "Death Ray" was published in the prestigious mainstream magazine *People's Literature* (*Renmin wenxue*) directly supervised by China Writers' Association in Beijing. With its socio-cultural influence and reader acceptance travelling beyond literature *per se*, this novella was soon adapted to a film of the same name in 1980 by Shanghai Film Studio.

From 1978 to 1983, there were dozens of magazines and newspapers thriving and playing their part in such an unprecedented movement of sf production, providing "the playground for thought experiments that create a sense of wonder" (Wu D. xxi), including *Kehuan haiyang* (*SF Ocean*), *Zhihui shu* (*Intelligent Tree*), *Kexue wenyi* (*Science Art and Literature*), *Kexue shidai* (*Science Era*) and *Kexue xiaoshuo bao* (*SF Newspaper*). Apart from the prosperity of publication, Chinese sf circles also started to seek a more engaged interaction with their international counterparts. While many classic European-American sf authors (Mary Shelley, Jules Verne, H. G. Wells, Isaac Asimov, Arthur C. Clarke and others) were translated into Chinese (Wu D. xxvi–xxxi), some "big name" sf writers and academics from abroad, such as Frederik Pohl, Roger Zelazny, Robert Heinlein, Brian Aldiss and Darko Suvin, were also invited to various sf-related events in China.[16]

However, alongside the ostensible dynamism of Chinese sf in the late 1970s and early 1980s, the New Enlightenment also saw the revival of the pragmatic and instrumentalist expectation of sf as a tool of science popularization. This purpose, which had been integral to its inception in the early twentieth century, led to a robust debate within the Chinese sf community about its inherent legitimacy. Once again, Chinese sf was seen as the medium to disseminate knowledge of modern science and technology (Tatsumi 331), as well as "a vehicle for expressing anxieties and hopes for modernization" to the cause of popular education and national renewal (Isaacson 2), and in this way it paid much more attention to *science* than *fiction*.

As a response, in the article "On My Understandings of Science Art and Literature" published in June 1979 in *Renmin wenxue* (*People's Literature*), the leading sf writer Tong Enzheng claimed that "in [sf stories], science mainly serves as the method and thus should be regarded as the supplement and background for the major plots and characters." His aims were "not to introduce scientific knowledge but, as in other forms of literature […] deliver a fact-based attitude, a truth-oriented spirit" (Tong 110). Together

16 The brief Golden Age of Chinese sf from 1978 to 1983 is covered comprehensively in Li Hua's 2021 book *Chinese Science Fiction during the Post-Mao Cultural Thaw*.

with other sf polemicists, Tong Enzheng attempted to distinguish sf from science popularization, only to find their voices muffled by popular science writers and even by senior scientists whose ideas carried much more weight in the "top-down" enlightenment discourse of elite culture.

In July 1979, paleobiologist Zhen Shuonan published an article in *Zhongguo qingnian bao* (*China Youth Daily*) where he launched a fierce attack against Ye Yonglie. Zhen pointed out the scientific errors in Ye's stories from a biological perspective and then turned his attack to a political level. He argued that valuable ideas should and can only be developed based on real rather than pseudo-science, which leads us nowhere but to mental chaos. One month later, Lu Bing, writer of children's literature, demonstrated in an article titled "Soulless Literature" that sf should be written as "fictionalized science," which is essentially a subgenre of popular science writing. *Science* fiction without science, for him, is a body without a soul (qtd. in Wu Y., *20* 144–7).

Among those who witnessed the rising popularity and impact of sf works reluctantly, Qian Xuesen the physicist (also known as Tsien Hsue-shen) was probably the most politically influential speaker. As one of the national heroes in twentieth-century China for his tremendous contributions to China's national defence projects and the then vice president of China Association for Science and Technology (CAST), Qian explicitly criticized the fictionality of sf in 1980. He argued that sf stories

> should indicate the rational imaginations of scientists, instead of those fictional fantasies without limitation, and need to focus on those potential scientific discoveries or technological inventions, although only rough conceptions by now, that can be made possible in the future. It has to concentrate on science [...] Science fictions, if detached from science, would become pollution. (qtd. in Wang W. 295)

He added in 1981 that these "scientific imaginations" would even become "valuable treasures" if they could anticipate "major scientific breakthroughs in the future" (Wang W. 308). Standing in line with Qian Xuesen, the majority of popular science writers were convinced that sf stories must deal with the knowledge of existing science and technology. They besieged sf production in China and targeted various sf writers and their works. One of the victims was Ye Yonglie's "Miracle on the World's

Highest Peak" (*Shijie zuigaofeng shang de qiji*) published in 1977. In this story, a team of scientists unearths a rare unfossilized dinosaur egg on Mount Qomolangma and then has it hatched. Unfortunately, this story was conceived as an unethical promotion of pseudo-science since bringing dinosaurs back to life was by then considered too dramatic and scientifically implausible to be true.

Intertwined with a broader change of cultural climate under the New Enlightenment, the criticism against Chinese sf had political connotations. In search for a socialist utopia of modernization expected to replace the fading Maoist utopia of revolution, Chinese society during the early 1980s "abound[ed] with high-minded zeal and idealist passion" (Xu J. 227) led by the intellectual elites. Concerns over the tendency towards spiritual liberation during the New Enlightenment gradually accumulated to an extent that any turbulence could result in an appalling response.

During a keynote report in March 1983 at the Central Party School to commemorate the centenary of Karl Marx's death, Zhou Yang, who was then the vice president of Chinese Academy of Social Sciences (CASS), former deputy head of the Publicity Department of the Communist Party of China (CCPPD), and an influential liberal-minded thinker after the Cultural Revolution, delivered an unauthorized speech. He discussed a range of sensitive subjects, including the intricate link between Marxism and "humanism" (*rendao zhuyi*), as well as the latent potential for alienation within socialist ideologies (Zhou n.p.).

This, however, caused a political storm because the political pressure had already come to a head before his speech. A cultural movement against the "'Rightist' views among Party officials [like Zhou Yang] and 'bourgeois' trends among intellectuals" was launched directly from the top (Sleeboom-Faulkner 69). At the Second Plenum of the Twelfth of CPC Central Committee in October 1983, Deng Xiaoping denounced in his speech "On the Organizational and Ideological Fronts" that "some comrades have only been interested in discussing humanism, the value of the human being, and alienation and in criticising socialism, not capitalism" (Deng 40). He also criticized the tendency towards "bourgeois liberalization" (*zichan jieji ziyouhua*) that may lead to "the spread of the corrupt and decadent ideas of the bourgeoisie and other exploiting classes and the spread of distrust of socialism, communism and leadership by the Communist Party" (Deng 41) – which was later referred to as "spiritual pollution."

Thus, a "top-down" crusade targeting a broad spectrum of "spiritual pollutions," particularly within the realms of literary and cultural production, heralded an abrupt downturn for Chinese sf starting in 1983. Following Deng's speech, during a meeting among the Standing Committee of CAST on 1 November 1983, Qian Xuesen reiterated his distrust of sf stories. He fiercely criticized those who "wrote, under the name of sf, ghostly, pornographic and pseudo-scientific stories to express their dissatisfaction towards socialism and to poison young people and our society" (Wang W. 335). Just four days later, on November 5th, an editorial titled "The Spiritual Pollution in Science Fiction should also be Eliminated" appeared in *Renmin ribao* (*People's Daily*), the newspaper articulating the sentiments of the influential intellectuals at the forefront of China's New Enlightenment movement. In this article, sf was considered an "anti-scientific" genre able to

> promote idealism and feudalism and disturb people's mind [...] some sf stories have even moved beyond "science" *per se* and indicated *politically problematic potentials* [...] which was resulted from the recent influence and erosion of the decayed capitalist and feudalist remnants and should be seen as the outcome of bourgeois liberalization and the complete commercialization regardless of its social consequence. (Shi n.p.; emphasis added)

With this severe political accusation, the short-lived prosperity of Chinese sf since 1978 came to an end, unlike other genres closer to the New Enlightenment discourse of high culture. Sf was, once again, considered utilitarian and instrumentalist, especially by the literary and cultural elites who endeavoured to establish a top-down totalized socialist utopia.

Not surprisingly, as documented by Wu Dingbo, Wei Yahua's story "Wenrou zhi xiang de meng" (translated as "Conjugal Happiness in the Arms of Morpheus," with an English version available in 1984) was accused of being cynical, sensual and anti-Socialist, displaying incorrect political inclination. Likewise, Ye Yonglie's works were also subjected to ideological condemnation for allegedly tarnishing "socialist society in China" and undermining "the values of socialism" (Wu D. xxxiii). Still traumatized by the memories of the Cultural Revolution and scared of another round of persecution, Chinese sf writers either ceased to write or moved to other forms of literature. Those dozens of sf magazines and newspapers that had once flourished as the ground for sf publication suddenly withered. All of them were shuttered due to an unspoken political influence, with only one remaining, *Kexue wenyi* (*Scientific Art and Literature*), grappling to endure in an era of socialist modernization that unfolded within a cultural narrative largely guided by a select group of political and literary intellectuals.

In this attempt of establishing a socialist or communist utopia developed from the New Enlightenment, science was considered the key to China's modernization and thus should not be fictionalized to any degree. However, such a sense of elitism gradually lost its dynamism and eventually faded away after Deng Xiaoping's "Southern Tour" in 1992. He cleared up the hesitations of regional governments by encouraging them to "be bolder than before in conducting reform and opening to the outside" and not to be afraid of "introducing too many elements of capitalism" (Deng 372) if they could serve well within the framework of socialist economic reforms.

From then on, China engaged much deeper in the process of commodification and privatization, "though still under the watchful eye of the party" (Harvey, *A Brief History* 125). Through this surge propelled by the market and capital, Chinese society from the 1990s onwards encountered various manifestations of commercialization, particularly in the realm of cultural production. While contesting the power of the "high modernism" standing for "the prophetic elitism and authoritarianism of the modern movement" (Jameson, *Postmodernism* 2), this transformation signalled the arrival of a "bottom-up" mass culture that challenged the "top-down" intellectual discourse of the New Enlightenment in the 1980s. This is what we will discuss next.

The Cat's Colour Does Not Matter: Deng's Reform and the Dawning of the Chinese Boom

During his famous Southern Tour to various cities significant to China's market reform, including Wuhan, Shenzhen, Zhuhai, Guangzhou and

Shanghai, Deng Xiaoping made it clear to local governments that "a market economy is not capitalism" and that the expansion of economy is crucial to "promote China's all-round development" (Deng 370–83). It was over this period that his "cat theory" ("it doesn't matter whether the cat is black or white, as long as it catches mice," a quote originally from a 1962 conference) was widely circulated among the public. In accordance with Deng's directives, China's reforms aimed at state-owned enterprises (SOEs) gained momentum, entering an advanced phase of privatization (often referred to as "ownership restructuring" or *gaizhi* euphemistically).

These reforms were deemed crucial to the Party's overarching strategy of fostering a "socialist market economy," a concept introduced by Jiang Zemin during the fourteenth National Congress of the CPC in 1992. With the enactment of the Company Law and the Unfair Competition Law in 1993, the groundwork for market competition was solidified. Small and medium-sized SOEs were encouraged to *restructure* in line with the policy of "*zhua da, fang xiao*" (grasp the big and let the small go) adopted in the mid-1990s, which was made possible by a myriad of methods such as employee shareholding, management buyout, bankruptcy, leasing and merging into joint ventures. Only "500 to 1000 large state firms" (Garnaut, Song and Yao 37) were exempt from the restructuring.

In this way, the social protection and job tenure that used to be guaranteed by the "iron rice bowls" were increasingly under threat and progressively stripped off given the fiscal pressure faced by the majority of SOEs.[17] Accompanied with the shrinking of employee welfare and benefits particularly in medical care, housing and education, the total number of SOEs between 1993 and 2002 fell from 104,700 to 29,449 (Song L., "State" 189) and more than 30 million workers were therefore laid off (*xiagang*) from SOEs, "receiving a reduced wage or basic living allowance but remaining on the factory's books – and thus avoiding classification as 'unemployed' " (Gittings 277). These laid-off workers, while forming a considerable redundancy of workforce, were largely absorbed in a dynamic

17 The term "iron rice bowl" (*tiefanwan*) is usually used to refer to the basic welfare system in China that guarantees job security and provides steady income. People who are considered to have such positions include members of civil service, SOE employees and military personnel.

and rapidly developing non-state sector that was engulfing the market share that was previously occupied by SOEs. As the slogan "*guotui minjin*" (the state retreats; the private sector advances) was commonly acknowledged at the turn of millennium, the share of urban employment fell remarkably from 78.3 per cent in 1978 to 31.9 per cent before China's accession to the World Trade Organization (WTO) in 2001.

Nonetheless, China's momentum towards denationalization and privatization has somewhat decelerated in the twenty-first century. After the State-owned Assets Supervision and Administration Commission (SASAC) was established in March 2003, the state reiterated the control of strategic industries where the dominance of SOEs will be maintained (Song L., "State-owned" 356) – including essential technology, non-renewable natural resources, national security, public utilities and infrastructure services. As the restructuring plan pressed forward, the conversion of pure SOEs into other forms of ownership continued. Preferential policies such as lower interest loans from state-owned banks and better access to land were introduced directly by the government to enhance the market competitiveness of those key enterprises, either through shareholding or administrative imperatives.

Such a reemphasized state influence over the market and economy, which allowed for the Keynesian monetary and fiscal expansion of an unprecedented scale to tackle downturn pressure during the 2008 financial crisis (Garnaut 41), has been effectively continued by the government led by Xi Jinping, who even increased the Party's involvement in the policymaking of state-holding enterprises. As outlined in the 2015 Guideline on Deepening SOE Reform issued by the State Council, state-holding enterprises were not only urged to improve their market presence and business performance but also to fulfil broader political objectives. These enterprises are expected to "serve political goals such as fostering indigenous innovation, supporting social stability and promoting economic initiatives abroad such as the Belt and Road Initiative (BRI)" (Song L., "State-owned" 362). The appointment of their top managers or chairs of boards of directors should now be approved by the SASAC under the supervision of the government.

However, despite the return of state control in the Hu and Xi administrations, as well as the pause of full-scale privatization and marketization in essential industries and social domains including welfare, pensions and health care, Deng Xiaoping's legacies did not completely fade away in these years. China's economic development is still believed to be the "central task" of the Party. As the slogan "to get rich is glorious" is now largely seen as the standard measure of individual success, the underpinning philosophy of Deng's Cat Theory was further reaffirmed, evident in a series of social changes. Decades of persistent reforms in favour of the market have fostered in China a considerable yet still expanding middle class accounting for 68 per cent of total urban households in 2012 and a predicted 76 per cent in 2022 – soaring from 4 per cent in 2000 (Barton, Chen and Jin n.p.).

The "producer's China," in line with Scott Newton's description of the UK, gradually surrendered to the "consumer's China." This process is realized through the currently ongoing supply-side reforms shifting the preference of the natural, financial and human resource allocation from the lossmaking and overproducing manufacturing to those more dynamic and promising industries of service, finance and high-tech innovation. In this way, as noted by David Harvey, "state withdrawal from social welfare provision and technically induced shifts in job structures that render large segments of the labour force redundant complete the domination of capital over labour in the market-place" (*A Brief History* 168).

The mouse has been caught, as China's substantial economic development shows, but the reforms beginning with Deng Xiaoping cannot be simply seen as neoliberal approaches like those prompted by Margaret Thatcher in the UK. Since the "authoritarian centralized control" of the state is still largely maintained (Harvey, *A Brief History* 120), this could be more appropriately termed "post-socialism" (Zhang X.) or "neoliberalism as exception" (Ong, *Neoliberalism*). However, some elements of neoliberalism have been quite apparent in this social transformation, where Chinese individuals were brought away from the collective communes of the past and thrown into an emerging discourse shaped by market forces and competitive principles.

Geographical unevenness, class conflicts, social stratification, the rising Gini index, and other "by-products" of marketization that can be identified in contemporary neoliberal Britain are also very much visible in China. People's obsession with consumerism configured in a capital-dominated discourse where individual choices, or even their personal security and livelihood, is now increasingly tied to their ability to purchase products. These transformations, with their partial neoliberal connotations, have broken "the social, conceptual, and imaginary totality of socialist modernity" and resulted in the "disintegration of a real or imagined national political, intellectual, and cultural discourse" (Zhang X. 3). It is in this denationalized, post-socialist cultural and intellectual field, as I will introduce next, that the Chinese SF Boom began to emerge.

This cultural transition aligns seamlessly with the deep-going marketization and privatization of China's economy and the profound political reforms encouraging new dynamism out of various social conundrums. In this new era when capitalist enterprises can both form and function freely, Chinese people have also developed a different sense of autonomy, indicating that the perceived dissolution and degeneration of the totality of a purported socialist reality opened "a narrow gate on a reconfiguration of economic, social, political, and cultural powers" (Zhang X. 18). Privatization has therefore travelled beyond market activities and been changed into a subjectivizing impulse that aims to prime the powers of the private self.

In the 1990s, Chinese citizens were urged to " 'free up' their individual capacities" to confront dynamic conditions in all areas of life "without seeking guidance from the state, society, or family" (Ong and Zhang 7) – a shift from "relying on the state" to "relying on yourself," which echoes the transformation taking place under the regimes of Thatcher and her successors. The collapse of the socialist totality, however, has also resulted in the breaking of the "iron rice bowl," made true via "the evisceration of social protections, the imposition of user fees, the creation of a flexible labour market regime, and the privatisation of assets formerly held in common" (Harvey, *A Brief History* 150). People in China during this period found themselves in turmoil where the previous stability projected by the socialist ideology and planned economy had been replaced by the uncertainty and insecurity associated with the competitive nature of the market. The gap between the rich and the poor widened, in line with the inequality among different social classes and the developmental unevenness between the favoured regions and the rest. In Harvey's words: "Someone somewhere and somehow is getting very rich" (*A Brief History* 142).

During this transition, publishers in China were financially detached from the state and urged to take care of their own finances. Suddenly, they found themselves in a brand-new situation in which they have to seriously consider what readers would like to read and pay for in order to survive under market pressure. Required in a commercial environment accompanied by various institutional and conceptual changes, "Chinese writers have become far more aware of their potential readers and the market's demands," their writings growing more "entertainment-oriented" (Kong 3). In this way, the high-modernist discourse in China, where sf was seen as spiritual pollution by a group of condescending intellectual elites in a "top-down" mainstream discourse, was shaken by a "bottom-up" mass culture.

Such a social transition from the enlightenment consensus of the 1980s to the fragmented discourse of commodification in the market economy urgently demanded a re-establishment of Chinese national identity and cultural norms that could fit the context driven by economic neoliberalism. This, in fact, forced a crisis upon Chinese intellectuals concerning their endangered social status. Since "the income differential between those employed within the state sector and those employed outside it grew exponentially" (Wang H. 85), the privileges that used to be enjoyed by Chinese cultural elites in the 1980s are gradually transferred to those capital-holding *nouveaux riche* who first rode the wave of marketization.

In response to this complex social transformation, left-wing intellectuals in the mid-1990s launched a nationwide debate mourning the fall of "humanist spirit" or "the spirit of humanism" (*renwen jingshen*) and the loss of the "grand narrative" framing the high-modernist quest for a socialist utopia. In June 1993, Wang Xiaoming, Professor in Chinese Literature at East China Normal University, published the transcript of his earlier panel discussion with his student in *Shanghai wenxue* (*Shanghai Literature*) entitled "Ruins in the Wilderness: The Crisis of Literature and Humanist Spirit" ("*Kuangye shang de feixu – wenxue he renwen jingshen de weiji*"), which is usually regarded as the beginning of this debate. As he confirms the crucial significance of literature in delivering humanist spirit, Wang observes:

> The crisis of literature today is already quite apparent. Several literary periodicals are losing their direction, the quality of new works is in general decline, and appreciative

> readers are growing fewer by the day, while those among writers and critics who realize they have chosen the wrong profession and "leap into the sea" [of business, *xiahai*] are ever more numerous [...] An all-embracing tide of "commodification" with Chinese characteristics is about to practically pull the literary world out by its roots. (Wang X. 63)

However, such a warning about the crisis of literature and the humanist spirit is sometimes considered the "clichéd laments" (Zhang X. 115) of those who felt nostalgic for the failing discourses of high modernism. The transition towards vulgarization and secularization resulting from people's indulgence in commodity fetishism marked a radical historical and contextual rupture from the 1980s when intellectuals were respected as "mentors" of the mass public. Recalling the "top-down" power dynamic between the elites and the public during the New Enlightenment, Cai Xiang rightfully yet regretfully points out "a bitter, sour fruit" cultivated in consumerism and mass culture. This is an unfortunate situation in which "the intellectuals' identity as 'advisor' has already gone through its own deconstruction" (Cai 47). To articulate this, Cai claims with melancholy: "The bell is ringing. Class is over" (Cai 47).

These "clichéd laments," however, are "the last mythology" (Zhang Y. 137–41) of the high-modernist, elite-preaching, centralized discourse where Chinese sf was accused of promoting pseudo-science and violating its science-popularization function expected in the grand narrative of enlightenment. As noted by a group of left-minded scholars pondering the wistful yearning for the "good old times" among left-wing intellectuals, a novel socio-political dynamism and a revamped literary production mechanism have arisen in the aftermath of China's high modernism ebbing and postmodern discourse spreading due to privatization and consumerism – that is the respect for the "reasonable albeit prosaic need of the majority" (Wang M. 115). During such a profound and complicated social transformation closely connected to the formation of "post-socialist modernity" (McGrath 7–9) that emerged in the 1990s and took shape in the first two decades of the twenty-first century, the pragmatic and elitist expectation of Chinese sf nurtured in the discourse of enlightenment was fading away.

Therefore, the Chinese SF Boom is freed from imagining socialist or communist utopias built on scientific advancement and therefore allowed to embrace a "bottom-up" impulse towards entertainment and even contain cultural/political criticism. In other words, the rise of Chinese sf since the 1990s can and should be considered part of the liberal response to the broader social transformation from the high-modernist discourse to the post-socialist modernity in which our everyday world, with the demise of "the lofty humanist-modernist rhetoric of the New Era intelligentsia," "surged into the cultural mainstream, offering itself as the chief mode of representing social life with its increasingly diverse yet flat, mobile yet pattern-forming activities of production and exchange" (Zhang X. 134).

In this case, the categorization of Chinese Boom as "rightist" is in relation to the "leftist" approaches of the British Boom, indicating its significance in the broader cultural transformation towards the mass culture, made possible by the denationalized publishing industry. But even so, many Boom writers in China still hold a critical eye to the proliferating logic of late capitalism and are set to challenge the developmental unevenness, the widening gap between urban and rural areas, the growing Gini index, the rising consumer culture, as well as other elements that have encouraged desires "in the Darwinian struggle for position" (Harvey, *A Brief History* 148). As the latest renaissance of Chinese sf has attracted attention from both fandom and academia after the sensational success of Liu Cixin's *The Three-Body Problem*,[18] the connection between the Chinese SF Boom and the common quest for a new "Chinese-ness" among the Chinese public is crucial to make sense of the post-socialist modernity.

The emergence of Chinese SF Boom can be marked by Liu Cixin's *China 2185* (Song M., "After 1989" 8) in terms of its different textual and narrative characteristics. Completed in 1989 but never published and only circulating online, this novel depicts a resurrection of the consciousness of six dead old men, including Mao, in a cybernetic space. These "ghosts" establish their own virtual nations experimenting various utopian possibilities of China's future and thus endangering the real government, who

18 Liu Cixin, as one of the leading writers of the Chinese SF Boom, can be understood as "the New Right" versus "the New Left" in China, according to Nathaniel Isaacson's panel speech in the symposium "Genre Fiction in Contemporary China, and its Reception in the West" hosted by the Leeds Centre for New Chinese Writing on 10–11 October 2019.

eventually shut down the entire Internet. As such, *China 2185* provides a sophisticated, subversive and mixed "representation of hope and despair, utopianism and its dystopian reflection, and nationalism and cosmopolitanism," witnessing a "collapse of idealism and optimism as well as a pervasive disillusionment with communism" (Song M., "After 1989" 8), which distinguishes *China 2185* from any previous Chinese sf story.

Meanwhile, regarding the literary or media platform for the promotion of the Chinese sf industry, the beginning of the Chinese Boom can also be dated to 1991 (Huss 95). In this year, *Kexue wenyi* (*Science Art and Literature*), the most important Chinese sf magazine surviving the repressed mid-1980s during the Anti-Spiritual Pollution Campaign, was renamed *Kehuan shijie* (*Science Fiction World*, *SFW*) and hosted the Annual Conference of the World SF: An Organization of SF Professionals (WSF). By emphasizing the "fiction" side of sf through such a name change and challenging the false accusation against sf of spiritual pollution, *SFW* embarked "on a solitary quest to establish the genre [of sf] permanently in China" (Huss 95) while acting as the dominant, if not the only, publishing platform fostering a robust group of Chinese sf writers with a diverse array of styles, including Wang Jinkang, Liu Cixin, Han Song, He Xi, Chen Qiufan, Hao Jingfang, Xia Jia – to name but a few.

Throughout the next thirty years, writers of the Chinese SF Boom persistently echoed a resounding assertion: Chinese sf should not remain confined within the role of a mere conduit or spin-off of science popularization, shackled by the pre-1990s paradigm. Instead, it possesses the potential to stand as a substantive augmentation to serious literature – what is commonly referred to as the literary "mainstream." This endeavour involves not only reflecting the fast-changing social and cultural values but also venturing into a broader literary territory that the "mainstream" often struggles to explore, an ambitious appeal culminating in Liu Cixin's renowned non-fiction piece, "Beyond Narcissism: What Science Fiction Can Offer Literature" (2013).

Based on his discussion of Arthur C. Clarke, Liu Cixin claims that sf may have "subverted and expanded the concepts of mainstream literature." Elements such as "macro-detail" and "species portrayal" are believed to be crucial for sf narrative. The former, he argues, allows sf authors "to sweep across time and space, crossing billions of years and tens of billions of light-years with a simple stroke of the pen, leaving the world and the history described in mainstream literature to appear as nothing more than a tiny grain of dust, hardly worth mentioning" ("Beyond" 25), while the latter superimposes "the image of an entire species over that of an individual character" ("Beyond" 27).

This, of course, is Liu Cixin's personal preference which probably cannot be applied to other writers who may hold different perspectives. But the point here is rather clear, directing our attention to a contradictory sense of doubleness: sf should not be simply viewed as a functional vehicle of science popularization as believed in the age of new enlightenment and elitism, nor as a pure market product made for consumption and entertainment despite its "bottom-up" nourishment drawn from the mass culture. Instead, there are considerable "literary" values connoted in sf writings deserving more serious readings. It blossomed forth from the ashes of spiritual pollution nurtured in the lofty discourse of enlightenment in the 1980s, which is itself a historical rupture that would not be possible without a broader socio-cultural transition reversing the "top-down" intellectual elitism.

So, this is how it begins, the tale of the Boom and the Boom. It seems, in a way, that the British and Chinese sf booms are independent. It seems their emergence roughly at the same time around 1990 is coincidental. But of course, they are not. When Timothy Morton introduces "hyperobject" in his discussion on the Anthropocene and climate change, he believes that a hyperobject is "massively distributed in time and space relative to humans," which is so vast that it is "almost impossible to hold in mind" (Morton 1, 58). In other words, it "showers us with effects and affects, even as it withdraws from our comprehension: we can see rain, but not climate; a banknote, but not the economy" (Bould, *Anthropocene* 14).

The sf booms are therefore the rain or the banknotes, the "local representation" (Morton 104) of a much larger phenomenon that is hard to be seen at first sight, or two of the numerous tentacles of the same hyperobject behind everything – the massive entity that can only be experienced locally. Although they were not aware of each other until very recently, the British and Chinese SF Booms, as fraternal twins already separated for too long, are in essence interconnected, both responding to, in different manners of course, specific political-economic transitions in a Thatcherite or post-socialist context. Respectively, each of them offers distinctive perspectives on the profound cultural and socio-economic shifts of an age where the state retreats from society, leaving individual men and women to bear the weight of their own destinies, and creating a ruptured historical discourse where social subjects are remade, forever redefined by market competition. Therefore, the two Booms should be perpetually intertwined in our reading, for only through this symbiotic approach can their profound political and historical import unfurl beyond the boundaries of our immediate perception – which, from the outset, is rooted in a crucible of alternatives and disruption: utopias.

CHAPTER 1

The Ones Who Walk Away: Disrupted Utopias in Han Song's *Red Star Over America* and Iain M. Banks's *Culture* Series

> In China, crime has been eradicated and divorce unheard of. The need for cloning has vanished, as people enjoy exceptionally long lives. In fact, many willingly request euthanasia before reaching the age of 120, driven by a desire to ease the state's burden. This is a noble spirit of collectivism.
>
> – Han Song, in *Red Star Over America*

> I still don't know why the hell you're fighting in the first place. The Idirans never were any threat to you. They still wouldn't be, if you stopped fighting them. Did life in your great Utopia really get so boring you needed a war?
>
> – Iain M. Banks, in *Consider Phlebas*

Disrupted Utopias

Ever since its coinage in the sixteenth century, the term "utopia" has always been bound to a vision of alternatives. It is a time-space with a sense of otherness – other landscapes, other worlds, other histories, other socio-political possibilities, other spectacles and much more. It serves as the canvas for our extrapolation beyond the confines of reality, our contemplation of what could have been achieved and what lies ahead, and our speculation of difference and deviance. Embedded in utopian principles, in Ernst Bloch's words, is "the philosophy of the New." At the core of its concerns, there is "conscience of tomorrow, commitment to the future, knowledge of hope" (Bloch 7). The tension between the real world and its utopian representation, in this way, could indeed remind us that "all forms of social organization – including our actual society – are provisional and capable of *being changed* [...] Utopias, like many modern texts, function to increase our awareness of the historicity of all values and of their human origin" (Ruppert 13; emphasis added).

Such an articulation of change and transgression is where utopian thoughts are connected to sf, a genre that also focuses on the sense of hope, dreams, newness and estrangement, that can be written "only between the utopian and anti-utopian horizons" (Suvin 61–2), which is always "located on the In-Front-of-Us, at the level of the Not-Yet-Being and in the dimension of utopian futurity" (Freedman, "Science Fiction and Utopia" 79). In this way, representing utopias in sf works is always an unending process, always leading to an implied vision that has not yet come into being and a continuous self-reformulation subject to "a critical examination of the utopian ideal itself" (Fitting 147).

This "critical examination," to an extent, can be traced back to what Tom Moylan called "critical utopia," which he uses not to envision idealized or perfect societies, but to interrogate the flaws those seemingly utopian societies may have retained, the shortcomings and injustices of the existing world. According to Moylan's own remarks in *Demand the Impossible* (1986) inspired from the works by Joanna Russ, Ursula K. Le Guin, Marge Piercy and Samuel R. Delany, critical utopia – mostly rooted to possibilities in the 1960s and the 1970s – appears to be self-reflective in nature. It stands for a shift "in anti-hegemonic culture and politics away from male-dominant, capitalist, hierarchical social structures," giving voice to "an emerging radical perception and experience that emphasize process over system, autonomous and marginal activity over the imposed order of a centre, human liberation over white/phallocratic control, and the interrelationships of nature over human chauvinism" (Moylan, *Demand* 201). Its central concern, therefore, is to be aware of "the limitations of the utopian tradition, so that these texts [of critical utopia] reject utopia as blueprint while preserving it as dream [...] [T]he novels focus on the continuing presence of difference and imperfection within utopian society itself and thus render more recognizable and dynamic alternatives" (10–11).

These alternatives, these visions of (retro-)futuristic possibilities put forth through a forever process of envisaging new utopias while questioning the old ones, are the desires most urgently needed in the cultural and social-political discourse of late capitalism. They are desired not in the sense of an absolute perfection as the placebo of despairing social problems but as a certain kind of hope calling for the alternatives that have "not yet" come true. In this way, the formation of utopia may have created a *disrupted* temporality and spatiality – a tear in the fabric of reality, a rupture with the known world, a deviation from normality or a transgression of boundaries. Although what Moylan sees as "critical utopias" seems to have gradually faded away under the fulfilment of neoliberalism since the 1980s, the sense of disruption remains crucial in sf writings, embedded in the ways utopias are constructed and, even more importantly, collapse in on themselves. As Fredric Jameson explains the connection between disruption and utopia in his *Archaeologies of the Future* (2005):

> Disruption is, then, the name for a new discursive strategy, and Utopia is the form such disruption necessarily takes. And this is now the temporal situation in which the Utopian form proper – the radical closure of a system of difference in time, the experience of the total formal break and discontinuity – has its political role to play, and in fact becomes a new kind of content in its own right. For it is the very principle of the radical break as such, its possibility, which is reinforced by the Utopian form, which insists that its radical difference is possible and that a break is necessary. (231)

In a similar vein, the "reinvention of the Utopian vision" that Jameson insists on in a broader context of the "end of utopia" or "end of history" (*Postmodernism* 159) here becomes pivotal and indispensable in our discussion of the British and Chinese SF Booms – both rooted deeply in the historical disruption and transition of the contemporary British and Chinese culture.

This chapter, therefore, focuses on two of the most influential critical utopias in China and the UK – both, however, are disrupted in their own way. One of the two utopias is the "harmonious society" (Song M., "Variations" 90) governed and supervised by an artificial intelligence named Amanduo in Han Song's 2000 novel *Red Star over America* (*Huoxing zhaoyao meiguo*). Despite its utopian façade, we will soon discover that Amanduo constantly teeters on the brink of its own demise, much like how the elitist discourse of enlightenment in the 1980s China was shaken, and eventually broken, by the marketplace in the following decade. This is a demonstration of people's melancholic farewell to the socialist utopia, one that is built upon a sense of certainty and centralization, and their tentative quest for a post-socialist, post-utopian future.

As the harmonious society collapses after the death of Amanduo that was once almighty, the protagonist Tang Long finds himself cast into a chaotic wasteland where all kinds of state protection, provision and supervision are suddenly stripped off, a new time-space where he can count on no one else but himself. In a way, Tang Long serves as an embodiment of China itself, though it is a China full of confusion, whose memories of the past utopia are still vivid and therefore always project into the future Tang Long has envisioned. During his safari in search of new orders, he comes across a number of possibilities that could fill the political and historical void left behind by the collapsed Amanduo, but none of them truly works because of their failure to detach from the grand narrative and universalism promised by the false utopia.

In contrast to this dying Amanduo, the other utopia, namely the Culture created by Iain M. Banks, appears far from its final termination. A rather intentional attack on Thatcherite neoliberalism that favoured "unrestrained competition and meritocracy" (Tew et al. 6), the Culture is a post-capitalist anarchy, a post-scarcity civilization where all humans and machines with self-consciousness are created equal, where they are endowed with the rights of life, liberty and the pursuit of happiness beyond capitalist exploitation and the alienation of labour. Banks does not buy the argument for the end-of-history or the sense of historical exhaustion, striving to articulate his own revolutionary desire and provide a constructive framework out of the pathology of left melancholia (Brown, "Resisting" 19–27; Fisher, *Postcapitalist* 55). In this manner, the utopian Culture represents a nostalgic commemoration for a future that has never arrived, narrated with a sense of wonder and the poetics of alterity, possibility and potentiality.

But even so, the moral ambiguity within the Culture can never be neglected. As it frequently interferes into the domestic affairs of other civilizations which the Culture believes should be guided or enlightened, and even wages wars against them, the Culture appears more like a utopia *within*, and an empire *without*. The post-racial, post-gender and posthuman diversity in the Culture, under a closer look, are hardly more than the delusions deriving from a hegemonic structure in which Banks's plan for social stability "is dependent upon a kind of social homogeneity" (Vint, *Bodies* 81). A manifestation of liberal humanism, the Culture behaves like Hardt and Negri's postmodern Empire that aims not to invade but to subsume, which substitutes the imperialistic logic of colonization with a rhizomic, decentred, nomadic framework of social formation. The child locked underground in Ursula Le Guin's classic Omelas finds new equivalence in the Culture.[1] And likewise, someone leaves, while others stay.

Demise of the False Utopia

When delving into the realm of contemporary Chinese sf, Han Song is an author whose work you simply cannot afford to bypass. In the introduction to *Exploring Dark Short Fiction #5: A Primer to Han Song* (2020) – the first and only anthology of Han Song available in English to date, editor Eric J. Guignard, with great enthusiasm, acknowledges his role in shaping the Chinese SF Boom:

> Han Song is lauded for works that bridge new developments in science and subjects of cultural and social dynamics with stories of dystopia, governmental conspiracy, and subversive horror, earning praise for his writing as "absurdly dark," while also reigniting a *science fiction renaissance*. (1; emphasis added)

1 In her 1973 story "The Ones Who Walk Away from Omelas," Ursula K. Le Guin describes a utopian city (Omelas), where everything is perfect, and the citizens enjoy a life of happiness, prosperity, and abundance. However, this utopia comes with a dark secret: the happiness and well-being of the entire city depend on the suffering and misery of a single child who is locked in a basement. It forces readers to confront the ethical dilemma of whether one can justify the happiness and prosperity of the many at the expense of the suffering of a single innocent individual. Some citizens of Omelas choose to walk away from the city, unable to accept this moral compromise, while others stay and live with the knowledge of the child's suffering.

In comparison to his fellow Boom writer Liu Cixin, Han Song has garnered considerably less attention among English-speaking readers. This relative obscurity primarily stems from the fact that his works have been less frequently translated and made available in English – which is usually considered a daunting job because of the complexity of the rich symbolic, metaphorical and especially political connotations in his stories always defeat any simple readings.

On top of this, Han Song also distinguishes himself through his unique writing style, regarded as a significant contribution to the Chinese Boom. As Li Guangyi observes, "one can use refined language, magnificent imagination, or any number of other adjectives to describe Han Song's unique literary style, but no phrase captures Han Song's writing better than 'eerie'" (29). Li's article was translated from Chinese by Nathaniel Isaacson and the original Chinese term for "eerie" is *guiyi*. *Guiyi* can also be translated as "strange," "alienated," "bizarre" and "grotesque" (see also Andolfatto 81–99). But here I follow Isaacson's translation of the term in order to set up a comparison between Han Song's aesthetic and Mark Fisher's discussion in *The Weird and The Eerie* (2016). In a similar vein, Wang Yao (Xia Jia) argues that Han Song's unique sense of eeriness, as well as his depictions of "the chaotic or deconstructed chronotope, the dark maze where history and memory intertwine, the grotesque ruins and tombstones," indicates the absurdity and uncertainty hiding behind the changing façades of modernity – for instance, "progress of civilization" and "scientific rationality" (Wang Y. 206). In other words, the eeriness in his writings "upends practically all of the established rules governing [the] content [of canonical science fictions] and is an important step forward for the nativization of [Chinese] science fiction" (qtd. in Jia, "Gloomy" 103).

One of the endeavours in this process of nativization, where China is placed at the centre of the narrative, is certainly Han Song's *Red Star over America* (2000), in which he envisions a utopian China that rises to become the superpower of the world, centrally governed by an omnipotent artificial intelligence named "Amanduo."[2] In contrast, America has become a dystopian wasteland. Born in what appears to be an impeccable society,

2 Amanduo is written as 阿曼多 in Chinese, a name that sounds like a transliteration from a foreign language but actually it does not seem to have real meanings.

the protagonist Tang Long is groomed as a professional *go* player and has spent his entire life under the protection and watchful eye of Amanduo. He is sent to the US to play in an international *go* competition as part of a grand mission to enlighten the American people by demonstrating the charms of *go*.

His mission has gone wrong, however. During the competition, Amanduo suddenly dysfunctions without warning, leaving Tang Long in the middle of a series of apocalyptic catastrophes caused by the absence of its control. Abandoned in a post-Amanduo world, Tang Long finds himself on a quixotic quest across America looking for an alternative order to replace his lost utopia. During his journey, he comes across a number of possible alternatives embodied by three characters – Suzuki, Newman and Colonel Sam – but none of these characters succeeds in truly bidding farewell to the past.

These characters are remarkable because each of them is consumed by a destiny that drives them: Suzuki is a perpetual traveller, on a quest for a "Sceptre" that he believes can foresee the future and grant him control over the post-Amanduo world, which, however, reveals itself to be a mere illusion. Newman has a bioengineered tail that functions like a biological hard drive, storing a wealth of historical and cultural knowledge for future access. Colonel Sam aspires to create a new, hybrid language called Aikemai, with which he attempts to write his own rules upon the dystopian wasteland and to make them universal. In short, Suzuki, Newman and Colonel Sam are all trying to build a new order following Amanduo's downfall.

Yet still, it is through their pursuits that they become disillusioned with their obsessive missions. They come to realize that, while presenting numerous proposals for new ideologies to replace Amanduo, they can never fully escape the looming shadow of the falling utopia. In truth, despite Amanduo's apparent malfunction, it lingers in an invisible form that few are aware of. Due to this ambiguity, Suzuki, Newman and Colonel Sam's beliefs in what they are chasing for are open to questions and challenges. In line with this, we can also revisit the historical metaphors of China's post-socialist transition that they embody, as well as the socio-political implications of their failed attempts at change.

What really matters in *Red Star over America* is an attempt to construct a scenario of difference, alternatives and transformation, indicating a release "from the mundane" and an escape "from the confines of what is ordinarily taken as reality" (Fisher, *Postcapitalist* 13). In his 2016 monograph *The Weird and The Eerie*, Mark Fisher teases out some of the nuances between these two often overlapping modes, with the former, "the weird," being constituted by a presence "of that *which does not belong*," and that may "exceed our capacity to represent it" (Fisher, *The Weird* 61). The eerie, on the other hand, "is constituted by a *failure of absence* or by a *failure of presence*," that is, "the sensation of the eerie occurs when there is something present when there should be nothing, or [...] there is nothing present when there should be something" (61; emphasis in original).

In line with Fisher's definition, Han Song's works can be classified as both weird and eerie, displaying the aesthetic and narrative elements of both genres that can evoke feelings of horror, strangeness and the uncanny. They also indicate features that Fisher proposes for the stories of the weird and the eerie – "a fascination with the outside, for that which lies beyond standard perception, cognition and experience," and the detachment from everyday urgencies that "can give us access to the forces which govern mundane reality but which are ordinarily obscured" (13). Creating such a space beyond "mundane reality" where a certain form of contemplation is developed from pain and unease, Han Song has managed to blend representations "of hope and despair, utopianism and its dystopian reflection, and nationalism and cosmopolitanism" (Song M., "After 1989" 8).

This "blended" utopianism, a combination of both utopian and dystopian spaces embedded in his eerie writings, has afforded Han Song a distinctive critical perspective on the enlightenment ideals of early twentieth-century May Fourth activists, most notably figures such as Liang Qichao (1873–1929) and Lu Xun (1881–1936), during the formative years of Chinese sf. Back then, utopian themes were quite prevalent in early Chinese sf (then called *kexue xiaoshuo*, that is, "scientific novels," emphasizing the *scientific* much more than the *fictional* side of sf). This is especially evident in, for example, Liang Qichao's *The Future of New China* [*Xin Zhongguo weilai Ji*, 1902] and Wu Jianren's *New Story of the Stone* [*Xin shitou ji*, 1905] (see Isaacson's *Celestial Empire*). In these novels, a utopian version of a futuristic and historically progressive China was commonly constructed by these enlightenment intellectuals in response to the chaotic reality in China, presenting "a pseudo-ethnographic mapping of the collision of internal and external pressures that faced Chinese society" (Isaacson 4). Sf was then a vehicle that could promote the public awareness of modernity and rationality.

This utopian vision, rooted in Enlightenment optimism, resurfaced in Chinese sf during the late 1970s and early 1980s. At this time, Chinese sf conveyed aspirations for a modernized and industrialized socialist utopia, which, however, was soon suffocated in the anti-spiritual pollution movement in late 1983 and early 1984 (see Introduction). After Chinese sf weathered this political winter and experienced a rebirth during the Boom era, utopianism was similarly rekindled along the journey – only taking on a far more ambiguous and inquisitive character. For this "variations" of utopia in contemporary Chinese sf, Song Mingwei has already provided a convincing summary in his 2013 article:

> Deeply entangled with the politics of a changing China, science fiction today both strengthens and *complicates* the utopian vision of a new and powerful China: it mingles nationalism with utopianism/dystopianism, mixes sharp social criticism with an acute awareness of China's potential for further reform, and wraps political consciousness in scientific discourses about the powers of technology and the technologies of power. (Song M., "Variations" 87; emphasis added)

These "variations," in a way, have blurred the boundary between utopias and dystopias, or, in other words, they guide us towards a distinct form of utopianism thriving on the ruins of the old one. As I have discussed in the Introduction, the New Enlightenment discourse in China in the 1980s developed upon "a system that was relatively stagnant economically and technologically" and on the "belief in a prosperous socialist utopia and the creation of a new socialist human being" (Kinkley 20), and therefore was closely connected to elitism and high modernism.

However, whereas such a discourse gradually collapsed in the following decade, the incoming trend of privatization and marketization from the 1990s onwards not only configured a nostalgic mourning for the lost certainty and predictability that used to be projected by the socialist utopia, but has also formulated "another utopian faith." And this is the one, according to Jeffrey C. Kinkley, where "economic growth […] would lead China to the best of all possible worlds" (20–1). The ostensible nostalgia towards a fading socialist totality, as Zhang Xudong observes, "became entangled with a utopian/dystopian fervor to embrace global capital and its ideology" in the 1990s (185) – which has eventually resulted in complicated and critical expressions of how utopianism is conveyed in contemporary Chinese literature. Of course, these elements are also evident in "serious writings" such as new historical and urban novels, but they can find much stronger voices and representations in sf, given the genre's potential for producing the Blochian "hope" as the utopian impulse.

The utopian China depicted in *Red Star Over America* appears, at least on first impression, to be a "good place" indeed. The novel is set in the year 2066, one hundred years after the Cultural Revolution, and China has become a gigantic "garden":

> Flowers bloomed all year round, trees cast their shade, a rainbow hung over the sky – every season was spring, manipulated by the National Climate and Emotion Management Bureau. People lived in buildings outfitted with eco-intelligent systems. These buildings would expand as the number of residents expanded, providing them with spacious and comfortable living space […] Everyone was guaranteed a decent and respectable job. (Han, *Huoxing* 234)

This "garden" is centrally supervised by Amanduo, a highly advanced artificial intelligence existing only in cyberspace, an omnipresent entity that, through the Internet, penetrates every corner of society. With Amanduo, "the unevenness of information distribution between the developed and developing countries have been eliminated; slogans such as 'democracy,' 'liberty,' 'equality' and 'justice' were no longer floating in the air like bubbles." Amanduo appears benign and benevolent, "like a sister-in-law […] whole-heartedly taking care of [people's] lives with its incomparable computing capability" (10).

In contrast to the harmony, order, peace and integrity promised by this utopian China, those countries rejecting Amanduo's supervision, the US in particular, constantly suffer from chaotic political disturbances, anarchic terrorism and even civil wars. For some readers – given that *Red*

Star Over America was published when the China-US relations were at a low point because of the US bombing of the Chinese embassy building in Belgrade – this story might be read as a rather radical manifesto for the growing nationalism of the Chinese people. But this is, I think, an unfortunate misunderstanding, because it is the powerful and harmonious society of the fictional China that teeters on the brink of its own downfall, while the dystopian wasteland of the US offers a canvas for the potential emergence of new orders.[3]

In fact, even though the names of various actual locations reappear throughout the novel – including Japan, Germany, Iran, South Korea and many others, along with China and the US – these places can and should be interpreted in a *denationalized* manner, that is, as a single yet hybridly cluttered time-space accommodating different social and ideological norms in China from different historical periods. This is illustrative of Mikhail Bakhtin's concept of "chronotope," which indicates

> the intrinsic connectedness of temporal and spatial relationships that are artistically expressed in literature [...] In the literary artistic chronotope, spatial and temporal indicators are fused into one carefully thought-out, concrete whole. Time, as it were, thickens, takes on flesh, becomes artistically visible; likewise, space becomes charged and responsive to the movements of time, plot and history. This intersection of axes and fusion of indicators characterize the artistic chronotope. (Bakhtin, *Dialogic* 84)

Therefore, Tang Long's quixotic adventures with Suzuki, Newman and Colonel Sam formulate a Bakhtinian "chronotope." After his interrogation of Greek romance narratives, Bakhtin argues that these Greek adventures, separate from each other and complete in themselves, "have no essential ties with any particular details of individual countries" (100). They are interchangeable in spatiality and reversible in temporality. In the same way, my reading of Han Song's *Red Star Over America* is *country-less*,

3 Such misunderstandings are not uncommon. According to Han Song, the manuscript of *Red Star over America* was turned down by four publishers – all of them believing that the radical descriptions of both China and the US could have a negative influence on real international relations and that it could trigger an even stronger round of nationalism among Chinese readers (*Xiangxiangli* 245). The story was eventually accepted and published by Heilongjiang renmin chubanshe.

seeing those geographical and, metaphorically, political labels as "spatial and temporal indicators" as suggested by Bakhtin. Or more precisely, the chronotope gradually mapped out through the protagonist Tang Long's journey (from the utopian, Amanduo-managed China to the dystopian, Amanduo-rejecting US) and through what he experiences there, including a flood, the Suzuki gang, Newman's friendship and the American civil war on the side of Colonel Sam is a highly symbolic, highly "fused" (Bakhtin, *Dialogic* 84) representation of the (sometimes hesitant) social and cultural transformation in China, and China alone.

In this case, the ambiguous nature of the "garden" society under Amanduo's supervision leaves us with a space for the critical scrutiny of the utopian imagination. "We have been under systematic training since [we were] two-and-a-half years old," says Tang Long to his Suzuki gang friends, "to be a person of perfection, to be an expert in a certain domain [...] Scientists have developed games of all kinds to satisfy people's desires, but my go teammates and I rarely played them. This is because, in China, the most important thing is to study and work, to complete the job assigned by the country" (Han, *Huoxing* 235). The work of planning and management is clearly evident in Han Song's Amanduo. As Song Mingwei observes, it has parallels with Jeffrey Wasserstrom's description of contemporary Chinese politics as a "soft" vision of authoritarianism ("Variations" 87) that stresses "the depoliticizing effort of keeping people apart and providing them with distracting forms of activity and entertainment" (Wasserstrom 110). Song Mingwei argues that the garden society might provide "a strong sense of self-reflection supporting modern intellectual criticisms of China's long tradition of authoritarian politics and culture," and Amanduo, therefore, should be perceived as "a completely efficient program for establishing a centralist system to which each individual will voluntarily submit" (Song M., "Variations" 88).

Under Amanduo's meticulous "caring" for the Chinese people, everything "will be smooth, trouble-free, and carefully arranged [...] People just need to enjoy their lives as always and complete the tasks that the country has assigned to them. The future will then come with no surprises. This is what happiness is" (Han, *Huoxing* 92). This understanding of happiness is, in a way, utopian indeed. But from a more critical perspective, it appears to be what Erika Gottlieb refers to as a typical "classic" or "western" dystopia – "the destruction of the individual's private world" (Gottlieb 11) – or what Kinkley describes as "the danger of totalitarianism and mindless social conformism furthered by technological progress" (Kinkley 13). Even more critically, the "utopian" Amanduo often filters the information passed on to individuals, in this way keeping them in an "infant incubator" for the sake of protection (Han, *Huoxing* 94). The structure of the "natural" family has long been dissolved in the Amanduo society. New-born babies, mostly from test-tubes, are grown in incubators and then assigned to non-genetic families. In the incubators they are imprinted with Amanduo's values and are protected from the miserable world beyond Amanduo's control. Tang Long realizes during his truth-seeking journey that

> although I am already sixteen years old, I have absolutely no idea of other cultures in the world. I inherited the genes of *go*, but not the knowledge that some foreigners are only interested in things like the horns on their head.[4] Does this have more a pragmatic utility than *go*? Amanduo didn't reveal this to me, nor did my teachers in the army. (Han, *Huoxing* 99)

In this "garden," there is no surprises, no uncertainty, no change, no sense of newness. Everything seems in order under Amanduo's supervision. But this garden created by Amanduo also forms what Bakhtin calls the "idyllic chronotope," where events are anchored around a small world spatially that "is limited and sufficient unto itself, not linked in any intrinsic way with other places, with the rest of the world" (Bakhtin, *Dialogic* 225). Meanwhile, such stability and predictability, also in Bakhtin's words, foregrounds "the unity of place," which "brings together and even fuses the cradle and the grave [...] and brings together as well childhood and old age [... and] the life of the various generations who had also lived in that same place, under the same conditions, and who had seen the same things" (Bakhtin, *Dialogic* 225).

As such, the idyllic, garden-like, harmonious society, where the forward impulse of time is constrained and therefore cannot generate the sense of

4 During Tang Long's journey, he meets an Iranian teenager who has horns on his head.

"becoming" (Bakhtin, *Dialogic* 210), will never experience any progression. The ostensibly utopian China overseen by the all-encompassing Amanduo, when subjected to meticulous scrutiny, reveals itself as profoundly problematic. As I will discuss next, this story serves as an interrogation of the socio-political transition taking place along with China's market-oriented reforms, a process that Han Song attempts to criticize, question and challenge, eventually undermining the Leviathan disguised by the utopian façade – a false utopia that is written to be disrupted in the first place. In fact, Han Song never shies away from such an effort, "in the context of technological civilization," to reveal the "cunning, meanness, and darkness in the Chinese people, a new ignorance characterized by information technology, rule of law, and wealth" (Han, qtd. in Jia, "Gloomy" 106), and critically to engage with the socio-cultural shift in China from a socialist utopia to a post-socialist wasteland.

Restoring Order in the Post-Amanduo World

As mentioned earlier, Amanduo, like the utopian and harmonious society it makes possible, is never far from its own collapse. Han Song's utopian imagination can be seen as a way to revisit both enlightenment and May Fourth utopianism. It also embodies a "parodied" version of China's rise through the "political utopianism and technological optimism" (Song, "New" 470–1) resurrected in the 1980s during the New Enlightenment movement. Amanduo's self-destruction foreshadows the tremendous historical rupture in China during the following decade, when the discourse of high modernism, "the 'enlightenment' consensus of the 1980s," was replaced by "the 'vulgarization' (*cubihua*) or 'secularization' (*shisuhua*) brought on by the commodification of culture in the market economy" (McGrath 32).

During the 1990s, a remarkable group of prominent critics lamented the decline of the "humanist spirit," as explored in the Introduction. They observed a trend that "surfaced with the rise of the great tide of the market economy and business: money worship, the sacrifice of principle for profit, the loss of ideals, the disintegration of ethics" (Zhang Z. 176). They were convinced that this process of marketization should shoulder the blame for the fading of the moral and technological utopia initially envisioned under socialism. For others, however, this mourning was merely a nostalgia for the period of new enlightenment when "liberal-humanist intellectuals believed that history had a message for *them* to deliver to the Chinese nation," though in the 1990s they realized that "the message was instead delivered to the market-place by joint forces of the state and global capitalism" (Zhang X. 116; emphasis in original). Han Song, a senior journalist at China's Xinhua News Agency, has borne witness to more than enough confusions, uncertainties, sufferings and struggles stemming from this significant historical disruption. Through his sf writings, he has performed as a social archivist, meticulously documenting the events and experiences that demand preservation.

I read *Red Star Over America* as a rather faithful representation of this disruption, charting China's historical trajectory through the experiences of the protagonist Tang Long and his search for an alternative to replace the collapsing utopia of Amanduo. The epochal transition of China is subtly encapsulated in the name "Tang Long" itself, which, unlike the transliteration "Amanduo," carries rich historical connotations. The Tang Dynasty (618–907 CE) is widely regarded as one of the most powerful periods in China and thus usually indicates China's historical prosperity. *Long* refers to the legendary and sacred animal the Chinese dragon, usually taken as the symbol for emperors.

Throughout Tang Long's odyssey, he is frequently addressed as *Longzi* (son of the dragon), suggesting his role as a harbinger of hope and the future, as well as the potential savior of order from chaos due to his prowess in the game of *go*: "[H]e is *Longzi* – a descendant of the dragon" (Han, *Huoxing* 378).[5] Unfortunately, however, Tang Long fails to evoke such hopes, nor does he manage to find an alternative to Amanduo's utopia. He even goes so far as to lose his proficiency in playing *go*, a vocation that was originally

5 The term *Long de chuanren* [龙的传人, descendants of the dragon] is a euphemistic synonym for the Chinese people, resonant with China's patriotism and nationalism.

designated for him by the now-defunct Amanduo, despite it being his life-long pursuit. In this context, the implications of Tang Long's name present an intriguing counterpoint to his tumultuous post-Amanduo experiences.

There are no explicit reasons in the text as to why Amanduo comes to an end, but there are some subtle clues. The omnipotent and self-evolving artificial intelligence, based on the hyper-advanced Internet with which so many people are interconnected, is considered "the First Life" or "Heart of the World" (Han, *Huoxing* 10). In this way, it is essentially dependent on a sense of centrality: civil affairs and people's lives in this apparently utopian society are centrally planned, arranged and supervised. This is a centrality made possible by Amanduo's extensive penetration into virtual space, "the super-intelligent system beyond human's control and imagination" (Han, *Huoxing* 81). Social development accelerated as a result, but at the same time and more importantly,

> Amanduo had created a huge amount of information entropy. It tore the world apart, step by step leading us to the eventual "heat death."[6] The world of the Internet, of the so-called "dream society," would cool down even before we can notice. People were increasingly clinging to the digital, non-human system. Everything, even emotions, was digitalized, constructed through zeros and ones, and every problem could be solved via the Internet. (Han, *Huoxing* 81)

In other words, the collapse of Amanduo is an inevitable consequence of its intrinsic conflict between the high-level "centrality" and the "fragmentation" resulting from the gradual accumulation of a myriad of piece-by-piece information and digitized data. It therefore becomes overloaded and, "as an intelligent entity, Amanduo became schizophrenic" (Han, *Huoxing* 80).

For me this evokes Fredric Jameson's use of the term "schizophrenia" standing for the postmodern subject's detachment from time and history and the postmodern condition in which people constantly live among the fragments of now and here. It is fairly evident in *Red Star Over America*

6 "Heat death" is a term borrowed from a physical hypothesis. In this novel, it means the "information entropy" in the virtual space governed by Amanduo will increase to a degree where no more information can be added. Thus it "cools down" during the process in which it was "heated."

that Amanduo's endeavour failed to reconcile the "top-down" rationale of elitism or high-modernist centralized control with the "bottom-up" drive. This drive stemmed from the increasing influence and prominence of the public voice, which was empowered by market forces and the circulation of capital. The "older frontier" between high culture and what is often referred to as mass or commercial culture, as noted by Jameson in his observation of high modernism (*Postmodernism* 2), encounters its own disruption. In this context, the dichotomy between these two contrasting discourses contributes to the debate surrounding the "humanist spirit" in China during the mid-1990s, which has been introduced in the previous chapter as the intellectual discourse that called for the emergence of the Chinese SF Boom.

This said, such a debate eventually faded away as the nostalgic longing for the revival of a vanishing humanist spirit gradually lost its appeal in light of the increasing prevalence of market-driven considerations and the growing influence of the general public. "Class is over," as Cai Xiang declared with melancholy (47), and so was the socialist utopia based on centrality and totality. The sense of certainty, arrangement, "top-down" management and the comfort of living in a "honey jar," an "infant incubator," a "garden" (Han, *Huoxing* 37, 94, 234) and a generally harmonious society, are all gone with the demise of the false utopia created by Amanduo, leaving an ideological void that urgently calls for other alternatives. In this way, Tang Long's initial elitist and educational mission to "save the souls of Americans" (28) who are not covered by Amanduo's arms turns out to be in vain. This should not be understood as Sino-centralism, however; the word "America" in this story is coded as an adventure chronotope with further connotations, including the power of a mass public rising in the post-socialist age. In fact, it is exactly in the absence of Amanduo and in the collapse of central management that Tang Long finds himself in confusion and uncertainty, in a position where "for the first time ever, [he] has a feeling that the future is not in [his] control" (17). Rather reluctantly, as the embodiment of China, Tang Long is forced to take up the task of conceptualizing a post-Amanduo world.

This post-Amanduo world, however, despite its chaos and anarchy, is still haunted by the ghost and shadow of the collapsed utopia. When Tang

Long is cast out of Amanduo's protection and almost killed in a destructive flood,[7] he is fortunately rescued by a group of well-armed teenaged orphans under the leadership of Suzuki. Suzuki believes that the new order to be established upon the ruins of Amanduo can be identified through the "Sceptre" that he and his gang-mates are looking for, a secretly developed device able to predict the future. "Whoever gets their hands on the Sceptre," says Suzuki to Tang Long, "will know what will be going on in this world. Once we can forecast when the apocalypse will come and how we can survive it, there will be no need to fear the disasters of the future" (123).

Even though Amanduo has already revealed its irreversible self-destruction, Suzuki remains captivated, not only by the certainty, predictability and the promise of a utopian future projected by such an entity but also by the top-down logic of centralization. As the only one in his gang who still has occasional connection to the struggling and weakening Amanduo, Suzuki regularly holds "press conferences" (102) to share selectively the information he collects from the remnants of the AI network. This process, in fact, has made Suzuki not a revolutionary pioneer striving to create a new order, as he firmly believes himself to be, but "an agent [or servant] of Amanduo" (119) who can only imitate the past.

For Suzuki and his gang-mates, such a nostalgic remembrance of the past is considered "the new belief" (180) after the tremendous transformation they have just experienced, a new belief that the Sceptre might provide the sense of security that used to be promised by Amanduo. When they eventually manage to find the Sceptre, it appears as "a stick, like a human thigh bone, of less than one-meter long, with a digital disc embedded in the middle and covered with a light-purple halo" (Han, *Huoxing* 172). They expect it to show them a way out of the current chaos (173), but this turns

7 When Amanduo reaches its termination, the coastal dam holding back the rising sea level (a result of global warming) and protecting the city where Tang Long plays in the *go* competition is also destroyed, resulting in a catastrophic flood. It is at this moment that Tang Long loses all contact with his teammates and with Amanduo, everything that can bring him back to the past. Han Song does not make it clear why the dam collapses – it might be a side-effect of Amanduo's demise or an intentional terrorist attack.

out to be nothing but an illusion, a false dream that confines Suzuki in his nostalgia for the fading utopia. In Tang Long's eyes,

> Suzuki looked at the Sceptre every day, wondering hard like a wall-facer.[8] He told us that the Sceptre was the only treasure that could save the world after Amanduo's collapse. But it kept silent, which was a huge disappointment to him. *Suzuki was so bewitched by the past that he was bound to be eliminated in the new era.* (202; emphasis added)

"The future predicted by the Sceptre has been broken," and Suzuki, who does not admit the Sceptre's failure, turns into a child-like old man whose hair becomes grey (242). Tang Long decides to leave Suzuki and to continue his journey in search of an alternative to Amanduo, and this time he does not need the Sceptre "to tell [him] about the future" (245).

Other attempts to restore order amid the chaos of the post-Amanduo world are associated with Newman and Colonel Sam. Newman is an extraordinary character that Tang Long meets after leaving Suzuki, who stands out for two features: his "magical" tail that can disseminate historical and cultural knowledge to the public and, like Tang Long, his ability to play *go*. Song Mingwei notes that *go* "contain[s] the ultimate means to peace and harmony" ("Variations" 89 in the novel). Under Amanduo's system of planning and arrangement, *go* is considered the embodiment of "calm, discipline, self-esteem and civilization" (Han, *Huoxing* 58), embodying Amanduo's utopian vision. It is also believed to be the only possible instrument to

8 The phrase "wall-facing" or "wall-gazing" is related to Buddhism and, specifically, to Bodhidharma, who in his meditation "always sat in silence facing the wall, so people called him the 'wall-contemplating Brahmin'" (McRae 113). As recorded in the *Two Entrances and Four Acts*, traditionally attributed to Bodhidharma, "wall-facing" can be applied to "those who turn from delusion back to reality, who meditate on walls, the absence of self and other, the oneness of mortal and sage, and who remain unmoved even by scriptures are in complete and unspoken agreement with reason" (Red Pine 3). In fact, anything can be a "wall" as long as it offers a focus to the meditator (van Schaik 117–18). In Chinese sf stories, "wall-facing" is in wide circulation thanks to Liu Cixin's *Three-Body* trilogy (2006–10; English trans. 2014–16), especially *Dark Forest* (2008), but it is also used here by Han Song to indicate the special connection between Suzuki and the Sceptre, as well as the utopian implications of predictability and totality hiding behind it.

save those who are not centrally supervised and supposedly protected by Amanduo, to educate those who are not covered in the glory of the enlightenment utopia.

It is quite surprising for Tang Long to find out that *go* playing, the vehicle to conduct the seemingly glorious, elitist, and educational mission of "saving the world" assigned by Amanduo, is nothing more than a gambling game to win food for Newman (253). As described in the story, the sublime significance assigned to Tang Long's *go* playing ability is subverted by Newman's secularized, vulgar and instrumental use of this skill. More importantly, Tang Long has a troubling feeling that Newman's way will become the new norm in the post-Amanduo world. "I felt jealous and unconvinced," says Tang Long, "however, the food caused my stomach to growl, and I almost rushed to have a go at him" (253). He is only stopped by his remaining pride as a former national *go* player for whom the game, as well as the spirit it connotes, used to be sacred.

In this way, the Lyotardian grand narrative to which Tang Long is originally attached through *go* playing is dispelled, replaced by the pragmatic and utilitarian post-Amanduo world to which Newman belongs. This post-Amanduo world indicates "a new condition" that Zhang Yiwu believes is established upon "the end of the grand narrative of Chinese modernity" and "the crisis of a mythological construction of knowledge based on the idea of enlightenment" (Zhang Y. 115–17). In this new condition, people's collective memories of history, of "the good old days of their nation" and "the past pride of their civilization" (Han, *Huoxing* 260), are stripped away from the elitist and enlightenment context of Amanduo; history and culture are converted into products and ruled by market principles of competition and calculation – these are the products provided by Newman's tail.

This tail was originally bioengineered by Newman's father, as a prosthetic storage or a biological archive of knowledge and history that is expected to become the basis of the post-Amanduo world. What can be extracted from the tail, however, is by no means the restoration of the grand narrative. So long as the knowledge extracted from Newman's tail can be bought and sold as commodity, what buyers actually receive is nothing like a factual history. It is only a stream of historical symbols that can be related to Jamesonian pastiche or Baudrillardian simulacra: "[N]umerous personae and events are floating within an agitating cloud [...] The harder [Tang Long] tries to look at [the symbols], the less meaningful they become" (Baudrillard 260).

Unfortunately, but unsurprisingly, Newman's attempt to restore order in the post-Amanduo era through the knowledge and memories stored in his tail also fails. *The Anthology of Newman* – based on his "newly conditioned" teachings (to recall Zhang Yiwu's terminology) which function as "the source of authority in people's thoughts, imaginations, understandings and beliefs" (Han, *Huoxing* 316) – is eventually and literally "run over" (338) by military units during the civil war, which is the final part of Tang Long's journey. After Amanduo's collapse, the US government attempts to maintain its control over the country by electing a new president, but numerous local military powers refuse to recognize it and rise with fire and violence. After witnessing Newman's death and the death of the elitist spirit that he represents, which proves unable to create the new order, Tang Long is then captured by the army of Colonel Sam, who is initially on the side of the government but later becomes an independent warlord.

In Sam's army, the sense of security that used to be provided by Amanduo has been transferred to a weaponized tank-like machine called a "land whale," leading to a Darwinian world based upon the law of the jungle (347). Here the shadowy Spectre of the utopian Amanduo seems to have retreated even further. When Colonel Sam points to the destroyed land whales and the dead soldiers in them, he tells Tang Long that "their endings have already been destined at the beginning – they will die, so they have to die [...] Look at them. There is no difference between dead bodies, no matter if they are revolutionaries or counterrevolutionaries" (353). The utopian discourses of enlightenment have given way to a new discourse, or a new "faith" (361), that welcomes or even encourages competition and killing and winning: "[T]hose who act more like beasts will triumph" (457).

This new discourse, namely "the environment of consciousness," a field "guiding everything in the world where people's behaviour would implicitly surrender to its energy" (355) – is constructed through a hybrid language that Colonel Sam has specially designed. The language is called Aikemai (a meaningless transliteration like Amanduo), "made of English, old-fashioned computer language, ancient Tibetan, and Shanghainese" (5).

Although Aikemai is created based on the fragments of several heterogeneous languages of the past, it is still designed to achieve totality, certainty and universality, to be "promoted to the entire solar system" (467) and to serve as the source of truth and knowledge.

As it turns out, such a discourse proves very tempting for Tang Long. He has developed an intrinsic resistance to *go*-playing and therefore also against Amanduo and the utopian China embodied by his own name. He changes throughout his entire quixotic journey in the post-Amanduo world, yet it is here with Colonel Sam that Tang Long achieves his final transformation. Fully devoting himself to Sam's war, to a discourse of killing, Tang Long's ability to play *go* is forsaken, for which he is then "liberated from such a dark dungeon," "giving up the 'shell' " that has confined his will, embracing his "true birth" and "living in a completely new way" (404–5, 430). Tang Long is no more, and with his passing, a new identity emerges – Black Tang. For this new persona, the once-promising terms like "Longzi" that symbolized a hopeful future under the utopian Amanduo have all become "decayed vocabularies" (415).

When Tang Long completes his transformation from a lifelong *go*-player to a true warrior in a competitive battlefield, moving from the utopia centrally supervised by Amanduo to a post-Amanduo world, it is still unclear whether Tang Long and China have achieved genuine liberation from the collapsing false utopia. The new order that Colonel Sam wishes to establish through the new hybrid language Aikemai is doomed to be a castle in the air. Unfortunately, again, in the post-Amanduo world that denies the Lyotardian grand narrative, Colonel Sam is assassinated with a *go* piece by someone whose identity is never overtly revealed (though some clues may point to Tang Long, or Blake Tang, as he now calls himself). Sam's dream of becoming the prophet of the new order, therefore, also comes to an end. "He dies when attempting to connect past and future" (472) – so this is inscribed on his tombstone.

At the end of *Red Star Over America*, however, it is Mars, the "red star,"[9] that "ascended to the midheaven, whose sword-like light poured down on

9 The novel's title "Red Star over America" can also be translated as "Mars over America."

our bodies" (496), illuminating the future towards which China is heading. Here I must point out that in the novel's title, Han Song intentionally parodies Edgar Snow's *Red Star Over China* (1937); Snow's first-hand interviews and his observations about Mao's communist regime provided an invaluable historical record of the early years of the Communist Party of China. Then, the "red star" referred to the mystery of the rise of Maoism, as Snow noted: "[T]here had been perhaps no greater mystery among nations, no more confused an epic, than the story of Red China" (Snow 35). In Han Song's novel, however, the political connotation of "red star" is changed, and it now indicates the emergence of a new order built on the ruins of the socialist utopia that Mao had once conceived.

Throughout Tang Long's journey, the red star, although remaining in the background, continues to cast its spell over people in the post-Amanduo chaos, even over the dead – "it hung in the sky coldly and arrogantly, its reddish light shining on the corpse, brilliant and greasy, stained with blood, like grease-soaked plastic film" (Han, *Huoxing* 111). As such eerie imagery suggests, every time the red star appears, such as when the flood hits the *go* competition, when Tang Long escapes from the Suzuki gang, and when Newman is killed, there is always death and destruction. As an external system of values outside the chronotope composed of the different fictional places in *Red Star Over America*, the red star destabilizes both the Amanduo-utopia and the post-Amanduo dystopia.

Han Song does not clearly explain what these new values are. They are encoded in a new discourse brought by aliens from Mars, a system called *fudi* (literally translated as "land of happiness" or "land of treasure"). According to Song Mingwei, "*fudi* is used as a metaphor for the land of the dead, referring to an afterlife of eternal rest or 'happiness'" ("Variations" 90). He goes on to argue that in Han Song's eyes, "China's future remains uncertain [… and] has become suspiciously inauspicious" (91). Despite the alien nature of *fudi*, the new order or new discourse it prefigures seems not very different from that of Amanduo. As *Red Star Over America* is written retrospectively as a memoir by Tang Long sixty years after his journey, through some scattered clues we realize that the old Tang Long, who has fully adapted to the *fudi* system, is "lying in [his] shell" (Han, *Huoxing* 5), something he had tried so hard to escape six decades ago.

This time, however, it is not a shell made of *go* playing or the centralized authority of the utopian Amanduo, but rather another country-less chronotope to be interrogated and challenged. It is hard to sketch the detailed structure of *fudi* based on *Red Star Over America*, since Han Song provides little direct description of it. But still, wherever China is heading in the end, whatever this *fudi* looks like and however it is constructed, one thing is for sure – that the world of *fudi* is future-less: "[P]eople's blind hope for the future," as Tang Long, embedded in the matrix of *fudi*, comments on his journey sixty years earlier, "was the biggest mistake of those who lived in the pre-*fudi* era" (394).

As far as back in 1954, Karl Mannheim reminded us that "in the future, in a world in which there is never anything new, in which all is finished and each moment is a repetition of the past, there can exist a condition in which thought will be utterly devoid of all ideological and utopian elements." Trapped in a constant state of "matter-of-factness," we are therefore left "without ideals [and become] a mere creature of impulses" (Mannheim 235–6). Tang Long's comments might recall Mannheim's warnings about the exhaustion of the utopian imagination to envision alternatives, as well as leftist concerns over the "end of history" celebrated by Francis Fukuyama's followers (see Fukuyama 3–18). But Han Song by no means wishes to advocate *fudi* in the story. Even though people's hopes for the future might be blind, even though the discourse of *fudi* as the replacement for Amanduo appears even more "critical" (as in Moylan's critical utopia) than its predecessor, "even though it might be a trap, we still have to go for it" (Han, *Huoxing* 394).

It is exactly the conceptualization of possible future alternatives that Han Song has proposed in this novel. It echoes with the Blochian principle of hope and can be read for its utopian impulse, which Jameson believes to be one of the most needed energies in our late-capitalist society. In Tang Long's journey in search of a new order to replace the illusory utopia of Amanduo, we can recognize the trajectory of the ideological and sociocultural transition in the real China during the 1990s. This period witnessed an accelerating momentum towards a post-socialist discourse and a competitive and economized environment of market imperatives, and eventually towards "a bigger thing beyond [Tang Long's] country that is hiding behind the curtain and casting influence upon us" (Han, *Huoxing* 181). In a way, this "bigger thing" that Han Song encodes in *fudi*, or the country-less chronotope projected by the red star, could be interpreted as a new form of sovereignty, or the new order that Tang Long strives to establish, "composed of a series of national and supranational organisms united under a single logic of rule" according to Hardt and Negri – one that they would call "Empire" (*Empire* 246), that can draw inspiration from the other utopia that exists in the shadow of its own disruption, namely the Culture in Banks's novels.

The Utopian Culture: The Political High Ground in New Space Opera

The Culture was born with a certain sense of anachronism. When Iain M. Banks's first Culture novel *Consider Phlebas* was published in 1987 as a space opera that featured a utopia, neither of these two basic elements seemed popular at that moment. "For whatever reasons," as Krishan Kumar writes in his article "The Ends of Utopia," "writers no longer turn to the utopian form or genre for imagining a better or more perfect future [...] The 'imagination of disaster' fares infinitely better, and this at least means that utopia's cousin – or alter ego – the dystopia, continues to flourish" (Kumar 555). This observation is a reminder of the general retreat of the Moylanian critical utopia since the 1980s when the majority of sf writers changed their course in a dystopian direction – to such an extent, in Lyman Tower Sargent's words, that "we need to think more seriously about the possibility of a 'critical dystopia' " (Sargent 9).

Following Sargent's coinage of the term, Moylan fleshes out his critical dystopia with political and historical sophistications in his 2000 book *Scraps of the Untainted Sky*. While he reiterates the significance of critical *utopias* in challenging "the political compromises of a Left authoritarianism and the theoretical strictures of both orthodox Marxist and structuralist analyses" (Moylan, *Scraps* 195), Moylan considers critical *dystopias* the other side of the coin: the reflection of "the bad new times of contemporary enclosure" that have been marked with "intensified exploitation and deprivation" during the Thatcherite or Reaganite neoliberal transition since the 1980s (Moylan, *Scraps* 276).

This was an era for dystopias not utopias, an era known for the triumph of the right-wing politics and the decline of the left. It witnessed a profound economic restructuring based on commodification, privatization, individualization and economization. The end-of-utopia discourse, empowered by a wide-spreading confidence in Western-style capitalism especially in the economic and political domains and the liberal democracy advocated by Francis Fukuyama, once again prevailed upon the weakening form of literary utopia and its representation in sf. Although dystopia, from a broader perspective, shares with "eutopia" the general vocation or function of utopianism that appealed to Bloch and Jameson and characterized by Sargent as an inherent part of "social dreaming" (Sargent 3), these dreams are portrayed, especially in the works of Margaret Atwood, Sheri S. Tepper, Octavia E. Butler and William Gibson, in a dark and nightmarish manner. This is perhaps one of Kumar's "whatever reasons" why writers refrain from writing about utopias. The sf of the 1980s had been therefore characterized by a strong sense of pessimism and ennui, suggesting a future, or a futuristic past, in which corporatist agendas and late-capitalist practices become so dominate that any alternative has become either impossible at all or suppressed as a marginal heterotopia.

Banks had had enough of this right-wing politics. He spoke to Michael Cobley in a 1990 interview for *Science Fiction Eye* and articulated his scorn and contempt for the Thatcherite regime. "I hate Thatcher and detest the Tories," said Banks. He has even suggested an analogy between Thatcher's party and hyenas: "[I]f you've ever noticed the behavior of hyenas; they tend to go for the young and the weak, the sick and the old, which the Tories seem to do as well" (Cobley 28). And this hatred for the right-leaning governments, which also extended to Tony Blair and New Labour, did not fade over the years. In 2013, after his announcement of his terminal cancer, Banks confessed to Stuart Kelly that "for half a second," he was "elated" to learn that Thatcher had died earlier in that year. But he also pointed out that her death was not symbolic in any sense. "Her baleful influence on British politics remains undiminished. Squeeze practically any Tory, any Blairite and any Lib Dem of the Orange Book persuasion, and it's the same poisonous Thatcherite pus that comes oozing out of all of them" (Kelly n.p.).

Throughout his career, from his earliest works to the very end of his life, Banks was consistently recognized for his strong leftist convictions. As Simone Caroti aptly describes, he remained "a lifelong advocate of left-wing political movements and a champion of Scotland's complete independence from the UK," the one who "found England in the Thatcher years a hard place to like, an impossible place to live in, and a dark place to observe from next door" (Caroti 12–13). In his political activism and desire for a better land, Banks re-invokes utopia during an age of dystopia, endeavouring to "make a world [he'd] like to live in" (Mitchell n.p.). This, as it turns out, is the Culture. His choice of genre for the Culture, however, seemed surprising back in the 1980s. He did not follow the market preference for the trendy cyberpunk novels, usually set in ruined places corrupted by consumerism and the money fetish. Instead, Banks rejuvenated a genre that had been in decline for decades, something seen as mediocre, archaic and dull. It was space opera.

The golden age of space opera, according to most sf histories, dates all the way back to the late 1930s and the 1940s, with *Astounding Science Fiction* (later called *Analog Science Fiction and Fact*) under John W. Campbell's editorship as the primary platform. But even during its heyday, space opera was never far from critical judgements. It was described as a "hacky, grinding, stinking, outworn, spaceship yarn" as early as in 1941 by Wilson Tucker (qtd. in Sawyer 505), which foreshadowed its generic exhaustion during and after the New Wave of the 1960s and the 1970s. Paul Kincaid writes in retrospect that, when Banks carefully selected his modules at the University of Stirling with an eye to becoming an sf writer, space opera was widely regarded as

> a conservative expression of the great man theory, in which one heroic figure, almost invariably a man, could set right all wrongs, defeating nasty, differently colored aliens, and change the world. Militaristic, its spaceships invariably modelled on naval vessels with hierarchical chains of command, space opera was clumsily written, naïve, and formulaic. (Kincaid, *Iain* 6)

Banks understood and acknowledged all these crucial blemishes of space opera and, more generally, of the hard sf written in the Campbellian manner. He is deeply inspired by M. John Harrison's 1971 commentary "A Literature of Comfort," an influential piece in which Harrison refers to hard sf as "a literature of shoddy, programmed pap" that provides nothing new but "the repetition of form and content" (Harrison, "Literature" 84). But even so, despite these condemnations of space opera for its irreconcilable dichotomies between "human and machine, human and (subordinate or doomed enemy) alien, male and (subordinate) female, good and evil" (Caroti 43) embedded in its formulaic, stereotypical, usually western- or anthropocentric ethos, Banks just cannot put it aside. He is intrigued by the genre's charm of flying outward, of moving beyond, of producing the awe for the sublime, so he does not align with those radical New Wave writers in cancelling space opera. He wishes, instead, for a reform.

Therefore, while he was immersed in the overwhelming criticism of space opera, Banks found someone speaking *for* it – Brian Aldiss. In his "Introduction" to his edited collection *Space Opera: An Anthology of Way-Back-When Futures* (1974), Aldiss proposes a rather different perspective on reading space opera:

> What space opera does is take a few light years and a pinch of reality and inflate thoroughly with melodrama, dreams, and seasoning of screwy ideas [...] Space opera was heady, escapist stuff, charging on without overmuch regard for logic or literacy, while often throwing off great images, excitements, and aspirations. (Aldiss xi–xii)

In line with this statement, Aldiss sends a call to both readers and writers to take a fresher look at this struggling genre. For him, stories told with extravagant settings and large-scale travelling could be defined with an intriguing term "Widescreen Baroque" which Banks has borrowed as the major source of inspiration and enthusiasm for his own world-building in the Culture novels. In an interview with James Rundle in 2010, Banks makes it clear that "I just loved the scope of it – again, to quote Mr. Aldiss, he came up with 'widescreen baroque space opera,' that was brilliant! And there were a lot of things that I was trying to do with it [...] I love space opera and I love the opportunity it gave me to work [on] a huge canvas" (Rundle n.p.).

On this huge canvas, armed with his left-wing political dedications, Banks becomes the pioneer of the New Space Opera, a revised genre that "appropriate[s] the scale and color of the old form while jettisoning its political baggage in favor of a more left-leaning, humanistic vision of our future in space" (Kincaid, *Iain* 151). Banks's generic reform, of course, does not go off without a hitch. Before *Consider Phlebas* (1987), which is commonly considered the inaugural novel of the New Space Opera and often the beginning of the British SF Boom, Banks had already completed the manuscripts of two of the other first three Culture novels – *The Player of Games* (1988) and *Use of Weapons* (1990) – and a novella "The State of the Art" (1989), but none were accepted for publication.

Although the specific reasons for their rejections may vary in each case, the general concerns of all the publishers are not hard to guess: to publish a utopian space opera during a time when cyberpunk dystopias like William Gibson's *Neuromancer* (1984) dominated the market would be a risky and therefore an unfavourable idea. Admitting a "partial defeat" (Banks, "Preface" x), Banks took a step back and devoted himself to publishing non-sf novels, where he succeeded. With *The Wasp Factory* (1984), *Walking on Glass* (1985), and *The Bridge* (1986), Banks had made his name for the blend of avant-garde and experimental narratives, supernatural horrors, gothic imageries and fantastic elements, becoming a representative figure of the New Scottish Renaissance among people such as Alasdair Gray, James Kelman, A. L. Kennedy, Irvine Welsh, Janice Galloway, Andrew O'Hagan and Alan Warner (Hames 496).

By this time, "Banks had established a reputation as one of the best young writers in Britain. He was controversial, challenging and unafraid to try new structures and new approaches. His books were guaranteed to receive substantial reviews and high sales" (Kincaid, *Iain* 25). With an increasing readership and fandom, Banks felt that he had got more leverage to argue with the publishers about his sf projects. He did so after being invited to an sf convention "Mexicon 2" by Paul Kincaid in February 1986, where he was well received. According to Kincaid himself, "immediately on his return" Banks proclaimed to his friend Ken MacLeod, "These are my people!" Soon after this, he found "the impetus to talk his editor into looking again at the sf novels, especially the most recent, *Consider Phlebas*" (Kincaid, *Iain* 26).

Consider Phlebas was eventually published by Macmillan, with a sensational success. It is received as "a splendid, rip-roaring adventure by an author who's clearly at home in the genre and well equipped to make the most of it" (F. Miller 13). For many readers and critics, *Consider Phlebas* is also a magnificent landmark for British sf in general. With the utopian Culture depicted in *Consider Phlebas* and the following volumes, Banks not only revitalizes the once exhausted genre space opera "singlehandedly" (Kincaid, *Iain* 2) and in this way writes his name as a trailblazer of the British SF Boom, but also uses it as a place for vengeance, for his retaliation against the cultural politics he disdained: Thatcherism. He builds the Culture as a laboratory for his thought experiments of non-Thatcherite, post-capitalist alternatives. He told Tim Metcalfe in an interview in November 1989:

> Look, there is a possibility of something really good in the future. Here's a genuine, humanist, non-superstitious, nonreligious, functioning utopia where absolutely no-one is exploited; where they don't have money, where they don't have laws to speak of, my idea of a perfect society – and it's obviously not capitalist – but it's so communist it's beyond anything in a way. Something like the Culture could just about evolve from capitalism. (qtd. in Martingale 441)

In other words, as he said to James Rundle, "there was a *moral high ground* in space opera, and I wanted to reclaim it for the Left! I was fed up with reading these otherwise enjoyable books that ultimately turned out to be ultra-capitalist, or almost proto-fascist at times. I wasn't having this" (Rundle n.p., emphasis added). This, in fact, is also a *political* high ground from which the British left has retreated for sophisticated historical reasons such as the decline of class consciousness in the face of post-Fordism and the articulation of personal aspiration to consumerism since the 1980s (see Chapter 4), which is also what Banks wishes to reclaim.

What Banks has painted on his galactic canvas is perhaps one of the wildest dreams for those on the left. There is no scarcity, no religious or political hierarchy, no government, no aristocracy, no monarch, no oppression or exploitation of any kind, no material deprivation, and therefore no need of labour or crime. There is no money, too, within the Culture's realm, because "money implies poverty" (Banks, *State* 142), and poverty is probably the last thing we can think about in the Culture. The Culture is "unmoneyed" (Banks, *Consider* 203) also because money is more than often connected to the circulation and accumulation of capital, and its ultimate material affluence has eventually fostered a "hedonistic" (Banks, *Consider* 336) civilization where "the humans of the Culture, having solved all the obvious problems of their shared pasts to be free from hunger, want, disease and the fear of natural disaster and attack, would find it a slightly empty existence only and merely enjoying themselves" (Banks, "Notes" n.p.).

There is "no real greed, paranoia, stupidity, fanaticism or bigotry" (Banks, "Notes" n.p.) in the Culture, nor inequality, stratification or the need to define values of material production in such a profoundly automated world, which undermines the very foundation of capitalism *per se*. As he writes himself in "A Few Notes on the Culture" (1994), the market-based capitalism, "for all its (profoundly inelegant) complexities, remains a crude and essentially blind system." It seems, therefore, that the Culture is indeed a post-capitalist utopia intended by Banks himself and endorsed by many critics, indeed a kind of "otherness" beyond the end-of-history discourse that Banks would have condemned.

Meanwhile, apart from the human hedonism in the Culture, the Minds take care of everything. They are entities of artificial intelligence with different personalities, sophisticated enough to develop an autonomy among themselves beyond human comprehension. But unlike the robot tyranny we might have seen in cyberpunk narratives, the Minds are friendly to human citizens of the Culture. It appears, as Banks describes in *Consider Phlebas*, "the Culture [...] relied profoundly on its machines for both its strategy and tactics" in their routine management and therefore it saw itself as "being a self-consciously *rational* society" (Banks, *Consider* 86–7; emphasis added). Culture humans, though incomparable to the Minds in terms of their intelligence and capacities, are all "well nourished, extensively educated and mentally alert" (87). It turns out, in this way, that the Culture stands on the opposite of those nightmarish "critical dystopias" where humans are oppressed, exploited or enslaved by their machine masters.

Relative to the Thatcherite reality where industrial unions and workers are sacrificed for market competition and economized calculation, this imagined civilization in which Banks himself would have liked to live can then be considered "quasi-technocratic" (Christie 28), "anarcho-socialist" (G. Miller 203), and in short, "utopian," through invoking the Blochian principles of hope (Kulbicki 40). Such a spacefaring, post-scarcity, post-capitalist utopia, according to Simone Caroti, is simultaneously "a secret garden" to contemplate a society gone right and "an engine for proactive advocacy of decency, non-violence, equal rights for all, and the chance to live a meaningful life" (Caroti 16). Among all the nine Culture novels, *Consider Phlebas* may stand out for two reasons. It is the first of them, marking the beginning of the British SF Boom and the generic rejuvenation of space opera, for which it has always been placed in a special historical position since its publication. But meanwhile, despite its utopian premises, *Consider Phlebas* provides a rather ambiguous image of the Culture itself, more ambiguous than the following stories in the series, therefore provoking a continuing debate about the *utopian-ness* of the Culture from the start of this series.

Here in this novel, our compassion and empathy are initially directed to the anti-hero Horza, a military agent working for the Idirans during the Idiran-Culture War. The Culture, however, only appears in the background, first portrayed as a seemingly hegemonic empire ruled by machines – "That's what the Culture's about: machines," says Horza, "it's the Idirans who are on the side of *life* in this war" (Banks, *Consider* 13). It is not until much later that the readers might finally realize that the Culture is not trapped in an "evolutionary dead end" as Horza suggests (Banks, *Consider* 29, 287). And the only mercy Horza has ever received throughout his struggle is from Yalson and Balveda, both Culture humans, and from Unaha-Closp, the drone he has captured on a Culture megaship, who tries, but fails, to save his life from Idiran soldiers.

Consider Phlebas concludes with a revelation of the latitude and magnitude of individual freedom of choice within the Culture, offering a glimpse of the Culture's inclusivity, tolerance and respect of all modes of lifestyle. This reminds Sherryl Vint of John Stuart Mill's liberalism to the extent that all Culture subjects, human or machine, retain the absolute right of ownership of oneself as the core to citizenship (Vint, *Bodies* 81), although practically there is no other property to *own*. Even so, however, the narrative ambiguity in *Consider Phlebas* provides a counter position for us to take against the Culture. We may have noticed that the Culture's benevolence and inclusivity are only available to their own people or those who have been admitted to their way of living. For others, the Culture is never a utopia. They are met by political pressure, electoral manipulation (as in *Use of Weapons*) and in the case of the Idirans, war.

The reasons that the Culture provides to justify its war is to defend itself from the religious, hierarchical, patriarchal and expansionary militant civilization of the Idiran, "to safeguard its own peace of mind: no more" (Banks, *Consider* 451). But as quoted in the epigraph of this chapter when Horza speaks to the Culture agent Balveda, "the Idirans never were any threat to you. They still won't be, if you stopped fighting them" (28). On the contrary to the hedonistic and materialist values the Culture endeavours to universalize, its "self-defence" eventually leads to the annihilation of 851.4 billion lives, 14,334 Orbitals, 53 planets and six stars (462) – which is a signal of the darker side of the Culture, from which some would rather walk away.

Therefore, these ambiguities that make the Culture less utopian and more critical have opened up further space for the academic engagements with Banks and his imagination of the Culture – an ambiguous totality that can be identified with both the Soviet Union (MacLeod, "Phlebas" 3) and the United States (Vint, "Cultural" 87) whose hedonistic and technocratic anarchist utopia is dependent on the judgemental, educational and sometimes violent rendezvous with other worlds beyond its ideological domain. It has also been read in relation to the Gulf War and Samuel P. Huntington's model of the "Clash of Civilizations": "a conflict between civilizations based on the incompatibility of their core values" (Duggan 559). This is a dirty job taken by the Culture's Contact section, and in particular, Special Circumstances established to solve problems when circumstances exceed the moral capacity of the Culture. It is a department comparable to Ursula K. Le Guin's "child in closet" in her famous short story "The Ones Who Walk Away from Omelas," a child enduring all the sufferings and deprived of all the comfort in exchange of the perfection of in general society.

In this way, the Culture as a left-wing attempt to foreground an alternative to the end-of-history capitalist discourse ironically suggested by Jameson yet faithfully inherited by Fukuyama has certainly continued in a critical utopian vein (Moylan, *Demand* xxiii). It is "critical," not just because Banks intentionally seizes the political high ground within the realm of space opera and uses the Culture to wage his own war against Thatcherism. It is also "critical" as the Culture, however utopian it might be, indicates its "self-contradictory" (Jacobs 51) nature on various occasions. Although the Culture's ideology, in Banks's own words, is "socialism within, anarchy without" (Banks, "Notes" n.p.), it tends to become less socialist and less anarchist if put under a closer interrogation. We will revisit this concept later in this chapter, contending that the Culture, initially conceived by Banks as an anti-capitalist utopia born out of his disdain for neoliberalism, can be associated with the socio-political framework of "Empire" put forth by Michael Hardt and Antonio Negri. Consequently, the war between the Culture and the Idirans should be understood in the context of the decline of imperialist empires and the emergence of the rhizomatic Empire in the late twentieth century.

Walking Away from the Culture

At the end of Le Guin's "The Ones Who Walk Away from Omelas" (1973), some people from Omelas may have realized that there is something terribly wrong with their city despite how utopian it looks. They have always been haunted by the child locked inside that room and left to take all the sufferings *alone* on behalf of the Omelas residents. So, they choose to leave. "Each alone," as Le Guin writes, "they go west or north, towards the mountains. They go on. They leave Omelas, they walk ahead into the darkness, and they do not come back" (Le Guin, "Omelas" 259). For Paul Kincaid, the Omelas metaphor is certainly not strange to the Culture and to those who, consciously or not, wish to escape from this critical utopia. Following his discussion of characters such as Gurgeh in

The Player of Games, Linter in "The State of the Art," and Genar-Hofoen in *Excession* (1996), he claims:

> En masse, as a community, the Culture appears very like heaven, a place, as we have seen, of great sex, extended lifespan, absence of worries, and there are machines to take care of everything from the massively complex to the tediously mundane. Who wouldn't want to live there? No wonder it is acclaimed as the great modern utopia of the political left. And yet, as in Ursula K. Le Guin's story, there are those who walk away from Omelas. (144)

Banks's political fervour in advocating for a post-capitalist alternative to combat right-wing politics is unquestionable. His endeavour in building a stronghold on the political high ground promised by the new space opera is far-sighted and courageous, especially at a time when neither utopia nor space opera was popular. His radical messages connoted in the Culture and in its contact with non-Culture worlds indeed can be interpreted as a Blochian call for a utopian hope of difference and transgression. But still, we are constantly reminded by those who walk away that the Culture is only utopian for some, not for all. In many cases such as the Culture's clashes against the Idirans and their religious society in *Consider Phlebas*, against the Empire of Azad and their monarchy in *The Player of Games*, and against the Chelgrians and their caste system in *Look to Windward* (2000), we are often told that the Culture is morally, socially and technologically more advanced and therefore its triumph is guaranteed. But apparently, this is not always true. Sometimes, the Culture as an alternative does not appear to be so different from what it stands against.

In one of the critical articles on Banks titled "Cultural Imperialism and the Ends of Empire," Sherryl Vint demonstrates the connection between the Culture and Michael Hardt and Antonio Negri's formulation of Empire, a regime that "seeks to regulate human nature through the control of what Foucault has called bodies and pleasures" (Vint, "Cultural" 86). She quotes them as saying that "Empire is formed not on the basis of force itself but on the basis of the capacity to present force as being in the service of right and peace" (Hardt and Negri, *Empire* 15). While focusing on the expansionary and penetrative nature of such a new regime, Vint goes on to emphasize the imperial potentials of Empire which "tends either directly or indirectly to penetrate and reconfigure the domestic law of the nation-states," a process that can be labelled as the "so-called *right of intervention*" of "the dominant subjects of the world to intervene in the territories of other subjects in the interest of preventing or resolving humanitarian problems, guaranteeing accords, and imposing peace" (Hardt and Negri, *Empire* 17–18).[10]

In this way, Vint establishes a parallel between the regimes of the US and the fictional Culture in terms of their indications of cultural imperialism, a parallel centred around, according to Mel van Elteren, the "social visions of US-style development, with its heavy emphasis on 'progress' in the form of unlimited, quantitative growth and economic-technological expansion" (180). As Vint continues, both of them

> seem to mean well and […] officially stand for values with which it is difficult to argue: democracy, freedom, and respect for human rights. Both also reveal a slippage between cultural imperialism as a method of converting others to one's values and more direct military imperialism when such cultural pressures are not efficacious. (89)

The Culture, of course, is not exactly the same as the United States. Their difference cannot be more obvious since the Culture is famously known for its lack of economy, market and capital, all of them essential to the proliferation of global capitalism where the United States performs as the leading power. But Vint reminds us that the Culture novels "offer important commentary on the way in which global capital spreads itself through spreading its values and way of life, much like the Culture increases its territory through spreading its values and way of living" (97n6). Based on such a comparison, the Culture is proven much less benevolent or "self-defensive" (as in the war against the Idirans) than it appears. The hedonism in the seemingly post-scarcity, post-capitalist civilization, in this way, also turns out to be questionable.

Despite its moneyless-ness, the Culture still demonstrates an impulse of internalizing the outside and homogenizing the differences as it contacts

10 This, as indicated in the previous chapter, is also what led *The New Statesman* to label many of the seemingly left-leaning British authors of the 1980s as "Blitcons" by the early 2000s.

other non-Culture civilizations beyond its reach – especially those like the Idirans in *Consider Phlebas* who do not yield to the Culture's ideology based on technological rationality, secularization and mechanization. And this, in fact, corresponds to what Hardt and Negri have framed for the Empire in terms of the process of assimilation and appropriation:

> Capital must therefore not only have open exchange with noncapitalist societies or only appropriate their wealth; it must also actually *transform* them into capitalist societies themselves [...] What is exported is a relation, a social form that will breed or replicate itself. Like a missionary or vampire, capital touches what is foreign and makes it proper. (Hardt and Negri, *Empire* 226; emphasis added)

This "transformation" is, in many ways, symbolized by the Idiran-Culture war in *Consider Phlebas*. It serves as a literary representation of the historical disruption in our real world – a disruption through which a new global order, referred to as Empire, gradually supplants and surpasses the old order based on imperialism and nation-states.

This replacement and transcendence, although not exactly what Banks has planned for the Culture as an intentional critique of Margaret Thatcher, are formulated based on the Culture's triumph over the Idirans during the war. In this war, what awaits the Idirans, as the embodiment of nation-states established upon locality and nationalism, is not only a military defeat. More than that, they are assimilated and become part of the Culture. Such an assimilation, rather than merely an elimination, has been clearly documented in the "Appendices" section of *Consider Phlebas*: "Idir [the mother planet of the Idirans] was never attacked, and technically never surrendered. Its computer network was taken over by effector weapons, and – freed of designed-in limitations – upgraded itself to sentience, to become a Culture Mind in all but name" (Banks, *Consider* 462).

Idir's surrender is not simply a result of the Culture's expansion. It is more generally a power transfer between two paradigms of power dynamics, from the imperial *empires* growing based on a power centre to the *Empire* that is decentred and deterritorialized. "In contrast to imperialism," write Hardt and Negri,

> Empire establishes no territorial centre of power and does not rely on fixed boundaries or barriers. It is a *decentered* and *deterritorializing* apparatus of rule that progressively

> incorporates the entire global realm within its open, expanding frontiers. Empire manages hybrid identities, flexible hierarchies, and plural exchanges through modulating networks of command. The distinct national colours of the imperialist map of the world have merged and blended in the imperial global rainbow. (xii–xiii; emphasis in original)

Indeed, it is precisely the impulse of "decentralization" and "deterritorialization" that has been driving the transition in the contemporary world – from modern nation-states to a postmodern "supranational" globalized entity. According to Slavoj Žižek, this "deterritorialization," though constructed quite ambiguously in *Empire*, refers to a process in which "victorious global capitalism pushes into every pore of our social lives, into the most intimate of spheres [...] which no longer is based on patriarchal or other hierarchic structures of dominance. Instead, it causes a flowing, hybrid identity" (Žižek, "Have" 192).

From this perspective, through the Idiran-Culture war, *Consider Phlebas* reflects on the inherent contrast between the "flowing, hybrid identity" that Žižek observes from the deterritorialized Empire and the centrality/locality usually attributed to nation-states and imperialism. The Idirans, in this case, are on the side of place and territory. "They believed in the destiny of *place*," as Horza finds out when introspecting on his own position during the war, certain individuals "would always belong in certain places – the high ground, the fertile lands, the temperate isles – whether they had been born there or not; and the same applied to tribes, clans and races," and even to species (Banks, *Consider* 158; emphasis in original). For the Idirans, "there was a place for everything, and everything ought to be in its place," and thus only through their territorial attachment to *place* can they restore the order to the chaos, so as to develop "eternal peace and joy" over their current struggles (158). On the contrary, the "mongrel" nature of the Culture (333) whose societies and civilizations are involved in an endless cycle of "falling apart and reforming" – who are always "self-altering" themselves (333), the Idirans resort to purity, continuity and spatiality.

Such a sense of continuity is established through an unbreakable connection, like an unbroken string, linking each of the Idiran warriors to the place of origin of their tribes and clans – their home world, Idir. During the war, the Idirans are "committed to taking and holding all they could; to maintaining frontiers, to securing planets and moons; above all, to keeping Idir safe, *at any price*" (461; emphasis added). While endeavouring to expand its territory, to "become stronger and stronger," and to "push their boundaries as far from the treasured planet of Idir as possible" (333), the militant empire of the Idirans is in fact anchored on various fixed places. In *Consider Phlebas*, that is non-artificial planets, moons and rocks. It operates similarly to the strategies employed by the British Empire to govern its overseas colonies in the nineteenth century, establishing a hierarchical structure with a central power hub – such as London, Idir and the like.

If we extend this discussion a little into *The Player of Games*, this clash of civilizations between the Culture and the Empire of Azad, rendered in the form of a board game, is very much similar to the Idiran-Culture war. As Gurgeh plays the final game with the Azadian emperor Nicosar, he finds that each of them represents the underpinning philosophy of their own societies. While Nicosar acts with an authoritarian power and deploys/sacrifices his pieces in a clear chain of command, Gurgeh habitually sets up something like "a net, a grid of forces and relationships, without any obvious hierarchy or entrenched leadership, and initially quite profoundly peaceful" (Banks, *Player* 269). More importantly, Gurgeh rarely kills the pieces of his opponent. He tends to absorb them and turns them into part of *us*. "They make them live like the people they set out to take over. The architecture of the system channels them, beguiles them, seduces and transforms them, demanding from them what they could not before have given but slowly grow to offer" (276).

For the Azadians, Nicosar is everything; for Nicosar, he has, and only has, his empire. For the Culture, however, Gurgeh is only a citizen good at playing games, reluctant to comply with the Culture's arrangement at the beginning, and there are many more like him. The Empire of Azad has a structure, a hierarchy, a pyramid where everyone is fixed in a certain place. The Culture, on the opposite, appears to have no visible structure, but such a sense of structureless-ness eventually forms a new structure through which the Culture is defined. This is why Colin Greenland reads the Azadians as "Victorian Britain" (Greenland 91), and why it is doomed to be superseded.

Returning to the Idiran-Culture war, the Culture "must seem like some fiendish amalgam of everything the Idirans have ever found repugnant"

(Banks, *Consider* 333). Instead of regulating themselves in a recognizable border within which the Idirans would "know exactly who they are: pure-bred, the one race, or nothing," the Culture does not have a clear boundary. "[It] just fades away at the edges, both fraying and spreading" (334). The Culture is, therefore, "deterritorialized" from the previous structure rooted in the sense of place. Without a power centre like the one for the Idiran *empire* based on locality and nationalism, the Culture *Empire* is "mobile in essence" (461). It is not located on a particular planet but made of numerous artificial Orbitals and megaships operated by the Minds. Therefore, freed from the sometimes pragmatically un-rewarding mission of protecting "home," the Culture, when battling against the Idirans, is able to simply abandon their residential Orbitals and transport its populations if necessary. In *Consider Phlebas*, Vavatch is chosen to be the sacrifice. According to the narrator Horza, then still an ally of the Idirans, the annihilation of Vavatch can be read as a sign of the Culture: "chaos from order, destruction from construction, death from life." This is "the final, grisly manifestation of the Culture's lethal idealism" (265).

Such a manifestation of the Culture's deterritorialization is, of course, not entirely the same as what Hardt and Negri's biopolitical perspective informed by Deleuze and Guattari. This said, one thing that links the post-capitalist Culture and the late-capitalist Empire is their decentred structure of power, "a non-hierarchical and non-centred network structure" labelled as a "rhizome" (Hardt and Negri, *Empire* 299). This rhizome stands in the opposite of what is called a "oligopolistic" model or a "tree structure" that can be borrowed to describe the place-based power hierarchy of a tribe, a clan, a country or a nation-state that has a power centre, just like the Idirans in *Consider Phlebas*. For them, as noted by Banks himself in "A Few Notes," "territory is all-important; resources, living-space, lines of communication; all are determined" by the nature of the place to which the nations belong. In this way, for Hardt and Negri, it is this commitment of nation-states to places and territories that lead to imperialism and imperial empires bound to a constant process of incorporating non-capitalist environments (*Commonwealth* 203).

However, the rhizomatic Empire, which transcends any fixed boundaries or barriers, is different. In the post-scarcity Culture, "the capacity of its means of production ubiquitously and comprehensively exceeded every reasonable [...] demand," which has consequentially dissolved the Culture's need "to colonise, exploit or enslave" on a material basis (Banks, *Consider* 451). What concerned the Idirans and urged them to expand their territories – a shortage of manufacturing resources and raw materials – are not problems for the Culture humans and machines. What matters in this Empire is the production of subjectivity – "the constant functioning of social machines in their various apparatuses and assemblages produces the world along with the subjects and objects that constitute it" (Hardt and Negri, *Empire* 28).

As the "subjects" in the Culture have become the products within its galaxy-spinning framework that penetrates every aspect in the Culture societies, the members of Empire find themselves in a *decentred* and *deterritorialized* power structure. And at the same time, to various degrees, they are attracted by and attached to the hedonistic living style that the Culture is set to protect during the war at a cost of infringing on or even eliminating Others when deemed necessary. Luckily, this cost is not borne by all. It is the liability only of the child in the closet – the agents of Special Circumstances in the Contact section, while ordinary living beings and machines can just enjoy their hedonistic lives happily in their utopia, governed by their guardians – the Minds.

This, however, is exactly what makes the Culture disrupted, an ostensible utopia built on a corrupt foundation, a false utopia from which many wish to walk away. The rhizomic Empire of the Culture can be considered a deterritorialized polity indeed in line with Hardt and Negri's conception, but certainly not in the Deleuzian sense – where the term "rhizome" originates (also with Felix Guattari's contributions). The Deleuzian rhizome is formed against the Cartesian, logocentric dichotomy of the One and the Multiple, subject and object, Self and Other, by which universality is deconstructed into folds and lines, turning into the intensities merging and flowing on the plane of imminence, always in the state of becoming and transition. But unfortunately, the Culture is still dependent on a kind of social homogeneity.

Banks claims in various interviews and, above all, in his "A Few Notes on the Culture" about the diversity and freedom that each individual is allowed to choose whatever way they live – switching between genders, modifying bodies, hibernating for a while, living as a robot or being uploaded to the cyberspace. Despite this, however, from the Culture we can see "a strange sort of *conformity* within diversity" (Vint, *Bodies* 81; emphasis added).

In other words, the Culture has never tried to undermine the dichotomy of the One and the Multiple. They have never found a line of flight to truly deterritorialize themselves. Instead, every time they make contact with other worlds, they strengthen this dichotomy to a further degree. They wish to build up a standard, for which they have the final say, and then make it universal and ubiquitous, with what they believe are good intentions. "They want other people to be like them," as Zakalwe is told in *Use of Weapons*, "They don't terraform, so they don't want others to either [...] The Culture believes profoundly in machine sentience, so it thinks everybody ought to, but I think it also believes every civilisation should be run by its machines [...] Again, who is to say that is correct?" (Banks, *Use* 254).

Unlike the dying utopia centrally governed by Amanduo in Han Song's *Red Star Over America*, the Culture does not have a structural pivot. It is managed by numerous Minds who run Orbitals and megaships and each of them can be distinguished from others by their unique personalities and hobbies. But again, upon their seemingly heterogeneity there emerges a certain sense of sameness, conformity and homogeneity. To borrow Zygmunt Bauman's comments on modern bureaucracy that views a nation's internal society as an object of administration, the Culture (empowered by the Contact department Special Circumstances), with the wars it engages in, tends to see the universe beyond its realm as "a collection of so many 'problems' to be solved, as a 'nature' to be 'controlled,' 'mastered' and 'improved' or 'remade,' as a legitimate target for 'social engineering,' and in general a garden to be designed and kept in the planned shape by force" (Bauman, *Modernity* 18).

The Culture's utopian-ness is very much dependent on its post-scarcity nature. You do not need to work and therefore will never be exploited. You can always trust the Minds to make the most appropriate decisions – even though sometimes they could hide something or some information from you for the sake of their grander missions. You can be whoever or whatever you want as long as it is possible technologically, and it seems the Minds are not so familiar with what "impossible" means. As Banks's intentional attack on Thatcherite regimes and their cultural politics, the Culture is an affluent society to its extreme, a dreamland built for left-wingers to reclaim the political high ground in space opera.

But from another perspective, the intrinsic and intricate injustices, flaws and contradictions that make this utopia critical and disruptive should also be acknowledged. People's freedom to switch between genders, to take on an organic or mechanical form of life as they wish, to choose a lifestyle without worrying about money, does not naturally resolve the hierarchies disguised behind the post-scarcity façade. What if the Culture's resources are no longer unlimited? What if they find their technology no longer capable of achieving what they desire? I will discuss the scenario of scarcity in the next chapter with Hao Jingfang's *Vagabonds* and Ken MacLeod's *Fall Revolution* quartet. But before that: bear in mind, after all, that "a staunch preacher and defender of rationality" like the Culture could be easily turned into "the most sinister, cruel, bloody-minded ruler" (Bauman, *Modernity* 203). This is why people in the Culture are walking away, from a utopia that is critical in nature, that can be disrupted anytime.

Meanwhile, what is also critical or disruptive in nature is Han Song's Amanduo. Although those who walk away from the harmonious society under Amanduo's supervision appear to be more reluctant than those from the Culture – who would rather have stayed if Amanduo had not collapsed – they do strive to build a post-Amanduo order as its replacement. In this way, *Red Star Over America* is not a nationalistic narrative predicting the rise of China as a global power and the relative decline of the United States, nor is it a manifesto calling for a certain sense of Sino-centralism. Rather, under the Bakhtinian framework of chronotope, Tang Long's journey from the utopian society governed by Amanduo to the dystopian post-Amanduo wasteland documents the fundamental ideological and social transition of the real-day China during the 1990s. The order-seeking journey of Tang Long, and of China, during the post-Amanduo and post-socialist era, is far from finished. It has just started.

CHAPTER 2

What's Past Is Prologue: Historical Rupture in Hao Jingfang's *Vagabonds* and Ken MacLeod's *Fall Revolution* Quartet

> […] they look like men who've been told they have cancer.
>
> – Ken MacLeod, in *The Stone Canal*

> Every age has its own diseases.
>
> – Hao Jingfang, in *Vagabonds*

Utopia as a Process

At the very end of *Red Star over America*, the phantom-like red star (Mars) appears for the last time, indicating a faint possibility of a new order in the post-utopian/post-Amanduo world. When Tang Long eventually completes his unsuccessful quest for utopian futures and makes his way back to Shanghai, he is presented with another ambiguous and uncanny image of Mars:

> At this moment, the red star rose in the middle of the sky, and its light shone down on our bodies like a sword with an aura that emboldened me. I shivered and went to kiss Susan, not even noticing the huge shadow the UFO was casting behind us. Only the dog barked in fear. (494)

This ending leaves more questions than the novel has solved. Which of the dual meanings of *fudi* gives a better sense of the new order – the land of happiness, of the dead, or both? Is it a promising social structure through which the liberty and freedom of its residents can be fully realized? These questions, of course, refuse a simple answer. Such a vagueness that Han Song gives to *Red Star* is, I believe, intentional – an intention to convey his *fin-de-siècle* concerns about China's fundamental changes, which is also a message coded in the "suspiciously inauspicious" ending of the novel convincingly interpreted by Song Mingwei: "Perhaps a utopian vision of China's rise constructed in the current political/cultural context is itself ambiguous: which direction it will take is impossible to foretell" ("Variations" 91).

"Impossible to foretell" – probably, but the extrapolative and speculative experiments of contemporary Chinese sf (interrogating various "utopian visions" formulated during China's post-socialist transformation) are in many ways possible and, more importantly, rewarding. During the Chinese SF Boom, a considerable number of emerging and established sf writers in China have followed in Han Song's footsteps, using Mars as a backdrop for their own utopian explorations.[1] For these writers, the red star may be considered a utopian referent for their own versions of the social, political, ideological or even ontological alternatives that serve as "non-alienated *enclaves* [that] suddenly light up in our hitherto contaminated environment" and "thereby converting Utopian representation into a critical and analytical method" (Jameson, *Archaeologies* 230; emphasis added).

Among this cohort, Hao Jingfang stands out, not only because of her achievement of winning the 2016 Hugo Award for Best Novelette with "Folding Beijing" – immediately after Liu Cixin's *The Three-Body Problem* was awarded Best Novel in the previous year – but also for her attempts to create various forms of utopia or dystopia. Through her writings, Hao Jingfang consistently emphasizes the inherent ambiguity within utopian

1 In September 2020, fifteen Chinese sf stories featuring Mars were collected and published in an anthology *China's Mars Chronicles* (*Zhongguo huoxing jishi*), edited by Liu Weijia, a boom writer who was mostly active from 1996 to 2002 and famous for his utopian/dystopian writings, now more dedicated to his editorship for *Science Fiction World*. Preeminent writers who have their work collected in this anthology include Wu Yan, Pan Haitian, Yang Ping, Su Xuejun, and Jiang Bo. Meanwhile, Mars-based novels during the Chinese New Wave, apart from Hao Jingfang's *Vagabonds* to be discussed in this chapter, also include Xing He's *Martian Genes* (*Huoxing shengming jiyin*, 2010), Liu Yang's *The Orphans of Red Planet* (*Huoxing gu'er*, 2018), and Han Song's own *Hospital* trilogies (2016–18).

visions, blurring the line between the bright and the dark side of the "social dreaming" that Lyman Tower Sargent has imputed to utopianism (3–4), where fond dreams and nightmares can easily turn into each other.

Not surprisingly, the award-winning "Folding Beijing" – an eye-catching example of Hao Jingfang's experiment of various possibilities beyond our realities – has attracted wide attention and academic study (Ren 54–7; Lyu, "Divide" 36–9). The utopian nature of this story can even be corroborated by her acceptance speech during the 2016 Hugo Award ceremony: "Science fiction writers like to take all possibilities into account, good or bad, fortunate or unfortunate [...] In 'Folding Beijing,' I also gave a scenario of a possible future that tried to tackle problems brought by automation, technological progress, unemployment, inequality and economic stagnation" (Hao, "Acceptance" n.p.). The First Space in "Folding Beijing" is portrayed with a utopian outlook, but as readers will find out, it is utopian only because it is built on the other side of the dystopian Third Space. Under such a spatial and temporal co-existence, this compressed society provides a critical stance to tackle the problems Hao Jingfang mentioned in her Hugo speech.

At the same time, in an interview with *Uncanny Magazine* where "Folding Beijing" was first published in English, Hao Jingfang also points out the inadequacy of short stories in providing a comprehensive explanation of utopian ideas and in proposing alternatives to "our hitherto contaminated environment" that Jameson speaks of:

> Any informed observer can tell that in a rapidly developing society like contemporary China, disparities of wealth and status are growing wider, faster, but no one has a good solution to the problem. During the last century, multiple attempts at creating fairer, more equal societies stalled [...] I think it means a more profound problem is present in the human condition, hinting at an eternal dilemma that will always be with us. *A short story can't resolve such questions*. (Stanish n.p.; emphasis added)

With this in mind, however, Hao Jingfang does make an endeavour to resolve these questions, or at least try to test out potential solutions through world-building, in her long-form writing *Vagabond* (*Liulang cangqiong*, 2016). Given its length, it was originally published as two separate novels – *Wandering with Maearth* (*Liulang ma'esi*, 2011) and *Return to Charon* (*Huidao karong*, 2012) – only combined for re-publication in 2016, and translated into English in 2020. In this novel, Hao Jingfang carries on Han Song's unfinished project of conceptualizing Mars as an "experimental laboratory" (Jameson, *Archaeologies* 184) of utopian visions. This is a world where a social structure unfamiliar to our reality can be formed upon different rules of politics, economy and ideology, a process of "thought experiment" (Caroti 14) that can be identified in the formation of Amanduo in *Red Star over America*, as well as in the techno-utopian Culture in Banks's novels.

Of course, the Jamesonian "experimental laboratory" is also a common theme found in the novels of the British SF Boom, with Banks's Culture serving as one of the most direct and radical examples. Reinventing space opera, a subgenre once in decline, Banks challenges the right-wing politics dominant since the 1980s that favours "unrestrained competition and meritocracy" (Tew et al. 6). He expresses concerns over the claim that the political right had triumphed in shaping the narrative of the end of history, striving to articulate his own post-capitalist aspirations and seeking to establish a constructive framework to move beyond the sense of despair often associated with leftist melancholy (Brown, "Resisting" 19–27; Fisher *Postcapitalist* 55). He wishes, in this way, to reclaim the political high ground the British left had long lost.

This political consciousness is also evident in the works of Ken MacLeod, Banks's close friend. This is not unexpected, given MacLeod's extraordinary enthusiasm for the Culture novels. In fact, he even posted the blog "A Few Notes on the Culture" online on behalf of Banks in 1994, which stands as the most comprehensive explanation of the Culture universe to date. But unlike Banks, MacLeod is more interested in political *debates* and *experiments* over different forms of utopian ideas, rather than proposing a once-and-for-all utopia as his ultimate political alternative. He makes it clear – "I very much don't set out to make a political point. Like most writers, I start from some ideas or even just an image. That can be a political idea" (qtd. in Christie 44).

One year after "A Few Notes," MacLeod published his debut novel *The Star Fraction* (1995), the first volume of his well-known *Fall Revolution* quartet to be followed by *The Stone Canal* (1996), *The Cassini Division*

(1998) and *The Sky Road* (1999). In these novels, the UK is presented in a disunited, balkanized manner, in that much of the country is in the hands of self-governing mini-states, or micropolitical groups guided by various ideologies. Each of these ideologies is given a moment and space to experiment with their unique social and ideological blueprints, constituting a scenario of multiplicity described as "a Darwinian selection of societies" (MacLeod, *Star* 91). They are taken to "uncompromisingly logical conclusions" (MacLeod, "Politics" 231) and then contested against each other. "Thus," as John Arnold and Andy Wood observe, "the four books [of the *Fall Revolution* quartet] build, but then interrogate, a large and complex history of human affairs across several centuries; and use this history to explore a variety of ideological ideas and political practices" (30).

Over the past nearly thirty years, MacLeod has risen to be one of the key writers associated with the conjunction of sf and politics. In response to both the right-wing discourse of historical exhaustion and the far-left utopia as in the Culture novels, he is known for "[disrupting] conventional progressivist notions of historical linearity and [destabilizing] any simple privileging of one of these possible worlds over the others as the culmination of a deterministic historical process" (Wegner 140). The simultaneous existence of multiple utopias in the *Fall Revolution* quartet and the constant contest among them have been widely acknowledged as another (apart from the Culture) critical paradigm to reflect on the rise of neoliberal globalism (Winter, "Moments" 335–44), especially against Margaret Thatcher's "There Is No Alternative" rhetoric that was becoming "the formative slogan of an emergent world order" (Nairn, "Break-up" 27). This is usually considered one of MacLeod's achievements through his formulation of parallel anarchies that "[reject] the state as the primary means of organisation" (Mendlesohn, "Impermanent" 18) and build a cradle of revolutions that may lead to something new, something alternative, something that could create a scenario of the Lukácsian *Augenblick* (Wegner 143) and then cure the melancholia of the British left.

Focusing on *Vagabonds* and the *Fall Revolution* novels, I am now extending our perception of utopias in the previous chapter as projects of "social dreaming" to a further stage, where utopia, one that may or may not be disrupted, is seen as a dynamic *process* rather than a fixed representation of alternative possibilities. With a dichotomy of two worlds and two opposite systems, *Vagabonds* formulates "a meandering philosophical parable about an ideological rift" (Alter 33L) between the libertarian Earth that becomes increasingly capitalistic and the egalitarian Martian Republic where resources and fortune are shared and allocated on a collectivist, centralized basis. The Martian Republic is built after a revolution against the Earth by a group of scientific elites following their disappointment of market fervour on their home planet, so it is itself a result of historical disruption, a violent rupture from capitalist realism. But for Hao Jingfang, this rupture is not simply a restoration of China's past. It is instead a transcendence towards a future beyond the post-socialist modernity of contemporary China, a *post-postsocialist* safari towards a land of hope where the contradictory top-down and bottom-up discourses – the intrinsic doubleness that has always troubled the Chinese SF Boom – may finally be reconciled with each other.

Likewise, MacLeod does not try to propose one true utopia in the *Fall Revolution* quartet. On the contrary, he invites everyone to constitute their own utopias as they see fit, based on the rules that differentiate themselves from the neighbouring utopias and in this way answering the call of Ruth Levitas made at a 1999 conference to embrace pluralism and to "envisage utopia as a *process* rather than representation" (qtd. in Mendlesohn, "Impermanent" 16). This process, MacLeod believes, is open-ended and will never end. It leads us not to a certain point where things turn to be ideal but to a horizontal plane embracing a constellation of possible ideologies. Some may flourish; others will fade.

Under such a sense of "meta-utopianism" conceptualized by Robert Nozick, I will argue that MacLeod's political experiments are deeply rooted in how he understands his own times from the 1970s to the 1980s and then the 1990s. They are connected to historical references to the decline of the British left, the rise and fall of anarchist movements, the dominance of Thatcher's big government, the influence of financial deregulation and the seeming triumph of the market. Despite the anarchies described in the novels, it seems that it is exactly through the absence of state that a state, or at least a quasi-state, might form in itself. This quasi-state as such is referred to as a *minimal state* by Nozick himself and can be perceived as the closest theoretical construct to a real-world instantiation of the meta-utopia. In this way, MacLeod manages to demonstrate his political critique of the immediate legacy of Thatcher's regimes – that is, as famously summarized by Murray Rothbard in his 1995 book *Making Economic Sense*: "free-market rhetoric masking statist content" (229; emphasis added).

The Martian Republic: A Utopian Enclave of Scarcity in *Vagabonds*

Similar to Amanduo in Han Song's *Red Star over America*, the Martian Republic Hao Jingfang envisions in *Vagabonds* also appears with a utopian façade initially, a single city under a glass dome and confined due to the material scarcity on Mars. It is built upon a central archive system where the artistic and scientific creations of every single resident can be shared, accessed, circulated, referred and respected without any man-made barrier in the form of marketing schemes, IP protection, competitions of profitability and so on and so forth. "All of our incomes," says Janet who works for the Martian Film Archive, "are set based on age, regardless of [...] our accomplishments. All of our films are uploaded to the central archive, and anyone is allowed to view them without paying for the privilege. *Money isn't something we worry about*" (Hao, *Vagabond* 68; emphasis added).

In the eyes of an Earth visitor, the central archive forms "a forum in which everyone was responsible for their own thoughts but no one would profit from their own language" (227), an enclave in which the Martians may stay away from the obsessive commerce of Earth where "everyone sold, bought, hid their own creations, and then enticed others with revelation of these secrets for money" (71). It can be considered "a contemporary version of the 'Red Mars' paradigm" (Hubble 5) that dates all the way back to Alexander Bogdanov's *Red Star* (1908), where Mars is rendered as an alternative world for communist or socialist societies.

Unlike the capital-dominated Earth where "commerce was the only rule, and advertisements would bombard the children day and night," the Martian Republic operates in an anti-capitalist manner. "Here the land was literally a thing of the people, managed for the commonweal. There was no private ownership in real estate, no smuggling, no buying on credit, no banking" (Hao, *Vagabond* 38–9). Instead of the dynamic and all-encompassing market on Earth, which appears to provide Terrans with diverse and ever-changing possibilities, the Martians are all affiliated to the "ateliers" they have chosen in their youth for their lifetime, producing a sense of stability and certainty. With these ateliers, the Martians believe they could be free from "worrying about the basic necessities of life," from the will of capital, and from selling one's "creative freedom for money" (179). In other words, it is the ateliers that guarantee their lifelong career and social protections – or even determine their very existence in the Martian Republic – since their identities cannot be recognized by the central archive without registration to one of the ateliers. Those who refuse to register would always be "someone standing outside the system" (123).

These ateliers, in this way, "had multiple social, political, and economic functions and [offered] a permanent 'membership' of workers with lifetime employment," resembling the "work unit" or *danwei* commonly adopted by state-owned enterprises (SOEs), government departments, schools and hospitals, which had played an indispensable role in urban China during the Mao era. Alone with the market-oriented reforms empowered by Deng Xiaoping's Cat Theory (see the Introduction) in the 1990s, however, the principle of "lifetime employment," usually referred to as the "Iron Rice Bowl," as well as a bundle of guaranteed social livelihoods including housing, health care, childcare and education, gradually withered away, replaced by short-term contracts. The collectivist sense of state protection gave way to an appeal to individual responsibilities.

But unlike the real *danwei* in post-socialist China, the ateliers of the Martian Republic in *Vagabonds* have not lost their power. Throughout the novel, they have been playing an indispensable role in maintaining the stability of the central archive system, particularly because of the environmental scarcity on Mars and its efficiency in distributing limited resources (nevertheless, such a stability promised by the ateliers does not go unchallenged, as explained later in this article). Thanks to the "fair, open, transparent distribution of resources," these Martian work units could then guarantee that "everyone receives what they should – not one penny more, not one penny less. No secrets or omissions" (128). Quite successfully, the Martian Republic manages to prevent the collectively owned wealth from being accumulated by private hands, a process of privatization deemed as the source of "corruption, hoarding, and greed" (129), as the root cause of "the terminal disease plaguing Earth" (29) to which Mars could provide an antidote.

In *Archaeologies of the Future*, Fredric Jameson argues that the utopian thought experiment may provide "[non-]alienated enclaves [that] suddenly light up in our hitherto contaminated environment" (230). In line with his argument, Mars in *Vagabonds* should then be seen as such a Jamesonian "enclave" free from the "contaminated environment" of the commercial revelry on Earth, which is made possible through Hao Jingfang's separation of the two seemingly disparate ideologies onto two planets. The Martian Republic, originally a colony of Earth, is founded with a military revolution against its Terran colonizers, some forty years before the story, launched by a group of ex-Terran scientists who grew disappointed by their market-prioritized mechanism that put corporate financial statements ahead of the well-being of individuals.

They wished to establish "*a completely free world* in which everyone was free to explore and discover, free to share their creations in the central archive, free to use the creations of others, supported by a stipend" (Hao, *Vagabonds* 478; emphasis added). Such a rupture between the representation of "the image of private property and exploitation" and that of "egalitarianism and communitarianism" refers to a form of "determinate negation of [the] past," which is the negation of the Martians' history of being colonized by the Terrans as well as their economized values of market. This form of "negation of the past" is not strange to sf studies, as it is evident in the dialectic between Anarres and Urras in Le Guin's *The Dispossessed* (1974) identified by John Fekete (132). Since its publication, Le Guin's novel has always been thought-provoking, in that it explores themes of anarcho-syndicalism, social and political structures, as well as the contrasts between two societies – one on an anarchist moon (Anarres) and the other on a capitalist planet (Urras). The story follows the physicist Shevek who becomes disillusioned with the limitations of life on Anarres, particularly the stifling orthodoxy of his own society and its lack of communication with Urras. But very soon, as he embarks on a perilous journey to Urras, he quickly realizes that the challenges and political complexities he encounters may be far removed from the utopian society he envisions.

Therefore, *The Dispossessed* is well known for its configuration of experimental socio-political alternatives, one of the most significant of its kind. In contrast to the abundant, pro-capitalist and market-driven Urrasti society, Anarres indicates "the presence of extreme scarcity" and "the absence of property and consumerism" (Fekete 131). It appears capital-free and is thus considered "a powerful and timely rebuke to present-day attempts to parlay American abundance and consumer goods into some ultimate vision of the 'great society'" (Jameson, *Archaeologies* 277–8). With the "barren, arid and inchoate" (Le Guin, *Dispossessed* 57) scenes on Anarres where "human solidarity is [the] only resource" of the Anarresti (139), Le Guin proposes a utopian hypothesis in response to Marx's and Trotsky's concerns whether an egalitarian society can ever be realized without the overwhelming material abundance that Iain M. Banks endows to his Culture Empire.

This "human solidarity" that Le Guin speaks of via Shevek chimes with Hao Jingfang's imagination of the Martian Republic, whose revolution against Earth erupts out of the rebels' "dissatisfaction with the way various factions on Mars [under Earth's domination] had been hoarding information, erecting walls to contain knowledge" (Hao, *Vagabonds* 362). They believe that "to survive in the harsh environment of Mars required the free sharing and exchange of discoveries and inventions" (363) – a Martian solidarity of sharing knowledge. In this way, through the "surgical excision of empirical reality" where the power of capital is taking over the world, a technique that Jameson calls "world reduction" (*Archaeologies* 271), Le Guin reveals to her readers "the inseparability of utopia and scarcity" (Jameson, *Archaeologies* 277) and points to the possibility of developing egalitarianism in a barren world not an abundant one.

Hao Jingfang does the same with her *Vagabonds*. In line with Le Guin's revelation of this "inseparability," the Martian Republic in *Vagabonds* shares with Anarres the potential of formulating a possible utopia. And more strikingly, both versions of utopia are established through a revolution. In John Fekete's discussion of *The Dispossessed*, he points out that "with the legend of revolution [of Anarres] there develops the illusion of a radical rupture between past and future, a rupture which separates Anarres from Urras and is supposed to have revealed the meaning of history" (131), a rupture that destroys the remaining connection to the old and calls for "a completely new society" (Hao, *Vagabonds* 361). Like the egalitarians on Anarres who claim to have broken with the libertarian ideology from the old world, and who determine "to insulate [themselves] as completely as possible from Urrasti corruption and injustice" (Freedman, "Science Fiction and Critical Theory" 238), people of the Martian Republic have also established an insular world, isolated and ruptured from the consumerist Earth. "The free world" its founders have envisioned – with the central archive and the atelier system designed to break any kind of artificial walls that could block the free circulation of information – gradually develops from their drastic refusal of the market and the sense of liquidity on Earth.

In contrast, the emphasis on stability and certainty through people's dedication to their ateliers in the Martian Republic calls to mind, again, Han Song's Amanduo, which has been analysed in the previous chapter. In *Red Star over America*, Amanduo, as a disrupted utopia, ultimately implodes, serving as a reflection of China's post-socialist transition characterized by the state's withdrawal from social protection and welfare provision. It seems, however, that Hao Jingfang's reconstruction of the egalitarian utopia, especially as the result of an anti-market revolution, reverses the direction of the historical transition that Amanduo embodies. It seems that the utopian "garden" falling apart in *Red Star over America* rises once again in *Vagabonds* and is pictured as "the last utopia of humankind, a place where crude commercial interests yielded to pure intellect" (Hao, *Vagabonds* 23). It seems that the historical rupture of the Martian Republic from its market-driven counterpart, made possible by the central archive and the fictional version of the *danwei* system (whose power is in decline in reality), can be considered a nostalgic return to China's past, before the arrival of its post-socialist modernity.

But again, this "nostalgic return" is by no means a simple restoration of the collapsed Amanduo, nor is it a melancholic mourning of the kind that Zhang Xudong describes as a "clichéd lament" of the elitist top-down intellectual field to a popular bottom-up cultural discourse (115). No matter how "utopian" Amanduo and the Martian Republic might be, there are still subtle differences in terms of their positions in China's historical transition. In *Red Star over America*, the belief that Amanduo is a utopia is most notably held by Tang Long, an "insider" who has always been living in that utopia, or in his own words, in the "garden" or "dream society" where things are centrally arranged, where people are allocated lifelong jobs (Han, *Huoxing* 6, 234). He is proud of this utopia, at least during his adventures with the Suzuki gang.

However, the Amanduo-utopia corrupts from within, because of the intrinsic contradiction between the logic of centrality it is built on and the fragmented, decentralized information it has collected from the mass public. This contradiction and the eventual collapse of Amanduo itself faithfully mirror the social change in China during the 1990s – the retreat of the state from welfare provision, the shift from "relying on the state" to "relying on oneself," the fading of the socialist sense of stability, and the emerging uncertainty and fluidity brought forth by the power of market. When *Red Star* was first published in 2000, all these changes were still underway and affecting society, and even Han Song himself was not sure where they might end up or what kind of future they might lead to. Hence, while he was writing the novel, he invited us to join Tang Long's journey and explore all the possibilities, calling for all auspicious or inauspicious alternatives.

But again, the Martian Republic of *Vagabonds* is considered a "utopia" most explicitly not by an insider like Tang Long but by an outsider, Eko, a documentary director from Earth who becomes disappointed with his own world, haunted by the power of capital and market. It is Eko who sees the red planet as "the last utopia," the "medicine" (Hao, *Vagabonds* 29) to cure the terminal disease plaguing his planet. From the Blochian perspective where the utopian impulse is to invoke the hope for "not-yet," Mars, therefore, does appear as a utopian enclave for Eko to diagnose the social symptoms on Earth he has identified. In this manner, Mars can indeed function as a beacon of hope in Hao Jingfang's novel, serving as an experimental space for conceptualizing a particular vision of utopia amidst the wasteland tainted by competitive market principles.

Different from the utopia in *Red Star over America* that marks the shift towards China's post-socialist condition, the Martian Republic, created more than ten years after Amanduo, carries on from where Han Song stopped. It is, instead, anchored in people's disenchantment with this post-socialist condition that allows for large-scale privatization and is governed by the all-encompassing rules of market competition, appealing to an alternative to that pro-capitalist paradise. Such a critique of China's increasing engagement with market principles, as Tom Moylan has put it in his discussion of critical utopia with *The Dispossessed* as an example (*Demand* 10), stands for a Hegelian process of negating "the negation of utopia by the forces of twentieth century history" (and of the twenty-first century for *Vagabonds*), an endeavour to formulate an enclave of hope accommodating what can be called the "post-postsocialist" possibilities.

This synchronic dialectic between Earth and Mars, each symbolizing a distinct period along the spectrum of Chinese history (one as an "already" and the other as a "not-yet"), situated in diverse locations or planets, reaffirms Jameson's assertion that sf is inherently a "spatial genre." Here, we can observe "a significant displacement in our reading interest from narrative in that sense, with its linear causality, toward spatial experience as such" (*Archaeologies* 312). Sf, therefore, emerges as a genre of "utopian hermeneutics," as exemplified by Hao Jingfang and *Vagabonds* in the context of the Chinese SF Boom.

Negating the Negation: A Nostalgic Return to the Future

This process of "negating the negation," this "spatial" extrapolation conceptualizing various historical alternatives relating *Vagabonds* to *The Dispossessed*, will never end. Since neither Urras and Anarres is flawless, Shevek, the protagonist in *The Dispossessed*, according to Wendy Gay Pearson, eventually comes to understand that "utopia is not about achieving perfection but about the quest for an egalitarian, communal society – a quest whose value lies in *working for* the goals of equality, liberty, and communalism, rather than in achieving them" (140; emphasis added). Through his tentative movements back and forth between the two worlds, Shevek perceives this dialectic as a utopia of *process*, an unending process.

Such a hesitation between two different (even opposite) possibilities can also be identified in Luoying, Shevek's counterpart in *Vagabonds* who is originally from the Martian Republic but sent to Earth at the age of 13, only to return to Mars five years later. Witnessing and experiencing both worlds like Shevek, Luoying develops troubling doubts over the seemingly utopian society that Eko sees as the last hope of humanity. Indeed, Luoying's fate "to be a vagabond" (*Vagabonds* 262), as emphasized in the novel, is irrevocably sealed. This sentiment is beautifully captured by the quote from Saint-Exupéry's *Wind, Sand and Stars*: "A simple village in our homeland would hide itself from us in the same manner. If we do not renounce the rest of the world for its sake [...] we cannot understand why it is someone's homeland" (262). And Mars, from Luoying's distant point of view, becomes problematic, turning into an illusory homeland to which she can no longer truly return.

In this way, along with the utopia formulated through the Mars-Earth dialectic, there also emerged a paradise-lost, especially for Luoying. She has seen the alternative, and thus her original hometown, the one regarded as a utopia in her memories, ceases to be. In the prologue of the novel, Hao Jingfang writes:

> Once, a group of children was born on one world and grew up on another.
>
> The world they were born into was a tower of rigid rules; the world they grew up on was a garden of rambling disorder. One was a magnificent, austere blueprint; the other was a wild bacchanalia [...]
>
> What had been put together in the tower was smashed to bits in the garden, what had been forgotten in drunken revelry was still memorialized in the blueprint. Those who lived only in the tower never suffered the loss of faith; those who lived only for the pursuit of pleasure had no vision to strive for. Only those who had wandered through both worlds could experience that particular stormy night in which distant mirages faded away and countless strange flowers blossomed in the wasteland. (3)

With such a Dickensian (as in *A Tale of Two Cities*) opening, Hao Jingfang directs us to the point she is trying to make in her own tale – "the tale of the fall of the last utopia" (4). She implies a sense of disenchantment with the seemingly utopian Martian Republic that Luoying gradually develops during her visit to Earth. This "disenchantment" is marked by Luoying's dialectical perception of the contradictory ideologies on the two planets. In response to Eko's anti-capitalist resentment of the "religion of consumerism" on Earth enshrining the power of the market, "where human nature has been turned away from *agape* and debased into covetousness" (175; emphasis in original), Luoying responds from a different perspective. She believes the so-called "desire" to consume that Eko blames for creating commodity fetishism is in fact the pursuit of individual uniqueness, a pursuit which would be otherwise overwhelmed by the Amanduo-ist sense of centrality and arrangement that is, in a way, also adopted in the Martian Republic. She goes on to justify her Terran friends' consumerist behaviours as a way of determining their own identity differentiated from others: "Even though they were shaped by their surroundings, they want to be unique [...] They can't choose the world they live in, or how that world operates, but they want to live their own lives, to find out who they are" (175).

I wish to clarify that Luoying's rebuttal does not glorify the libertarian and market-based Earth itself. As indicated later in *Vagabonds*, Hao Jingfang is very much aware that the ostensible consumerist freedom of the Earthlings to strive for individual uniqueness is still confined by the market. Earth's seemingly kaleidoscopic reality, enriched by the countless choices promised by various forms of commodities, including artistic creations, actually follows a "big supermarket" logic where, in essence, "everything had the same content, the same packaging, the same themes and subjects that had been done a million times" (223) (reminding us of the Jamesonian pastiche in postmodern, post-industrial and late-capitalist society). In Hao Jingfang's Terran society, this is the only way for a film, or any other product intended for consumption, to become a "blockbuster" (223) and be deemed successful. Even though Eko launches a left-wing countermovement against these big supermarkets, denying market preferences and producing the works favoured by "minorities" and the "artisanal market," he eventually realizes that in so doing he is not resisting the process of commodification but only "strengthen[ing] it" (224). His "pursuit for the personal and unique" has, therefore, never truly departed from "the mold of his commercial society" (224).

Luoying is also aware of the hypocrisy of the market in its claims for individual uniqueness because the repetitive, non-creative nature of cultural and artistic production that Eko identifies on Earth is exactly what feels flawed for her. No matter how dynamic she might find her life on Earth, Luoying cannot forget "the sense of sacredness in the act of *creation*, planted deep in her heart by her homeland" (151; emphasis added). It is, after all, such a treasured "act of creation," protected by the central archive providing an unbiased, unlimited sharing platform accessible to everyone based on their need and interests rather than affordability, that forms the core of the egalitarian Martian Republic and would lead to true, un-alienated freedom.

But Luoying does not find it truly free. Having seen the diversity of people's livelihood coloured by the numerous options of commodities, she is no longer "to imagine [herself] living the life [she] was *assigned* to" (177; emphasis added). In line with her reluctance to conform to the system of atelier assignment, her plea in favour of individual uniqueness in consumerist society against Eko's all-encompassing criticism is not a libertarian proposal for transplanting the Terran ideology on Mars without change. Instead, Luoying proposes to challenge the rigidity of the Republic's atelier system – a system of the state arrangement and assignment that, both in theory and in practice, guarantees their social stability. She says to Eko, in a regretful tone:

> You don't know that an atelier is for life. Though switching isn't forbidden, it's extremely rare for anyone on Mars to change ateliers. Everyone climbs the career ladder rung by rung, spending a whole life within the confines of two parallel lines. If I had never been to Earth, I suppose it wouldn't bother me. But I have been there. You know the lifestyle of everyone on Earth: free to come and go, free to hop from profession to profession. I've grown used to that kind of life, filled with fluidity and experiments. I don't want to live in a pyramid. (177)

With a sense of disenchantment over the utopian Martian Republic, Luoying appeals to "shatter what has ossified" (387), to "untether people from their ateliers so that they can move about freely" (389), and to "advocate for the free transfer of housing" (456) that used to be dependent on people's marital status and their atelier affiliations. She begins to question whether Mars and Earth, in essence, are truly different beneath the surface elements such as the political and economic structures, people's lifestyles, the dominant ideologies and so on. Despite all these superficial differences, however, as the group of young revolutionaries gradually realizes, the underpinning philosophy that had been implicitly guiding the two societies was, rather surprisingly, the same – that of competition and calculation.

This competitive and calculative logic is clearly apparent in the market-empowered society on Earth. The new technologies introduced from Mars are first tested out not in scientific labs but on the stock market, rendered as the futures and options for trading, driven by the calculations and strategies employed in these financial endeavours. Each artistic creation has an extremely limited turnover period, competing for market acceptance and profit. As Eko finds out, everything, when entering the market, "was like a bottle of milk with an expiration date. Unless it found a buyer, it would be mercilessly removed from the shelves and thrown away. Three days, or maybe thirty days; commerce or death" (100). This echoes Wendy Brown's summary of the expansion of market values, that is "the financialization of everything and the increasing dominance of finance capital over productive capital in the dynamics of the economy and everyday life," and the normative socio-economic structure where "competition replaces exchange as the market's root principle and basic good" (W. Brown, *Undoing* 28, 36).

As I mentioned earlier, the Martian Republic is founded in the hope of building "a completely new society" (Hao, *Vagabonds* 361), a hope of breaking with all these market competitions and financial calculations. But in fact, even though they have established the central archive and the atelier system to avoid the privatization of the public/collective capital and the means of production (129), the Martians are never far away from the same logic for a single moment that prevails on Earth, though rendered in a different manner. The competition is not directly among the individual-enterprises as in neoliberal societies, but initially between different ateliers, namely people's *danwei* that is supposed to protect them. Since their annual budgets are centrally allocated and supervised based on the degree of success of the project each atelier has proposed, "the competition for the next year's budget is a critical moment for each atelier" (289), influencing the fate of everyone in the community. Therefore, the Martian Republic can be seen as "a carefully managed enterprise in which the return on every investment and the potential for loss in every eventuality are calculated to three decimal places" (289).

This entrepreneurial drive on Earth is also apparent in the competition for budgets among the ateliers, which can essentially be regarded as autonomous "enterprises" striving to strike a calculated balance between cost and profit. Each of the ateliers operates as a shrewd participant in this exhaustive game, making every effort to secure favour from the state and acquire the necessary grants, often eliciting disappointment and envy from competing ateliers. During this process, unfortunately but inevitably, forgery and bluffing may appear because to win a share of the budget, an atelier "must make bold pronouncements and airy promises [...] the higher the costs of production for a project, the higher the allocated share of the budget" (370).

Meanwhile, individuals associated with these ateliers also find themselves deeply entrenched in an environment where they engage in a parallel competition. They vie for higher citation rates within the central archive for their respective works, often driven not by genuine interests in scientific exploration, artistic creation or the pursuit of "creative expression and wisdom" (388), but by the relentless pressure of this competitive milieu. Instead, for most if not all people involved in this competition, the citation rate they attempt to boost could lead the way towards a greater reputation and a higher rank within their atelier hierarchy. They would then be entitled to more resources and public acknowledgement. In other words, the citation rate can be seen as the Martian capital. Although the reward for competition on Mars, whether among the ateliers or individuals, is not necessarily in a monetary form like that on Earth, people's enthusiasm for the process of self-recognition and self-promotion still reminds us of Michel Feher's perception of "self-appreciation" as a fundamental feature of "human capital" in a fully economized social structure (Feher 21–41).

Underneath the utopian vision of the Martian Republic seemingly built upon equality, stability and equitable distribution, "the only thing that matters is [still] selfish gain" (Hao, *Vagabonds* 388). The egalitarian garden that they used to be proud of appears compromised at its very root. But even so, even with such rather painful revelations, Luoying does not ask for a regime change through a full-scale adoption of the libertarian values stimulating the commercial dynamism of Earth. Nor does she promote overturning the state once and for all to establish anarchism or anarcho-syndicalism to free up the ateliers from the rigid constraint of the budget allocation. Instead, she proposes moderate reforms, increasing the "fluidity" for people to transfer from one atelier to another, to exchange their house with others and, in general, to detach the responsibilities of welfare provision and social protection from the ateliers and introduce individual incentives.

Such a scheme that Luoying fights for does not sound strange to readers in China. It reflects, in a realistic way, on China's post-socialist transformation in terms of housing and the *danwei* compounds. For housing, according to John Gittings, it has indeed "encouraged social mobility" in the post-Deng era, when "millions of [urban residents], obliged to leave public housing due for redevelopment, bought apartments of their own [... and] Those who already owned their own homes in the cities were able to sell without incurring official disapproval" (262). In a similar vein, the "organized dependency" (Walder 51–76) of those *danwei*-affiliated workers, who "relied on their respective work unit so much that they even developed a work-unit identity and a culture of personal dependence on their work unit and their leaders" (Yan Y. 19–20), has also dissolved during China's historical transition.

Along with the systematic denationalization targeted at the *danwei* compounds, what was also challenged in this era was a special socialist concept "*bianzhi*," referring to the *authorized* number of *established* working posts in Party and government administrative apparatus, public institutions (*shiye danwei*) such as public hospitals, schools, universities, research institutes, state-run media and SOEs (Brødsgaard 363). But in the recent decades, the *bianzhi* system has become increasingly "redundant" (Delman and Yin 98) during the ongoing marketization and decentralization. The fixed, pre-settled working posts supervised directly by the state were gradually replaced with conditionally renewable contracts, first among the

SOEs (which created millions of "laid-off" workers in the late 1990s who moved to the non-state sectors), and then in the domain of education and health care.

Hence, Luoying's call for revolution appears more like an entreaty for a movement towards "individualization," rooted in the central archive and the pre-existing atelier system within the Martian Republic. In essence, it advocates for internal reforms aimed at enhancing social mobility and fluidity, all while upholding the Republic's efficiency in resource allocation and its mission to shield Mars from the market-driven contamination discussed by Hao Jingfang during her Hugo Award ceremony: "the disparities of wealth that are growing wider and faster." Through *Vagabonds* and her work in crafting the dialectic between Earth and Mars, Hao Jingfang underscores the importance of this ideal of individualization, which, in the words of Zygmunt Bauman, "carries the emancipation of the individual from the ascribed, inherited and inborn determination of his or her social character [… and] consists in transforming human 'identity' from a 'given' into a 'task'" (Bauman, *Individualized* 144).

But meanwhile, Luoying's revolution does not produce a paradise-lost like the dying Amanduo in Han Song's *Red Star over America*. The Martian Republic, as the consequence of its *de facto* historical rupture breaking with the former libertarian regime from Earth, cannot travel backwards. A utopia itself, it has indeed offered hope for an alternative and a supposedly better world for left-wingers on Earth. But it is also an ambiguous utopia open to challenge and introspection, thus invoking its own hope for the Blochian sense of not-yet.

A utopia upon another utopia; a negation to another negation, Luoying does not realize this point until she learns, in a later part of this novel, that what she opposes is exactly what her parents supported at the cost of their lives, that is "the fairness of absolute equal distribution" (Hao, *Vagabonds* 532); what she proposes is what her grandfather rebelled against at the start of everything. She comes to understand that "there are only two systems in the world: the solid and the liquid" (472), each at the opposite ends of the same spectrum and neither flawless. The process of "negating the negation" in which Luoying is involved is endless, reminding us of Shevek's never-complete journey in Le Guin's *The Dispossessed*. This leads

Luoying to her permanent residence on neither of the planets but on the spaceship drifting in between (which is literally named "Maearth"). In so doing, with the ability of comprehending both worlds, Luoying has become a permanent vagabond at the end of *Vagabonds*, forever trying to formulate a "truer" sense of freedom and forever envisioning a new utopia upon the fall of old ones.

The *Fall Revolution* Quartet: A Nozickian Framework of Meta-Utopianism

But in fact, the process of negating the negation, or in other words the establishment of new alternatives through a historical rupture or disruption, is not always made possible via the collapse of previous utopias like Amanduo in *Red Star over America* and the Martian Republic in *Vagabonds*. It is not always a violent and rebellious rupture like the Idiran-Culture war. Utopias with heterogeneous features and ideas can, in many ways, co-exist with each other, each forming a distinctive community among a diversity of communities based on different roles and values preferred by those who choose to live within. This chimes with Robert Nozick's well-known argument of "meta-utopia" conceptualized in his monograph *Anarchy, State and Utopia* (1974), which refers to "the environment in which utopian experiments may be tried out; the environment in which people are free to do their own thing; the environment which must, to a great extent, be realized first if more particular utopian visions are to be realized stably" (Nozick 312).

To elaborate on the relations between the notion "meta-utopia" and the subordinate "particular utopian visions" he mentions, Nozick invites us to engage in a thought experiment about the formation of utopia:

> Imagine a possible world in which to live [...] Every rational creature in this world you have imagined will have the same rights of imagining a possible world for himself to live in (in which all other rational inhabitants have the same imagining rights,

> and so on) as you have. The other inhabitants of the world you have imagined may choose to stay in the world which has been created for them (they have been created for) or they may choose to leave it and inhabit a world of their own imagining. If they choose to leave your world and live in another, your world is without them. You may choose to abandon your imagined world, now without its emigrants. This process goes on; worlds are created, people leave them, create new worlds, and so on. (Nozick 299)

As we proceed with this cycle, we will eventually come up with a series of stable, parallel "associations," that is "a wide and diverse range of communities" in our actual world (Nozick 307), each occupied by a certain group of like-minded dwellers (in their own utopian enclave) who may in this way live as they wish, to pursue their own good and to test out their values and ideals. Therefore, the Nozickian "meta-utopianism" does not pre-set a single form of utopia of changeless universality, but instead it allows for a variety of sub-utopias subject to the assumptions and preferences of different people and invokes the possibility of formulating a "framework of utopia" in which "utopian experimentation can be tried, different styles of life can be lived, and alternative visions of the good can be individually or jointly pursued" (Nozick 307). In these pursuits, some of the communities could be strengthened, others abandoned, some thriving, others on the verge of breaking apart.

No doubt, such a framework of meta-utopianism is exactly the narrative foundation of Ken MacLeod's *Fall Revolution* quartet. Apart from the balkanized London in *The Star Fraction* where we can see numerous political enclaves from libertarian capitalists to the greens and the Trotskyists, from fundamentalist Christians to Islamic militants (among which the libertarian Norlonto stands out as the most influential), we are also presented with other forms of utopia in its sequels such as "a libertarian, anarcho-capitalist society [...] in *The Stone Canal*, a socialist Stirnerist anarchy in *The Cassini Division*, and in *The Sky Road*, an ecotopia which may or may not be anarchic or libertarian, depending on one's definition" (Mendlesohn, "Impermanent" 18). It does not culminate with the realization of a particular utopian vision or a permanent triumph of any stable order. On the contrary, for MacLeod, "utopias are travelled towards, briefly glimpsed, but never at rest" (Arnold and Wood 42). In this way, Fredric Jameson's comments on Kim Stanley Robinson's *Mars* trilogy can also be applied to MacLeod's stories:

> Unlike the "monological" utopias of the tradition, which needed to dramatize a single utopian possibility strongly because of its repression from Terran history and political possibility, this more "polyphonic" one includes the struggle between a whole range of utopian alternatives, about which it deliberately fails to conclude. (Jameson, *Archaeologies* 410)

Of course, it should be noted that Jameson is not entirely convinced by Nozick's conceptualization of meta-utopia. He believes that the framework of meta-utopianism indicates what he calls "modernist symptoms" (Jameson, *Archaeologies* 218). That is, no matter how multiple, how diversified those sub-utopias within this framework could ever be, each of the sub-utopias generated from it is still a "solution," an achieved utopian construct rather than the story of its production or the process of its formation like in Robinson's writings (218). Utopias, for Jameson, should be autonomous, non-communicating, appearing as "a constellation of discontinuous centers" as he draws on Yona Friedman's multiplicity of utopian communities (219–21). But in this case, the Nozickian meta-utopianism is fleshed out further in the *Fall Revolution* quartet, since we have witnessed Norlonto and New Mars being built from the ground up and directly confronting their neighbours or rivals, which can be perceived as a rebuttal to Jameson's critique.

Despite this, Jameson agrees with Nozick about considering the meta-utopian project "the answer to repressive unities and identities of all kinds" (218). In fact, it is exactly this "variety" of the political insights presented in these stories, instead of their loosely connected narrative plots, that truly links them as a "quartet." It is also this multiplicity of utopian voices and political configurations, according to Andrew M. Butler ("Introduction" ix), that grants MacLeod's quartet the character of a heteroglossia, a term sitting at the core of Bakhtin's dialogical theories developed through his reading of Dostoevsky. "The prose writer," writes Bakhtin, "does not destroy the seeds of social heteroglossia embedded in words" (Bakhtin, *Dialogic* 298) and therefore everything in heteroglossic novels (of MacLeod and Dostoevsky alike) "tends toward dialogue, toward a dialogic opposition, as if tending toward its centre. All else is the means; dialogue is the end. A single voice ends nothing and resolves nothing. Two voices is the minimum for life, the minimum for existence" (Bakhtin, *Problems* 252).

In line with this polyphonic sense of heteroglossia, the *Fall Revolution* quartet is itself a political dialogue in which different or even opposing ideas can be proposed and contested. "Any mode of totality," any attempt to build a universal utopia of perfection and stability, must be "subjected to subversion" (Luckhurst, *Science Fiction* 229), whether it emerges from the Norlonto (the left-libertarian anarchic enclave in the fractured London in *The Star Fraction*), the anarcho-capitalist New Mars in *The Stone Canal*, or the money-less Solar Union in *The Cassini Division*. With none of the above leading to the one true solution that overwhelms the rest, these utopian visions are put in a constant dialogue with each other.

Developing from this dialogue, these visions provide different possible answers to the same question Luoying and Eko have pondered in *Vagabonds* through the dialectic between the egalitarian Mars and the libertarian Earth: in which society can its residents really achieve their freedom, "determine [their] own fate" (Hao, *Vagabonds* 455) and create a world where they will never feel "owned" (MacLeod, *Cassini* 134)? But meanwhile, unlike *Vagabonds* where Luoying and Eko have to fight for a new society with their new utopian blueprints responding to the negation against the previous one, characters in the *Fall Revolution* quartet seem to be a bit luckier under MacLeod's Nozickian framework of meta-utopianism. They do not need to rebel against and wishfully overthrow Terran neoliberalism or the atelier system of the Martian Republic. They can just leave the current community and look for another that meets their expectations. They are expected to "diverge in the values they have and have different weightings for the values they share" and thus there is "no reason to think that there is one community which will serve as ideal for all people and much reason to think that there is not" (Nozick 309–10).

It is exactly such a process of leaving and joining that formulates the individual "freedom" in this quartet. "From each as they choose, to each as they are chosen" (MacLeod *Star* 135) – Janis Taine's libertarian assertion in *The Star Fraction* may well indicate a synchronic heterogeneity of parallel utopias, among which people are provided with more than one ideological order they can *choose* to follow rather freely and find themselves in a scenario where, "Every man under his own vine and under his own fig tree, and no one to make him afraid" (MacLeod *Cassini* 170). This process, of course, is far from untroubled when put into practice in reality, because moving between enclaves is subject to the limitations of border-crossing if said enclaves have not reached their eventual respective stability. According to Nozick himself, "in the actual world communities *impinge* upon one another, creating problems of foreign relations and self-defense and necessitating modes of adjudicating and resolving disputes between the communities" (307; emphasis in original).

Nozick also points out that reality is different from his theoretical configuration of meta-utopianism. There are temporal and financial costs involved in moving and traveling between and locating other communities. There is also a possibility that "some communities may try to keep some of their members ignorant of the nature of other alternative communities they might join, to try to prevent them from freely leaving their own community to join another" (Nozick 307). Because of these limitations, the ultimate outcome of meta-utopianism as well as people's free flow among different communities of alternatives that, according to Nozick's model, will lead to the eventual stability and harmony, may never come into being – it is an ideal, after all, an ideal calling for "a place where people are at liberty to join together voluntarily to pursue and attempt to realize their own vision of the good life" (Nozick 312).

But even though the Nozickian framework of utopianism is as abstract and unreachable as any of the conventional utopian visions of universal or homogeneous perfection, it still points at a difference: Nozick acknowledges the possibility of a stable co-existence of diverse utopian communities with diverse values and ideals, none of which would erode the border of its neighbours. It is exactly such a co-existence that differentiates MacLeod's utopianism from the utopias we have discussed so far – Han Song's Amanduo, Banks's Culture and Hao Jingfang's Martian Republic. The libertarian Norlonto is itself a wonderland of diversity and non-conformity. These are not the "separate fiefs" of a united regime with a universal order but "layered, interwoven properties and neighbourhoods" that are privately managed:

> Some welcomed anyone passing through. Some had gates on the streets, or took a toll, or turned back anyone who hadn't been invited by a resident. Carrying weapons on the street might be prohibited, permitted or required. It was a matter for the street-owners, like wearing ties in restaurants. Smoking or non-smoking. There were sinister, seedy areas that had been all bought up by nazis and made most of their money from tourists and memorabilia. There were women-only territories. There was a whole district [...] consisted of experimental communities being crawled over by sociologists. (MacLeod, *Star* 174–5)

Likewise, on the New Mars established upon trade, commerce and short-term contracts there is still room for a certain group of "abolitionists" appealing for the equal rights of humans and androids (MacLeod, *Stone* 12), a group that later becomes an important left-wing political power. In the classless, market-less and anarchic Solar Union, there is also a community of "non-cooperatives" for whom it is "considered all right to exchange coins with them for their odd handicrafts and eccentric nanofactures" (MacLeod, *Cassini* 21). In this way, instead of overturning the previous utopia guided by one single order, to produce a historical rupture and therefore to consolidate a new order that governs all, the *Fall Revolution* goes the other way: any attempt that aims to create (or bring back) such a universal order and to weaken or even eliminate the internal discrepancies under the meta-utopian framework will eventually prove futile.

In a conversation between Moh Kohn and Jon Wilde in *The Star Fraction*, they both attempt to convince each other of their own political views, indicating what John Arnold and Andy Wood (42) consider "much of the Fall Revolution Quartet comprises a development":

> Kohn tried – and felt he failed – to articulate the inchoate vision he held of a socialist society that would be even wilder and more free-wheeling than Norlonto, freer than the free market, where the common knowledge that could not but be common property would become the greatest wealth, shared without sacrifice or stint. Wilde countered with his own vision of a world where the market was only the framework, but the only framework, for ways of life as diverse as human inclination could devise. (MacLeod, *Star* 91)

It seems as if Kohn, to some extent influenced by his father's Trotskyite beliefs, is inspired by an idea of a market-less society in which information and knowledge can be shared and circulated without constraints.

But as the story proceeds, we gradually realize that Kohn has no problem at all with the market itself, especially since he recognizes the success of Norlonto. "Anarcho-capitalism works," he says, "[as] much as any kind of capitalism works" (MacLeod, *Star* 176). Instead, as revealed later, his preferred social structure "wasn't something you forced on people." "It was people organizing themselves *as they pleased* into co-ops, collectives, communes, unions" (332; emphasis added).

Here "as they pleased" is in fact the essence of MacLeod's perception of what freedom should look like in the quartet – a meta-utopia consisting of various utopian communities "in which the free development of each was the condition for the free development of all" and among which people could "*wander about* with [their] eyes and opinions open" (MacLeod, *Star* 227, 241; emphasis in original). Of course, as I mentioned earlier, the promise of "wandering about" as such probably cannot actually be achieved due to the practical limitations not included in the Nozickian framework of meta-utopia. But still, in this way MacLeod presents a unique vision for utopia different from the Culture, Amanduo or the Martian Republic, indicating not a sense of universality but diversity, not a place of isolation or perfection but connection and option, not an appeal for a strong yet benevolent state but for a libertarian domain where individuals may truly realize their freedom, a domain that denies the presence of the state and thus produces various forms of anarchy.

In other words, these stories build up a world "where monolithic authority seems irredeemably splintered" and "where people use whatever bits and pieces of political insights and ideas they can lash together to make some sense of it, and some contribution to guiding it" (J. Brown 67). MacLeod's endeavour to create anarchies (Norlonto, New Mars, the Solar Union or even the posthuman Fast Folk) grants him an authorial persona as polemical and significant as that of his friend Iain M. Banks. Their reputations are built upon the drafting of social and ideological alternatives in sf. These anarchic alternatives (as well as MacLeod's state-less political outlines, to some extent) can be further interpreted as a critical reaction to the strong governments under Thatcherism that at times resorted to authoritarian or even populist principles. MacLeod's anarchies can also be seen as the literary/science fictional response to the historical exhaustion of the "most politically tedious decade" (Segal 142) when, according to Philip Tew and others, "pastiche replaced [the] sense that the new could make a positive intervention in the world which could make the future different from both the past and the present" (Tew et al. 17).

A "MacLeodian" Contractarianism and the Formation of the Minimal State

Naturally, in these anarchies developed in the *Fall Revolution* quartet, the actions and decisions of people as social subjects seem free from state intervention. As we have discussed in the last chapter, before the *Fall Revolution* (1995–9), Iain M. Banks has already begun his anarchy-building, namely the Culture series starting with *Consider Phlebas* in 1987. His money-less, post-capitalist Culture as an anarchic utopia has been widely acknowledged not only as a remarkable contribution to the British Boom but also a left-wing political alternative interrogating the proliferation of Thatcherism and neoliberalism in socio-cultural domains. However, the state-less scenario of MacLeod's stories, unlike Banks's, is most comprehensively presented in Norlonto and New Mars. They are the places where money – useless as in the Culture – functions as "freedom's own passport" (MacLeod, *Star* 70).

Here individual freedom is promised and established upon libertarian values marked by privacy, property and people's natural rights to protect them. And this protection, likewise, will not be provided by any form of state or law enforcement, but by the residents themselves and through their *contractual cooperation* with each other, just as Jordan Brown describes Norlonto in *The Star Fraction*: "You can get anything with money. *Force* has no purchase there" (MacLeod, *Star* 17; emphasis added). In this way, since MacLeod's libertarian or capitalist anarchies such as Norlonto and New Mars are set to deny all state intervention and encourage contractual cooperation among individuals, there also emerges, as Farah Mendlesohn claims (18–19), a unique sense of "contractarianism" in these political enclaves.

Despite its anarchic façade, however, this MacLeodian contractarianism, as I will elaborate later, eventually leads to the formation of a minimal state internalized in the meta-utopian framework and thus a quasi-authority to guarantee contract enforcement. Apparently, the term "contractarianism" originally refers to a political paradigm where human morality may give way to people's own contractual agreements in their own best interests. Certain features of this ideology are generally aligned with those of a-moral dystopias, such as violence, bonded labour, prostitution and even slavery, which may be intrinsic to MacLeod's utopias under the meta-utopian framework. To be more precise, the contractarianism that can be identified in Norlonto and New Mars "empowers individuals (and sometime groups) to negotiate agreements over services [... which] assumes two things: that enforcement of contracts emerges from the need to negotiate future contracts in good faith, and every individual is in a position to negotiate as an equal" (Mendlesohn, "Impermanent" 19).

Obviously, the contractarianism adopted by MacLeod in his novel is by definition different from the social contract that stemmed from Thomas Hobbes and was later revisited by various scholars including Baruch Spinoza, John Locke, Immanuel Kant, Jean-Jacques Rousseau and more recently John Rawls. "Contract" in Norlonto and New Mars, however, does not stand for the process in which individuals have all *consented* to renounce part of their freedoms and submit to a sovereign authority in exchange of the protection for their remaining rights and for the maintenance of social order, which in turn provides a reasonable justification for the existence of a state. For the "free-market anarchism" (MacLeod, *Stone* 140) conceptualized in the *Fall Revolution* quartet, such a process of political representation "signifies the delegation of power from one group or individual to another, and with that delegation comes the risk of exploitation by the group or individual to whom power has been ceded" (May 47). This is exactly what should be rejected together with "all legislation, all authority, and all privileged, licensed, official, and legal influence" (Bakunin 35). Since people's unanimous agreement over the same idea, in turn producing an ideal state, may never be truly reached under the meta-utopian framework, neither of the two most significant elements of orthodox contractarianism – morality and the legitimate authority of government – is present in MacLeod's anarcho-libertarian communities.

On the contrary, these communities follow the MacLeodian sense of contractarianism, where honouring fair contracts is considered essential and indispensable. For example, the Stone Canal, the water supply and thus the lifeline of Ship City – the major human colony on New Mars – is itself the product of this kind of contractual cooperation between David Reid and those workers who had earned their freedoms by building the wormhole Malley Mile, the stargate through which they have reached this new planet in the first place. Each acting as "an independent contractor" (MacLeod, *Stone* 301), they all do their job required by a contract, in exchange for promised payments. Once the job is done, while some might enjoy a few moments of satisfaction, many would just walk away with indifference, "signalling their availability for another contract" (307). In fact, this logic can be further extended to basically every corner of New Mars and Norlonto, where the right to adjudicate contractual disputes is retained in the hands of individuals rather than submitted to an overall authority. In other words, in the absence of state, "there is no facility for the rich (in power and/or capital) to enforce their will," and more importantly, "none of the false reasoning of laissez-faire reserved to the government" (Mendlesohn, "Impermanent" 19) could be granted with legitimacy.

Therefore, unfairness, exploitation and abuses that would typically arouse concern among anarchists (May 47) are extremely costly, because economic abusers risk losing future contracts and customers, or even being "hunted down like dogs" (MacLeod, *Stone* 176). This is how Dee Model, the android girl who develops her self-consciousness and personhood, takes her revenge. "You're a person," she is told by her friend Ax, "You're free. Have you ever thought – what you would like to do to people who've treated you like *meat*?" (MacLeod, *Stone* 95; emphasis in original). She has indeed thought about this and accomplished this under the libertarian freedom made possible through the absence of state intervention. Although there are no protective laws or legitimate regulations in favour of contracted workers, there is also nothing to protect those who hire them from potential violence and vengeance.

In MacLeod's novels, money, capital, commerce, trade and the consequential lack of empathy when carrying out these contracts establish a fluid network of social connection. In other words, both Norlonto and New Mars are founded upon a sophisticated matrix linked up through potential contracts and the contractual relationships among individuals. Such a "contractarian" matrix that MacLeod proposes through his configuration of Norlonto and New Mars may find a niche for itself through re-examining "wider libertarian political initiatives circling in the orbit of an expanding anarchist core" (Cross 133) and proposing "anarchist alternatives" against the neoliberal, strong-state Thatcherite regimes that have run Britain since the late 1970s.

However, it is also because of such a matrix that Norlonto and New Mars become, over time, less anarchic than they might initially appear. On top of their seemingly state-less anarchism, the social relationships in the two societies established upon the MacLeodian contractarian network will eventually lead to other Nozickian political frameworks, namely "ultraminimal state" and "minimal state" – each a negation of both anarchism itself and the strong state promised by the social contract theory. Out of all the characters in the *Fall Revolution*, Jon Wilde is probably the only one aware of or even expecting the ultimate formation of a minimal state. During his conversation with Moh Kohn in *The Star Fraction*, he regretfully points out that the balkanized London is a "travesty" of his political ideal, a place consisting of "mini-states instead of *minimal states*" (MacLeod, *Star* 91; emphasis added).

I have briefly mentioned earlier that the orthodox contractarianism, espoused from Hobbes to Rawls, prefigures a strong authority based on and justified by the common good and the unanimous consent of all members of society. This is, however, problematic for Nozick, who firmly claims that an ideal regime should maintain only a "minimal" authority. While acknowledging Locke's "state of nature" – where "all mankind [… are] all equal and independent [and] no one ought to harm another in his life, health, liberty, or possessions" and where the natural rights to punish the transgressors of the law of nature are "put into every man's hands" (Locke 102–3) – Nozick goes on to argue that in these scenarios, an individual can of course defend himself and enforce his rights. But more importantly, during this process, "others may join with him in his defense, *at his call*" (Nozick 12; emphasis added).

In line with such an "at-call" responsibility, individuals will gradually form certain groups or "mutual-protection associations" in which "all will answer the call of any member for defense or for the enforcement of his rights" (Nozick 12). It strikes me that this sense of mutual protection that Nozick conceptualizes, echoes – curiously enough – the shibboleth that Kohn is asked to articulate when he requests help from the Army of the New Public (ANR) during the Fall Revolution:

> As a citizen of the United Republic I claim the protection of its armed forces and pledge on my honour to exercise when called upon by its lawful authority the Army Council of the Army of the New Republic all the rights and duties of such citizenship including but not limited to the franchise and the common defence. (MacLeod, *Star* 193)

In the oath of ANR, the mutual protection of its citizens is realized through a shared recognition of honour and duty. But in other places, once this pure honour and duty are replaced by something else of general equivalence that is also commonly recognized, such as money, the mutual protection can then be handled in the usual manner by division of labour and exchange. In other words, "some people will be hired to perform protective functions, and some entrepreneurs will go into the business of selling protective services" which would offer different sorts of protection at different prices "for those who may desire more extensive or elaborate protection" (Nozick 13). In theory, in a certain geographical area there will eventually emerge, through market competition, a "dominant protective association" (Nozick 13). In MacLeod's novels, we have the Invisible Hand Legal Services on New Mars whose supervision guarantees an unbiased trial over the disputes between ordinary individuals like Tamara Hunter and those in power such as David Reid, regardless of their fortune and social status. (It is also indicated that there are other defence agencies providing similar services, but the Invisible Hand is apparently the most influential one for major characters.)

For Nozick, the dominant protective association (like the Invisible Hand) is then inclined to become an "ultraminimal state." In his own words, an ultraminimal state "maintains a monopoly over all use of force except that necessary in immediate self-defense, and so excludes private (or agency) retaliation for wrong and exaction of compensation; but it provides protection and enforcement services only to those who purchase its protection and enforcement policies" (Nozick 26). This raises two questions: Firstly, what if one of the two parties involved in a dispute is under the protection of the dominant protective association while the other is not? Secondly, can an "independent" individual seek for their own justice in the domain of an association to which they do not belong?

Here, Nozick believes that if this independent is a "reliable enforcer," their natural rights should of course be fully respected (104–5). However, he admits that there would also be "unreliable enforcers" who might over-punish the guilty or even those who are not guilty at all, and thus impose risks upon others. To prevent such uncertainties, the dominant protective association should take a step further to forbid all kinds of personal retaliation within its domain, including those from the independents and in this way, now as an ultraminimal state, establish the "*de facto* monopoly" where it may "punish a wielder of an unreliable or unfair procedure who (against the client's will) has punished one of its clients, independently of whether or not its client actually is guilty and therefore even if its client is guilty" (Nozick 107–8).

Because of this *de facto* monopoly, the Invisible Hand Legal Services stands out as an ultraminimal state on New Mars. Everyone within its reach will be put under its protection in terms of their property and natural rights. When there is a dispute, the Invisible Hand will then coordinate both parties to take that dispute to a court that they both acknowledge as fair (MacLeod, *Stone* 99). Of course, everything comes with a price. Even if someone does not comply with the Invisible Hand's coordination (whether they do not want or are unable to), they still cannot bypass its general supervision to enforce their own justice since, in such a contractarian society (in the MacLeodian sense), in doing so they could lose not only one lone trial but all future contracts with others. The Hand has become a "generally effective enforcer of a prohibition on others' using unreliable enforcement procedures (calling them as it sees them), and it oversees these procedures" (Nozick 114). The wise move, therefore, as Dee Model does after her escape from David Reid, is to "register an autonomy claim" with the Invisible Hand and to have "a gang on your side" (MacLeod, *Stone* 36).

However, the story of another stranger to the Invisible Hand, Jonathan Wilde, is more dramatic. While being chased by Reid's hitmen, Wilde – an independent not covered by any defence contract – still receives help from an Invisible Hand defence robot. After fulfilling its duties, the robot speaks to Wilde:

> Good morning [...] You called for help, within the domain of Invisible Hand Legal Services. I intervened in response [...] Although no binding contract has been entered into, it would be a matter of courtesy to make a payment to Invisible Hand. As a reciprocal courtesy, Invisible Hand would like to offer you a ten-week defence policy, with that payment written off against your first bill if you choose to pay in advance. (MacLeod, *Stone* 102)

This is how the Invisible Hand moves to the final stage of Nozick's configuration of the minimal state. Theoretically speaking, the essential issue concerning the transition from ultraminimal to minimal state is the question of who ought to pay for the temporary "membership" of the independents. Nozick claims it should be the current clients of the protective association, based on the principle of *compensation*: "[T]hose who act in self-protection in order to increase their own security [should] compensate those they prohibit from doing risky acts which might actually have turned out to be harmless for the disadvantages imposed upon them" (Nozick 114). If an independent is not allowed to seek for justice according to their own judgement within the realm of an ultraminimal state, they are entitled to compensation for their loss, and the most economical form of compensation, Nozick believes, is to take the independent under protection. The cost, then, will be shared by all current members.

Therefore, a dominant protective association such as the Invisible Hand could be considered an ultraminimal state once it gains the *de facto* monopoly and may eventually evolve to a minimal state through the principle of compensation, which, interestingly, is termed by Nozick "the invisible-hand mechanism." This, I believe, is certainly more than a serendipitous echo of the *Invisible Hand* Legal Services on New Mars, especially given that MacLeod also borrows other Nozickian terms in his stories such as Reid's *Mutual Protection* Company and Wilde's explicit endorsement of the "minimal state" in *The Star Fraction*. As we read from Wilde's experience, it seems that the Invisible Hand still requires a payment from him, but again, this requirement is out of "a reciprocal courtesy," which we can reasonably perceive as optional. Although Wilde agrees with the robot about how much he should reimburse for the sunk cost of the agency, he also retains the choice not to pay and renounces the "ten-week defence policy" he is offered. In the latter case, Wilde is able to maintain his identity as an independent and the invoice generated in defending him would have to be shared by all the current clients of the Invisible Hand.

In this way, the Invisible Hand, as the dominant protective association portrayed in *The Stone Canal*, eventually becomes the minimal state. This is the ideal form of authority for Nozick, limited to "functions of protecting all its citizens against violence, theft, and fraud, and to the enforcement of *contracts*, and so on" but meanwhile able to develop a *de facto* monopoly on all kinds of enforcement and thus protect all individuals within its domain (Nozick 22–3, 26; emphasis added). Upon the ostensible "insanely logical outcome" of anarcho-capitalist theories (MacLeod, *Cassini* 147), New Mars manages to develop the minimal state that Wilde fails to build in Norlonto. A contract in the context of the MacLeodian contractarianism still requires third-party enforcement, which does not necessarily take shape as a state but as the Nozickian mutual-protection associations or minimal states. It is, therefore, no longer a free-market anarchy as almost all characters believe it to be. Instead, it suggests the formation of an authority, but this authority is nothing like the Thatcherite strong state that strove to centralize power away from local governments, to invoke nationalism and even populism (Lawson 64) and to weaken the power of trade unions. It promises, as Reid speaks to his contracted labourers who build New Mars: "[A] new world, a clean slate [where] you're all free, and together we'll live in freedom" (MacLeod, *Stone* 298).

What's Past Is Prologue

However, as you may have noticed, the *Fall Revolution*'s critique of Thatcherism mainly focuses on state, whereas the "free-market rhetoric" carried out through financial deregulation and privatization is attributed with a striking dynamism. In previous studies, this quartet has been described as a demonstration of "left-wing struggles against neoliberal consensus" (Winter, "Moments" 325), which is true to some extent, but it also presents MacLeod's concern over the ideological exhaustion of non-capitalist and non-market alternatives, since "the logic of free market has been extended into all spheres of life" for both Norlonto (and the US/UN dominated world it belongs to) and New Mars (Arnold 135). In the quartet, even the nuclear deterrent itself can be financialized and traded as futures and options "available to anyone willing to pay for it" (MacLeod, *Stone* 151). Human lives become commensurable through money, as killing someone can be repaid through the economic equivalence of the victim's "emotional distress, loss of life-experience, earnings, loss of society for those close to them – add all that up and multiply it by the down time" (MacLeod, *Stone* 155). On top of these points, the adaptability and penetrability of such an economized logic can be best elaborated in this paragraph when Norlonto is about to surrender its anarchic autonomy to the ANR:

> But if you let the Army in, what do you think will happen? The Army will get sucked into our way of doing things – the economic way, not the political way. They'll have to do deals and trade combat futures and take disputes to court companies and swap laws and all the rest of it […] They don't want a fight on their hands. They don't want to conquer us, they want to buy us off. In fact it looks like they already have bought off the defense companies. And what's bought can be sold. Before they know it they'll be practicing anarcho-capitalism without believing a word of it. (MacLeod, *Stone* 209)

And this is exactly what "capitalist realism" stands for, a term MacLeod uses as the title for Chapter Eight in *The Stone Canal*.

It is true that there *are* a few utopias amidst the MacLeodian meta-utopianism presented in the *Fall Revolution*, envisaging non-capitalist ideas and alternatives, most notably the Solar Union in *The Cassini Division*. But throughout the novels, the Solar Union in most cases only hides in the background; instead, the plot centres largely on Ellen May Ngwethu and her interaction with the Fast Folk and New Mars. Though at certain points in the novel we can indeed learn that the Solar Union is a classless anarchy, that is, "a world without money" (MacLeod, *Cassini* 177) where "the capitalist system was abolished" (11), there is little elaboration of the details of its social structure and the premises on which it is founded – an especially meagre offering when compared to Banks's profoundly imaginative conception of the Culture's post-capitalist society. We do not exactly know how the economy of the Solar Union is managed and operated, nor are we made aware of how different social communities or communes cooperate with each other. What we can notice, however, is how canny, opportunistic and penetrative capital and markets can be. To obtain the permission to land on New Mars, Ellen's group has to convert to the capitalist manner and *bargain* with different protection companies over "collateral against any damage" (MacLeod, *Cassini* 164).

Such a lack of a feasible and sustainable plan for a non-capitalist alternative may well fit in with the in-text interpretation of the quartet's title "Fall Revolution" *per se*: "Without a socialist revolution, in the next historical period at that, a catastrophe threatens the whole culture of mankind," and in that case, "if we didn't get [...] a new society. A saner world. We'd go back, to an older kind of society. Pre-capitalist [...] instead of post-" (MacLeod, *Star* 42, 170). This is the meaning of the "Fall," and it seems, in the actual world, we are indeed falling because the sense of historical exhaustion we live under has already dispelled all possibilities eschewing market and capital, which we can see reflected in MacLeod's work by David Reid's conversion from a staunch far-left Trotskyist to an anarcho-libertarian.

The fall of the British left since the late 1970s resulted from an array of complex reasons – the rise of post-Fordism, the decline of class identity, the decade-long stagflation, etc., which, altogether, led to Margaret Thatcher's ascendancy. Consumption was articulated as the supreme realization of individual aspiration. Personal efforts were rewarded in an economic structure that became increasingly privatized and competitive. Internationalization was welcomed by financial elites in the City of London – at the cost of massive redundancies and closures in manufacturing industries across the UK. Trade unions were put in shackles after their fiasco during the Miners' Strike of 1984–5. Government expenditure on social welfare saw a substantial cut under Thatcher's watch. Left-wing local authorities had their powers increasingly contained. The gap between "producer's Britain" and "consumer's Britain" (Newton 25) has widened to an extent that the break-up of the Kingdom, which was “almost inconceivable” in the mid-1970s (Nairn, “The Twilight” 3), has now become a serious issue at stake. This is why Thatcherism, having shaped British society in the mould of its neoliberal values, remains firmly in place as the underpinning philosophy guiding the governments that followed Thatcher and why a non-capitalist social design is now a lot harder to imagine.

“What’s past is prologue” (MacLeod, *Star* 42). So long as the capitalist-realist claim of “the end of history” genuinely hinders people from looking for non-capitalist alternatives, the better future we might hope for will be unavailable – nothing new will come forth, merely pastiches of the past. The clash between Wilde and Reid, therefore – as well as their seemingly oppositional political stances which determine the ideological foundation of New Mars far in the future – is in fact the product of “a bygone age” (dating back to the mid-1970s), a relic “contaminated by the long-established politics of the past as they strive to influence and conduct the direction of the future” (Christie 59). It is exactly because of this paralysis that Jameson insists on reiterating the urgency and significance of recovering a sense of utopia in line with the Blochian hope for the not-yet. Therefore, instead of proposing a “one true utopia” in the *Fall Revolution* quartet, MacLeod invites us to constitute our own utopias as we see fit, based on the rules that might differentiate these imagined societies from their neighbouring utopias.

“What’s Past is Prologue.” This is also the point that Hao Jingfang is trying to make in *Vagabonds*, only in a different sense. The dialect between the libertarian Earth and the egalitarian Martian Republic, between “the garden of rambling order” and “the tower of rigid rules,” and between the liquid system (that “features freedom of movement […] in which the units are relatively independent”) and the solid system (that “features stable structure in which every unit is fixed in its position”) will never truly complete (Hao, *Vagabonds* 472). As Luoying eventually realizes, there would always be someone living in one world while thinking of the other. Through their longings for change and transition, the two sides of the dialectic will then become an unending process of negating the negation, like a Mobius loop for which one side is at the same time the other and through which the other can be travelled to. And that is the place accommodating the true knowledge of freedom and utopia.

CHAPTER 3

Long Live the Vampire: Exploitive Heterotopias in China Miéville's *Perdido Street Station* and Chen Qiufan's *Waste Tide*

> All I want is for you to treat us as people, not waste.
>
> – Chen Qiufan, in *Waste Tide*

> In some lands the [khepri] refugees were butchered in terrible pogroms. In others, like New Crobuzon, they were welcomed with unease, but not with official violence. They had settled, become workers and tax-payers and criminals, and found themselves, by an organic pressure just too gentle to be obvious, living in ghettos preyed on, sometimes, by bigots and thugs.
>
> – China Miéville, in *Perdido Street Station*

Science Fictionalizing Here and Now

"I'm a classical Marxist." In his interview with Joan Gordon (363), China Miéville identifies himself once again as a dedicated left-wing activist. By the time the British SF Boom finally broke into the horizon of sf studies, Miéville had already gained a reputation for pursuing his doctorate degree in Marxism and international law at LSE and for his involvement in the Socialist Alliance during the 2001 UK general election (apparently, he did not make it to the Number 10, receiving 1.2 per cent of votes cast as he stood for Regent's Park and Kensington North).[1] But different from

1 Data available at <https://api.parliament.uk/uk-general-elections/elections/24263>, accessed on 28 September 2023.

Banks and MacLeod who tend to experiment their political ideals by reviving space opera, Miéville engages in a different genre. He believes that the political high ground that Banks has spoken of can also be reclaimed from novels that are set in strange places with strange characters – rather than the grandiose canvas of space baroque. He resorts not to galactic civilizations but the monstrous and the uncanny. Magical, horrific, mysterious – such adjectives that are not conventionally associated with sf are now frequently used to describe his extraordinary way of storytelling and world-building.

In this way, Miéville revisits what was also prominent in the early twentieth century but soon began to decline: the Weird, which is endowed with a Lovecraftian sense of alterity and otherness that, in his own words, bridges "fantastic genres and the anti-realist avant-garde" (Miéville, "Afterword" 244). Since the early 2000s, Miéville has become well known for his "New Weird" aesthetic, incorporating "the sublime terror of [... an] early pulp monster, mixing it with an updated sensibility that had become fascinated with the monsters themselves, in addition to the supernatural terror they inspired" (Edwards and Venezia 3). A significant strand of the British SF Boom, the New Weird is clearly political savvy like the new space opera, one that "mimics the 'absurdity' of capitalist modernity" and questions the "ironically (capitalist) modern distinction of high and low culture" (Miéville, "Symposium" 41, 42). He blurs and transcends the conventional boundaries of sf, fantasy, noir and urban gothic, giving rise to a speculative genre that emerges from endless possibilities, mirroring the radical transformation not in a far future, but of the *real* world.

Such a real-world concern is also what has driven the Chinese writer, Chen Qiufan, to immerse himself in the domain of sf. At the 2007 Chengdu International SF/Fantasy Conference, Chen Qiufan expressed his firm belief in the importance of realism as an element in sf, instead of the oft-mentioned futurism. He argued that contemporary China's social life should be carefully examined through speculative genres because, in recent decades, "reality has surpassed science fiction" (Chen Q., qtd. in Ren 55). This was further elaborated during the International Science Fiction Forum in 2012 when he claimed that "science fiction is the greatest realism of our time" and that it provides a unique platform for imagination through its open realism, allowing for the portrayal of (retro-)futuristic realities untouched by mainstream literature.[2]

This chapter, therefore, with a comparative reading of China Miéville's *Perdido Street Station* (2000) and Chen Qiufan's *Waste Tide* (2013), highlights their common focus on *reality*. It strives to shift our attention away from utopian futures (as we see from previous chapters) and directs it towards a speculative exploration of the current state of affairs, of what is happening *here and now*, which observes the rapid normalization of exploitative biopolitics in the present moment.

In *Perdido Street Station*, the sense of historical rupture remains significant, represented in a hybrid city named New Crobuzon. It is home to various political, racial and species communities, each with their own histories and political appeals, and together, they have formed a dynamic discourse of solidarity and conviviality. This, however, is often problematized. Along with the interwoven relationships between various human and non-human species, New Crobuzon gives rise to various heterotopic spaces, akin to ethnic enclaves. These spaces act as strongholds for social and cultural conventions that are traditionally affiliated with marginalized communities, frequently relegated to the social margins and categorized as the underclass. Beyond the confines of these heterotopic spaces, a haunting presence pervades the narrative of *Perdido Street Station* – the vampiric monsters known as the *slake-moths*. They do not prey on the physical bodies of their victims, but rather, they feed upon their sentience – the essence of consciousness itself. This portrayal transforms them into what could be described as "capitalist monsters," serving as a new-weird embodiment of the Jamesonian cultural logic that characterizes late capitalism, that governs not a futuristic utopia but the present-day reality of London and the UK.

Out of the same concern of reality, Chen Qiufan's *Waste Tide* also revolves around heterotopias – in this case marginalized communities of

2 The International Science Fiction Forum is the annual awards ceremony for Xingyun Awards for Global Chinese Science Fiction, which was founded in 2010 and is now one of the most important awards focused on science fiction writings in China.

waste people. They leave their homes in search of fortune and affluence, migrating to places like Silicon Isle and major cities due to the regional disparities in China's economic development. However, they quickly become victims of market exploitation and alienation, rendering themselves as one of the most vulnerable social demographics. In a way, China's double-digit economic boom since the 1990s is fundamentally based on labour-intensive industries, as the cheap labour force provided by migrant workers guarantees the price advantage of the commodities for export labelled "made in China." But despite their economic contributions, these migrant workers are usually denied access to various social welfare, mostly including housing, education, childcare and medical care, because of the Household Registration System (*hukou*).

In Guy Standing's term, they become "denizens," trapped in the interstice between economic acceptance and social rejection. Compared to the urban locals, the denizens have "a more limited range of rights, or weaker entitlement to them" (590), struggling from social margins where they may develop an identity based on victimhood. From this perspective, although *Waste Tide* is more frequently interpreted as an eco-critical interrogation of China's economic boom at the cost of environmental degradation, it is also an important text for us to understand China's unique political-economic condition built upon its internal labour migration (Tao 73–95; Chan and Selden 259–71).

With this in mind, I will now embark on a side-by-side exploration of Silicon Isle in *Waste Tide* and New Crobuzon in *Perdido Street Station*. Within these imaginative cities, crafted by Chen Qiufan and China Miéville, I intend to uncover the metaphoric layers that shroud their social commentaries, each infused with the authors' personal ties and recollections of their native locales. Drawing inspiration from Michelle Foucault's concept of "heterotopia," I will investigate the sense of duality that shapes both cities: the interplay of economic inclusion and social alienation that marks the waste people's pursuit for acceptance on Silicon Isle, and the complex conflict of human and non-human creatures in New Crobuzon, torn between embracing their unique species identity and integrating into mainstream society.

Vampiric Cities: Silicon Isle and New Crobuzon

In August 2019, the London Chinese Science Fiction Group (which I co-convened with Angela Chan) invited Chen Qiufan to speak about his writing career and his debut novel *Waste Tide* (2013), a few months after its English translation was published.[3] During his lecture, titled "Why Did I Write a Science Fiction Novel About E-waste?" Chen Qiufan shared with us his personal trip in 2011 to Guiyu (*guìyǔ*), a town in Guangdong province situated on the South China Sea coast (one-hour drive from his hometown Shantou), which is also the archetype of the highly polluted Silicon Isle (*guīyǔ*) in *Waste Tide*. Benefitting from its geographical location and favourable state policies to boost economy and trade after Deng Xiaoping's South Tour in 1992 (see the Introduction), Guiyu flourished as one of the international hubs of e-waste recycling. It had become the world's largest e-waste site by 2013, creating significant economic growth for the local government. However, as observed by Chen Qiufan himself, behind such an economic prosperity there lay profound social sufferings and ecological crises. Everything

> is chaotic and disorganised, and the waste disposal workers are unprotected and directly exposed to this polluted environment. They try to find recyclable metal components containing a certain amount of rare earth among the discarded cables or electronic parts. This business has caused serious damage to the local environment of Guiyu. Soil, water and even the air are all contaminated and eroded by the electronic wastes, not to mention the impact on unprotected workers, who are the most direct victims of environmental pollution. ("Why Did I Write" n.p.)

From here, Chen Qiufan went on to explain that in sf stories, especially in his *Waste Tide*, "environmental concerns can be generalised to a broader social context, and readers are more likely to think about how their individual reactions can affect our environment, as well as the lives of those vulnerable waste workers they have never met" in person (n.p.).

3 This talk was moderated by Angela Chan, co-convenor of LCSFG, and Ma Chen (Mia), then PhD candidate in the Department of China and Inner Asia at SOAS. It was held at Goodenough College in London.

In a way, Chen Qiufan's own reading of *Waste Tide* as an elaboration of such "environmental concerns" has been widely acknowledged. The novel is hailed by Simon Ings as "a dark mirror held up to our Anthropocene selves" that stands out as an eco-thriller with its "spoiled and toxic beauty" – inscribed right on the cover of its British edition. Drawing on the sophisticated eco-critical concerns of *Waste Tide*, literary and cultural scholars have examined this novel from the perspectives of ecological degradation, the toxic sublime, and posthuman ecocriticism (Li H., "The Environment" 270–82; Ma 67–80; Healey 1–33). Others have analysed the uneven global distribution of ecological costs and risks (Sun, "Imagining" 289–306) or seen cyborg and human-machine hybridity as a response to environmental failures (Song M., "Representations" 546–65; Xiong 75–89). All of these environmental readings of *Waste Tide* have contributed to the scholarship on this novel and on the Chinese SF Boom in general.

Despite this, however, what I am interested in here is not only the novel's eco-critical narrative. Beyond its interrogation of ecological degradation and environmental failures caused by the e-waste recycling industry on Silicon Isle, *Waste Tide* also provides a speculative version of the real Guiyu that has expanded and thrived during China's economic boom since the 1990s, featuring the same social conflicts and miseries emerging along with the city's developmental glories. One of these conflicts, in fact, was also mentioned in Chen Qiufan's speech quoted above, but not elaborated further, that is the tension between "waste workers" – usually the internal labour migrants from the less-developed regions in China – and the local residents of the city. While the accelerating process of urbanization in China is an undeniable consequence of the country's economic restructuring, urban conditions become increasingly complex due to the spaces formed to accommodate newcomers, such as waste villages surrounding Silicon Isle in *Waste Tide*. As a result, there is a pressing need for a fresh perspective on our living spaces and a new approach to understanding the dynamics between recent arrivals and those who have lived here for generations.

According to Rachel Murphy, the demographic influx of migrant workers to Chinese cities is usually coupled with social exclusion. "Migrants [in China]," she writes, "are often viewed as economic labourers rather than as complex social beings. Migrants are perceived to belong to a homogeneous economic group or stratum [...] rather than recognised as heterogeneous individuals [... with] various social relations" (Murphy 1). Above all, either in literature, films or reality, it seems that they are also frequently connected to an array of particular places: "construction sites, production lines, tunnels, streets, small enterprises, households, temporary dormitories, abandoned old factories, basements, and urban villages (similar to shanty towns or urban slums), which inscribe their experiences of exploitation, inequality, displacement, and marginality" (Lu 8).

Similar to the waste people depicted in *Waste Tide*, numerous migrant workers left their hometowns, which lagged behind in China's economic growth, with aspirations of finding prosperity in thriving urban centres. However, their dreams are often shattered by overwhelming feelings of estrangement and alienation. Unfair payment, wage arrears, unpaid overtime and discrimination in the labour market, on top of other forms of mistreatment, have become the common concerns for all 293 million migrant workers in mainland China (in 2021). "Many migrant workers," observes Kinglun Ngok, "worked hard for the entire year, and did not even have the money for transport to go back home [...] In order to get back their wage arrears, migrant workers in desperate situations sometimes resorted to violence" (Ngok 252). To some extent, although they are accepted by cities like Shenzhen, Guangzhou, Beijing and Shanghai due to their economic contributions, primarily through the provision of cheap labour, they are not genuinely embraced as full-fledged citizens. They are, instead, "denizens" or "insider outsiders" lacking basic social and economic rights (Standing 597). As an "underpaid, unprivileged underclass" (Solinger 177) usually treated as "transient guests" (Pun 19), they are more institutionally excluded because of China's household registration system (*hukou*) and can only access very limited resources in terms of education, housing, job security and other types of welfare as a result.[4]

4 Under China's population policies, a citizen must be registered with only one specific place, a process usually known as household registration (*hukou*). Generally speaking, people's social welfare resources (medical care, childcare, housing, education, among others) are directly connected to where they are registered, not where they live. Switching *hukou* is possible, but for that there would be additional requirements for different places (such as education degree, wage level, personal

In this sense, Silicon Isle in *Waste Tide* serves as more than just a speculative representation of Guiyu; it encapsulates the essence of all Chinese cities where we can witness the shattered dreams of migrant workers. Under the manipulation of three local clans, chiefly led by the Luo clan, Silicon Isle's economy thrives solely on the e-waste recycling industry. This has transformed a place that was once described as "poor but lively" (Chen Q., *Waste* 41) into an ecological dystopia, "a polluted and ruined homeland" (171). Wealth has been amassed, as the locals of Silicon Isle are busy reaping all the economic benefits through environmental exploitation, but the migrant workers from other less-developed regions are not treated fairly.

These waste people toil amidst the hazardous detritus of electronic waste, their labour devoid of adequate safeguards, their recompense insufficient for both their economic contributions and the perils they embrace. They endure meagre wages, inadequate training and unrelenting work hours. They confront entrenched discrimination at the hands of Silicon Isle's native inhabitants, who expel them from the urban centre to distant satellite villages. They are turned down by the very place that is built upon their economic contributions. Within this spatial segregation, Mimi, the novel's heroine and one of the "waste girls," becomes infected with an artificial virus due to her close contact with the toxic materials in the waste village. This infection spawns a secondary consciousness distinct from her original mind, gifting her with posthuman abilities. Empowered by this transformation, Mimi emerges as a leader among the waste people, igniting a rebellion against the local clans. Their battle is waged to secure the equal rights and recognition they rightfully deserve.

Most of the waste people in *Waste Tide* are drawn to the significantly higher wages offered in comparison to what they could earn in their underdeveloped hometowns. This wage gap reflects China's escalating regional unevenness, both among different regions and between urban and rural

property, and more). It would be extremely difficult, if not impossible, for migrant workers to get a *hukou* in cities like Beijing and Shanghai. They are usually registered with their underdeveloped hometown and cannot meet the basic requirements to switch to the city in which they work and live. In this way, they are denied the social protection granted by the *hukou* they can never earn. See Chapter 2 for the connection between *hukou* and the atelier system in Hao Jingfang's *Vagabonds*.

areas. However, despite their economic contributions, they still find themselves in an uncomfortable predicament – they are not acknowledged by the Silicon Isle locals as "part of us" and are therefore destined to be perpetual "outsiders." They are trapped in a process of "double alienation" (Pun et al. 116) where the Marxist sense of alienation of labour in the capitalist mode of production is joined by an alienation of identity. These migrant workers, in this way, are always "branded as second-class citizens and inferior laborers" (Pun et al. 116) and treated as the reserve army of labour to be exploited by their employers with no necessary additional responsibilities. They are even forced to relocate to "densely-populated communities" in suburban areas (Pun 92), which are typically the primary focus of government oversight and clean-up efforts.

Consequently, they can only develop "limited social interactions" with the local population (Frenkel and Yu 272), who often exhibit subtle forms of discrimination against them. The migrant workers in China, and Chen Qiufan's waste people alike, should be perceived as examples of the duality between "economic acceptance" and "social rejection" suggested by Kinglun Ngok:

> "Economic acceptance" meant that local government accepted the influence of market forces which caused rural migration, and migrant workers were treated as a source of cheap labor – although even then, this acceptance had its limitations, as migrant workers were forced into the dirtiest, toughest and most dangerous jobs while receiving minimal wages. "Social rejection" was also a result of the official policy which denied migrant workers various public services. (252)

In this way, the "social rejection" of migrant workers and the "subtle discrimination" from the locals mentioned above can both be considered "the most serious form of social exclusion that exists in China" (252).

In *Waste Tide*, Chen Qiufan amplifies the open hostility and violence directed at the waste people on the fictional Silicon Isle in a more exaggerated manner. The affluent downtown residents hold a deep belief in their superiority over the migrant workers and in their right to harbour an unshakable conviction of their own supremacy over the migrant labourers and a sense of entitlement to harvest all the fruits of economic prosperity, even if it means exacting a heavy toll on the environment. Nestled within the luxurious heart of Silicon Isle, these "nouveaux riches of contemporary China" are surrounded by numerous expensive automobiles and "boutiques specializing in luxury brands" that can only be seen in China's most bustling metropolises. They are keen to buy "the best material goods the world had to offer and used them to fill their own empty lives" (Chen Q., *Waste* 29–30). Whereas the waste people, "all of them migrants from elsewhere in China," are left flitting between the toxic piles of "metal chassis, broken displays, circuit boards, plastic components, and wires" in the neighbouring villages, where "everything was shrouded in a leaden miasma, an amalgamation of the white mist [...] and the black smoke from the unceasing burning of PVC, insulation, and circuit boards" (31).

The stark divergence between these two renditions of Silicon Isle, coupled with the resulting isolation – both geographical and social – between the native population and the marginalized waste people, exacerbates the already profound levels of discrimination experienced by the latter. Not a single Silicon Isle local could claim to be fully innocent:

> Everyone had benefitted in some manner by exploiting the blood and sweat of the waste people [...] Everyone had, at one time or another, looked at the waste people with contempt or disgust, or insulted them with a careless or hurtful word. Everyone had had the thought, even if only momentarily, that the waste people were born low and that they were fated to live in the company of trash, destined to be filthy until their deaths. (263)

Placed in such an unthinkable predicament, tens of thousands of migrant workers in this doomed land, trapped in a web of local corruption, deadly environmental degradation and economic exploitation, are turned into waste people just like those recycled wastes with which they have to work and live. Anxious, bewildered and bereft of hope, the waste people and their tumultuous emotions converge around a singular figure, Mimi. She finds herself unable to quell the pervasive tension stemming from life on Silicon Isle – a tension born from "the unfamiliar surroundings," "the enmity of the natives" and "the malicious looks from the local hooligans" (92). The waste people are not only overlooked but, even worse, shunned, victimized and subjected to discrimination by the native inhabitants of Silicon Isle, despite the natives' wealth acquired through the physical and mental sacrifice of the migrant population.

Of course, Chen Qiufan is not the only one who writes about exploitive biopolitics and labour competition in speculative cities, nor is he the only one who finds creative inspiration in his own place of origin. Among the writers of the British Boom, China Miéville should also be named for his personal attachment to his home, which was in Willesden, "a working-class, ethnically-mixed area" in North-West London (Gordon and Miéville 355) that became the main setting of his debut novel *King Rat* (1998). London in his eyes, however, is not a city for royalty, politicians or business elites. It is "a London of council estates and dirty walls, black youth and white youth, Armenian girls" (Miéville, *King* 67), a place where people of various ethnicities and from various cultures may cohabit. As he spoke to Nick Gevers in late 2002:

> London is *big enough* that unlike a lot of smaller cities it has a very large ring that's neither central nor suburban. That's the zone I grew up in, and it's really the zone that defines London for me [...] I always enjoy describing it. And in general, the city landscape is something that constantly inspires me [...] It's also because London, unlike a lot of other cities, isn't defined by one historical moment [...] Instead, you walk down a street in London, you're walking from the 16th to the 21st century, through a patchwork of history. That I love. (Gevers n.p.; emphasis added)

In a way, London's "bigness" is not only in a geographical or demographical scope. Despite its vast expanse of nearly 1,600 square kilometres and a population exceeding 9 million people, making it the largest city in the UK by all measures, London is predominantly recognized for its rich cultural and ethnic diversity. In the past three decades, this diversity has only grown further. "Since the 1990s," writes Steven Vertovec, "there has been a marked rise in net immigration and a diversification of countries of origin" (1028). During this period, it is not surprising to note that there is a rough alignment with what Scott Newton conceptualizes as the historical shift from "Producer's Britain" to "Consumer's Britain" under Thatcher's regime (see the Introduction), a transformation that unfolds as London extends its embrace of a service-centric economy, evolving into the epicentre of the nation's financial vitality. For Roger Luckhurst, such a proliferation of financialization indicates "the full opening of London markets to the borderless flows of international capital and their final severance from the social fabric of London itself" (Luckhurst, "The Contemporary" 537).

Consequently, the influx of immigrants into London during this period beckons us to cultivate a fresh comprehension of the city's cultural and ethnic fusion, pushing us to reevaluate established paradigms in ethnic studies like multiculturalism and community cohesion. Multiculturalism, Stuart Hall claims, becomes an "enemy" that should be contested (Hall, "Old" 55). It turns into the "exotica of difference," where minority cultures are fetishized and treated as mere spectacles to be observed and disciplined (56). In other words, multiculturalism views a certain ethnic community as "a kind of stable, only very slowly-changing ground inside the hectic upsets, discontinuities and ruptures of history" (43), which in essence ignores that fact that ethnic and cultural identities are always in the process of formation – a process that is never completed, never finished.

Ethnicity and identity, therefore, are neither pure nor fixed. They should not be used as biopolitical categories designed to distinguish us from them, insiders from outsiders and those we trust from those we don't. In this way, if we follow Hall's ideas about ethnic intersectionality and fluidity, we are then able to interrogate Trevor Phillips's provocative speech in 2005 about ethnic segregation from a critical perspective. "We are sleepwalking our way to segregation," he said:

> We are becoming strangers to each other, and we are leaving communities to be marooned outside the mainstream [...] these marooned communities will steadily drift away from the rest of us, evolving their own lifestyles, playing by their own rules and increasingly regarding the codes of behaviour, loyalty and respect that the rest of us take for granted as outdated behaviour that no longer applies to them. (Phillips n.p.)

Phillips's speech quickly drew intense criticism, primarily focused on his careless use of the term "ghetto" and the dubious demographic data he cited from Michael Poulsen's 2005 conference paper, "The 'new geography' of ethnicity in Britain?" The data had been collected and analysed using a controversial methodology to assess ethnic diversity and segregation in urban residential neighbourhoods, sparking a heated debate (Peach 1381–95; Wright et al. 167–76).

Quite contrary to Phillips's argument, ethnic studies in recent decades have revealed that the cohabitation of multiple ethnicities in London does not lead to social isolation. Usually considered "one of the world's greatest cosmopolitan cities" (White 143), London is formed not upon total segregation but a process of merging and becoming that leads towards a context of "super-diversity," where "multi-dimensional conditions and processes" affecting immigrants in London (Vertovec 1050) will be recognized as part of their identification as "Londoners" rather than "Londoners with foreign/exotic elements." This is described by Paul Gilroy using the term "conviviality," which refers to the processes of "cohabitation and interaction that have made multi-culture an ordinary feature of social life in Britain's urban areas" (Gilroy, *After* xi).

Despite this, however, Gilroy also cautions us that conviviality "does not describe the absence of racism or the triumph of tolerance" (xi). As indicated in Susanne Wessendorf's empirical research on the London Borough of Hackney, this hyper-diverse context is often "characterized by a fine balance between building positive relations across difference and keeping a distance" (Wessendorf 393). Being open, but sometimes closed – such a tension among Londoners of various ethnic and cultural backgrounds brings to the fore the significance of formulating a sense of "London-ness" articulated by ethnic multiplicity and hybridity.

Miéville, with his particular perception of London as an "ethnically-mixed" metropolis, also joins this conversation about conviviality by creating a speculative version of the city where he was born and raised, that is New Crobuzon first appearing in *Perdido Street Station* (2000) and further developed in *The Scar* (2002) and *Iron Council* (2004) (together known as the *Bas-Lag* trilogy). A "mongrel" city in nature (Miéville, *Perdido* 617), New Crobuzon accommodates, apart from human beings as the most common residents of this place, an incredible variety of non-human species, represented with different appearances, outlooks, cultural norms, religious rituals, behavioural patterns and internal social structures. A *khepri* can be identified by their beetle head and human body, whose saliva might be used for artistic creation; a *garuda* has feathers, a beak, a pair of wings and other eagle-like features that grant them the ability to fly; a *cactacae* is known for their cactaceous characteristics, inhabiting a gigantic glass house that produces the climate of desert; a *vodyanoi* is an amphibious frog-like race able to perform "watercraeft" by which water can be temporarily shaped like clay. And of course, New Crobuzon is also inhabited by a multitude of non-human species known as "xenians." The collision, integration and interaction among these xenian races, as well as their respective communities, give rise to a complex ethnic landscape reminiscent of London's real-day diversity.

"This is what makes the world, Ms Lin" (Miéville, *Perdido* 51). As the crime boss Mr Motley commissions Lin, the *khepri* artist, to make a statue of himself, he elaborates what he believes is the fundamental dynamic of New Crobuzon: "Transition. The point where one thing becomes another. It is what makes you, the city, the world, what they are. And that is the theme I'm interested in. The zone where the disparate become part of the whole. The hybrid zone" (51). For Miéville, New Crobuzon is not only an imagined city with New Weird aesthetics. He tells Joan Gordon that it is "clearly analogous to [...] London," with "the danger, the intricacy, the mystery, the rich fecundity, [and] the semi-autonomous architecture" (Gordon and Miéville 362).

At the heart of New Crobuzon, the detailed fictional imagery of London is carefully established, especially the worries, concerns and conflicts emerging along with ethnic cohabitation and conviviality. In other words, New Crobuzon offers "a phantasmagorical doubling of contemporary London" (Edwards and Venezia 21) or an urban representation that mimics "a metaphorically hybrid London" (Gordon 457). From "the industrial to the residential to the opulent to the slum to the underworld to the airborne to the modern to the ancient to the colourful to the drab to the fecund to the barren ..." (Miéville, *Perdido* 51), various races carve out niches for themselves within this city of hybridity, each with their own hopes, ambitions, dreams and relentless efforts to turn them into reality.

But unfortunately, hybridity is not equivalent to fairness and equality. The multicultural New Crobuzon is not a utopia for xenians. It is a realm where equitable chances for social engagement and involvement, especially education, employment and even personal connections remain elusive for them. In this social structure where native-born humans still hold sway, xenian newcomers often discover themselves ensnared within a web of prejudices, discrimination and bias. As a consequence, they are relegated to the periphery, subservient to and reliant upon the dominant social narrative that favours the local population. In the renowned New

Crobuzon University, "xenian students had only been admitted as degree candidates [...] for twenty years" (Miéville, *Perdido* 16), who can only build up "occasional defensive tight-knit group" (231) dodging and hiding on a campus "overwhelmingly" occupied by humans. *Vodyanoi* stevedores working at the Kelltree dock are not paid fairly compared to their human co-workers, leading to a strike that eventually ends up brutally suppressed by the government (a miniature of the Miners' Strike in 1984–5). Anti-xenian religions and political parties can always retain a large group of supporters whose social influence steadily swelling with each passing day.

The romantic relationship between Lin the khepri artist and Isaac the human scientist, to a certain degree, can sometimes be seen as a dialectical hybridity (Gordon 456–76) developed upon a mutual understanding of their partner's values. Nevertheless, a sense of unease and disquiet pervades their relationship. Isaac is hesitant to publicly acknowledge their relationship out of concern for the potential repercussions on his academic standing and the prevailing social discourse developed upon "the regime of formal or informal policing [...] invested in reinforcing the structures of racial inequality" (Wood 83). This invisible barrier between different races, originally rooted in biological differences and fortified by biopolitical forces, remains a formidable obstacle to the development of a unified sense of "New Crobuzon-ness."

Heterotopias: Transcending the Space of Outsiders

However, this unified sense of New Crobuzon-ness, or of Silicon Isleness, is never made possible. As observed by Song Mingwei, the victimized waste people in *Waste Tide* often find themselves confined to isolated neighbourhoods, effectively creating a population of "invisible masses" ("Representations" 560) within segregated waste-processing villages hastily constructed for migrant laborers. To some extent, this invisible wall dividing the urban natives and migrant workers can be likened to the boundaries of the "protective shell" introduced by Peter Sloterdijk. In his influential book *In the World Interior of Capital* (2013), he claims that nowadays, people's "social life in its entirety would have to be integrated into *a protective shell*," namely "a domestically organized and artificially climatized inner space" that distinguishes the privileged "insider," beneficiaries of market competition, against those disadvantaged "outsiders" trying to break in (Sloterdijk 171; emphasis added).

These "outsiders," embodied by the waste people as discussed in Sun Mengtian's essay ("Imaging" 296), resonate with Zygmunt Bauman's concept of "human waste." In Bauman's book *Wasted Lives*, he claims that the production of human waste is in fact an inevitable and inescapable side-effect of economic progress, casting "some part of the extant population as 'out of place,' 'unfit,' or 'undesirable' " under the new economic or socio-political order (Bauman, *Wasted* 5). These discarded humans, these lives left to waste, are deemed as "excessive" and "redundant," congregating as a community of "those who either couldn't or weren't meant to be acknowledged or permitted to endure" (5). Expanding upon Bauman's later argument that "immigrants embody – in a visible, palpable manner – the unspoken yet painful and distressing premonition of our own expendability" (56), Sun Mengtian extends this concept to the tension within *Waste Tide*, between the waste people and the urban natives. She posits that the natives' hostility towards the waste people stems from their anxieties. They fear that one day these outsiders might supplant them, rendering them expendable in turn (Sun, "Imagining" 296).

Sun Mengtian here correctly points out the inevitable conflict and violence between Chinese migrant workers and the local urban residents. But I am not convinced by her endeavour to draw a parallel between the waste people of Silicon Isle and Bauman's concept of "human waste," as they are far from "excessive" or "redundant" in nature. In fact, they are indispensable to China's economic progress. According to Ingrid Nielsen and Russell Smyth, "the continued flow of migrant labor to the urban centers is vital to the sustainability of China's rapid economic growth [...] their cheap labor costs have, in-part, underpinned the competitive advantage of operating out of China" (Nielsen and Smyth 248). Sun Mengtian quotes Mimi's worrying thought in the story – "human lives are so much cheaper than machines" that the price for an equally-functioning machine "was enough to hire a hundred young workers like her" (Chen Q., *Waste* 70) – to justify the "disposability" of the waste people. However, it can also be read in the opposite way: it is precisely their disposability, their role as a source of inexpensive labour, that has propelled China into the position of the "world's factory," particularly in cities like Guiyu in the labour-intensive south-eastern regions. As Ngok's suggests, the waste people on Silicon Isle, despite their social marginalization by the locals, do not conform to Bauman's definition of "human waste," as their economic contributions are acknowledged and accepted. But even so, they remain excluded from entering the Sloterdijkian "protective shell" that bestows privileges upon the downtown district of Silicon Isle at the expense of the suburban waste villages.

This shell, emblematic of the demarcation line between the two delineated facets of Silicon Isle, takes centre stage in *Waste Tide*. Through this lens, it unveils the heterotopic essence of those inhabitants dwelling in the profoundly contaminated waste villages, estranged from the flourishing heart of the city – a realm steeped in otherness, metamorphosis and divergence. In Michel Foucault's "Of Other Spaces," heterotopias are distinguished from utopias. Unlike utopias, which are encapsulated, immutable realms isolated from their surrounding environments and existing as "sites with no real place" (Foucault, "Of" 24), heterotopias are dynamic spaces that embody both mythical and tangible elements, challenging the conventional spaces within which we reside. Foucault believes that virtually every culture worldwide forms heterotopias, suggesting their widespread existence within various cultural, social and political contexts.

In his understanding, there are two types of heterotopias: crisis heterotopias, which are "privileged or sacred or forbidden places, reserved for individuals who are, in relation to society and to the human environment in which they live, in a state of crisis;" and heterotopias of deviation, "those in which individuals whose behavior is deviant in relation to the required mean or norm are placed" (Foucault, "Of" 24–5). He asserts that in contemporary society, the heterotopia of crisis is progressively giving way to that of deviation, but meanwhile, there are still spaces that straddle the boundary between these two types of heterotopias. In these spaces, elements of both crisis and deviation are evident among the inhabitants.

Foucault cites retirement homes as an example, where old age signifies both a crisis and a deviation. Likewise, in the case of *Waste Tide*, the suburban villages surrounding Silicon Isle also serve as the heterotopia of both types, where migrant workers with a deviant "outsider" identity are endangered by severe environmental crisis as well as by their unfortunate social status as an underpaid underclass.

The relatively enclosed yet approachable communities in *Waste Tide* is, in a way, different from Foucault's original examples of heterotopia such as prisons, schools and hospitals, often intentionally built by the state or the dominant social group. The waste villages for migrant workers are established less "deliberately" and thus developed and expanded more informally. Still, the boundary distinguishing the heterotopic villages at the periphery and the Silicon Isle downtown at the centre is also very much evident, though in a less concrete yet more abstract manner. The social stratification that favours the locals of Silicon Isle and the alienation or marginalization of waste people is derived from the inherent differences between the two groups – especially in terms of the sense of belonging to the city, the languages they speak (the Guiyu dialect is unintelligible to outsiders), and the unequal access to social protection and welfare (such as healthcare, education and housing).

In essence, by examining the two distinct versions of Silicon Isle, characterized by the prosperous city centre and the exploited waste villages, we can discern an ambiguous boundary that distinguishes between the privileged and the marginalized. This boundary is ambiguous because it lacks a solid wall or border guards enforcing a division, and it does not rely on a physical isolation method like a ghetto. Instead, it manifests through social and economic disparities, creating a separation between *us* and *them* with a boundary that appears both invisible and intangible. According to Kevin Hetherington's exploration of heterotopia, each of the two versions of Silicon Isle can be seen as being "constituted in relation to other sites by their difference" and able to "organize a bit of the social world in a way different to that which surrounds them" (Hetherington viii). For Hetherington, heterotopias are spaces of "alternative ordering" and "deferral" where "ideas and practices that represent the good life can come into being, from nowhere, even if they never actually achieve what they set out to achieve" (ix), which allows for the potential of transformation within the heterotopic communities (though the eventual outcome of this pursuit is not always promising).

This interpretation remains a subject of debate, as the aforementioned "potential of transformation" or transgressive power should not be automatically ascribed to the connotations of Foucault's heterotopia. As David Harvey points out, although heterotopia may enable us "to look upon the multiple forms of transgressive behaviors (usually normalized as 'deviant') in urban spaces as important and productive," it is only "superficially attractive" because in this "banal multiplicity [...] an eclectic mess of heterogeneous and different spaces within which anything 'different' – however defined – might go on" (Harvey, "Cosmopolitanism" 537–8). But even so, for the waste people in *Waste Tide* trapped in the duality of economic acceptance and social rejection, this potential for change and transgression can still provide us with an inspiring way to interrogate their endeavour for resistance and liberation in the place of otherness.

Drawing on the boundary between the isolation and penetration of the two versions of Silicon Isle, as well as the fine line between acceptance and exclusion, *Waste Tide* manages to establish, to use Slavoj Žižek's words,

> a frontier between those who succeeded in remaining "within" (the "developed", those to whom the rules of human rights, social security, etc., still apply) and the others, the excluded (the main concern of the "developed" with regard to them is how to contain their explosive potential, even if the price to be paid is the neglect of elementary democratic principles). (Žižek, *Universal* 21)

This narrative unfolds with the drive for resistance and transgression initially cultivated within the heterotopic realm of the waste people, considered "deviant." Ultimately, it permeates into the privileged enclave of the locals, seen as "insiders," culminating in a tumultuous eruption of violence – a full-blown conflict between us and them (Chen Q., *Waste* 153).

This impulse of transgression, in *Waste Tide*, emerges in response to the pervasive suffering and profound humiliation experienced by the waste people, leading to a collective victimhood that can be conceptualized with Jing Tsu's "mentality of failure." Based on Frantz Fanon's understanding of violence that "remains the brooding fantasy of the oppressed," Jing Tsu goes on to investigate the consequential failure of the violence and oppression in Fanon's claim. She believes that "the embrace of failure belies not a mentality of submission but a strategy of negotiation" – an "unexpected solution to prevailing anxieties about national and culture identities" that brings forward "a discursive possibility for considering the value of the struggle for identity" concerning the deprived and marginalized social groups (Tsu 20–1).

In this manner, the potent forces arising from feelings of failure, trauma and self-doubt become a source of remarkable productivity for the waste people. These emotions create a space for liberation, allowing them to break free from the oppressive and exploitive work conditions and the humiliation imposed by the locals. From this viewpoint, the migrant workers on Silicon Isle face overt hostility, which results in fear, confusion and despair that weigh heavily on each waste work, producing a "state of tension" (Chen Q., *Waste* 92). Many times, these waste people find themselves on their knees,

> begging for mercy; strong, weak, old, young, dirty, helpless – they knelt before the Silicon Isle natives because they had dirtied his clothing, unintentionally stared at him for too long, touched her child, brushed against his car, or even for no reason at all, *simply because they were waste people*. (211; emphasis added)

The seemingly baseless sense of superiority among the natives, along with their deep-seated prejudice, emboldens them to regard the waste people "as if they belonged to a completely different species whose birth-right was to gaze down upon these people like animals" – the "animals" who have "sacrificed their health and lives in exchange for insignificant scraps to fill their bellies and distant dreams, built up the extravagant prosperity of Silicon Isle, and yet they were seen as only slaves, bugs, disposable trash" (211–12).

Bit by bit, these failures and humiliations accumulate within the heterotopic community of waste people, eventually kindled by the torturous experiences of Mimi, a waste girl who, like most of the waste people on Silicon Isle, embodies the usual submissiveness and timidity often associated with China's migrant workers. In *Waste Tide*, the son of Luo Jincheng – head of the most powerful clan on Silicon Isle – gets infected with an incurable disease due to the toxic environment in the neighbourhood. Helplessly,

Luo resorts to a shamanic local faith, one that needs a sacrifice to save his son. Mimi becomes the chosen one here unfortunately, and is mercilessly beaten, abused, raped and almost buried alive by Luo's hatchet men. Yet it is exactly from such a tragedy that Mimi embraces her transformation. Because of her instinct for survival, Mimi unconsciously activates the artificial virus with which she has accidentally been infected and creates a new consciousness apart from her original mindset as a waste girl: "Something had changed inside Mimi [...] Her habitual timidity tinged with anxiety was gone, replaced by a calmness that seemed to come from deep inside, the confidence of someone fully in control of the situation" (200).

Mimi's miraculous return from the brink of death is facilitated by her newfound consciousness, referred to as Mimi 1, which exists alongside her original self, Mimi 0. The latter was once wary and guarded, but Mimi 1 transforms into a beacon of hope, a symbol and a poignant reminder for all waste people. It conveys a powerful message that, regardless of the social dominance wielded by the natives of Silicon Isle, the waste people must not relinquish their dignity and identity in the face of oppression and degradation. The sense of failure and trauma of the fictional Chinese migrant workers throughout the years of being humiliated by the locals who see them as outsiders brings about a tremendous transformative impulse of their heterotopic communities within or around economically developed cities.

Eventually, under the guidance of the awakened Mimi 1, all the waste people's virtual consciousnesses "commingled, conversed rapidly, and reached a compromise, coalescing into *a unified force*" (291; emphasis added) – a collective victimhood enabling them to transcend their terror and uncertainty as waste people. Indeed, the segregated communities established for migrant workers in *Waste Tide* stand as potent Foucauldian heterotopias. They serve as wellsprings of transformative energy emanating from society's fringes, and this energy ultimately surges into the heart of mainstream social discourse. The violent metamorphosis of the waste people on Silicon Isle, fuelled by their profound failures and traumas, carries tremendous potential. They bravely confront entrenched biases and discrimination, culminating in their heroic act of rescuing the locals from a devastating flood. This action symbolizes their unyielding determination to "awaken the souls of the Silicon Isle natives" and unequivocally affirm their shared humanity: "we laugh, we cry, we pity, we sympathize" (314).

Just as Silicon Isle bears witness to the fight for recognition amidst the waste people, an analogous desire to bridge the invisible chasms separating outcasts from insiders, inhabitants from citizens and the privileged from the disenfranchised can be detected within the xenian domains of New Crobuzon. These exceptional communities weave their existence through a complex fabric of conviviality and species mingling, creating ripples of change across the city's tapestry. In Foucault's article, heterotopias are defined as "counter-sites" allowing for the cultural norms that do not fit in the human-favoured mainstream, identities deemed alien and rituals performed only by a certain ethnicity.

These notes of discord, validated and justified within the (often invisibly) bordered spaces in which they emerge, "are simultaneously represented, contested, and inverted" in a mechanism of opening and closing that "both isolates them and makes them penetrable" (Foucault, "Of" 24, 26). Heterotopias, therefore, maintain a constant dialectical interaction with the bigger and more general social environment in which they are embedded as well as other counter-sites taking shape at the same time. Such a dynamic interaction coincides with China Miéville's own views of dialectics:

> The point about dialectics is that the postmodern fascination with hybridity and miscegenation too often blurs into a fetishistic and sometimes quite self-indulgent *celebration* of marginality *for its own sake* […] the point of dialectics as about movement, dynamism, tendencies within an overall, comprehensible, and total system is incredibly illuminating to me, in terms of the tensions that drive it being simultaneously *within* the system, and overthrowing it […] the social tensions and contradictions […] is always-already-in-transition. (Gordon and Miéville 364; emphasis in original)

The very essence of New Crobuzon is rooted in this notion of "transition." This sprawling urban behemoth, a mosaic woven with an astounding array of races, cultural customs, faiths and architectural wonders, persists despite enduring the ever-present divisions arising from their disparities and preconceived notions. Its foundation rests resolutely on the potential for transformation and fusion – an impetus of transition that distinguishes it from the stagnant utopia and aligns it with the transgressive heterotopia.

The latter embodies and delineates the "fundamental dynamic" (Miéville, *Perdido* 51) that underpins the interplay between marginalized and mainstream societal factions. Just as the observation of the crime boss Mr Motley: *transition*, "from one state to another's affected by taking something – a social group, a piece of wood, a hex – to a place where its interactions with other forces make its *own energy* pull against its current state" (207; emphasis in original), is "what makes you, the city, the world, what they are [...] The zone where the disparate become part of the whole" (51).

The process of assimilation into the broader social fabric finds a poignant embodiment in the receptive listener of Motley's monologue, none other than Lin, the *khepri* artist who has cultivated a self-identity that transcends the confines of her khepri kinship. She succeeds in learning and borrowing the heterogeneous elements that belong to other social groups in the hybrid New Crobuzon, and eventually "stop[s] trying to be khepri" (263), stops being confined in a marginalized heterotopic community so as to engage in the general social matrix to which *khepri* communities are attached. However, in this case, Lin's transition within the *khepri* heterotopia, as well as her continuous efforts to get involved in the multicultural and multifarious context of New Crobuzon – a hybrid entity – is subject to a sense of "double consciousness." Through an intricate process of "the dense cultural syncretism" (Gilroy, *Black* 27), this double consciousness gives rise to a profound disarray in terms of her self-identity.

The concept of "double consciousness" was first introduced by Du Bois in his seminal work, *The Souls of Black Folk* (1903). He coined this term to elucidate the internal struggle experienced by many individuals of African descent in North America. It is characterized as "a peculiar [...] sense of always looking at one's self through the eyes of others, of measuring one's soul by the tape of a world that looks on in amused contempt and pity" (Du Bois 8). This "two-ness" or "doubleness," which aptly characterizes the distinctive mindset of the black community in Du Bois's narrative, or the xenian minorities in *Perdido Street Station* serving as symbolic representations of marginalized urban groups, alludes to the presence of "two souls, two thoughts, two unreconciled strivings; two warring ideals in one dark [or xenian] body, whose dogged strength alone keeps it from being torn asunder" (Du Bois 8).

In this case, a thought-provoking parallel can be drawn between Du Bois's "Veil," which obstructs white individuals from perceiving their black neighbours as fully autonomous members of their society, and the "invisible wall" segregating humans from xenians in New Crobuzon, hindering the latter from being acknowledged as active agents. Nevertheless, individuals from the margins, such as Lin the *khepri*, endeavour to forge their identity by continually assessing themselves against the prevailing discourse – "a maladaptive response [that] could be to change your reality and to take on the characteristics of the oppressor" (O. Moore 753). Therefore, double consciousness, as Paul Gilroy observes, "emerged from the unhappy symbiosis between three modes of thinking, being, and seeing" (Gilroy, *Black* 127). This symbiosis is considered "racially particularistic [... and] nationalistic in that it derives from the nation state in which the ex-slaves but not-yet-citizens find themselves, rather than from their aspiration towards a nation state of their own" (127).

For Lin herself, the *khepri* communities are cultivated upon "a culture that was blind to itself" with "bankrupt imaginations falling back on cod-heroic grandiosity" (Miéville, *Perdido* 263, 25). She draws upon the transformative energy inherent in the dialectical xenian heterotopias, emancipating herself by rejecting some, if not all, conventional *khepri* values and acclimating to the prevailing social and cultural norms of human beings. Lin intentionally lives outside typical *khepri* communities, opting for "human fashion" over the traditional ballooning pantaloons favoured by those in the ghettos (26). However, she remains aware that she can never fully assimilate into the privileged groups, recognizing that she is forever marked by her *khepri* identity in the eyes of the city (263). Yet, she also cannot completely shed her unspoken solidarity with her fellow *khepri* social activists.

Lin's transformation, marked by her double consciousness, places her in a precarious position, straddling the divide between the khepri communities and the broader discourse of New Crobuzon under human dominion. Regrettably, she finds herself an "outsider" to both her *khepri* sisterhood and the heterogeneous fabric of the entire city (26). In *Black Skin, White Masks* (1957), Frantz Fanon explores and critiques the misguided pursuit of equality by black communities with Europeans, which is often manifested through "the wearing of European clothes [...] using European furniture and European forms of social intercourse, adorning the Native language with European expressions; using bombastic phrases in speaking or writing a European language" (Fanon 25). Building upon Fanon's insights, the mere emulation of human languages, behaviours and social conventions falls short in granting true liberation to the *khepri*, *garuda*, *vodyanoi* and other xenian minorities inhabiting *Perdido Street Station*. Their persistent double consciousness, where they are constantly observed by humans, keeps them under the watchful "eyes" that can deceive individuals into believing they can fully immerse themselves in someone else's reality.

So far, we have come to a point that the new-weird city New Crobuzon serves as a speculative urban setting that mirrors the complex dynamics of a multicultural and multi-species society, which itself functions as a Foucauldian heterotopia, characterized by a hybrid cartography of different cultures and races. This exploration of heterotopia and xenian experiences in New Crobuzon draws parallels with *Waste Tide*, where migrant workers flock to Silicon Isle in search of economic opportunities but face social rejection and exploitation. These waste people form heterotopic communities in segregated villages, and their dual consciousness emerges as they strive for recognition and liberation. Both novels cast a penetrating light on the trials endured by marginalized communities dwelling within the heart of urban landscapes and the indomitable spirit that stirs within their heterotopic realms. However, as we shall discover soon, beyond this dynamic interplay lies an ominous force, a sinister malevolence that ensnares not only the conflict between humans and xenians, Silicon Isle's citizens and denizens but all who dare to tread upon its shadowy path – a vampiric entity that consumes with no limit.

Capitalist Monsters and Vampiric Victims

In the pages of *Perdido Street Station*, Lin's endeavours to distance herself from her *khepri* heritage and integrate into the predominantly human society of New Crobuzon ultimately prove futile. Risking life and limb, she collaborates with the crime boss, Mr Motley, in the creation of his portrait statue. This venture, intended to showcase her artistic talents beyond the *khepri* community, instead entangles her in a perilous web. Very soon, she finds herself becoming nothing but leverage that Mr Motley wields to manipulate her partner, the human scientist Isaac who inadvertently acquires an object of great importance to Motley, who will stop at nothing to reclaim it.

What Isaac takes is the larvae of a *slake-moth*, a creature that undergoes a mesmerizing yet horrifying metamorphosis. Starting as a harmless grub, it transforms into a formidable monster, boasting three pairs of legs, a menacing tail and, in Miéville's words, "a huge, prehensile, slavering tongue" (Miéville, *Perdido* 441). But the slake-moth's most captivating and deadly feature is its wings – magical, mesmeric wings, vital to the vampire, fatal to the victims. In the city of New Crobuzon, these creatures reign as apex predators, unrivalled in their dominance and prowess, "at the top of their food chain" (462). They become a nightmare hovering above the weird city, but more importantly, the unfathomable, hypnotic patterns adorning these wings that hold a mesmerizing power.

These hypnotic patterns, as described in the narrative, twist and curve in enigmatic ways, "each as random and inconstant as oil on water, each a perfect reflection of the other, kept gently moving, their patterns changing, flickering in a seductive tide" (441). It is through their wings that the slake-moths wield their powers to mesmerize any sentient beings whose eyes fall on them. By unfolding their magical wings to enthral their hypnotized prey, these incredible predators slip their "slavering tongues" into the victim's head, drinking "not the meat-calories slopping about in the brainpan, but the fine wine of sapience and sentience itself, the subconscious" (457). Such a feast of sapience is produced by the endless "self-reflexive" thoughts based on people's (and xenians') "instincts and needs and desires and intuitions" (457).

In other words, the slake-moths feed on "dreams," leaving their mindless victims in a zombie state, regarded as "already-exhausted sources of value, former vessels of creative activity and self-reflexivity that have been entirely consumed and cast aside" (Shaviro, *Connected* 168–9). The victims' "spirits could not roam in spectral form. They had been metabolised. They had been drunk and shat out, converted by vile oneirochymical processes and become fuel for a slake-moth flight" (Miéville, *Perdido* 670). This affliction of mindlessness knows no discrimination, placing everyone at risk.

The terror and dread of falling prey to the slake-moths extend across all species and ethnicities inhabiting New Crobuzon, each possessing a human-like sentience that grants them the capacity to dream. They face the fear of losing not only their sanity but also their very essence to these dream-devouring monstrosities, therefore being materialized, dehumanized and alienated. In this process, there occurs "the appropriation and accumulation of human mental creativity" (Shaviro, *Connected* 170), resulting in the erosion of the victims' subjectivity, a threat that looms over anyone who has transitioned from their original heterotopic community and become attached to the dominant capitalist discourse that governs both humans and xenians.

As they siphon the psyche and sentience of their victims, the slake-moths also produce a tangible substance – a liquid that is "*thick* with distilled dreams" (Miéville, *Perdido* 460; emphasis in original). This valuable by-product can be processed into a potent psychedelic drug known as "dreamshit," which is eagerly consumed by both humans and xenians. In this way, the victim's individuality, creativity and subjectivity are transmuted into a standardized commodity, measured by its market value and consumed by those who, in turn, risk becoming depleted sources themselves. This, according to Carl Freedman, is a "ruthless transformation by capital of labor into labor-power," namely "the transformation of the free productive capacities of the worker into a mere commodity to be bought and sold for wages" (Freedman, *Art* 33). Therefore, the slake-moths should be considered the embodiment of the capitalist social structure itself, aptly termed by Steven Shaviro as "capitalist monsters" (*Connected* 168–71).

By portraying the vampiric nature of capital through the creation of the slake-moths, China Miéville sheds light on the unsettling facets of a bizarre capitalist world that often masquerades as normal, natural and unalterable. He employs the fantastic genre of New Weird to challenge the notion of "grotesque realism," which merely mirrors the "absurdity" inherent in capitalist modernity (Miéville, "Symposium" 42). In the city of New Crobuzon, which is permeated by the dominant capitalist discourse, commodities that bear a human or xenian resemblance may stand upright and vocalize their grievances. Meanwhile, the vampiric forces of capital continue to drain the dreams and worth of the labouring populace.

However, the slake-moths as "capitalist monsters," though originally from an unknown place (presumably from the mythical Fractured Land), are not entirely strangers or aliens to New Crobuzon. They are deliberately brought into the city by Mayor Rudgutter and his supporters and introduced to a select group of scientists. The goal is to conduct experiments on mind-control technologies that could be employed to manipulate the city's inhabitants and maintain the advantageous and profitable position of the ruling class. Yet the project has soon been terminated, as "the money people" (Miéville, *Perdido* 435) who back it grow apprehensive about its progress and their financial investments, so the slake-moths are then sold to "the highest bidder" (436).

The highest bidder, in this case, is Mr Motley himself. He decides to exploit the slake-moths to produce dreamshit, extracting surplus value or capital from the consumers addicted to the drug. This exploitative capitalist logic, facilitated by these monstrous creatures, initially seems to function smoothly. However, everything takes a nightmarish turn when the slake-moths break free and run amok, which becomes a threat to the overall capitalist order in New Crobuzon and "have started to metastasise and proliferate uncontrollably, like a cancer" (Shaviro, *Connected* 170–1). But in fact, such a "cancerous pathology is [...] nothing more than a monstrous intensification of the 'normal' functioning of the system infected by it" (171).

"Capital," argues Jodi Melamed when discussing racial capitalism, "can only be capital when it is accumulating, and it can only accumulate by producing and moving through relations of severe inequality among human groups" (Melamed 77). The segregation and discrimination faced by marginalized social communities, rooted in the racial divide between humans and xenians in *Perdido Street Station*, already foreshadow the flow of capital and the exploitation of labour. These heterotopic communities, borne out of these marginalized groups, are spaces with transformative potential where xenian minorities attempt to engage with the mainstream discourse, which is predominantly controlled by humans. However, these efforts ultimately fail to free these individuals from becoming the "prey" of the "vampiric" capitalist monsters that loom over everyone, be they xenians or humans.

From this perspective, the hybridity between different ethnic communities is reduced to a miscellaneous stasis, represented by Mr Motley's "motley" body – a random combination of various species in a chaotic order of transition (Miéville, *Perdido* 134, 51). As Lin finds out about Motley's body:

> Scraps of skin and fur and feathers swung as he moved; tiny limbs clutched; eyes rolled from obscure niches; antlers and protrusions of bone jutted precariously; feelers twitched and mouths glistened. Many-coloured skeins of skin collided. A cloven hoof thumped gently against the wood floor. Tides of flesh washed against each other in violent currents. Muscles tethered by alien tendons to alien bones worked together in uneasy truce, in slow, tense motion. Scales gleamed. Fins quivered. Wings fluttered brokenly. Insect claws folded and unfolded. (52–3)

In a similar vein, although the raw materials for the dreamshit produced by the slake-moths is the memories, sentience and the producing capacity of social subjects that the monsters have consumed, they are no longer connected to what the victims of the slake-moths have gone through before. They become ahistorical, schizophrenic, a pastiche under the capitalist framework "without ulterior motives [and] amputated of the satiric impulse," a "blank parody," which Fredric Jameson argues is one of the characteristics of late capitalism (Jameson, *Postmodernism* 17). Such a sense of pastiche is not strange to Isaac, since he has tried the dreamshit by mistake, and this is how he feels about the pastiched memories that are rendered as the commodities of the late-capitalist cultural production:

> A magic lantern was flickering in his head, bombarding him with a succession of images. This was no zöetrope with an endlessly repeated little visual anecdote: this was a juddering bombardment of infinitely varied moments. Isaac was strafed with a million scintillas of time. Every fractioned life juddered as it segued into the next and Isaac would eavesdrop on other creatures' lives. He spoke the chymical language of the khepri crying because her broodma had chastised her and then he snorted derisorily as the head stableman listened to some half-arsed excuse from the new boy and he closed his translucent inner eyelid as he slipped beneath the cold fresh

> waters of the mountain streams and kicked towards the other vodyanoi coupling orgiastically. (Miéville, *Perdido* 222–3)

This "succession of images," this "zöetrope" of visions and memories taken from the human and xenian communities does indicate the ethnic hybridity in New Crobuzon, but certainly not in a desirable manner. The cultural norms and identity emerging in these ethnic heterotopias that are simultaneously segregated and connected to each other, according to Robert Wood, are homogenized in line with the logic capitalist exploitation connoted in the slake-moths, preying upon both the exploiter and the exploited. Such a sense of homogenization may lead to, in Wood's words, "the domestication of its resistant heterotopic margins, while undermining the subversive nature of the forms of social life created within those margins" (Wood 75). The conviviality wished by any multicultural society, most representatively that in London and New Crobuzon, is therefore undermined before it could be formed.

Here, the domestication of heterotopic margins is also part of Silicon Isle. The waste villages in *Waste Tide* have indeed provided a heterotopic space for the marginalized community of waste people on Silicon Isle to transcend their original peripheral status and in so doing get involved in the mainstream social discourse. But in the process, they find themselves trapped in an even more complicated web. China's economic success in recent decades, to some degree, depends on its increasing involvement in the global market, and therefore can be bound to a new world order, one that is termed "Empire" by Michael Hardt and Antonio Negri (referring back to Chapter 1). In *Waste Tide*, the impulse of change developed in heterotopias of both deviation and crisis is therefore subdued under the market-based social structure in which the "penetrability" of heterotopic community of waste people is very often dependent on capital's capability to "[separate] populations from specifically coded territories and [set] them in motion" (Hardt and Negri, *Empire* 326). As capital usually tends to "reduce all previously established forms of status, title, and privilege to [...] quantitative and commensurable economic terms" (326) and links all these values through money, the transformation of the "heterotopic margin" (in Wood's words) in *Waste Tide* will "surrender to the laws of the rate of profit, the rate of exploitation, the realization of surplus value, and so forth" (326).

The waste people in this novel are often enticed away from their inland, and likely impoverished, hometowns with the false promise of Silicon Isle's prosperity. Much like the migrant workers in real cities endorsed by Chinese state policy, they too are trapped within the rigid quantitative logic of money. "Living on the margins of the prosperity that did not belong to them, they toiled day after day in the most mechanical, repetitive, and trivial assembly line work," earning only "a pittance for their labour while they harboured dreams of someday making enough to return home in respectable circumstances" (Chen Q., *Waste* 224).

The "someday" they hope for, however, may never come true. To the affluent natives, particularly the leaders of the local waste-processing oligarchs, the waste people are nothing more than refuse, akin to the chaotic electronic landfill in which they reside and toil. Consequently, these marginalized individuals are viewed as expendable means of accumulating capital. Their existence is marked by a continual struggle for basic necessities, and their intellectual worth, if any, is largely reduced to monetary gain, profit and commercial exploitation. In this manner, they are objectified, consumed and ultimately depleted.

The clan leader, Luo Jincheng, justifies his exploitation of the waste people with the phrase "winner takes all" (Chen Q., *Waste* 251), which mirrors the fundamental logic that entraps all migrant workers in China. They migrate to economically developed cities with dreams of achieving success and making fortune, only to discover that they are involved in a market-driven discourse defined by competition and the law of the jungle. Their individual productive abilities are reduced to quantifiable and monetizable commodities. For the majority of privileged native residents of Silicon Isle who benefit from the capitalist production process, this perspective on their economic structure as a zero-sum competition serves as a convenient and timely justification. It allows them to rationalize their "vampiric" actions in dispossessing and dehumanizing the waste people, as well as the ecological degradation they incur as a cost.

In this context, Luo Jincheng can be viewed as an emblematic figure. As the leader of the largest and most powerful among the three clannish corporations on Silicon Isle, Boss Luo has been deeply influenced by his perception of their society, one that operates on the principles of "the law of the jungle and survival of the fittest" (Chen Q., *Waste* 162). His actions and decisions are driven by a rather straightforward belief, summed up as "an animal has to be strong enough to prevent its offspring from being hunted … it's the same with mankind" (191). With this spirit, Luo seeks to extract the surplus value from the waste people, minimizing their living costs to control the expense, exploiting them with money as the leverage, casting them aside like discarded waste once their values are fully exhausted. In other words, Boss Luo, together with other powerful locals endeavouring to defend the protective shell in which they are *insiders*, regards Silicon Isle as a hunting ground where his family should be protected, a place in which people are dehumanized by the emotionless symbols of capital, and thus, as in Wendy Brown's explanation of the process of economization, seek to "strengthen its competitive positioning and appreciate its value" (Brown, *Undoing* 33).

The process of such dehumanization and economization, as well as the "perpetual cycle of looting, exploitation, and forceful extraction" taking place on Silicon Isle, which strongly resists "a fair system [where] everyone would benefit" (Chen Q., *Waste* 45), is called a "disease" in the novel. That is to "think of life as some zero-sum game in which there must be winners and losers, even at the expense of the interests of the others, including their lives" (326). In this case, emerging from the waste people's heterotopic transgressions and their resistance against feelings of failure, prejudice and discrimination, the transformed Mimi 1 envisions herself as the antidote to this disease. Serving as the embodiment of revitalized subjectivity and self-awareness for the waste people, as well as for migrant workers in China more broadly, she successfully reunites what was once a fragmented group fighting for recognition as human *beings* rather than mere human *waste*.

Therefore, within the heterotopic waste villages, Mimi 1 assumes the role of a subversive or revolutionary figure who sparks and personally leads their rebellious "war" against the self-centred, money-driven locals. In the eyes of the waste people, the image of the girl inhabited by Mimi 1's consciousness begins to "blur and flicker, as though some invisible, distant light source were illuminating her: warm, serene, and radiant." She seems to have "grown much taller and acquired an awe-inspiring aura that made it impossible to stare at her" (250). Unlike her innocent and fragile counterpart Mimi 0, Mimi 1 surpasses her original marginalized identity as an abandoned or used-up "object," isolated within the heterotopic community of waste people and thus possesses greater power, knowledge and connection to the overarching discourse that governs Silicon Isle. Nevertheless, this transcendence does not equate to genuine liberation but rather a deeper entrapment. Mimi 1 is unavoidably bound to the zero-sum competition prevailing on Silicon Isle, guided by the Social Darwinian principle of "winner takes all." Amid the upheaval of the waste people's struggle, Mimi 1 resorts to acts of violence, murder and anything she deems necessary to ensure victory in the war between the waste people and the Silicon Isle locals – just as Boss Luo had done to them.

She believes, like every other participant stuck in such a hunting game of market competition and capitalist exploitation, that "human weakness is going to be the death of you someday" (Chen Q., *Waste* 339). Here, weakness alludes to the excessive consideration for other subjects within the framework of capitalist social discourse and the hesitance to seize and exploit their surplus values. This sentiment may readily evoke Friedrich Engels's timeless observation in "Outlines of a Critique of Political Economy" (1843) regarding the liberal economic system – a system that "had done its best to universalize enmity, to transform mankind into a horde of ravenous beasts (for what else are competitors?) who devour one another just *because* each has identical interests with all the others" (Engels 423; emphasis in original).

Although Mimi 1's appeal to rescue the natives in the eventual fatal flood seems to indicate some benevolence, her point in such an act is never only to save lives (Chen Q., *Waste* 313). Rather it is in this way that the waste people can be "socially accepted" by Silicon Isle, qualified to be involved in the "vampiric" capitalist logic dominating the city no longer as the "victim" but sometimes as the "vampire" itself. "All the costs have been carefully calculated" (178) – through the fictional characters, Chen Qiufan here explicitly demonstrates the truth of Silicon Isle, a truth also applicable to Guiyu, and China.

Long Live the Vampire

Mimi 1 is not the antidote to this "disease." Instead, she is part of it, embodying and representing what the waste people have always wished to be in this market-based hunting ground – educated, canny, resourceful, with the ability to overturn their marginalized social status as victims of capitalist exploitation. In this way, *Waste Tide* should not only be read as an eco-critical narrative calling for environmentalist readings. It is, to a certain extent, a realistic tale that reflects the suffering and hardships endured by China's 293 million migrant workers today. While it unfolds on Silicon Isle and epitomizes the capitalist characteristics of places like Guiyu, it also mirrors other cities that have thrived due to China's market-oriented reforms in the post-socialist era.

The transgressive forces of the heterotopia formed by the migrant workers on Silicon Isle and various other real Chinese cities, although seemingly enabling those who live in the periphery to be involved in the mainstream discourse, have failed to exterminate the general vampiric logic of capital accumulation. *Waste Tide* interrogates the severe violence, bias and discrimination against China's migrant workers. Yet, even as the waste people, in one way or another, manage to breach the invisible barrier that separates them from the locals, they can never truly break free from the grip of vampiric capitalism that reduces their heterotopic transformations and resulting social hybridity into a homogeneous zero-sum competition centred on money, capital and profit.

In New Crobuzon, just as in *Waste Tide*, the vampire can be vanquished, but the vampiric society endures. Although the slake-moths, now regarded as capitalist monsters by Steven Shaviro, are eventually ambushed and slain by Isaac's hunting squad, New Crobuzon, the new weird city, remains largely unchanged. After all, the slake-moths are not only predators but products of the city itself. They are bred, hatched, raised and sustained by the minds, sentience and, above all, the subjectivity of both humans and xenians living there, transcending the sense of conviviality and multi-species cohabitation that the city claims to embody. In many ways, New Crobuzon is a city of hybrids, a weird place where weird races walk as normal, but all have an uninterrupted connection to their historical past. Some came willingly, while others were driven by disasters or personal guilt. Nevertheless, they are all an integral part of the city's complex tapestry, a testament to the mingling of cultures, histories and identities in this unique metropolis. In other words, they are natural.

The slake-moths, however, are *un*-natural. Despite their origin in the near-mythological Fractured Land, they come to New Crobuzon, while still cocoons, as a biological commodity sold first to the government for developing mind-control weapons and then to the criminal underworld for the dreamshit industry. They are here because New Crobuzon needs them, a materialization of the city's most implicit desire, "an omen that examines an ethical and moral dilemma that prevails in modern society – that of capitalism and commodity exploitation" (O'Connor 275). This is the reason why Shaviro believes the slake-moths are more like "Lovecraft's Cthulhu rather than Stoker's Dracula" ("Capitalist" 285), since the latter is still in many ways part of *us* – with his human shape, gentle charm and reference to his historical archetype Vlad the Impaler – while the former is absolutely inhuman, unrecognizable, unfathomable, uncanny and therefore completely *other* to us.

As one of the most fearsome monsters in sf and New Weird, as the embodiment of the vampiric city New Crobuzon, the slake-moths arrive because they are summoned, as soon as the inhabitants of New Crobuzon (both humans and xenians) chant the shibboleth or spells made of the signs and symbols of money, value, capital and the market. The slake-moths can be killed, their bodies destroyed, but not their *presence*. After their demise, there will always be new forms of the vampiric logic. As we shall see in the next chapter, we will explore how these reimagined interpretations of the Marxist concept of the vampire can expand beyond its traditional emphasis on capitalist production and labour, focusing on more contemporary relations of production intertwined with evolving forms of consumption and even "prosumption," thus entangled with new senses of historicity and, in sf, futurity.

CHAPTER 4

From Consumption to Prosumption: Spectacle of Political Economy in James Lovegrove's *Days* and Long Yi's *Earth Province*

> We make the *symbols* of Sterling and Dollar and Yen [. . .] three ordinary letters ennobled, raised to a state of grace by that which they represent, to remind us that money transfigures all [. . .] We make the symbol of Days to remind us of the source of our wealth.
>
> – James Lovegrove, in *Days*

> Murder is equivalent to stealing the assets of the Earth – a crime worse than robbing a bank.
>
> – Long Yi, in *Earth Province*

Beyond the Vampire

Among all the weird creatures and monsters in Miéville's novels, the slake-moths stand out as perhaps the most memorable. The fact that one of these creatures graces the cover of the critical anthology *China Miéville: Critical Essays*, published by Gylphi in 2015 and edited by Caroline Edwards and Tony Venezia, serves as visible proof of their significance. Conceptualized as "capitalist monsters," these flying vampires prey on not blood or flesh but sentience and conscience, connoting an exhaustive logic of capitalist exploitation, hovering over the ethnically diverse city of New Crobuzon.

The victims of the slake-moths in New Crobuzon, condemned to irreversible mindlessness as the living dead, evoke the harsh reality witnessed by Karl Marx in Victorian London, for which he wrote "Capital is dead labour which, vampire-like, lives only by sucking living labour, and lives the more, the more labour it sucks" (Marx, *Capital* 342). In this way, Miéville's portrayal of the slake-moths that suck dreams is rather deliberate. It is an intentional reference to Marx's vampires haunting the exploited in the nineteenth century, an embodiment of the production relations of, in the novel, the dreamshit industry in New Crobuzon, and also a demonstration of Miéville's political concerns from a position as – in his own words – "a classical Marxist" (Gordon 363) who refuses to be identified as a postmodernist.

Despite Miéville's self-identification as a classical Marxist, however, *Perdido Street Station* does suggest an alternative lens for interpreting contemporary London's class consciousness rather than its Victorian counterpart. Marx argued, in an era when the critique of political economy was still very much centred on industrial production, that capitalism tends over time to polarize society into two classes of owners and manual workers, between those who own the means of production and those who sell their labour power for wages and between those who profit from vampirism and those who are victimized. This is considered the basis of class formation. But in New Crobuzon, class formation gets complicated, as the sense of belonging and collective identity is less developed from people's positions in relation to social production. Industrial actions, therefore, could be compromised by the micro-politics fuelled by the inequality and uneven privileges favouring a particular social community over the others, though they are all part of the working class. Consequently, the unity of labourers is jeopardized by internal conflicts of interest, eroding the solidarity essential for effective collective action.

This shift is starkly evident in the ill-fated strike of the *vodyanoi* dockers in New Crobuzon, which protests against the "vicious attacks on wages by the dock authorities" (Miéville, *Perdido* 154). This endeavour, met not only with forceful suppression by the government but also denounced by some of their human workmates, illustrates that class consciousness no longer serves as the unifying force among all wage laborers. It seems the exploitive relations of production, from the perspective of "classical" Marxist critique and embodied by the slake-moths and the dreamshit industry in New Crobuzon, is coupled with other themes in the last decade of the twentieth century – a time when Miéville was educated as a left-wing polemicist, a time envisioned as "New Times" by contributors to *Marxism Today* in the late 1980s, spearheaded by Stuart Hall and Martin Jacques. It seems that class struggle does not maintain a power dynamic sufficient *in itself* to provide an alternative to the capitalist realism dominating the *fin-de-siècle* end-of-history discourse. In fact, a crucial aspect of the operation of capitalist realism lies in the deliberate disavowal of class, effectively neutralizing its inherently oppositional content and rebranding it as a matter of style or identity rather than a fundamental structural relation.

Nevertheless, class was in decline. The powerful days of class-based unions during the heyday of "organized" (Lash and Urry 2–7) or "managed" (Fulcher 2) capitalism have become the glory of the past. The identity of working class and organized labourers was reshaped under the impact of a series of "disorganizing" changes including the falling profits of heavy industries, the deregulation of financial and economic sectors, the privatization of public provision, the flexibility or "casualization" of employment relations and the rise of globalization that allows production to be moved to areas where unions are weak or cooperative. This transition, then, "is epochal" (Hall and Jacques 12).

"Social life, culture and politics," writes John Urry in his contribution to the *New Times* project, "are no longer predominantly organised in terms of social class [...] because current inequalities of income, wealth and power do not produce homogeneous social classes which share common experiences of class deprivation, or even vote the same way at elections" (Urry 99). His observations that the class of male manufacturing workers will be decentralized into smaller units, that people are to be organized around other concerns such as race, gender, environment, social amenities, lifestyles and ways of consuming are accurate. Such a change in class formation and the restructuring of the prevailing mode of production, however, were *articulated* (in Hall's terminology) more to the interest of Thatcher's right-wing campaigns. She spoke in March 1988, in line with her appropriation of personal aspirations for autonomy, choice, better life, greater responsibility and fulfilment of desires: "In the world in which we now live, divisions into class are outmoded and meaningless. We are all working people who basically want the same things. We all share the desire for higher standards of living, of health, of education, of leisure" ("Speech to Conservative Central Council" n.p.).

In a way, it would be arbitrary to attribute the withering of class-based politics solely to Thatcher's undisguised attempts to sideline class imagery and her tough reactions to union protests and strikes. It is true that the void left by the disintegration of class consciousness was immediately filled by Thatcherism, but Thatcherism *per se* is hardly the reason for this ideological change in the first place. It is also the result, or product, of the historical/epochal transition due to the economic transformation during the post-Fordist decline of organized capitalism. This said, Thatcherism does stand opposite the class mentality. It tends to invoke political awareness from the ordinariness of people's everyday life and their attempt to "get to the heart of what people seem to want" (McRobbie 250). It has a resonance with people's desire for the "right to buy" and the "right to choose" as forms of self-expression, resorting to the "economic populism" driven by social affluence and a compulsion to consume (Mort 161–3). The problem of British left, as Mort points out, lies in their "over-identification" with production and class and their underestimation of consumption as an alternative approach to understand post-Fordist politics and culture (164). The political high ground connoted in the ideology of affluence and in the way in which people spend for a lifestyle chosen by themselves has since then become a stronghold of the Thatcherite governments.

Trying to reclaim this political high ground, the *New Times* polemicists sought to change from within, struggling towards a hard road to renewal. Far from "occupying a different world from that of Thatcherism," as Hall reflects, "we can only renew the project of the left by precisely occupying *the same world* that Thatcherism does, and building from that a *different* form of society" (Hall, *Hard* 15; emphasis in original). This is a world undergoing an epochal transition from Fordism to post-Fordism, a world "increasingly characterised by diversity, differentiation and fragmentation, rather [than] homogeneity, standardisation and the economies and organisations of scale which characterised modern mass society" (Hall and Jacques 11). This is a society where political identities are endorsed by consumer demands in favour of greater choice, compelling the left to ponder what the market is and what role it plays in forming the sites of belonging and collectivity in the relative absence of class. This is a time when lessons for the left should be drawn from the triumph of Thatcherism to understand "what it is, why it arose, what its historical specificity is, the reasons for its success in redrawing the political map and disorganising the Left" (Hall, "Thatcher's" 20).

Despite the expected controversies stirred by the New Timers and the ensuing critiques against them (Pollert 42–72; S. Clarke 59–92; Sivanandan 1–30), this project cannot be simply dismissed as a capitulation to the Thatcherite values. It was proposed with full awareness that "New Times are [not] necessarily and inevitably 'good times' ":

> New Times, after all, is still new times for capitalism, which remains in place, untranscended in all its fundamental rhythms and tendencies. Capital is still deeply entrenched – in fact, more so, globally, than ever before. And the old inequalities associated with it remain, defining the life-experience and limiting the hopes and aspirations of whole groups and classes of people, and whole communities. Alongside that the New Times are producing new social divisions, new forms of inequality and disempowerment, which overlay the old ones. (Hall and Jacques 17)

It was these "new forms" of inequality and disempowerment overlaying the old ones that the New Timers set out to interrogate and diagnose. This project was rather an introspection of the left on their denial of consumption in the formation of collective identities, arguing that it was of equal if not greater significance than the relations of production, especially during a decade when industrial unions were losing their influence. It was the recognition of a new political discourse where individual aspirations were articulated through leisure and style of life more often in the marketplace than factory compounds. The political dynamic of capitalist production found expression in new forms of spectacle built upon affluence and consumption.

This chapter, therefore, starts from consumption and consumerism, discussing how the right to buy and the right to choose are intertwined with the formulation of political identities, how the things we possess – never passive or inert in themselves – affect people's social and political engagement, and whether the rise of market, based on consumer demands rather than standardized production, can protect us from the lurking tongue of the slake-moths or just trap us in the same exploitative or vampiric logic displayed in another form.

One of the novels I find particularly inspiring for interpreting the relation between consumption and identity is James Lovegrove's *Days* (1997), in which the mesmeric magic of the slake-moths' wings is represented in a way familiar to everyone in the consumer society – the shopping windows of a gigantic shopping mall known as "Days." Compared to other writers of the British Boom such as Iain M. Banks, Ken MacLeod and China Miéville, Lovegrove seems to be quieter in terms of political articulation. He has even turned away from writing about the Boom *Zeitgeist* since around 2005 and devoted more time in publishing shared-universe novels and young adult fictions, including the *Pantheon* Series (2009–16), *Sherlock Holmes* Novels (2013–18), The *Cthulhu* Casebooks (2016–18) and *Firefly* Novels (2018–20). But even so, his earlier works, especially *Days* and *Untied Kingdom* (2003), have already made a space for him in Andrew M. Butler's "(Partial) Census" of the Boom writers (Butler, "Thirteen" 376). He is also mentioned in Roger Luckhurst's article in the same *SFS* special issue, which acknowledges Lovegrove's post-Thatcher responses to John Major and Tony Blair.

Published in the same year when New Labour ascended to office with its own interest in these questions of choice, *Days* depicts an idealized marketplace in its purest form, a landscape "dominated by the consumer dreamlands of gigantic shopping malls, [which is an] entirely self-sustaining capitalist environment" (Luckhurst, "Cultural" 427). In this novel, Days is named after its founder Septimus Day, who passes it on to his seven sons upon his death. With its 777 departments, Days provides not only what people *need* but also what they *desire*. "If it can be sold, it will be bought, and if it can be bought, it will be sold" (Lovegrove 24). This slogan printed on the Days shopping catalogue appears like a manifesto of a contemporary "Universal Provider" promising anything from a pin to an elephant, reminding us that the Mall has everything; the Mall *is* everything. Although some part of *Days,* such as the narrator's frequent complaints about the decadence of British society and expression of nostalgia, could be read as a representation of "melancholic Englishness," which indicates "a hesitancy about using [the Mall] for political satire" (Luckhurst, "Cultural" 427), the novel's emphasis on the semiotic hollowness behind the *appearance* of commodities still demonstrates a critical stance against consumption as the source of political subjectivity.

Such a critique of consumption, as well as consumption's role in identity formation, could not have been better timed especially given New Labour's electoral victory that established the first Labour government in nearly two decades, for which the Labour Party was forced to make fundamental changes to its values and programme. For political historians, the rise of New Labour was never an isolated incident despite Tony Blair's personal charisma. It was rather suggested to be heavily influenced by the left-wing journal *Marxism Today* and deeply connected to what was termed the New Times project – an intellectual debate traced back to the late 1980s in response to the dominance of Thatcherism and to the disarray of Labour for much of that decade (Finlayson, *Making Sense* 116–19). Of course, the New Times project was not at all a homogeneous movement. It was sophisticated and divided, consisting of different, even opposing voices and ideas. Some of the New Timers tended to identify themselves with Blair's New Labour, such as Geoff Mulgan and Charles (Charlie) Leadbeater who formed part of the network of think-tank gurus with close connections to New Labour in the mid-1990s; others, such as Eric Hobsbawm, Stuart Hall, Martin Jacques, took issue with it from the outset to an extent that they revived *Marxism Today* (initially collapsed in 1991) for one last special issue in 1998 just to denounce the Blairite project.

Observing such a troubled "kinship" between New Times and New Labour, in the first half of this chapter, I will read James Lovegrove's *Days* within a context where speculative fiction in the UK was considered a preferred source of left-wing critique and where New Labour was proven more electable. I will look into the socio-political influence of consumption in the process of identity formation since the 1980s, a transformative decade marked by the considerable weakening of industrial unions and the gradual displacement of factories by the marketplace as the locus of personal aspiration.

Meanwhile, I will also relate *Days*'s interrogation of consumption to Guy Debord's postmodern critique, which perceives the penetration of television and mass media into people's everyday life as an ideological transition leading to the society of the spectacle, where authentic social life is to be replaced by symbolic representation, material things by spectacular images. Therefore, I am now calling attention to the representation of Debordian spectacles in Lovegrove's *Days*, especially those connoted in the window display and people's shopping preferences manipulated by marketing, discount and advertisements. I will then move on to amplify his critical reflections on the idea that the social subject and collective identity are increasingly developed through consumption, an idea that the New Times contributors deem to be crucial to the UK's historical turn in the face of post-Fordism, disorganized capitalism, the decline of class, and "the return of subject" (Hall, "Meaning" 119), though its belated outcome, New Labour, was not always what they had expected.

A Days Membership: A Vision of Affluence for the Ordinary

During the second term of Thatcher's regime, the old maxims of save and prosper and the austere morality that she introduced to cope with stagflation were replaced with a propaganda for hedonism and consumer pleasure as the result of economic recovery. It was a time of national growth when real GDP increased on average by 3.5 per cent per annum between 1983 and 1989, reaching 4.4 per cent in 1987 and 4.7 per cent in 1988 (Gilmour 75). It was also a time of personal prosperity when living standards "improved faster than at any time since 1945, with average personal incomes increasing by 20 percent between 1983 and 1987" (Newton 162). It seems that Britain was indeed booming again, but this economic boom did not lead to an increase of personal savings. In fact, it went the other way, as the ratio of personal savings to income slumped from 12 per cent in 1979 to 5.5 per cent in 1988 while non-housing loans grew from £7 billion to £28 billion over the same period (Vinen 206; Newton 164).

This "credit boom" was not totally unexpected, especially in a society where all restrictions of hire purchase had been removed in 1982 and where people were encouraged to *buy* into a vision of hope, affluence and success with either paper or plastic money. In his oft-cited article "The Politics of Consumption" as part of the *New Times* project, Frank Mort regards the seductive marketing slogans of NatWest (a UK retail and commercial bank) in the late 1980s – such as "No Spending Limit," "Gold Card Service," "Moneycare: Making It, Spending It, Enjoying It" – as examples of this boom of credit and consumption. Even some of the major high-street retail chains, including M&S, Dixons, and Next, contributed to the expansion of credit by providing their own financial services. "[Spending] on the never-never has never been so acceptable – and for some so necessary" (Mort 162).

However, along with the boom of credit, credit scoring became particularly important in an age when the purchasing power brought by the creditworthiness of a person can be bound to identity formation and political engagement. While those with high earnings are granted more credit and more options in the marketplace, which may lead to a better vision of personal aspiration and the future, those with a less promising financial condition, and therefore registered in the "sub-prime sector," are excluded from this politics of consumption. Although financial exclusion is not new, its consequences "are much more serious now than they were in the past" (Kempson and Whyley 22) because of its unprecedented entanglement with other forms of social marginalization, exclusion and stratification.

In this way, paying with plastic money was considered not only an indispensable method of consumption since the late 1980s but also an entrance qualification of being admitted as a subject into a society where consuming is increasingly taken as a source of power and pleasure. "For most people," writes Lovegrove in his novel, "the limit on a credit account is a goal rather than a boundary, something to race for rather than keep as far away as possible from" (Lovegrove 128). Transaction with credits may be too swift and too easy for consumers to feel the financial burden of shopping. Hire purchase may create a temporary sense of affluence or even pride by casting debts into the future so that they could be underestimated at the time when they were credited. But people do feel one thing immediately, that is their privilege over others in the hierarchy of credit, a privilege of buying the items that others cannot.

Like the real society in the UK, which favours some while discriminating others in the financial and, by extension, cultural and political sectors,

Days also discriminates. An entrance ticket, that is a membership card, is awarded only to qualified customers after a rigorous background check. The Days membership is made of a hierarchy of eight layers, each referring to a certain level of credit that can be used for purchasing in the Mall and to their in-store privileges. It is also a visible embodiment of the social values, status and recognition of card holders themselves. Even the lowest level of the membership hierarchy, Aluminium, is hard to acquire; the second lowest, Silver, is worth showing off. Linda and her husband Gordon are lucky enough to earn a Silver, for which they have spent "five years of struggle, of hard graft, of sacrifice and self-discipline, of pennies pinched and corners cut and weekends worked" (Lovegrove 20).

Compared to Gordon who appears more hesitant to apply for a Days membership, Linda is far more decisive in fighting for a way into the Mall. She knows exactly what she wants, pursuing a Silver card with all her hard work and endeavours, instead of an Aluminium which most others would have started with, because in her eyes "an Aluminium was common, in both senses of the word" (Lovegrove 21). In this way, she manages to construct an identity differentiated from that of her neighbours and friends who are unlikely to earn a Silver. She demonstrates little compassion for her next-door neighbours, the Winslows, and upon learning of their failure to apply for the Days membership, Linda comments that "if only they would try a little harder, if only they would not wear their defeat so openly, a Days card could be theirs as well" (50). She shows little sympathy to those who are turned down by Days due to their misbehaviour in the Mall (mostly related to theft and failure to pay off the debts; violence, however, may be tolerated) or lack of stable income, because she believes "if you don't know how to behave while you're there, and if you lack the self-control not to take anything you can't pay for, then you thoroughly deserve the consequences" (55).

You will reap what you sow. You will get what you deserve. You will take the consequences of not working hard and of your own misdeeds. These doctrines grant Linda a Thatcherite charisma, especially related to Thatcher's invocation of "Victorian values" in her run-up to the 1983 election – values whose importance to the Conservative Party was also evident in the Major years (Evans 608). It was an encouragement of individual responsibility, a distinction between the "deserving" and the "underserving poor," and a critical reflection on the "dependency culture" in the UK. "I never felt uneasy about praising […] 'Victorian virtues,'" says the Iron Lady in her autobiography *The Downing Street Years*, "the purpose of help [from the government and society] must not be to allow people merely to live a half-life, but to restore their self-discipline and through that their self-esteem" (Thatcher, *Downing* 627).

Of course, such a distinction, in Thatcher's words, between those who have "genuinely fallen into difficulties and needed some support till they could get out of them" and those who have "simply lost the will or habit of work and self-improvement" (627) has been seriously challenged by leftist critics. The selectivity of Thatcher's Victorian vision and its innate ambiguities have been proven problematic since it neglects the other Victorian values that do not contribute to the Thatcherite propagation of the individual and consumption-based social discourse. For Raphael Samuel, for example, the phrase "Victorian values" is more like something Thatcher had "stumbled on" as her rallying cry, something conjured "out of nowhere." As he traces the coinage of this term to an interview with Weekend World on 16 January 1983, Samuel continues with a tone of sarcasm: "Only those who are privy to the secrets of the television studio will know whether it was an inspiration of the moment, or a premeditated plant" (Samuel 12).

In either case, however, people *were* in effect pushed to be self-dependent, to take care of themselves and their own families and to realize what they wished for through personal endeavours. Thatcher's call for a restoration of Victorian values coincided with a consumer-led boom that empowered individuals as autonomous agents in the marketplace and amplified their personal desires and aspirations. According to another New Timer Charlie Leadbeater, this was a time when people could determine, through consuming, not "just what they want in the supermarket, but what they want for their lives, what kind of people they want to be, where they will live, how their children will be educated" (Leadbeater 17). All may prosper if they work hard and stay disciplined as required by Thatcher's biased invocation of Victorian virtues. All sacrifices will pay off. All hard times will be treated with gains. This is why Linda is so determined to earn a Days membership to achieve prosperity, so eager to be admitted into the consumer dreamland and so bewitched by the vision promised by the credits granted to her household.

But still, Linda's determination and eagerness in pursuing a membership do not mean she is a free agent. Somehow, she is compelled by a momentum that she might not be aware of. The Mall is enshrined as the most significant entity in the society, to an extent that anyone excluded from it would become "one of the overlooked, the disregarded, [and] the discounted" (Lovegrove 28). A life without Days, as Lovegrove puts it, is "a monotonous tangle of dead ends and drudgery" (145). Therefore, it is Linda's fear of being financially excluded from Days like her deprived neighbours that fuel her desire for the membership. This is a fear of another Victorian value that Thatcher forgot, one that produced a society in which "a few got rich and most got hell" (Kinnock; qtd. in Samuel 13). A Silver card may have indeed provided Linda with an immense variety of consumer choices that are politicized as the source of power and identity formation, but meanwhile it also eliminates the very choice of *not* engaging in such a politics of credit and consumption. Everyone, including Linda herself, is involved in the same competition that none shall escape, though she is one of the lucky winners who must always be watchful not to violate the rules of the Mall, not to be kicked out.

From this perspective, the Mall is both inviting and enclosed. Its inviting façade extends a warm welcome to potential customers, showcasing a dazzling array of consumption possibilities and diversities through its shop windows. Yet, woven into this enticing display is an imperceptible barrier – an invisible wall that bars entry to those who fail to meet the stringent entrance requirements. The grandeur *inside* the Mall, connoted as images in advertisements and marketing campaigns, is delivered to the outside through window display deliberately to attract those like Linda who see consumption as the way to realize their dreams and aspirations. But here comes a paradox: it seems that people are bewitched not by the commodities on the shelves, not the *things* they really need, but by the *vision* of affluence that sometimes can be detached from physical items. Their desires are driven by what they see through the windows, the shopping catalogue and the advertisements, which are not always equivalent to the commodities they can purchase. Therefore, the moment when Linda and her husband Gordon finally have a chance to enter the Mall after all these years of hard work, the moment when they see the miraculous shopping windows, appears particularly interesting. Here, in front of the windows,

> Gordon is *mesmerised*. Whether by the sight of clumps of ragged, hunched, wind-blown human beings sitting or squatting or reclining before the one-storey-high windows along the edge of the building, or by the displays themselves, Linda cannot tell, but as she reaches his side, she finds her eye drawn to the window immediately to the left of the South-East Entrance, and all at once her eagerness to enter the store melts away, to be replaced by rapt, acquiescent fascination. (Lovegrove 73; emphasis added)

Linda's "acquiescent fascination" and the fact that Gordon is mesmerized are signs of their capitulation not to the things they are about to purchase, but to the *symbols* of "custom and commerce, of margins and mark-ups, of retail and revenue, of sales and success, of profit and plenty" (66–7), and to the immense possibilities they feel they can afford with money or credits. Their self-identities, in this way, are defined by what card they hold and how much they can spend in advance, and Days, similarly, transcends its original function as a shopping mall and becomes a temple of awe, wonder and spectacle that gives meanings to the pilgrims who "treat the Days logo with almost religious reverence" (11). Along with the mesmerization of the shoppers, there is also a fetishization of the shop windows, and of the Mall itself.

The shop windows, of course, are not something newly invented by Days. They have been important for interrogating urban transformation for centuries, such as in Charles Baudelaire's poem "The Eyes of the Poor." For Marshall Berman, the transparent "wall" standing in between the couple sitting inside the café and the poor family gazing from the outside as a "manifestation of class divisions" (Berman 153). The illuminated appearance of the dining couple by the light of the café has made them part of the window spectacle and forms a private space visible to the public, igniting a sense of envy and admiration from the passersby who do not belong to the class that can be allowed in.

By the end of the twentieth century, however, although the glass panel is still there to separate the privileged insiders and the excluded outsiders, the relations between the two sides have changed profoundly. During the

Thatcher years marked by the declining centrality of class and the boom of consumption, "ordinary" households that were not previously privileged like the couple in Baudelaire's poem were given an opportunity to climb up and become the insiders. Working families such as that of Linda and Gordon are frequently described by Thatcher with a "diffuse, mutable language of 'ordinariness,' hard-working respectability and family-centred individualism" (Lawrence and Sutcliffe-Braithwaite 134), for whom independence and self-responsibility are considered the most rewarding merits in a culture of enterprise. The Mall – the consumer dreamland, the place where people are differentiated by their credits, with a discourse built upon the politics of consumption – is no longer a house where, as Baudelaire wrote through the son in the poor family, "only people who are not like us can go." Instead, it is open to everyone, to every *ordinary* couple or family, because the entrance qualification is measured not by the wealth bound to class but by people's financial condition that can be improved through self-reliance, hard work and pursuit of personal aspirations.

Linda is certainly *ordinary* in a Thatcherite way. Like others, she has always yearned for a better life and a brighter future promised by the visions of affluence in the shop window. These visions, however, are more often endowed with semiotic or symbolic meanings that exceed the advertisement of commodities, indicating a utopian alternative to the financially excluded normality outside the Mall. If we borrow Rachel Bowlby's analogy between the shop window and a painting – which is "clearly framed, set off behind its exhibiting glass" and "draws spectators to it as something designed to be looked at" (Bowlby 59) – then what captivates Linda is in fact not the framed *painting,* but the *frame i*tself. When she was little, Linda and her mother often made "the pilgrimage [at Days] to see the Christmas displays" every year and stop at "*any* window that caught their eye and gaze in at [...] a cosy, firelit interior scene where the living mannequins would be busy decorating the hearth or wrapping gifts or singing carols" (Lovegrove 75–6; emphasis added).

These scenes of domestic harmony and happiness form a temporary hideaway or sanctuary where they can stay away from Linda's father, "a cold, distant brute of a man who kept his wife in her place" (51) but ended up being an annoying character no one likes. He is, in a way, a remnant of the past denied by the New Times, a personified reminder of the falling influence of working-class masculinity amidst a culture based on the shop floor. For Linda, as well as all the ordinary people she represents fighting for their aspirations, the actual commodities displayed behind the windows are considered less important than the very fact that something is there. What they look for through the windows is not a particular scene that narrates the story of a better life. What they care about are not the nuances between various window displays, which are "all essentially alike" (Lovegrove 73). They are, instead, pursuing the possibilities envisioned by the painting frame that is resonant with Guy Debord's conceptualization of "spectacle."

The Rise of the Spectacle: Collective Actions in Lightning Sales

At the very beginning of *The Society of the Spectacle* (1967), Debord claims: "In societies dominated by modern conditions of production, life is presented as an immense accumulation of *spectacles*. Everything that was directly lived has receded into a representation" (Thesis 1; emphasis in original).[1] In this rather short statement, two keywords appear to be essential to understand the spectacle: "modern conditions of production" and "representation," introduced based on Debord's word play on Karl Marx's "immense accumulation of commodities." For traditional Marxist critique, the capitalist mode of production has in its nature a tendency to alienate the workers from their products, from the act of production, from other workers and from their *Gattungswesen* (usually translated as "species being"). Marx, articulating the nature of alienation in "Economic and Philosophic Manuscripts of 1844," contends that labour does not only produce commodities:

1 Debord's *The Society of the Spectacle* (1967) consists of 221 numbered "theses," and therefore what appears in the bracket referring to this book are the numbers of the theses being quoted.

> it produces itself and the worker as a commodity [...] This fact expresses merely that the object which labour produces – labour's product – confronts it as *something alien*, as a *power independent* of the producer. The product of labour is labour which has been embodied in an object, which has become material: it is the *objectification* of labour. Labour's realisation is its objectification. Under these economic conditions this realisation of labour appears as *loss of realisation* for the workers; objectification as *loss of the object and bondage to it*; appropriation as *estrangement*, as *alienation*. (*Karl Marx* 272; emphasis in original)

In this way, as Marx elaborates further in "Comment on James Mill" (1844) since the means of production is rendered private and the conflict between the property owners and the propertyless workers remains irreconcilable,

> my work is *an alienation of life*, for I work *in order to live*, in order to obtain for myself the *means* of life [...] my individuality is alienated to such a degree that [the activity of working] is instead hateful to me, a torment, and rather the semblance of an activity. (*Karl Marx* 228; emphasis in original)

Labour is thus no longer a pleasure, no longer the way in which we can fully realize our potential as a social subject. It becomes forced, coerced and involuntary. For this, Marx famously points out that the alienating nature of labour in capitalism "emerges clearly in the fact that as soon as no physical or other compulsion exists, labour is shunned like the plague" (*Karl Marx* 274). According to Marx's theory of immiseration, while labour in the capitalist mode of production is considered a process of self-sacrifice, of mortification, while the tools and machines we use for working have turned against ourselves, becoming the master to whom we must all be subordinate, we might find, quite sorrowfully, that the more we produce, the deeper we are enslaved; the more wealth we create, the poorer we will become. Our labour capacities *per se*, embodied in and evaluated by the objects of our production, will then be regarded as materialized commodities that can be sold on the market like Days in Lovegrove's novel – an *estranged* place where social relations between people are perceived as the relations among things and *depersonalized* products.

From this point, Debord goes further. He describes this process of alienation as "an evident degradation of being into *having* – human fulfilment was no longer equated with what one was, but with what one possessed" (Thesis 17; emphasis in original). Beyond the first stage of alienation centred on labour and production, Debord borrows the term "spectacle" to conceptualize the second stage of alienation concerning "representation," that is the alienation from *having* to *appearing* where "all 'having' must now derive its immediate prestige and its ultimate purpose from appearances" (Thesis 17). Like the way in which social relations are mediated through things, this time, the world of things is mediated by images. Debord believes:

> When the real world is transformed into mere images, mere images become real beings – dynamic figments that provide the direct motivations for a hypnotic behaviour. Since the spectacle's job is to use various specialised mediations in order to *show* us a world that can no longer be directly grasped, it naturally elevates the sense of sight to the special pre-eminence once occupied by touch: the most abstract and easily deceived sense is the most readily adaptable to the generalised abstraction of present-day society [...] It is the opposite of dialogue. Wherever *representation* becomes independent, the spectacle regenerates itself. (Thesis 18; emphasis in original)

Of course, this "independent representation" that Debord discusses here, which will eventually lead to the formation of the spectacle, is neither entirely new nor unique to his time. To some extent, it can be traced all the way back to the Great Exhibition of 1851 and to Victorian England (Richards 17–72) and finds resonance in Walter Benjamin's discussion on the flâneur and arcades in the mid-nineteen-century Paris in *The Arcades Project*. But still, the difference between the Debordian Spectacle and its earlier forms is substantial. "The society of the spectacle" as Debord calls it, during a new age when the institutional and technical apparatus of mass media (especially television advertising) penetrates basically to every corner possible in our life, witnesses a structural transition towards an "upside-down world" based on an "inverted" reality. "In a world that is really upside down, the true is a moment of the false" (Thesis 9). This rather mystifying statement actually reveals to us the triumph of images and representation over the material form of commodities. The sense of *being touched* gives its way to the sense of *being seen*.

While such a sense of being seen can be quite typically represented by the window display of Days – which people from the ordinary households misperceive as the end of their pursuit for individual affluence – it is certainly not the only form of the spectacle in the novel. In fact, the Days spectacle appears long before the customers come to the Mall, before they are mesmerized by the live advertisements going on in the spectacular shop windows (and by the windows themselves), and even before they get in the cab or bus to start their shopping journey. The spectacle comes at the moment when they receive the envelope from Days after their membership application is approved, which contains not only the membership card but also the legal documents indicating their liability to honour the debt owed to Days and potential punishments for those who cannot behave themselves. The most important item in this envelope is a detailed shopping catalogue in which the spectacle is formed of the pictures, descriptions and advertisements of the commodities for sale.

The catalogue is immense, and supposed to be immense, because "it purports to list, and in many instances depict, *every single item* available at Days" (Lovegrove 23; emphasis added). Whatever you can imagine – be it daily necessities, exotic foods or costumes, reproductions of antiques like the exquisite carriage clock that looks exactly the same as the one damaged by Linda's father in her childhood (24) – it has been included in the catalogue for your reference. It can be taken as a considerate gesture from Days for its customers to prepare their shopping list in advance rather than to spend hours wandering in between the departments looking for what they might like to purchase. The "immensity" of the catalogue might indicate the incomparable ability of Days to buy and sell "anything you can possibly want, anything in the entire world [… and any] piece of merchandise in existence" (24).

But in an "inverted world" as Debord suggests, the relation between the Days catalogue, the actual goods and people's desire over specific commodities is also inverted. For those who have received a copy of the Days catalogue (which can be seen as a window to preview what they may want to buy), the window is not merely a window anymore. It is granted with an ontological commitment to define the very existence of what can be really sold. The "all-inclusiveness" of the catalogue from a pin to an elephant may have amplified the omnipotence of Days the shopping mall, but from an "inverted" perspective, we can also interpret it in the opposite way: only those items included in the catalogue can be considered commodities for sale.

The catalogue is no longer a faithful record nor is it an aesthetic presentation of Days's inventory. It *is* the inventory *per se*, since the visibility of commodities has become so significant that the production of things is transformed into the production of images; that the consumption of things should be firstly taken as the construction and spread of symbols, signs and representations. As Mr Bloom, head of Days security, says to Frank, an experienced store detective considering resignation: "Everything we have, everything we are, belongs to the store [...] And if you want to abandon all that, that's your prerogative, but bear in mind that without Days you'll be nobody" (Lovegrove 222). In this way, "commodification is not only visible, we no longer see anything else; the world we see is the world of the commodity" (Thesis 42). Our needs and desires are entwined so intricately to the Days catalogue that the definition of "everything" is reduced, narrowed and limited to "everything collected in this catalogue."

We are what we can buy; we buy what we can see; we see what we are guided to see – not the thing itself but the image of it; and we are guided by the "constant presence" of the spectacle that, as Debord claims, lies in the heart "of this real society's unreality" (Thesis 6). Image prevails over materiality, the spectacle over the product. It seems that, along with the rise of the society of the spectacle, the "inverted reality" may also lead to inverted relations of production that bring to the fore the voices of consumers, which coincides with the emergence of post-Fordism. Based on the example of Sainsbury's, Robin Murray has elaborated on the increasing influence of post-Fordism especially in the retailing industry, where "the emphasis [of production] has shifted from the manufacturer's economies of scale to the retailer's economies of scope" (Murray 43). Production priorities are no longer determined by the producer's prediction of the market trend but by consumers who can now increase their influence in market activities through their collective choices, behaviours, preferences and, mostly essentially, purchases.

Therefore, through the "vertical integration" from manufacturers to retailers and to consumers, "it is retailers," writes Daniel Miller, "who inform marketing and advertising as to trends in demand, and this in turn is fed back to producers and designers who *are told* to come up with a new [...] version of a familiar commodity in order to fulfil this aspiration" (4; emphasis added). What can be seen will be desired; what can be desired will be produced. Social subjects, in this post-Fordist discourse, are met with a different definition. They are not only the producers who make the product for *others* to consume but also the consumers themselves who work, at the same time, "to constitute [their own] desires and needs" (Best 48).

Considered another important factor of the *New Times* debate, post-Fordism is clearly the underpinning philosophy of the daily management of Days in Lovegrove's novel, with the retailer at the centre. One of the Day brothers, Sato, is such a faithful follower of numbers and the law of mathematics. Known for his enthusiasm in sitting "in front of the terminal watching takings from every department float up on the screen" and in cross-referencing the weekly report of profits and losses against other "gigastores" like Days around the world (Lovegrove 43), Sato reaches "a sensible decision" to resolve the conflict between the Books Department and the adjacent Computers Department. He believes that "Computers has a larger turnover of product and therefore demands a greater amount of display area. Books has been consistently running at a loss, so it seemed logical that it should surrender floorspace to its immediate neighbour" (99). Similarly, the landscape of all departments in Days is largely shaped according to their popularity among consumers:

> A kind of commercial vortex holds sway on the floors of Days: the closer you get to the centre of the building, the more popular the departments become. The most heavily in-demand departments with the fattest profit margins are clustered around the tiered hoops overlooking the Menagerie, while, at the opposite end of the retail scale, the departments that constitute the Peripheries are consigned to the far-flung edges by the slightness of their sales figures. (83)

Although some of the items on offer in the areas of the Peripheries could be of great value, they are, as Lovegrove puts it, "obscure, exotic, inessential, or just plain arcane," and thus, without enough customers interested in them, "trade is always slow and sales figures always low" (83). Dividing the heterogeneous market into hundreds of market niches that focus on a specific subgroup of targeted customers, the Day brothers are able to collect the accurate and timely first-hand data from their customers to keep a proper balance between demands and supplies.

Of course, post-Fordism not only concerns commodity supply. It is a broader term, "suggesting a whole new epoch distinct from the era of mass production, with its standardised products, concentrations of capital and its 'Taylorist' forms of work organisation and discipline" (Hall, "Meaning" 117). For some involved in the *New Times* project, this new epoch, marked by the decline of class-centred solidarity, signalled the emergence of a new identity developed upon the maximization of personal choices through consumption – a new collectivity based on individuality. One of the representatives of this strand of argument is Charles Leadbeater, who first came to widespread notice in the 1980s as a regular contributor to *Marxism Today* and later served as an advisor of Tony Blair's New Labour government concerning the knowledge economy. He wrote in 1988 that "Thatcherism has appropriated the individual and choice" and therefore "the Left needs a new progressive individualism if we are to win them back" (Leadbeater 14). This "progressive individualism," as Leadbeater stresses, appears necessary for a "renewed" version of socialism based on the expansion not of the public sector but of "the sphere of individual rights and responsibilities" (Leadbeater 14). It calls for not the individual consumerism that is usually related to the Thatcherite individualism (rendering people as independent atoms) but a vision of an "individually-based collectivism" (Leadbeater 15).

In this way, Leadbeater recognizes the importance of choice in consumption. This means that "the Left has to acknowledge the obvious: the market, competition, can be useful economic tools to deliver consumer choice" (Leadbeater 18). It provides a promising and efficient way to co-ordinate an array of decentred economic decisions in the post-Fordist era. Even more remarkably, the growing visibility of consumers and their socio-cultural influence (in contrast to the retreat of manual workers), at the same time, can be politicized and democratized as a justification of collective social actions:

> The Left has to renew confidence that collective social action is accountable to, and designed to fulfil, *individual needs*. It has to renegotiate the contract between those

> who finance collective services, those who provide them, and those who consume them, to ensure they provide value for money, efficiency, flexibility and choice. (Leadbeater 15; emphasis added)

But unfortunately, in Days – the "Universal Provider" taken as a fictional miniature of the consumption-based society – these collective actions that Leadbeater is convinced should be formed by individual choices in the marketplace also appears as a *spectacular* vision focusing more on the "frame" of the actions than the "paintings" they may contain. Even if some keen consumers like Linda find their way into the Mall (luckier than those "undeserving poor" gathering outside yet denied entry by the invisible wall made of transparent shop windows), they are still confined within the territory of the Debordian unreality. These collective actions, brought forth by the "individual needs" as Leadbeater has argued in the New Times project, are represented as nothing but an illusion embodied by what Lovegrove describes as the "lightning sale." It is nowhere near the rational appeals of consumer-individuals that Leadbetter expects to restore social justice but rather a blank collective unconscious.

The rules for a lightning sale at Days are simple. A certain discount would be applied in a random department for a random (usually short) length of time. In the novel, the announcement of a lightning sale is granted with a similarly mesmeric magic to the one that can be identified from the shop windows, the Days catalogue and other forms of the spectacle. As Lovegrove describes in great detail, after announcing such a lightning sale with a 15 per cent reduction in Dolls:

> The hush that descends on the store for the duration of the announcement is absolute. Then, as [the announcement] is repeated, shoppers begin to move. They drop whatever they are doing, and hoisting up their handbaskets or swinging their trolleys around or stamping down on the Go pedals of their motorised carts and spinning the steering wheels, they make for Dolls. Never mind that few of these people, if any, had the urge to buy a doll until now, and never mind that a fifteen percent discount hardly amounts to the offer of a lifetime, a lightning sale is a lightning sale, and it summons bargain-hungry customers like an aid convoy summons the starving. (Lovegrove 107)

During a lightning sale, customers may feel an unstoppable urge to rush to the department and buy the discounted items, even though they probably have never thought about buying them before. It is a promotion that only concerns the format rather than the commodities on sale, the frame rather than the painting.

Linda is involved in one of these lightning sales. While she tries to find a special tie for her husband as the souvenir for their first Days adventure, a lightning sale of five minutes takes place in the very department she is in. And once it is announced,

> The emotion that wells up in Linda Trivett then is too pure and blinding to sully with a name. It surges through her in a great white wave, clarifying her thoughts, sharpening her senses, purging her of uncertainty. She knows what she has to do, but more than that, she knows that this is what she was *born* to do. Never has she felt such an undiluted sense of purpose before. It races through her veins, as cold and clear as a subterranean stream. Deep in her being she is suddenly connected with all that is and all that was and all that is meant to be. (189; emphasis in original)

As we can see from here, what Linda wants during the lightning sale is not what she wanted before. Her rationality, self-discipline and clear life-planning that have earned her a membership from Days in the first place, which to a large degree fits the neo-Victorian society that Thatcher called for and forms the basis of collective social actions, suddenly gives way to blindness and even insanity. In these scenarios, people literally fight over something they would barely glance at elsewhere or in another time. The seemingly civilized dreamland of consumerism, during the lightning sales, becomes uncivilized, turning people into enemies, competitors and predators who resort to the economized logic of market calculation.

Therefore, the lightning sale at Days, as an embodiment of the collective social actions that Leadbeater observes from the consumption-based, post-Fordist society, constitutes another form of the Debordian spectacle. It creates isolated and fragmented bubbles of temporality and extends the Foucauldian concept of heterotopia (space of otherness) into the realm of time (time of otherness). It can thus be differentiated from the spatial spectacle such as the shop windows and the catalogue, formulating the "temporal" spectacle that is equally, if not more, narcotic, equally unreal, than the former. At the moment when a lightning sale ends, like when a window display is covered by curtains, there is "a collective sigh of disappointment from unsuccessful customers as they turn away from the cash registers, disgustedly discarding the [commodities] that only seconds ago they were frantic to buy" (Lovegrove 109). Some of them would even exchange apologies afterwards for their previous misconducts and antagonism when coerced in such alienated temporal bubbles, feeling confused because "*they don't know* what came over them" (109; emphasis added).

They don't know – that is the point, like the victims of the slake-moths in Miéville's *Perdido Street Station* who do not know how they are mesmerized and thoroughly exploited by these capitalist monsters; like the window shoppers lining up outside Days who do not know (or are not even aware of) why they are so interested in (and bewitched by) the shop windows *per se* regardless of what is really being displayed. This sense of confusion, especially for people finding themselves in the temporal spectacle such as the lightning sale at Days, chimes with Debord's own observation in his *The Society of the Spectacle*: "[T]he more [one] contemplates the less he lives; the more he accepts recognizing himself in the dominant images of need, the less he understands his own existence and his own desires" (Thesis 30). The second-stage alienation of the spectator from having to appearing as Debord argues can reinforce "the contemplated object that result from his own *unconscious* activity" (Thesis 30; emphasis added).

Here in a world governed by the production of the spectacle, here in the unreality where things are defined by the Days catalogue, the collective social actions developed upon individuality and the logic of consumption (which Linda embodies) apparently cannot provide the "culture of social responsibility to overcome the poverty, deprivation, insecurity, and inequality" (Leadbeater 17). The politicized consumers, in a similar manner, are granted with not a political subjectivity as promised but a collective unconscious (which the lightning sale represents) when they are involved in a seemingly progressive social action. Hiding behind these actions, behind these narcotic lightning sales, is the Days management – the Day brothers. They stay on the highest floor of the Days building, making themselves invisible to all their employees and customers, only showing up when a dispute has to be resolved (if they deem this profitable). They are, as I believe, in many ways as monstrous as the slake-moths, rendering the shop windows and the lightning sales as their mesmeric wings of the spectacle.

Money May Buy Life: Money Fetish in *Earth Province*

When Stephen Brooke revisits the *New Times* in retrospect, he connects the factors underpinning the project such as the decline of heavy industry, the fall of class mentality and the curtailment of union power to "the increasing presence of new technologies at the workplace" (Brook 23). He recalls his own personal stories back in the 1980s from using a manual typewriter to an Apple portable computer. This, he believes, is "a small example of the swiftness with which everyday life was reshaped in the eighties by global developments in technology" (Brook 25). In line with Brook's observations, scholars in previous decades have already emphasized the significance of technology in giving new meanings to the phenomena that had always existed. It was information technology that empowered retailers like Sainsbury's to quickly feed their everyday sales data back to the producer and in so doing make themselves the centre of post-Fordist transition (Murray 42–3). It was the credit scoring facilitated through new surveillance technologies that repositioned financial exclusion to make it so significant to so many ordinary households (Burton et al. 6). It was the new communication technologies that enabled an immediate transmission and circulation of transnational information and experiences (Struck et al. 575), which eventually contributed to the process of globalization that substantially reshaped the local manufacturing industries in the UK and sabotaged production-based unionization.

These non-fictional novums have all played a part in changing the political landscape where *New Times* scholars must also relocate themselves to understand the new mechanisms of identity formation and political engagement. However, technological progress never stops. As we have moved well into the twenty-first century, dramatic technological development in terms of the Internet, machine learning, cloud computing, big data analytics and social or algorithmic media in the last twenty years has formulated a newer discourse in politics, economics and culture, as well as newer forms of the spectacle. Therefore, our perception of the production-consumption dynamic should be modified to a further degree to acknowledge the emergent platform economy, digital labour and prosumer economy.

With this in mind, I will now move beyond the *New Times* vision for the 1980s and the 1990s and extrapolate into the new millennium represented in a novel of the Chinese Boom – *Earth Province* (*Diqiu sheng*, 2018), written by Long Yi. It prefigures a world where money is not merely the entrance ticket to the society of affluence but the God who governs all, where production and consumption converge to the extent that people shall literally pay for what they produce. It expands the shopping mall portrayed in *Days* to a planetary level, where people are no longer self-reliant subjects trying to buy into the spectacle through consumer choices – they are themselves placed on the shelf behind the shop windows and listed in the catalogue side by side with the other commodities.

While Long Yi is better known as an author of detective and spy fictions set in the 1940s Sino-Japanese war, *Earth Province* marks his inaugural venture into sf, and is yet to be translated into English. The novel's fictional city Xijing, divided into two parts (the Underground and the Overground), is solely established upon people's obsession with money, amounting to its literal deification. Meanwhile, under the "Life Extermination Law," men over 45 years old and women aged over 40 are sent to various "extermination centres" where they are killed by a special device embedded on their spine, a monitor of biological data called a "scorpion." As the protagonist, Qiao Wude, attempts to buy his way off the death list thirteen days before his scheduled extermination, he gradually realizes the shocking truth behind the Law and the scorpions: all the residents in the Underground city are merely products, to be *sold* as consumable meat to aliens after their legal extermination.

As Long Yi writes in the afterword of the novel, the reason why he wrote an sf novel is because of his "worries over the future" (Long Yi, *Diqiu* 309), a future where "people would see money as religion, greed as glory" (311), where the criteria of moral judgement and evaluation are reduced to merely a mathematical calculation of wealth and capital. *Earth Province* can be read as a manifesto against money and the world under its control, sketching out a world that Long Yi seeks to challenge and criticize where money is "rendered as the *only* form of value" and has penetrated literally every aspect of our lives (310; emphasis added). In a way, *Earth Province* is deeply connected to the author's observation of social concerns since the

1990s: "Even if we are not historians, economists, or other professionals, if we turn on the television or casually scroll through the Internet news, we often have the strange feeling that the world is no longer the same as it was a few decades ago, but rather a rigid and regressive version of that world" (309). And this "rigidity" and "regressiveness" of our contemporary world, Long Yi believes, should be both attributed to one single reason – money, together with its mesmeric powers to homogenize different things that are originally and essentially heterogeneous to each other.

Long Yi's self-explanation can be read as an anachronic continuation of the debate over the fall of "humanist spirit" (*renwen jingshen*) from around 1993 to 1995, which I have introduced in Introduction when mapping out the intellectual field for the emergence of the Chinese Boom. Although the intellectual elitists involved in this debate fail to agree on a single definition of what "humanist spirit" stands for, what they have argued for or against is clearly contextualized within the general cultural transition in China ignited by marketization and economization. It speaks to the phenomena that have surfaced "with the rise of the great tide of the market economy and business: money worship, the sacrifice of principle for profit, the loss of ideals, the disintegration of ethics" (Zhang Z. 176). It seems that people's concerns over money prevail upon their pursuit for spiritual richness, leading us to a world that is commercially prosperous yet spiritually barren – a world in which money transcends its material and physical origin and penetrates the spiritual domain in people's psyche.

In line with these arguments, Long Yi rejuvenates older critiques of the money fetish by sanctifying it as a new religion. "To live for God of Money is glorious; to die for God of Money is great" (Long Yi, *Diqiu* 11). The worship of money and the belief in what it can achieve formulate the basis of the ideology and social structure of Xijing. Perceiving money as an abstract and neutral form of value through which people can pursue the goals that usually cannot be pursued with direct and obvious actions, Long Yi expands the power of money beyond the pure market exchange of commodities and extends it to fields that are not normally covered by monetary transactions. Everything including social relations and human spirituality, is objectified, commodified and reduced in accord with the logic of money. Vacant positions in the government are open for the highest bidder. Friends and colleagues can be betrayed for a sufficient price. The loyalty of local warlords depends on how generous the emperor can be. Numerous kinds of taxes are levied not only for people's incomes but also for their very basic biological needs. With money, people can even escape death, getting away from their arranged extermination:

> Look for the clinics in the underworld. Two thousand yuan [monetary unit in the novel] for the surgery. One thousand for each extra year you live. And you can buy a scorpion of others and have it transplanted into your body [...] In this way, you can earn more money during your extra life and pay for even more years. (Long Yi, *Diqiu* 54)

Money may buy life. This claim, in *Earth Province*, is no longer a metaphor or an overstatement, but a realistic observation of what is literally happening in the fictional Xijing when people attempt to survive the Life Extermination Law. Here in this city, people's obsession with money and their practices according to the logic of the money economy in their social interactions is represented by their fetish of *Idioms of the Tribune*, a collection of sayings they quote so as to rationalize their self-interested, money-oriented decisions and behaviours. Here, the word "Tribune" in the title is detached from its Roman origin. The people living in the Underground city are told that Xijing is governed by a Tribune, which, however, is just a lie, as the Tribune is overtaken long ago and the city is now ruled by an emperor (Long Yi does not explain the nuances between the regime of the former Tribune and that of the current emperor). But still, the title "Idioms of the Tribune" is maintained, becoming an instrument of biopolitical governance. The "Tribune," therefore, can be seen as an imaginary embodiment of the God of Money.

Although Long Yi does not systematically list all the idioms in any clear order, he does cite more than forty-five entries to demonstrate how much the characters in the novel are influenced, captivated and even bewitched by the sayings. We can develop a general impression of the idioms through a few examples: "There is only one word for our core values – money" (Long Yi, *Diqiu* 33), quotes Doctor Mei Dusi when he bargains with the protagonist Qiao Wude for a fake scorpion; "One would be condemned by the God if not performing selfishness" (72), quotes Qiao Wude when he takes advantage of his unreliable colleagues; "Benevolence is like the human appendix, which has no function nor profit in it" (80), also quotes Qiao Wude, when he considers abandoning his partner and attempts to escape his extermination alone, a thought he gives up very soon.

People's intense enthusiasm for the idioms they cite to defend their belief in the God of Money, as a sign of devotion, reminds us of another compilation of sayings that has been worshipped and enshrined to a similar extent in China. That is *Quotations from Chairman Mao*, also known colloquially as the "Red Treasure Book" or the "Little Red Book" (*hong baoshu*). Considered "the most prominent icon" of the Cultural Revolution in China (1966–76) and "the ultimate guide to political action and moral behavior" for the Chinese populace (Leese 23), the Little Red Book was printed and reprinted numerous times, with at least billions of official and unofficial copies. Although the accurate publication figures can never be ascertained, what can be confirmed is its enormous political, social and cultural impact in Maoist China. Anything justified by a statement beginning with "Chairman Mao teaches us" would be put on the moral and political high ground, becoming the ultimate truths that invalidate any potential critique and challenge:

> Mao's Little Red Book represented a scriptural authority and emanated a sacred aura during China's Cultural Revolution. An intense religious atmosphere surrounded the activities and rituals of Mao's words. Everyday life was immersed in study sessions, discussions, lectures, public performances of Mao's poems and quotations, ritualistic confessions of one's errant thoughts, and nightly diary-writing aimed at self-criticism. (Wang Ban 266)

In line with this observation, *Idioms of the Tribune* in *Earth Province* can also emanate such a "sacred aura" and therefore indicate the "scriptural authority" in the name of money, leading to a cult not of a particular personality but of a "spectacle" embodied by the God of Money, a satirical reincarnation of the Little Red Book in a post-Maoist, market-based world. Through various ritualistic forms, money as "the God of our times" has converted everyone in Xijing into the modern religion developed upon the money economy.[2] As Charles Fitzgerald noted in 1976, Mao's writings by that time had "become to his own people in his own age what the *Sayings of Confucius* [i.e., the *Analects*] were to the Chinese people for the past two thousand years: the source of inspiration and guidance in matters social, political and moral" (Fitzgerald 1). And in a similar vein, we can also say that the idioms quoted from the God of Money, likewise, have become to those who live in a money-oriented society what the Little Red Book was to those involved in the Cultural Revolution, before the series of post-socialist reforms in the following decades.

By setting up this comparison between the Little Red Book and the idioms, however, I am not suggesting any direct historical or political reference to the Cultural Revolution in this novel. Also, it is certainly not a nostalgic attempt to re-establish the Maoist discourse out of the contemporality of vulgarization and marketization. Instead, by relating the idioms to the glorification of Mao's teachings and the consequential socio-political impact, we can notice a new round of revolution taking place in the cultural domain. This time, it is brought forward by people's obsession with money, together with the calculative or competitive logics behind it, which could reduce our pursuit for spirituality to the pursuit for the universal equivalent. The world based on money is the one in which "the highest moral aspiration is to gain one's profit at another's expense" (Long Yi, *Diqiu* 307) as indicated by the last idiom appearing in the novel – the central topic that concerns those intellectuals involved in the debate of the decline of humanist spirit.

Paying to Work: "Synergic Implosion" of Production and Consumption

Despite the presence of this overhanging debate on his novel, Long Yi also incorporates the social impact of technologies since 2000 and

2 Please see Georg Simmel's 1900 book *The Philosophy of Money*.

prefigures a new discourse where production and consumption are integrated to a further degree. In *Earth Province*, the foundation of individual autonomy for political engagement is no longer consumer choices over commodities in the marketplace nor a vision of affluence that they could buy into with credits. Instead, the residents of Xijing become simultaneously the subject and object of consumption, and in this way find themselves articulated with the politics of "prosumption," where the boundary between producers and consumers dissolves. Qiao Wude is one of those aware of their awkward situation in the society under the gaze of the God of money. As he reflects:

> He has to admit that he had been living like an "object" when looking back on his lifeline of forty-five years. Eating, drinking, assisting women to reproduce, offering bribes, taking bribes – and that's it. Even if he could get the big money and run away from his extermination with [his girlfriend], he would still feel like an "object," a rich "object." (Long Yi, *Diqiu* 107)

In fact, Qiao Wude is not only *like* an object. He *is* an object in the literal sense, and so is everyone else in the Underground city of Xijing. The cruellest truth he realizes as the plot develops is that the pillar industry of the Earth is officially stock farming, but here the stock being farmed and exported to alien worlds is actually human flesh, as well as the related sideline products. They are called "the Earth lamb" (*diyang*), which etymologically can be related to the phrase "two-legged sheep" or "two-legged lamb" (*liangjiao yang*) that was originally used to refer to victims of cannibalism in ancient China. Therefore, the so-called Life Extermination Law in this novel is executed in order to guarantee the "organic growth and timely maturity" of all the Earth lambs to be slaughtered (Long Yi, *Diqiu* 119), rather than because of resource scarcity as they are told by the Xijing government. And in this case, the slaughterhouses turn out to be the Extermination Centres where people are expected to spend the last few days before their planned extermination. After being terminated by the scorpions embedded in their spine, these people, killed just in time to satisfy the quality requirements of the alien importers, are sent to a mechanized meat processing sector, nothing short of the meat industry in our reality.

In this way, the boundary between human and animal livestock becomes ambiguous since the human bodies *per se* are considered consumable commodities, rendered as another material form of capital exploitation. According to Rosi Braidotti, this ambiguity that Long Yi builds up in his novel could lead to a new understanding of advanced capitalism. Based on Deleuze's concept of "becoming," capitalism is seen as "a differential engine that promotes the quantitative proliferation of multiple options in consumers' goods and actively produces deterritorialized differences for the sake of commodification" (Braidotti 41). All that lives, from us human beings to the animals we take as food, are therefore placed under a framework of "opportunistic commodification" (35) that forms the political economy of our times, which bio-genetically incorporates both human and other species into the logic of insatiable consumption. Human subjects are therefore reduced to such a degree, via the homogenizing power of money, that they are objectified to the same level as any other living and non-living objects around them, thus becoming nothing more than the potential sources of capitalist profits.

In other words, people find suddenly that the items that used to be displayed behind a shop window like those of Days are in fact themselves. The "Earth lamb" industry in *Earth Province* does not waste any profitable parts of the livestock. The high-quality "lambs," farmed in the Underground city and fed with nutritious, costly energy bars, go to the meat market and create a considerable trade surplus with alien buyers; while the low-quality "lambs," that is those who live in the Overground half of this city and suffer from famines, food shortage, over-population and pollution, can only be made into fertilizer and sold for grain cultivation (Long Yi, *Diqiu* 119). This business even includes their excretions, which are collected and "exported to the planet of Dung Beetle" (120) as an important nourishment for the aliens' reproduction. Eventually, and unsurprisingly, it leads to a discourse of necro-politics (Mbembe 11–40), where the survival of some (the ruling minorities of the Earth) depends on the death or even consumption of others (all the Earth lambs).

But meanwhile, we cannot and should not neglect the inherent differences between the "products" made of the Earth lambs in *Earth Province* and the commodities sold in Days. According to the consecrated *Idioms of the Tribune*, "One will be punished if not paying taxes on time and if preventing pregnancy" (Long Yi, *Diqiu* 6). And this, notably, indicates two essential obligations for the commoditized human subjects in the novel that other forms of commodity do not have to undertake: paying taxes and reproduction. People living in the Underground city of Xijing are required to pay taxes for literally everything in their life – not only for the money they earn through some difficult, dangerous or even nasty jobs but also for their biological needs for basic survival – eating, excreting and reproducing.

If we follow the same logic of the Earth lamb industry, having sex is in fact an indispensable "working procedure" to (re)produce livestock in a sustainable fashion, which can be considered a certain form of labour that should have been rewarded rather than taxed. Similarly, since human excrement is also a profitable commodity in the government's interplanetary business with aliens, the act of excreting could also represent people's active participation in social production. In such a productive process, the money people spend for taxes, consumption and relaxation is actually invested in the process of self-growth and self-cultivation, and in the making of satisfactory products – in this case, themselves.

Therefore, the necessary investment to maintain the Earth lamb industry in this novel, a burden that should have been taken by the emperor and other privileged aristocrats, is now dispersed to, and shared by each of the products through their daily cost to stay alive, until their planned slaughter required by law. Although money in the Underground city of Xijing may also bring the hope or possibility for some to survive beyond their legal extermination, by implanting a fake scorpion bought on the black market, this is still a temporary solution because a fake scorpion can only last for several days or at most several years (depending on the price). Before the termination of the fake scorpions, people will have to pay for another one with the money they have earned during the extra time of their lives.

Here, the hope that money may bring appears as nothing more than a dangling carrot. The more they are involved in such a cycle of paying for new scorpions, the deeper they are trapped in an endless process to keep postponing the day when they will be killed, processed and shelved for aliens. And they do this as a producer, a consumer and a product at the same time, contributing to the surplus value to be taken by the capitalists without being paid properly (or at all) for their labour. This indicates a new strand of political economy and identity formation, one that emerges as a "synergic implosion" of both production and consumption in a context termed "prosumer capitalism" (Ritzer and Jurgenson 14), a process "toward unpaid rather than paid labor and toward offering products at no cost" (19).

Consumption is certainly never independent from production, but the act of shopping usually requires some time out of work and thus draw a boundary between being a consumer in the marketplace and being a producer in their workplace. If we look back at Lovegrove's *Days*, we notice that to venture inside the Mall, Linda and her husband Gordon have to spend the time and energy that could have been invested in their daily jobs. At an early point in the novel when they just received their membership card, Linda, a hairdresser, and Gordon, working in a bank, have an unhappy argument on which day they should begin their maiden trip in the spectacular Days:

> Gordon pointed out that he couldn't afford to take a day off work [on a weekday], not if they were to maintain the level of income necessary to keep the use of the card, so therefore if they went, it would have to be on a Saturday or not at all. Linda replied that Saturdays were her busiest – and therefore most lucrative – hairdressing days, and that if *he* took a day off sick he got paid, whereas she did not. (Lovegrove 22; emphasis in original)

As we can see from this conversation, Gordon's reluctance to ask for a day off is in line with a solid and apparent reason, especially during a time when he needs to work extra hard for a potential promotion and when, in a broader context, "missing a day can […] mean the difference between employment and the dole queue" (23). But the same reason can also be applied to Linda's hairdressing business which, equally apparently, expects more customers and therefore more income during weekends. No matter which day they choose (a Thursday eventually), at least one of them must temporarily stop offering their services and sacrifice their occupational roles in the general social production. Although this conversation mainly arises as an implication of Linda and Gordon's different personalities and to insinuate their later behaviours at Days, it has also indicated a fact that since shopping malls like Days can be considered an urban heterotopia of consumerism, being in this heterotopia means being out of the rest of the city.

The transparent shop windows, therefore, stand in between the world of producers and that of consumers, separating the capitalist exploitation of each of them into isolated time-space. In prosumer capitalism, however, this window is broken. And upon the absence of this borderline, there develops a new mechanism that George Ritzer terms "synergistically double exploitation," through which the respective exploitations of labourers and consumers are "increasingly likely to take place in the same setting (including online, at home amidst the family, as well as in other elements of the social factory) and often at about the same time" (Ritzer, "Prosumer" 426). From this perspective, this "synergy" of exploitation in such a prosumer society forms the basis of the Earth lamb industry in *Earth Province*. People living in the Underground city of Xijing, on the one hand, have to pay numerous kinds of fees and taxes in excess of what they can afford, while on the other hand, by keeping themselves alive (particularly including the acts of excreting and making love) they are in fact engaging in the process of production and reproduction.

This is probably the future that the author Long Yi is truly afraid of as he has noted in the afterword of *Earth Province* (Long Yi, *Diqiu* 309). His worries and concerns have also been elaborated further in an article he wrote for *Wenyi bao* (*Literature and Art Newspaper*) in March 2018 titled "The True Terror Comes from Ourselves," two months after the novel's publication:

> When I first started to think of *Earth Province*, an industrial giant in the Internet economy just claimed: "Big data is becoming the future currency." This claim was euphemistic due to its high-tech premise, which, when translated into the vernacular, meant "big data is money." The potential value of data has now been well perceived, but the subtext underneath this "claim" is so obvious that it goes unnoticed. This subtext is the very old idea that "money is power."
>
> Thus, with years of thinking and reflection, I wish to present a novel based on the claim "money is power," design a related social structure, then try to break it. This is *Earth Province*. (Long Yi, "True" n.p.)

In a way, Long Yi's critique of the money fetish and its socio-cultural impact, to a large degree, keeps to the traditions dating back to the debate over the humanist spirit in the 1990s. But here, I would like to emphasize the historical context that draws Long Yi's attention towards "big data," in which the economics based on social or algorithmic media increasingly dominate people's lives (Tapscott and Williams 2006), a trend which has also foregrounded the significance of prosumption in the past decade.

The economic norms of "prosumption," though, predate the twenty-first century. Its precedents, under the logic of self-service, had already appeared in various forms such as the McDonaldized fast food industry that incorporates customers themselves into the process serving food; the supermarkets that encourage shoppers to use the self-checkout kiosks; the call-in radio show that needs the active participation of the callers; the ATM machines that turn the customers into bank tellers and even require extra fees. But still, a turning point is not reached until the age of participatory virtual platform with extensions into our realities, such as Facebook, Twitter, YouTube and Wikipedia, where people are allowed, and in some cases requested, to generate their own content and creations on an un(der)paid basis and contribute to the commercial success of these companies. In the ninth version of Ritzer's 1993 book *The McDonaldization of Society* (2018), he explains why digital businesses have achieved so much in promoting the prosumer economy online compared to their traditional counterparts:

> While brick-and-mortar sites have long done this, most notably McDonald's efforts to get consumers to perform tasks traditionally performed by paid workers, this is accomplished much more easily and extensively on Internet sites where it is hard, if not impossible, for consumers to find workers to help them. In the main, if prosumers online want something done, they have little choice but to do it themselves. (Ritzer, *McDonaldization* 51)

These Internet giants have managed to collectively formulate a market in which people's creativity and sociality can be commodified and sold in a virtual shopping mall where users have to pay to consume what they have produced, a mall that can be called "Me-Mart." At the beginning of Aleena Chia's provocative essay, "Welcome to Me-Mart" (2012), she parodies the propaganda put about by the Internet platforms to invite contributions from the users:

> Welcome to the participation revolution, the peer-production revolution, the mass collaboration revolution. Welcome to the future, of books, music, television, and

> computers, where you can be your own author, musician, performer, programmer, publisher, broadcaster, and publicist. Welcome to the new Internet, where you can create anything, with anyone, at any time, at minimal cost, for everyone to see, read, hear, comment on, buy, and recommend. You are your own news empire, your own media conglomeration, your own public relations giant. (Chia 422)

Although China did not quite go through the age of McDonaldization in the mid-twentieth century when, as Ritzer observes, the prosumer economy began to be institutionalized, the propaganda calling for such a Me-Mart has nonetheless become extremely popular in China, especially since the 2010s.

Encouraged by favourable policies from the government, China has developed an incomparable market in terms of scale and user-generated content circulated through various participatory virtual platforms such as Weibo, WeChat, Bilibili, Douban, Douyin (TikTok), Xiaohongshu and other places for user co-creation. According to *The 47th China Statistical Report on Internet Development* published in February 2021 by China Internet Network Information Center (CINIC), the number of Chinese netizens, including those who use mobile phones and cellular data, reached 989 million by December 2020, an increase of 43.7 per cent during the past five years. Also, by the end of 2020, the aggregate market value of Chinese listed companies in the Internet industry amounts to 16.8 trillion *renminbi* (2.6 trillion US dollars). Apart from the listed companies there are 207 Internet "unicorns," privately-owned start-ups worth over one billion US dollars. Given this market prosperity, these companies, with their surprising creativities, have designed and promoted numerous forms of prosumption that aim at drawing users into the process of content production where it is consumers who are expected to invest money, time and energy to produce the immaterial commodities that will be sold back to themselves – a process represented quite faithfully by the Earth Lamb industry in *Earth Province.*

The Politics of Prosumption

A shocking example of marketing in the prosumer economy, as well as the "synergistically double exploitation" (Ritzer) involved here, is a promotion campaign on Weibo launched by Tangdaren, a well-known brand for instant noodles in China. On 27 April 2021, they released an unfinished video advertisement starring Wang Junkai (Karry Wang) in which the visual effects are still left in a primitive stage.[3] Relying on Wang's enormous celebrity influence among his fans and across society, Tangdaren sent out a call-for-contributions to invite the public to propose their ideas on animation design and participate in the process of video production. The contributor with the best-received ideas was promised a "handsome" award – a signature photo of Wang Junkai – while others would be listed in the "special thanks" at the end of this video. We are not entirely unfamiliar with the prosumer economy after all we have witnessed in the age of, to use an old-fashioned term, Web 2.0. But in this case, it is still surprising to realize, and hard to believe, how effective and how convenient the monetary cost (outsourcing the video production to commercial partners), which should have been borne by the company, can be transferred to Wang's fans, the users of Weibo, or in another word, prosumers: a process pretty much resembling the Earth lamb industry in *Earth Province* where people should pay (money, time, their lives) for what they produce.

Although this campaign immediately provoked widespread controversies online, with the marketing team of Tangdaren quickly declaring that they have hired a group of properly paid professionals to work on the rest of the video and soon released the finished version, the underpinning philosophy had already penetrated other industries long before this public relations crisis.[4] The idol economy, the enthusiastic production of fansub and fan literature and even our voluntary efforts of adding to our online personal profiles such as LinkedIn and ResearchGate – for all these domains where the prosumer economy may take place, there will always be active and passionate contributors willing to do unpaid work. Usually they do this for worship (for idols), for hobbies, leisure, skill training, self-publicity or just for updating their CVs. These should all be acknowledged. But even so, we

3 This video is available at <https://www.bilibili.com/s/video/BV1cK4y1Z7S1>.

4 The finished version of this video is available at <https://www.youtube.com/watch?v=nuE6ASdpQ3w>.

still need to be vigilant and alerted to a new form of capitalist exploitation, one that interpenetrates both production and consumption, that dissolves the boundary between our producer and consumer identities, and most importantly, that incorporates what used to be excluded or neglected into the gaze of capital.

Therefore, Long Yi's novel can be read as not only an intentional critique of the money fetish in contemporary society, as he points out himself in the afterword and in the interviews. Beyond this, however, *Earth Provinces* also indicates the rising influence of prosumption in political economies that could lead to another socio-political transition concerning the formation of individual autonomy and identity. Since the entire planet is turned into a mall-like Days, since commodities are now required to (re) produce themselves, the political landscape in this novel transcends both the politics of class and of consumption that have been debated by the *New Times* scholars in the 1980s. It proposes the politics of prosumption.

With a dissolving boundary between production and consumption, between work and leisure, the victims of the Earth lamb industry find themselves being exploited as consumers who resort to the money fetish that Long Yi has intentionally criticized and as producers who produce their own bodies and excretions to be sold to aliens. Sleeping, eating, breathing and having sex are therefore commoditized and supervised by the data-collecting devices (like the scorpions). People have no other choice but "to pay for the privilege of doing the work as well as for what they gain from it" (Ritzer, "Prosumer" 434). The unchanged momentum of capitalism to colonize non-capitalist territory is then pushed to its spatial and temporal extremes in *Earth Province*; exploitation extended to twenty-four hours a day and seven days a week, for which the production site and the marketplace converge into one, not some factories, not the shopping malls like Days, but Earth itself. The lingering spirit of the slake-moths grows even more enormous and formidable, from which no one can ever escape, and this, as I will argue in the next chapter, will lead us to an age of, in Liu Cixin's popular phrase, the Dark Forest.

CHAPTER 5

Past the Point of No Return: Economization and Deterritorialization in Liu Cixin's *Three-Body* Trilogy and M. John Harrison's *Kefahuchi Tract* Trilogy

> Anything sufficiently weird must be fishy [...] I'm saying that there's always someone behind things that don't seem to have an explanation.
>
> – Da Shi, in *The Three-Body Problem*, p. 133

> Uncertainty is all we have. It's our advantage. It's the virtue of the day.
>
> – Lens Aschemann, in *Nova Swing*, p. 21

Finally, it is now time to move towards Liu Cixin's *Three-Body* trilogy (2006–10), the most influential piece of the Chinese SF Boom so far, second to none in terms of its literary achievement, scholarly acknowledgement and, most remarkably, market success. In this chapter, my discussion begins with an anecdotal reflection on the impact of the *Three-Body* trilogy. It explores its emergence as the source of a market boom and its resonance with readers who view it not merely as fiction, but as a reflection of their market-driven reality. The messages conveyed through the Dark Forest discourse in this trilogy call for a winner-takes-all mindset in a Social Darwinian cosmology and formulate a binary dichotomy between the Self and the Other, between the centre and the periphery, between us and them. Everyone else apart from the Self is turned into enemies lurking around. Everything else apart from our own survival is considered unimportant and can be sacrificed anytime. Surprisingly, however, an alternative to this discourse can be abstracted from M. John Harrison's *Kefahuchi Tract* trilogy (2002–12) which, according to my PhD supervisor James Kneale in an email, "could not be more different" to Liu Cixin's works.

The Dark Forest considers our universe a dark place where "the only moral imperative is the recognition of zero morality, and all intelligent species *compete* to *destroy* other species" (Song M., "Liu Cixin's" 116; emphasis added). According to Liu Cixin's poetic and oft-cited description in *The Dark Forest* (2008):

> The universe is a dark forest. Every civilization is an armed hunter stalking through the trees like a ghost, gently pushing aside branches that block the path and trying to tread without sound. Even breathing is done with care. The hunters have to be careful, because everywhere in the forest are stealthy hunters like him. If he finds other life – another hunter, an angel or a demon, a delicate infant or a tottering old man, a fairy or a demigod – there's only one thing he can do: open fire and eliminate them. (Liu, *Dark* 484)

Such a sense of destruction and elimination can be identified in every civilization of the *Three-Body* universe, especially the Earthlings and the Trisolarans, alongside other worlds that are technologically more advanced.[1] The key to the eventual triumph in the game of survival, therefore, is related to one of the most frequently quoted lines from the *Three-Body* trilogy: "If I destroy you, what business is it of yours?" (Liu, *Dark* 417).

To be or not to be – this classic Shakespearean dilemma takes on new meaning in the Dark Forest, transformed into another choice: to see or not to see. In the discourse of zero morality, where all are enemies and therefore should be eliminated upon discovery without hesitation, boundary becomes crucial for the Dark Forest hunters. Any attempt to breach the boundary and breaking into the horizon of other civilizations, voluntarily or not, would be a fatal offence. To "hide well" and to "cleanse well" (Liu, *Death's* 468), to protect themselves and to destroy others, this is the key that will eventually lead to survival. In Deleuze and Guattari's terminology, the subjects in the *Three-Body* trilogy – embodied not by individual characters but by the general entity of different rival civilizations – are

1 The Trisolaran world is the most important alien civilization in the trilogy, appearing as the enemy of humanity in *The Three-Body Problem* and *The Dark Forest*, and eventually driven away because the location of both Earth and the Trisolaris are exposed to more powerful "hunters" in the universe.

"territorialized" as a place where the Multiple always originates from the One in a "tree" structure, where the Other is always reduced to the Self and where the Dark Forest cosmology itself appears hegemonic because an invisible hand is pulling subjects of diversity into the abyss of sameness (see Deleuze and Guattari 3–25). It is also a place of battle where the dark forest hunters are turned into "human capital," whose major preoccupation is "capital growth or appreciation" (Feher 27), or at least the prevention of their own depreciation.

The Kefahuchi Tract in Harrison's novels, however, provides a site of "deterritorialization," an alternate place where the molar line in Liu Cixin's *Three-Body* trilogy is no more, replaced by the "line of flight" emerging along with the formation of a "rhizome." As the narrative focus of Harrison's trilogy, the Kefahuchi Tract refers to an unfathomable area in the universe beyond the comprehension of sentient creatures in all forms. It is a weird heterotopia in which all rules are annulled, all science invalidated and all structures deformed and merging into one another. It is "a singularity without an event horizon" (Harrison, *Light* 93), "a kind of light-years-wide interstellar *honeypot* whose epistemological and ontological mysteries have created rifts/riffs in reality that have haunted Alien species for aeons, and humans more recently" (Clute, "Harrison"; emphasis added). In a way, Harrison's imagination of the Kefahuchi Tract can be traced back to Arkady and Boris Strugatsky's *Roadside Picnic* (1972), in which six Visitation Zones, appearing after an extra-terrestrial event, provide an inexplicable place that exhibit weird phenomena and contain artefacts with seemingly supernatural properties. As John Moore argues, in these Zones portrayed in *Roadside Picnic*, "the ultimate semiotician, whose very survival depends on the correct interpretation of signifiers, rejects signs for immediacy" (J. Moore 75).

Likewise, in the Kefahuchi Tract, the meaning of the system – borrowing from Brian Massumi's comments on the *rhizome* conceptualized in *A Thousand Plateaus* (1980) – has been changed "from closed to open, univocal to rhizomatic, simple to complex, clarifying to problematizing" (Massumi, "Deleuze" 566). It has composed a plane of immanence where there is no beginning nor end, where any single point can be connected to any other without being converged to "the One" in the logic of sameness, where things are always in-between, always in transition and always *becoming*.

This chapter, therefore, is centred on the term "rhizome." Based on the unprecedented market boom of Liu Cixin's *Three-Body* trilogy, I will introduce the alienation, or economization, of social subjects not as human beings but as human-capital and human-enterprise, not only in post-socialist China but also other countries embracing privatization and marketization. This will reveal the molar, binary logic of the Self and the Other in the process of economization through close reading and explain why the competitive, calculative and eventually, bestial nature of the dark forest is so widely welcomed by the beneficiaries of our increasingly neoliberalized society.

Such a transition from human beings to human capital is usually credited to neoliberalism as Michel Foucault suggested during his lectures at the Collège de France. As I mentioned in Introduction, while post-socialist China does not neatly fit into the mould of a neoliberal state akin to Thatcherite Britain, certain neoliberal elements, such as the permeation of market competition into various social spheres, have undeniably exerted a profound influence on Chinese society. To probe into this transition further, I will then bring in Deleuze and Guattari's ideas of rhizome, line of flight, deterritorialization and haecceity, discussing how these ideas are represented in Harrison's *Kefahuchi Tract* novels and how they can be borrowed to challenge the Dark Forest mindset, formulate an alternative social order other than that of capitalist realism, and invoke the hope for a Blochian *not-yet*.

Behold the *Three-Body* Boom: Dark Forest as the Bible

When Liu Cixin won the Arthur C. Clarke Award for Imagination in Service to Society in November 2018, I was, purely by chance, in the middle of writing a book chapter on both names. I realized instantly that Liu Cixin probably would have to deliver a speech as the awardee, one that I could use as a reference. He did indeed make a speech, reiterating his long-time respect for Clarke, the man he sees as his mentor in writing sf. Although I could have guessed what Liu Cixin might have to say on this occasion, I was still struck by the way he described reading Clarke's works:

> My mind opened up like it has never before. I felt like a narrow stream finally embracing the sea. At midnight when I finished reading *2001: A Space Odyssey*, I walked out of the house and stared at the starry sky. I was able to see the galaxy, thanks to the unpolluted sky of China back then. That night, I noticed that the starry sky looked nothing like before. For the first time in my life, I was awed by the magnitude and mystery of our universe, the feeling which you only get [when] facing religion. (Liu, "Remarks" n.p.)

Liu Cixin's words precisely echoed my sentiments upon completing his *Three-Body* trilogy one winter evening in 2013. In the following years, I witnessed Liu Cixin win awards, become a phenomenon, gain a global reputation and popularity and achieve what Yan Feng anticipated as early as in 2008: "single-handedly elevat[ing] Chinese science fiction to a world-class level on his own" (Yan F., "Chuangshi" 74). In fact, Yan Feng's observation of Liu Cixin's achievement was a little exaggerated. Already an important writer in Chinese sf since the 1990s, Liu Cixin was not well recognized outside this genre until the late 2000s. This is related to the general marginalization of sf in a literary spectrum dominated by "serious" or "realistic" works. As Fei Dao (another writer of the Chinese Boom) recalls his experiences of attending an academic conference in 2008, sf back then was "one of the keywords tagged by most people's [mental] firewalls as useless information," one that had to be tossed over the firewall "so that they had to evaluate it anew instead of automatically ignoring it" (Fei Dao 475). Therefore, Yan Feng's compliment was also part of this "tossing-over" endeavour to make sf visible in a larger horizon, where Liu Cixin can be found in a "subtle and complex relationship with mainstream literature that is both continuous and paradoxical, and this relationship could in turn offer significant insights into our understanding of the qualities and dilemmas of Chinese literature and its future direction" (Yan F., "Chuangshi" 73).

Yan Feng and Fei Dao did not have to wait too long to see *Three-Body*'s sensational success, as well as its social and cultural impact both in and outside China, both in and outside sf fandom. The third instalment

Death's End sold a hundred thousand copies within one month of its initial publication in November 2010, and by the end of 2020, the whole trilogy had sold twenty-nine million copies worldwide, including three million in twenty-six non-Chinese languages.[2] The trilogy was nominated for multiple international sf and fantasy awards such as the Nebula, Locus, Prometheus and John W. Campbell Memorial Awards, with the first volume – *The Three-Body Problem* (2006), translated by Ken Liu – winning the Hugo Award for Best Novel in 2015. According to the thirteenth "Writer Rich List" released by Great Star Media in 2019, Liu Cixin has become the most profitable writer in China with his annual copyright income of 18 million *renminbi* (2 million GBP, mostly generated from the sales of the *Three-Body* trilogy), 16 per cent more than the runner-up Yu Hua, author of a series of highly acclaimed works of "serious" literature such as *To Live* (1993) and *Chronicle of a Blood Merchant* (1995).[3]

Such a *Three-Body* Boom in the market can be cross validated by the IPO prospectus of Shanghai Duke Book Co., Ltd, the current copyright agency for the e-books of the *Three-Body* trilogy. According to their information disclosed to the China Securities Regulatory Commission, in 2019 the agency has paid 12.28 million *renminbi* (1.37 million GBP) to Liu Cixin, which means they would expect a gross income of at least 27 *renminbi* (3 million GBP) from their contract with Liu Cixin (Shanghai Duke Book 336). I should point out here that apart from the *Three-Body* trilogy, Duke Book has also purchased the e-book copyrights for Liu Cixin's *The Supernova Era* (2004) and *Ball Lightning* (2005) as a bundle of contractual agreements. But still, the *Three-Body* trilogy accounts for the majority of their e-book market. Although the copyright agency for the trilogy's paperback publication (*Science Fiction World* and Chongqing Publishing Group) has not disclosed the relevant sales data to the public, the fact is obvious: the *Three-Body* trilogy has become *the* bestseller of the last decade in China's sf market, one that forms a cultural mark and niches itself well

2 I would like to thank Dr Zhang Feng (also known as San Feng), visiting scholar at Centre for Science and Human Imagination, Southern University of Science and Technology, for providing the relevant information.

3 Please see <http://zuojiabang.cn/Rangking/List?n=13&t=47>, accessed on 4 July 2021.

in a wider social context. As Cao Xuenan puts it: "[T]he wide accessibility afforded by the book form found Liu gaining visibility as a *writer*, rather than an *sf* writer" (188; emphasis in original).

Witnessing such an unstoppable *Three-Body* Boom from the 2010s onwards, I find myself, on the one hand, excited for the trilogy's popularity and market recognition. On the other hand, however, I also remain sceptical and concerned about the ecstasy expressed by the trilogy's rapidly expanding readership, one that has exploded far beyond its original fan base. Apparently, the *Three-Body* trilogy is not the beginning of the Chinese SF Boom, but it is certainly the highlight. I begin to wonder: why *Three-Body*? Why is this trilogy so popular in China that it has travelled beyond the domain of sf and into various mainstream cultural spheres? How could we make sense of the general social background in which such a popularity emerged in the first place?

There have been a number of academic discussions of the ways in which Chinese and Anglo-American readers have received the *Three-Body* trilogy. People tend to focus on the representation of the Cultural Revolution and the publisher's self-censorship (Cao 187), techno-progressivism as a method for achieving Chinese socialist realism (Moran 120), or Liu Cixin's ecocritical reworking of Rachel Carson (Erney 85). Yet, as I mentioned earlier, it is the Dark Forest theory that has led to the most profound, irreplaceable socio-cultural impact within mainland China. In Liu Cixin's own words, the Dark Forest prefigures "the worst of all possible universes [… where] existence is as dark and harsh as one can imagine" (Liu, "Worst" n.p.).

The Dark Forest metaphor has found an unexpected dynamism in China and new interpretations of the metaphor continue to emerge outside the realm of canonical sf or even literature in general. Established entrepreneurs in China or CEOs of listed companies often evoke this metaphor as a timely justification for their competitive and calculative mentality, with the social subjects reproduced and redefined in a post-socialist discourse. One of the keen advocates of the Dark Forest is Lei Jun, CEO of Xiaomi, a leading electronics company in China that makes and invests in smartphones, laptops, consumer electronics and home appliances. During a panel discussion in 2018 organized by Morningside Venture Capital, Lei Jun claimed: "It is the *Three Body* trilogy that I would recommend most eagerly to other people in the last ten years [...] it serves as an important source of inspiration for commercial and market strategies."[4] Unsurprisingly, this declaration echoes that of many other successful entrepreneurs in China, including Ma Huateng (Tencent), Zhou Hongyi (Qihoo 360) and Li Yanhong (Baidu).

For a time, especially after *The Three-Body Problem* won the Hugo Award in 2015, the Dark Forest has become a fashion in China. Numerous blog articles about this imagined universe written by business commentators and practitioners circulated on various social media platforms. These articles advocated for a rationalization of the winner-takes-all Social Darwinist conceit of business and social competition that accompanied the fundamental socio-cultural transformation in China since the 1990s, alongside a new wave of Chinese sf. As I discussed in Introduction when mapping out the historical background of the Chinese Boom, this marks a transition from "relying on the state" to "relying on oneself," where a series of social welfare programmes that used to be collectively provided via SOEs and public institutions (*shiye danwei*) have now been gradually stripped off in the process of privatization. In this context, the Dark Forest has even been considered "the Bible" (Ji and Zheng 259) not only for profit-driven businesses but also for "economized" (Çalışkan and Callon 369–98) individuals and post-socialist subjects who were inescapably embedded in the decentralized society without social protection.

These post-socialist subjects, losing their "iron rice bowl" as well as the sense of socialist centrality attached to it, are rendered as the "hunters" of Liu Cixin's Dark Forest. "Hunting" here alludes to the ongoing process of marketization in China, where guaranteed tenures are being replaced in SOEs, hospitals, schools, universities and research institutes by renewable, short-term contracts to maximize employers' flexibility. Employees can only earn contract renewals by demonstrating immediate and foreseeable productive outcome. This casualization engenders an eerie sense of uncertainty, confusion and stress, arising from workers' concerns of losing and being eliminated from social competitions, just like all the civilizations in

4 A video clip of his panel speech is available at <https://www.sohu.com/a/279849713_378279>.

the *Three-Body* trilogy. No matter how advanced these civilizations may become in terms of technology, they forever live with the fear of being destroyed by other hunters in the Dark Forest. In a similar vein and under the slogan "to get rich is glorious" developed upon former state leader Deng Xiaoping's "cat theory," wherein economic development became the prime directive, China has witnessed a dramatic economic boom since the 1990s.

The unprecedented popularity of Liu Cixin's Dark Forest theory both within and beyond the domain of sf and literature, therefore, becomes less unexpected once interrogated under the broader socio-cultural transition in post-socialist China that fostered the Chinese Boom. Previous studies of the *Three-Body* trilogy have commonly considered the competitive and Social Darwinist nature of the Dark Forest and its "zero-morality" situation as among Liu Cixin's key areas of focus. These include his generally critical, but sometimes melancholic, reflections on the Cultural Revolution (Song, "Liu Cixin's" 116–22), his pessimism about human morality in the face of apocalyptic crises and technological determinism (Li H., "Twentiy-First" 658–63; Liu Cixin, "Beyond" 22–32) and the irreconcilable tension between his configuration of the Self and the Other that is usually connected to the violence of modernity (Sun, "Alien" 610–44; Lyu, "Dark" 175–92). What these studies have not commented on, however, is how the Dark Forest fits into the larger context of market competition in China's socio-cultural transition since the 1990s and how the Dark Forest may offer ways of addressing the impact of "economization," as well as the remaking of social subjects into human capital.

Liu Cixin refrains from explicitly discussing politics in his works. Even so, it is also noted that "in spite of Liu Cixin's protestations of artlessness and his politically prudent assertions of being an unpolitical writer, his novel has both more political depth and more aesthetic sophistication than its author appears inclined to claim" (Erney 82). He tends to create various forms of thought experimentation that depict "humanity's relationship with the natural world" and "the effects of extreme situations on human behaviour and social systems" (Liu, "Beyond" 26, 29). From this perspective, the *Three-Body* trilogy may be considered a successful experiment; however, the question remains of why it is this series, and no other work among the fairly large corpus of the Chinese Boom, that has gained such high popularity precisely during a time of market-oriented socio-cultural transition and privatization in China. Why does the Dark Forest mentality work so well in the context of commercial and market competitions?

These are the questions my reading of the Dark Forest cosmology attempts to answer. The Dark Forest, I suggest, should be read as an allegory for the post-socialist reality in China, where the logic of market competition and calculation have penetrated all social spheres. It is exactly for such reasons that the Dark Forest is so famous and influential among Chinese entrepreneurs and economized individuals, who, inspired by the *Three-Body* trilogy, see contemporary China as a hunting ground where one needs to fight, to kill and to take. Considered the "Bible" for and a justification of their business rivalries, this trilogy can also be read as a reflection of the sense of stress, risk and uncertainty that post-socialist subjects in China have been suffering from.

People as "Non-people": The Dehumanizing Impulse of the Dark Forest

> "You mean that in this environment, people will become new people?"
>
> "New people? No, Lieutenant Colonel. People will become … non-people." (Liu, *Dark* 447)

This conversation, taking place in *The Dark Forest*, serves as a crucial demonstration of the transformation of humans in Dark Forest discourse. Before the military encounter between the Earth and Trisolaran civilizations, the seemingly well-prepared, overconfident Earth space fleet is easily eliminated by a single Trisolaran probe – a weapon poetically named "the droplet" – due to the fleet's tremendous technological deficiency. However, a handful of spaceships survive the fiasco, temporarily escape from the droplet's chase, and eventually find themselves stuck in another fatal situation. Their journey will never end, but their available resources are extremely limited. In such a scenario, the survivors yearn for a home they can no longer return to and for their lost utopia that is forced to be given away to the Trisolarans.

Very soon, the survivors realize the true terror of their situation. Their "comrades" on other surviving ships, suddenly, are turned into enemies, competitors or "hunters," throwing away, to use Michel Foucault's words, the "warm" moral and cultural values that are presented "precisely as antithetical to the 'cold' mechanism of competition" (Foucault, *Birth* 242). In the Dark Forest, people as social subjects are remade into the contributors or beneficiaries of the essential logic and "formative power" of an "enterprise society." This society follows the "impassive, calculating, rational, and mechanical [principles] in the strictly economic game of competition" (242). In this way, as indicated in the conversation quoted at the beginning of this section, these "new people" – who manage to survive the droplet's destruction but are forever disconnected from their authentic home – will finally become "non-people," waging war against each other for a better chance of carrying on the legacy of human civilization, which is referred to as "Battle of Darkness" later in the trilogy.

This transition from people to non-people, from the "warm" values of the innocent Earth, which are developed upon a friendly astronomical cycle leading to certainty, stability and abundance, to the "coldness" of the Dark Forest constructed upon uncertainty, competition and scarcity – can be read in relation to the sophisticated transformation in real-day China from socialist to post-socialist modernity. In fact, the tension between these two forms of modernity in China has already been presented in an early description of the Trisolaran society in the trilogy. With three suns orbiting randomly around each other, their unpredictable and chaotic movements result in an extremely unstable climate in the Trisolaran world. Frequent apocalyptic disasters urge the Trisolarans to prioritize the survival of their civilization and deny the impact of "weaknesses," such as emotional impulses, "moral" considerations and the "pursuit of beauty and enjoyment" (Liu, *Three-Body* 353).

These, as the Trisolarans believe, could put them in grave danger in the competitive game of survival. They are, in this way, "de-humanized," "without wealth, without status, without love, and without hope" (354), rendered not as independent subjects, but as disposable and exploitable resources participating in social production, their value measured according to their quantified, commensurable contributions to the Trisolaran civilization. Here of course, the Trisolarans are not "human beings," but here I still use the term "dehumanization" to indicate a process in which their individual uniqueness, subjectivity and autonomy are sacrificed for the survival of their civilization. For the Trisolarans, those who "have lost the ability to work productively" because of age or injury "would have been forcibly dehydrated, and the resulting dry fibres cast to the flames. *Trisolaris did not keep the idle around*" (350; emphasis added).

This quantified and utilitarian logic behind such a process of dehumanization in the Trisolaran world is exactly the same as the one that leads to the "Battle of Darkness" among the surviving human spaceships – that is, to see other survivors in a dehumanized shape and as potential competitors fighting for usable resources. In line with this, Luo Ji, the first human being who understands the Dark Forest cosmology and thus becomes the "Sword-holder" by establishing a "Mutual-Assured-Destruction" (MAD) deterrence with the Trisolarans,[5] observes that the "factors of chaos and randomness in the complex makeups of every civilized society in the universe get filtered out by the distance" (Liu, *Dark* 13).[6] These vigilant hunters are "identical" to each other in the Dark Forest discourse, becoming "just a collection of points in space with a clear mathematical configuration" (222), trapped in an endless competition that yields winners and losers, while their inherent uniqueness and subjectivity are destroyed in the process of dehumanization. This is a process, in Zygmunt Bauman's words,

5 The term "Mutual Assured Destruction" (MAD) originated from the Cold War armament race, referring to a delicate situation where the use of apocalyptic weapons by either of the opposing sides will lead to the complete annihilation of both (Brodie 264–304; Schelling 1–30). In the *Three-Body* trilogy, a temporal, fragile peace between the Earth and the Trisolarans was realized by such an MAD deterrence, with the "Sword-holder" threatening to broadcast the location of the Trisolaris. In the Dark Forest, this broadcast will surely attract deadly attacks from other more powerful "hunters" in the universe, targeted against both the Trisolarans and the Earth given their close distance.

6 These words are originally from Ye Wenjie, Luo Ji's mentor and main character of the first instalment *The Three-Body Problem*, but later Luo Ji agrees with this idea and extends it in a further place.

that "starts at the point when, thanks to the distantiation, the objects [...] can and are reduced to a set of quantitative measures" (*Modernity* 102).

In this way, the Dark Forest discourse, one that not only encourages but also justifies exploitative competition, can be understood as a vehicle to interrogate the spread of the calculative market rules into other social and cultural domains in contemporary China. Because of the market-oriented reforms initiated by Deng Xiaoping, the influence of an ever-expanding market economy has transcended the economic sphere and become dynamic in forming "an order of normative reason that [...] takes shape as a governing rationality extending a specific formulation of economic values, practices, and metrics to every dimension of human life" (Brown, *Undoing* 30). A variety of market principles and mechanisms, in this way, effectively intrude into those domains formerly supervised by the state and erode the foundation of welfare provision and social protection. These new principles, in fact, are not only instrumental in inducing structural transitions of China's economic and fiscal policies but also in formulating a "calculation-based" discourse, where the "cold" equation of supply and demand, of investment-costs-profit, triumphs over "warm" cultural and moral values.

In other words, almost all areas of social life in post-socialist China have been constructed upon economic productivity. Everything is seen as "social capital" that can be invested and reinvested. Social entities and individuals, in this case, will have to surrender to the logic of "enterprise" in which they are rendered as calculative agencies in a process of economization (Çalışkan and Callon 378), and then cast into a Hobbesian battlefield of all against all. Therefore, the Dark Forest has in itself crystallized a transition from the fading socialist utopia (like Han Song's Amanduo) towards the emerging post-socialist modernity marked by the economizing impulse of remaking, or dehumanizing, the social subjects into "human capital" (I will expand on this later).

As recorded in the *Three-Body* trilogy, the overwhelming victory of the Trisolarans over the Earth space fleet, the "old" Earth seen as "home" – the place where social protection and welfare provision can be expected – ceases to be. The "new people" born in this transitional situation have to fit themselves into the Dark Forest discourse defined by omnipresent competition and endless uncertainty, a discourse that has become the new norm. It is, in fact, the formation of this specific and normative mode of reason, one that favours capital efficiency and configures human beings as market actors, that differentiates the Dark Forest discourse from the ethos of the pre-Deng ages. Such a discourse promotes a social matrix where winners may prosper while others will lose. It defines the significant features of post-socialist China (embodied by the Trisolarans and other civilizations familiar with Dark Forest theory) and marks a historical rupture with the past.

So far in this chapter, I have demonstrated the competitive essence of the Dark Forest that, in a way, echoes the market-oriented, privatized transformation in China in the past three decades. But merely revealing the competitiveness of the Dark Forest and of post-socialist modernity in China has not explained the surprising, cross-generic popularity the *Three-Body* trilogy has gained, nor does it account for the trilogy's unique status as *the Bible*, providing its neoliberal worshippers with clear spiritual and behavioural inspirations. These inspirations, connoted in Liu Cixin's story, are straightforward and powerful, widely circulating among its readers within and beyond the sf community. It calls for a "cold" mindset, in the age of the *Three-Body* Boom when the principle of the Dark Forest is enshrined: "If we lose our human nature, we lose much, but if we lose our *bestial nature*, we lose everything" (Liu, *Death's* 459; emphasis added). Therefore, in the following section, I will elaborate on how these dehumanized subjects (or the hunters) cope with the potential apocalypse they might have to encounter, how they will upgrade their arsenal and enhance their competitiveness in the face of such a risk and at what cost they are willing to do so.

Human as Capital: The "Bestial" Nature of "Hunters"

The powerful manifesto calling for "bestial nature" is one of the most well-known statements of Thomas Wade, an important anti-hero in the last instalment *Death's End*. Despite his cold instrumental rationality (that, in most cases, stands against the "warm" values of morality and humanity), he has managed to gain recognition and aroused strong sympathy among the *Three-Body* fandom. As a Wade supporter noted a few years ago in an online book review, "we can no longer see Thomas Wade merely as a character – what he represents is the desire of human beings for survival in the Dark Forest and the cosmic battlefield" (Heartsweet n.p.). For similar reasons, his wicked charm as a "bastard, devil, murderer, careerist, political hooligan, technophilic madman" (Liu, *Death's* 416) has attracted a large group of enthusiastic followers who explicitly articulate their affection through social media, blog articles and idea-sharing websites such as Douban and Zhihu.

But before I discuss Thomas Wade in greater detail, I will first take a detour to briefly introduce Foucault's idea of the competitive essence of market and human capital. "Competition is an essence," Foucault claims, "Competition is an *eidos*. Competition has an internal logic; it has its own structure. Its effects are only produced if this logic is respected. It is, as it were, a formal game between inequalities […] Competition is therefore an historical objective of governmental art" (Foucault, *Birth* 120). Wendy Brown agrees with Foucault's perception of competition as the inherent logic of neoliberalism which has been disseminated across society through the meshing of political and business (and, in the Dark Forest, science fictional) lexicons. From this point, Brown emphasizes the "cannibalizing" tendency of dehumanized subjects – or in other words, human capital. This shifting of responsibility, therefore, eventually leads to "the combination of devolved authority [from the state] and responsibilization of the subject," whereas "the socialization of risk accompanying the privatization of gain" has resulted in a situation where "inequality and competition unto death replace equality and commitment to protect life" (Brown, *Undoing* 62–72).

It is in such a "competition unto death" that Thomas Wade's bestial nature is celebrated, especially for those who take the *Three-Body* trilogy as the Bible. Wade's extremist rationality, based on his "cold" and utilitarian cost-gain calculation, often defies the "warm" moral concerns embodied by Cheng Xin, a character on the opposite side who stands in favour of the equality and well-being of all living souls. She does not press the MAD button in the face of the Trisolaran invasion because she cannot bear the moral burden of mass killing, surrendering the Earth to alien dominance. Throughout the trilogy, her repetitive "softness" and reluctance in making sacrifices during the encounter with other "hunters" in the Dark Forest directly results in the apocalypse of the Earth civilization.

For Wade's supporters, the moral high ground Cheng Xin holds onto is considered the source of human weaknesses that must be eliminated from the Dark Forest competition. This echoes the ideas of the Trisolaran "Princeps," who believes that "this type of civilization [like Earth] was the weakest and most short-lived" (Liu, *Three-Body* 354). In this way, Cheng Xin's innocence and moral purity have even earned her a rather sarcastic title among the fandom: The Blessed Mother. In fact, in the *Three-Body* novels, Liu Cixin has already established the reference between Cheng Xin and the Blessed Mother. Against the Dark Forest,

> humanity was exposed to the cruel, cold universe, where Death's scythe may fall at a moment's notice [...] human civilization had been abandoned in a sinister, terrifying dark forest; it cried, hoping for a mother's love incarnate. As the public's feelings for Cheng Xin gradually melded with the thickening atmosphere of religiosity, her image as the Saint Mary of a new era once again gained prominence. (Liu, *Death's* 287)

But in the online context in contemporary China and among the *Three-Body* fandom, "the Saint Mary" or "the Blessed Mother" (translated from 圣母 *shèngmǔ*) is not relevant to its Christian origin. Instead, it is usually used to refer to those who, either in reality or fiction, like to make a show of being morally superior to other people. In their eyes, Cheng Xin has become the embodiment of human weakness, of the inability to make hard decisions at crucial times.

In contrast to Cheng Xin's seemingly excessive benevolence, Wade stands for the other side of the dichotomy. He claims that he "[has] to advance, advance without regard for consequences" (Liu, *Death's* 127) in pursuit of his ultimate goal – survival of Earth's civilization in the Dark Forest – even if this involves assassination, mass killing and other measures that Cheng Xin would doubtless protest against. In line with his "cold" determination, Wade attempts to murder Cheng Xin to become the Sword-holder and thus to maintain the MAD deterrence against the invading Trisolarans, believing that she could never succeed at this job. He attempts to declare war against the rather short-sighted Earth government that stands in his way of developing light-speed spaceships, putting tens of thousands of people in grave danger. To escape from the rifles of other hunters in the Dark Forest, sacrifice must be made, no matter the cost.

In fact, Wade is not the only character in the *Three-Body* trilogy to demonstrate this bestial nature. Zhang Beihai in *The Dark Forest* also commits murder to make sure the technological development of human civilization keeps on the right track. He even sees the deaths of his targets as "their final contribution to the cause of humanity's endeavours in space" (Liu, *Dark* 257). Contrary to Cheng Xin's mocking title "the Blessed Mother," Zhang Beihai is given a title of admiration: "The Watchman of Humanity" (*Three-Body* Community n.p.). I have no intention of justifying their calculative-based, competition-led and sometimes inhumane decisions and behaviours, and I believe many would not. However, we cannot ignore the fact that a sizable group of readers have indeed fostered compassion for and resonated with these "cold" anti-heroes whose decisions have come to resonate with them, which can be seen in various book reviews, blog articles and other forms of fandom culture.

This has opened a window to investigate how the post-socialist subject, rendered as "human capital" in the process of economization, reacts to the proliferating logic of market competition in contemporary China. The economizing and enterprising impulses connoted in the contemporary transformation of Chinese society, while constructing a logic of "economic calculation" outside the pure economic domain, have been steadily changing and eventually determined a new set of social norms that governs the shaping of the subject (Foucault, *Birth* 148). As mentioned above, the dehumanizing nature of the Dark Forest has indicated that in such an economized society, subjects have become "calculative agencies" or "market actors" activated through economic competition. Meanwhile, even more importantly, they have also turned into "human capital," whose success depends on a persistent process of self-appreciation and self-investment.

The difference here between "human capital" in post-socialist China and "free labourers" connected to a "liberal" economic model lies in whether there is a clear, concrete boundary between what can be negotiated in the marketplace and what cannot. According to Michel Feher, from such a liberal perspective,

> love, religion, and culture cannot be reduced to a mere calculus of interests: they delineate an existential realm where human desires are not optimally managed through bargaining and the interplay of self-interested exchanges but are either met or humbled by the manifestation of disinterested feelings – such as divine charity, parental and spousal devotion, social and national solidarity, love and compassion for humanity, and so on. Such a realm is not only meant to complement that of the market, that is, to supplement what market relations can deliver; more than just a safety net, it is required for the formation of subjects who can distinguish between the negotiable and the inalienable and may expect to be treated according to this distinction. (23–4)

Therefore, free labourers in this case will see a divide between their subjectivity in reproducing new subjects (whether in its biological, social, cultural or moral senses) and their production, circulation and consumption of tradable labour power and commodities. In this way they manage to draw the line that guards other realms outside the marketplace from those competitive, calculative values taken for granted by *homo economicus*.

This boundary, or divide, however, is deconstructed. Everything is now tradeable, and this contributes to the "self-appreciation" and "self-investment" of the subject. As Feher continues, when the subject is considered human capital, they will be identified with the following characteristics:

> (1) The subjects that it [human capital] defines seek to appreciate and to value themselves, such that their life may be thought of as a strategy aimed at self-appreciation;
> (2) All of their behaviours and all the events affecting them (in any existential register) are liable to cause the subjects either to appreciate or to depreciate themselves;
> (3) And it is therefore possible to govern subjects seeking to increase the value of their human capital, or, more precisely, to act on the way they govern themselves, by inciting them to adopt conducts deemed valorising and to follow models for self-valuation that modify their priorities and inflect their strategic choices. (28)

Therefore, with market principles and calculative logic as the underpinning philosophy behind the behaviours and decisions of the "human-capitalized" subject, their education and various other forms of vocational training should all be considered a certain kind of up-front investment that could contribute to their employability and marketability. The "economic" return of previous investments, measured on a competitive basis, becomes the only thing that matters. Volunteering, charity and other ostensibly "non-profit" engagements in the discourse of human capital are perceived less as an altruistic benefaction to their surrounding community. Instead, these figure more as just another referenceable item available in the subject's *curriculum vitae* that will be reviewed by entrepreneurial employers. These "investments" and "returns" exist not only in monetary forms quantified by the subject's expected wages, but also appear as intangible values such as affect, time and knowledge. They manage to create an invisible balance that defines the calculative mindset of the altered subject, that forces everything to "comport increasingly with a business model and business metrics" (Brown, *Undoing* 123) and that dominates the contemporary cultural politics of the post-socialist China.

Such a "business model" or "business metrics" have become the guidance for the decisions made by the Dark Forest hunters in the *Three-Body* trilogy. They are compelled to comply with the principles of self-appreciation based on the competitive market logic. Their basic survival is then dependent on a constant process of self-evolution, and their attacks "all share two qualities: one they're casual; two, they're economical" (Liu, *Death's* 277). As Liu Cixin elaborates these two qualities further through Sophon (the Trisolaran military agent):

> By "casual," what I mean is that the only basis for the attack is the exposure of the target's location. There will be no reconnaissance or exploration conducted against the target beforehand. For a supercivilization, such exploration is more expensive than a blind strike. By "economical," what I mean is that the attack will employ the least expensive method. (*Death's* 277–8)

From this perspective, the Dark Forest attacks are the results of careful calculation, constituting an economic structure that maximizes the outcome with minimum investments. This is the mentality of *homo economicus*, the active participant of social production who always maintains their rationality, able to achieve their predetermined goals with optimal decisions.

In previous readings, the sense of techno-progressivism has become definitive of Liu Cixin's novels, which are often endowed with a Clarkean sense of techno-optimism that makes him, as Liu Cixin claims himself after the publication of *The Three-Body Problem*, "a technocrat who regards science as the solution to problems of all kinds" (qtd. in Yan F., "Ping" n.p.). Although such an obsession with science and technology is in many ways related to his professional identity as a hydraulic engineer, it has also been connoted with a nationalist grand narrative where techno-scientific problem-solving would come into play, a narrative that is crucial for China in the process of "global repositioning" (Dougherty 41, 58). But on top of these readings, Liu Cixin's techno-progressivism, especially its popularity and impact among the readership, among those who find more personal connection to anti-heroes such as Thomas Wade and Zhang Beihai rather than Cheng Xin the Blessed Mother, is called forth by the economized, entrepreneurial society of human capital in China.

To eliminate and hide from other hunters, to survive in the Dark Forest, anything or anyone standing in the way should be removed according to the cold calculation represented by Thomas Wade and Zhang Beihai. This is because, in a society encouraging competition, in the universe of scarcity where "civilization continuously grows and expands, but the total matter in the universe remains constant," survival is the primary need of all subjects (Liu, *Dark* 13). It is the bestial nature, in contrast to the "warm" moral concerns that could lead to weakness and hesitation, that should be considered the prime directive in the Dark Forest, and this has been taken as a "biblical," ultimate truth by a great number of readers.

The *Three-Body* trilogy is not only a series of novels. It conveys a particular mindset that is welcomed in the decade of the *Three-Body* Boom. It should be read along with the historical transition that leads to individual stress, concern and insecurity resulting from the retreat of collective arrangement and national protection. This is metaphorically represented in the trilogy since the Earth – a utopian home of human beings, which "remained always in a Stable Era" and "had been born [with] a paradise where the climate was eternally mild" (Liu, *Three-Body* 349) – is increasingly involved in the Dark Forest cosmology and therefore cast into a battlefield of constant competition.

Social subjects after the post-socialist transition have been remade, or dehumanized, into homogeneous human capital, and only through relying on their "bestial nature" can they triumph over their competitors, namely other hunters in the Dark Forest. In this way, the post-socialist society which has gradually, but surely, developed in China since the 1990s denies a sense of stability and state protection. Instead, it welcomes the "responsibilization" or "entrepreneurialization" that "aimed at transferring almost everything provided by the social state to individuals" (Brown, *Ruins* 38). It is in such a marketized and privatized environment that the subject is required to maintain their bestial nature and to compromise a certain degree of moral concerns in their human-capitalized process of self-appreciation. This is why the hunters' survival in the Dark Forest depends on their constant armament against each other. This is why the *Three-Body* trilogy is adored, worshipped and enshrined, serving as a justification of people's "killings" in their own life.

"If I destroy you, what business is it of yours?" Carved above the gate leading to the Dark Forest era, this quote becomes the hunter's creed, radiating its impact and efficacy from Liu Cixin's novels into our reality, into all social domains being conquered by the army of human capital in the process of economization.

From the Dark Forest to the Kefahuchi Tract

Realizing this, I have now developed a newer yet disenchanted understanding of the *Three-Body* trilogy. And it is because of this disenchantment that I strive to explore other possibilities beyond the Dark Forest battlefield, that I start to notice M. John Harrison's *Kefahuchi* trilogy. In *The Dark Forest*, I find myself more empathetic with the character Luo Ji (who discovers the Dark Forest theory for the human beings) when he "saw the truth of the universe" in the "dead, lonely, cold blackness" on a frozen lake (Liu, *Dark* 223). He becomes aware of the Dark Forest cosmology as he plunges in an ice hole and sinks in the water, where starlight appears refracted and the starfield retreats from its familiar, stable formation and, in a van Gogh manner, "curl[s] up into a vortex and scatter[s] into turbulent, chaotic waves of silver" (Liu, *Dark* 223).

Through this turbulence caused by the starlight refraction, stillness shatters, certainty turns uncertain, and what used to be solid melts into air. From that night on, Luo Ji no longer sees these "fuzzy" stars with awe or wonder or respect like when David Bowman arrives at the Star Gate in *2001: A Space Odyssey* (1968). He sees them with fear. From such a sense of uncertainty and fear brought by the Dark Forest, the *Three-Body* trilogy resorts to another kind of certainty to deal with people's confusion and insecurity, that is the prevalence of the subjectivity of the Self, as well as the logic of sameness.

Earlier in *The Three-Body Problem*, several Earth scientists become suicidal due to unexplained experimental failures that seem to invalidate modern physics. The experimental results they collect become random and chaotic, impossible to apply to any proper theory. Involved in the incidents rather involuntarily, the protagonist Wang Miao also becomes psychotic as he is shown a series of mystical manifestations beyond his scientific comprehension. Before he mentally gives in to the "flickering universe" (a massive energy fluctuation of the cosmic microwave background), which in his eyes is caused by "a strange, perverse, immense presence that could never be understood by human intellect" (Liu, *Three-Body* 127), the detective Da Shi intervenes, saying to the nano-scientist: "Anything sufficiently weird must be fishy" (133).

Da Shi's phrasing reminds us immediately of one of Clarke's well-known laws: "Any sufficiently advanced technology is indistinguishable from magic." Originally published in a letter to *Science* (Clarke, "Clarke's" 255), this statement has been quoted to refer to the techno-optimism in his works. In *2001*, for instance, omnipotent alien beings beyond human imagination demonstrate unfathomable magics, inviting Bowman through a mystical Star Gate before turning him into a Star Child. In *Childhood's End* (1953), the Overmind moulds human children into a single entity before absorbing them, or it, into its own realm. These technologically advanced and morally developed beings, while performing their miracles, act as guardians or saviours able to lead humans to their ultimate revelation, to "a lifting of the veil on some profound truth" (Luckhurst, *Science Fiction* 133), to a sense of wonder and eventually to the human transcendence. It is such a fictional journey towards the sublime that differentiates Clarke from other writers of the Golden Age with whom Clarke is also categorized on many occasions.

But even so, Clarke is certainly not an advocate for this transcendent ascension of human beings in a religious sense. Despite the mysticism in his oft-cited assertion about "sufficiently advanced technologies," this can also be interpreted the other way around: *any inexplainable magic can be explained with sufficiently advanced technologies*. I am aware that such a reversion might not be flawless based on strict logic, but with this we are able to reveal Clarke's "anthropocentric" confidence in the rationality and subjectivity of the Self. No matter how weird or how miraculous an event might seem to be, there is always a plausible scientific explanation behind all these mystical curtains, always someone responsible for those "fishy" events.

In novels such as *2001* and *Childhood's End*, although human beings have to "evolve" into a non-human form to make sense of the truth behind miracles, they are still confined in the narrative based on the absolute privilege of the Self over the Other – the same power dynamic also evident in anthropocentricism. Here the prefix "anthropo-" refers not only to human beings but also to the alien Self (like the Overmind) who feels obliged, with their advanced technologies, to enlighten primitive civilizations (like human beings) who are situated as the Other. That is, alien encounters for both Clarke and Liu Cixin not only happen "between terran self and alien other" (Malmgren, "Self" 15), but also between "alien self" and "terran other." Because of this, the "intense, near religious, transcendence" that Luckhurst references in his reading of Clarke (*Science Fiction* 133) is in fact a one-way journey towards disenchantment, where science-based modernity takes the place of spirituality, where, as Clarke writes himself, "Civilization and Religion [becomes] incompatible" (Clarke, *3001* 141).

This Self/Other dynamic resonates in the *Three-Body* trilogy. Along with Liu Cixin's techno-optimism that equals that of his mentor Clarke, Liu Cixin also parodies, probably unintentionally, the Clarkean belief in disenchantment. The detective Da Shi laughs at Wang Miao's overreaction to the ostensible miracles that have shattered his scientific worldview.[7] It

7 Li Hua has systematically discussed Liu Cixin's techno-optimism in her 2017 article "Spaceship Earth and Technological Utopianism." But she also argues that his "naïve" optimism can be categorized as a kind of "cruel optimism," in Lauren Berlant's terms, because technological supremacy could lead to severe environmental exploitation and an "over-confidence" in science and technology

turns out later in the trilogy that these miracles are indeed "fishy" (as Da Shi puts it). They are not performed by a higher being beyond human comprehension. They are just gimmicks made by the Trisolarans' advanced technologies that seem "magical" compared to contemporary human science. In line with this, the Trisolarans have nothing in common with the Overmind or the Builder of the Star Gate, who wish to enlighten Earth about their eventual transcendence. They are just one of the vigilant hunters in the Dark Forest who happens to take the first shot. As I note in "Dark Forest or Grand Central," the Dark Forest discourse requires "every civilization [to see] themselves as the only subject with agency [… and] become the absolute Self while other beings are reduced to mere points, identical to one another, unreachable and incommunicable that should be eradicated" (Lyu, "Dark" 186). In other words, the Dark Forest is a place where otherness (that is the internal diversity and randomness within other hunters who keep threatening the "hunter-self") must always be reduced to the sameness of the Self.

As human *beings* are constantly alienated and transfigured into human *capital* in the age of economization, the Dark Forest mentality favoured by "entrepreneurialized" subjects (who tend to follow the mindset of competition and calculation originating from the marketplace) is built upon the tyranny of the Self, or *Self-capital*. They expand their territory by absorbing the resources of the Other and thrive upon the relative depreciation of their capital-competitors. Faced with the sense of uncertainty emerging in the increasingly entrepreneurialized and marketized Dark Forest era, social subjects tend to resort to another kind of certainty as they strive for survival. But in this case, the new sense of certainty no longer derives from collective distribution, state protection, various forms of social welfare or "the iron rice bowl." Likewise, the Self no longer refers to the centralized socialist utopia such as the totalized Amanduo seen in its decline in Han Song's *Red Star Over America* to which social subjects are all affiliated.

Instead, the Self is transferred to individuals, now entrepreneurialized to be responsible for themselves. They realize that in the Dark Forest,

---

throughout Chinese history since the early twentieth century (H. Li, "Spaceship" 17–31).

beneath the infinite units of the *hunter-self* which appear to be variant yet in essence identical to each other, there is an unvarying constant that guides them all – the binary distinction of Self and Other. This is exactly what Gilles Deleuze and Felix Guattari wish to challenge. They have made every endeavour to undermine such a tree structure in which "the One" is always the origin of "the multiple," a structure that nourishes all kinds of exploitation, and to replace it with the non-binary concept of "rhizome." As they write in *A Thousand Plateaus* (1980), the making of the multiple can be achieved

> not by always adding a higher dimension, but rather in the simplest of ways, by dint of sobriety, with the number of dimensions one already has available – always n - 1 (the only way the one belongs to the multiple: always subtracted). *Subtract the unique from the multiplicity to be constituted; write at n - 1 dimensions.* (6; emphasis added)

The new non-binary system of "rhizome" that they propose

> pertains to a map that must be produced, constructed, a map that is always detachable, connectable, reversible, modifiable, and has multiple entryways and exits and its own lines of flight [...] In contrast to centered (even polycentric) systems with hierarchical modes of communication and preestablished paths, the rhizome is an acentered, nonhierarchical, nonsignifying system without a General and without an organizing memory or central automaton, defined solely by a circulation of states. (21)

Therefore, a rhizome will lead to the deconstruction of all pre-settled structures, especially binary oppositions such as the Self-Other dichotomy that appears so frequently in Liu Cixin's and Clarke's works. It prefigures a land of transition, movement, diffusion and dispersibility, instead of centrality, hierarchy or hegemony. It is anti-linear, anti-certain and anti-methodological.

In the *Three-Body* trilogy, after the Earth has become a lost utopia, after the sense of stability is endangered by the Dark Forest ambush, Luo Ji's realization of the cold-blooded truth of the all-against-all universe might have led to a process of "deterritorialization," in Deleuze/Guattari's terms, through which individual social subjects can be freed from being subordinate to a collective centrality.[8] Unfortunately, in the context of uncertainty

8 For Deleuze and Guattari, deterritorialization is crucial to the process of becoming. They believe the world is constituted by nothing but a "virtual" flow of intensities

and insecurity created in the Dark Forest era, this deterritorialized field is soon "reterritorialized" into another binary system, one that encourages competition and calculation, that renders previously incommensurable qualities as quantitative variants and that justifies the market competition not only in the post-socialist China but also the post-Thatcherite UK. What I wish to do here is to go further, to deterritorialize the Dark Forest common sense of competition and calculation, which should be channelled again towards its own "transcendence." I strive to imagine something that can create a Deleuzo-Guattarian "multiple" and "ontological heterogeneity" (Guattari 61) beyond the tree and the fascicular-root dialectics and to invite "schizoanalytic" subjects, that is, "body without organs" (BwO), who defy any molar structures and call for alternatives along the line of flight.[9]

In pursuing the line of flight and then deterritorializing the Self-Other dichotomy, we need to go to the Kefahuchi Tract to look for inspiration and for an alternative to the fetishism of certainty and competition of the *Three-Body* trilogy. We need to challenge the epistemology based upon an economized or entrepreneurialized subjectivity that welcomes calculation, vengeance and hostility, replacing it with a new mechanism of transgression and becoming. This dynamic between destruction and creation is one

---

that give rise to "actual" and perceptible objects, as well as various forms of beings, a flow without a start or an end. In this process of becoming, the territory is considered a node, a twist, a moment that remains stable temporarily and interrupts the flow of intensities. In this way, what is promised in Deleuze and Guattari's rhizomic plane is a deterritorializing from the previous territory, a process in which existing structures and systems are expected to change and become, open to all possibilities. The way in which the process of becoming can be realized is therefore defined as the line of flight.

9 Deleuze and Guattari stand against Freudian psychoanalysis. Desire, they believe, should not be suppressed or contained in a certain territory (familial or social or even Oedipal). In response, they propose their "schizoanalysis." It aims not to encode subjects and their bodies within a certain structure or hierarchy, but to lead them back to "the area of the unborn," a state of being that is amorphous and undifferentiated. The undifferentiated body is referred to as "the body without organs" (BwO). "The BwO," write Deleuze and Guattari, "is what remains when you take everything away. What you take away is precisely the phantasy, and signifiances and subjectifications as a whole" (151).

of the major features of M. John Harrison's *Kefahuchi Tract* trilogy: *Light* (2002), *Nova Swing* (2006) and *Empty Space: A Haunting* (2012). Unlike Liu Cixin, who writes the *Three-Body* trilogy with a liner narrative and with an aesthetic of conventional hard sf, Harrison tends to smash temporality and generic boundaries. "Harrison pierces, rends, tears, defaces. Reading him is like standing in the quiet aftermath of a volcanic eruption, as a once-familiar landscape reveals its molten underbelly, and soft falling ash obscures all around" (Williams and Bould 14). His works are often considered "absurdist and grotesque," sometimes "concerned with the topological," and overall, a subversion/deconstruction of the fantasy genre (Blackmore 22).

These three novels draw upon the elements of both space opera and the New Weird, and even inherit the legacy of the New Wave of the 1960s and 1970s. Beyond the representation of "a taking stock of the status quo" in contemporary London, the trilogy is also well known for "projecting existent possibilities into the future" (Scholz 1150) – a future four hundred years from now illuminated by the mysterious Kefahuchi Tract. Unlike what is presented by Liu Cixin and Clarke, the Kefahuchi Tract is a region of chaos, randomness, and above all, *uncertainty*. It is the limbo where all rules fail, where all kinds of physics are no longer valid, and all endeavours to make sense of it turn out to be in vain. Paul Kincaid argues that Harrison's trilogy is "the most significant work of science fiction to have appeared so far [in the twenty-first] century," and it is "precisely [the] balance between creation and destruction that makes this such a major work":

> The balance is more subtly represented by the creation and destruction of characters, a recurring theme throughout the three books. Harrison makes it explicit that the science-fictionality of the novels is embodied within his key central characters, that they bring the future into being and sustain it. And yet these characters are constantly being torn apart and remade, so that the universe into which these works plunge us can never be more than contingent, hesitant, *open to doubts and uncertainties*. (Kincaid, "Jetsam" n.p.; emphasis added)

Harrison's influence on the British SF Boom is immense. "He is an author's author – without Harrison, no China Miéville perhaps, no New Weird, no contemporary post-genre or slipstream in quite the same way – and the thinker's author, lauded by the likes of John Gray and Robert McFarlane"

(Williams and Bould 15). Even so, however, he has never been a bestseller. In fact, he has more in common with Han Song, whose eerie, uncanny and ambiguous writing style always denies a simple reading, and inevitably scares away a certain group of potential readers. For "reasons perhaps all-too-obvious," as Williams and Bould continue, Harrison "has never fitted comfortably into the genre market, nor the mainstream market" (15). And this, in 1999, won him the Richard Evans Memorial Prize, a small grant awarded to genre authors who have made considerable contributions to this field but not gained concomitant commercial success. Although he has won the James Tiptree Jr. Memorial Award for *Light* and Arthur C. Clarke Award and Philip K. Dick Award for *Nova Swing*, his works are still very much underestimated by the market.

When he presents us with the inexplicable mystery as the Kefahuchi Tract – a "magic" that looks even more paranormal, more inscrutable than the gimmicks performed by the Trisolarans that terrify scientist Wang Miao – Harrison does not make it "fishy," nor does he fit it in a *self*-centric discourse in which all magics can be comprehended through certainty, rationality and modernity. Instead, he welcomes uncertainty. Chaos and order in the Kefahuchi Tract are switchable, "like an optical illusion," and both images are always inherent – it is the viewer who will create one fixed state (Scholz 1155). Just like the *Three-Body* trilogy, there is also a detective in the Kefahuchi novels (particularly in *Nova Swing*), Lens Aschemann, who perhaps speaks for the author himself. Aschemann is dedicated to investigating "site crimes," that is, crimes related to the Saudade event site. The event site is part of the Kefahuchi Tract that has invaded on the planet Saudade, a bubble of emergence, blending and transition, "a stationary vapour of uncertain physics" (Harrison, *Nova* 89), a transformative heterotopia where "streets transposed on one another," where "there isn't a single piece of dependable architecture" and where everything struggled "to keep afloat" (11).

During his investigation of the human-shaped creatures originating from the event site – "people [who] came out of the Saudade site who had never gone in" (21) – Aschemann does not back off because of the uncanny sense of uncertainty and weirdness. He embraces it, feeling curious about what is really happening inside the site, inside the Kefahuchi Tract. He is enchanted with it. "Uncertainty," says Aschemann, "is all we have. It's our advantage. It's the *virtue of the day*" (21; emphasis added). The Saudade event site, as well as the Kefahuchi Tract from which it originates, provides an alternate epistemology that undermines the anthropocentric views in Liu Cixin's and Clarke's works, calling for a magic that cannot be disenchanted by sufficiently advanced technology. It emerges and develops not through the tree dichotomy between the One and the multiplicity, but to become a smooth space of nomadism, a plane of immanence.

Science prevails – this is the underlying truth faithfully held by the benevolent Clarkean aliens and the hunters in the Dark Forest. They believe that science can only evolve in one certain way, that there is only one set of principles of nature. This is the reason why the human scientists in *The Three-Body Problem* are so desperate after the Trisolarans cripple their experiments and why the Overlords in *Childhood's End* have to enlighten humans about the *proper* evolutionary path towards merging with the Overmind. But here in the Kefahuchi Tract there is no one true way of formulating science. There is no *proper* path to engage with the Kefahuchi Tract, nor to develop the *right* technology to get close to it.

Instead, Harrison focuses on possibilities: "Anything worked. Wherever you looked, you found" (Harrison, *Light* 140). He abandons the *punctual system* in Liu Cixin's and Clarke's works that requires a point of origin as the source of meaning, a scientific explanation behind magics. He suspends, questions and challenges the logic of sameness that is, in Deleuze and Guattari's words, "arborescent, mnemonic, molar, structural" in nature – the systems of "territorialization or reterritorialization" (Deleuze and Guattari 295). There is never the One. There is always multiplicity. Therefore, as Harrison writes in *Light*:

> Every race they met on their way through the Core had a star drive based on a *different* theory. All those theories worked, even when they ruled out one another's basic assumptions. You could travel between the stars, it began to seem, by assuming anything. If your theory gave you a foamy space to work with – if you had to catch a wave – that didn't preclude some other engine, running on a perfectly smooth Einsteinian surface, from surfing the same tranche of empty space. It was even possible to build drives on the basis of superstring-style theories, which, despite their promise four hundred years ago, had never really worked at all. (139–40; emphasis in original)

All roads lead to the Kefahuchi Tract. All kinds of physics and mathematics are equally valid. All species in the universe have their own way of making things work. But no one can really grasp the essence of its magic.

Light is told in three loosely connected strands of narrative, each focusing on a certain character – Michael Kearney, a physicist in contemporary London; Seria Mau, who abandons her biological body and has become a "k-captain" of a "k-ship" in the 2400s, flying around the Beach (the area adjacent to the Kefahuchi Tract); and Ed Chianese, Seria's younger brother, who works as a "prophet" in a circus and has a reputation for "surfing" (flying as close to the Tract as possible). They are all haunted by the presence of a sentient alien creature that they call, variously, the Shrander, Dr Haends and Sandra Shen. This creature, from an ancient and advanced civilization tens of millions of years ago, intervenes in their lives, performs what seems like magic to them and step by step leads them closer to the secrets hidden in the Kefahuchi Tract. Even more strikingly, as we realize towards the end of *Light*, it is the *creator* of human beings. "Because we built you," as the Shrander explains to Ed Chianese why it brings to him the Tract, as well as the reasons for the problems, miseries, confusions and uncertainties he has suffered: "We built you from the amino acids up" (Harrison, *Light* 315).

This, again, reminds us of Arthur C. Clarke, in particular his powerful aliens in *2001* who build the Star Gate and the Grand Central Station of the universe, who see themselves as the mentor of "Mind." There is nothing they cannot achieve. They are "the lords of the Galaxy," capable of existing beyond "the reach of time" and becoming "the tyranny of matter" (Clarke, *2001* 209). They are the sower of civilizations. They are the point of origin, the One from which the cosmic multiplicity derives, the almighty Self to which the Other is subordinated. But the Shrander's species is different. They are not omnipotent, since their technological powers fail in the face of the weird halo of the Kefahuchi Tract. They are not even someone special, only a normal one whose ambitions fade away as they see the failures of those who came before them.

"[The Kefahuchi Tract] was old when we got here," says the Shrander to Ed Chianese. "The people who had been here before us, well they were old when we were nothing. We stole their ideas as fast as we could, the way you're doing now. We had our try at that thing [...] and it failed" (Harrison, *Light* 314). The reason why they create human beings is not to enlighten one more sentient civilization as they see fit,one more branch of the arborescent structure in which they are the centre. They do this because they hope that human beings might become better than they are at perceiving the imperceptible; humans will inherit the mission that they themselves have inherited from their predecessors: "We are missing something, we had to admit. But that in itself gave us our big idea. We couldn't know the Tract; but we decided to build something that could" (Harrison, *Light* 315).

In this eons-long journey of making sense of the Kefahuchi Tract, there is no God-like initiator such as the Star Gate builders who started everything in the first place, and there will always be followers striving to continue what is left unfinished. The neighbours of the Kefahuchi Tract come and go, travelling across the universe to try their luck on this ultimate mystery and all failing to make sense of it. It remains, with no beginning nor end. It welcomes all possibilities, none of them subordinated to any other. It defies the Self, the One, the point of origin, and breaks up the stasis of the Self-Other dichotomy enshrined in the Dark Forest cosmology. It calls for the nomad, going from "point to point only as a consequence and as a factual necessity" and embracing uncertainties in an open space, "one that is indefinite and noncommunicating" (Deleuze and Guattari 380). It invalidates the Cogito – "I Think," "a point of subjectification" (587) – and liberates itself from "the edifice of an ordered interiority," and thus moves freely "in an element of exteriority" (Massumi, "Translator's" xii). In Massumi's terms, "It [does] not repose on identity; it [rides] difference" (xii).

Therefore, the Kefahuchi Tract appears in the novel to become a nomadic space that tore the restrictive analogy held by the hunters in the Dark Forest, a Deleuzian *intermezzo* that denies sameness and competition while advocating succession, transition and the dynamic state of being in-between. With all these transgressive and transformative impulses, this unfathomable space, both mysterious and mystical, becomes a beacon for the deterritorialization of the Self.

"Michael, We're None of Us Here at All": Becoming, and the Line of Flight

When the Kefahuchi Tract is first discovered by humans at the turn of the twenty-first century, Michael Kearney, the protagonist of the contemporary narrative strand in *Light*, and his colleague Brian Tate find something strange in their mathematical model displayed on their computer: "A cascade of fractals like a bird's wing, so tiny Kearney barely noticed it" (Harrison, *Light* 5). They think it is a glitch, leaving it alone. But before long, this "glitch" grows by itself. It expands its territory, gathers itself up "behind the code somewhere and shot out across the screen," appearing on their monitor as "a million coloured lights, boiling and sweeping about like a shoal of startled fish" (119). The light of the fractals even "leaks" from virtuality into reality, melding the two spaces into one, where the physics we are familiar with are "off" (216). The event horizon protecting *our* world from the colonization of the fractals dissolves as Kearney and Tate run their formula, just like what Ed Chianese observes from the Kefahuchi Tract – a singularity where "the wrong physics [got] loose in the universe" and where anything "could come out" (237). The leaking light pours out into the room, constructing a continuum linking the real and the virtual, where binary differentiation between body and code, man and animal, presence and simulation is undermined. Along this continuum, the cat in Kearney's laboratory goes *inside* the monitor after the lights. "She just walked through the screen and into the data" (215). Realizing that such a process of merging and transition threatens to shake up all previously known structures and knowledge, Tate says to Kearney, out of fear, astonishment and confusion: "Michael, *we're none of us here* at all" (216; emphasis added). And after this, even more shockingly, Tate himself melts and follows the cat into the light.

Of course, this scary scene that Kearney believes he is witnessing seems to be only a delusion, since his memory and mental condition, as suggested throughout the trilogy, are disordered because of his schizophrenic relationship with his ex-wife Anna. But even so, Tate's last words are worthy of closer contemplation – we *are* and *aren't* at the same time, existing not in a space of stillness, but of change and mobility where we are always becoming something different. Such a sense of alteration and deformation is also evident in Kearney himself as well as many other characters in the *Kefahuchi Tract* trilogy. At the end of *Light*, after decades of seeking and hiding, Kearney finally has the courage to face the Shrander, the inescapable nightmare haunting him since childhood. This is his destiny, to respond to the call of the Kefahuchi Tract four hundred years into the future and to be part of the light like his colleague Tate and the cat that walks through the screen. As the Shrander brings him to the Tract, the inexplicable source of the light,

> Everything was too bright to see. The light roared in on him unconfined: he felt it on his skin, he heard it as a sound. It was light unburdened, light like a substance: real light. Great walls and arcs and petals of it hung and flickered, they hardened, they endured a moment, they tumbled and fell towards him, they somehow passed through him and were gone in a second, only to be replaced. He had no idea where he was. He felt the most extraordinary sense of surprise and wonder and delight [...]
>
> He saw the raging glory of the light. He felt himself slipping away into it, here in this fabulous place. He was so amazed. He wanted the Shrander to know. He wanted it to be certain he had understood. (298, 300)

Similarly, Seria Mau, the k-captain, is freed from the *machinic assemblage* of the k-ship she is attached to, from the matrix of codes that has replaced her biological body, or from the *reterritorialized* state after her initial *deterritorialization* from a human to a ship (Jarvis 177). Through Dr Haends's surgery, Seria is turned into a formless, bird-like creature staying forever in metamorphosis. After Seria's rebirth, Dr Haends says to her: "Now you *can be* what you *are*" (Harrison, *Light* 308; emphasis added), in this way sublating all the rules and structure that would determine what she can or cannot become and allowing for infinite possibilities projected by the Kefahuchi Tract. "It will maintain any shape you want," as Dr Haends continues, "[you] can be this, or you can be something else. You can be a white cat [her previous k-ship] again, and pounce among the stars. Or why not try something new?" (309)

The detective Lens Aschemann also tries something new in *Nova Swing*. During his investigation of the Saudade event site, he feels increasingly that he is summoned by this place of uncertainty and transition. All "site crimes" in his eyes, that is, intrusions into the site and the smuggling of artefacts that do not belong to the outside world, "are crimes against continuity – continuity of life, continuity of ownership, systems continuity" (Harrison, *Nova* 239). With this realization, he becomes empathic with the criminals he is investigating and with the event site itself. He walks into it, breaking the continuity as a detective in Saudade, a "corporate planet" known for its "black market hothouse of illegal new technological innovation [and] its exploitation and entrepreneurial speculative experimentation producing new bodies, goods and experience" (Botting 238). As he wanders in the site, he also feels what Brian Tate warns everyone in *Light* – we're none of us here at all:

> He felt enlarged – swollen, but not exactly sick. Some time on the third, or perhaps the fourth day, he looked down at himself and saw the lower part of his legs dissolving into thousands of bright, energetic white sparks. He felt no pain. Despite that – and though no sound accompanied the process – he had a lively sense of himself as part of the entertainment. He was fizzing and crackling into the dark like a firework [...] The sparks blew away uphill on a light breeze, and out over the lip of the cliff. (Harrison, *Nova* 216)

And it is at this moment that he sees his late wife, whose memory is always with him, and she guides him to his eventual fate. She speaks to him: "Is that you? Aschemann, always something new! You'll never change!" (216)

Never change yet always be something new – this, again, echoes Deleuze/Guattari's concept of "becoming." It is not a simple process of change from one point to another, nor an evolution that lifts the subject to a higher level of being. Instead, it is an expression of pure speed, a state of being in-between, in-transition. "Every becoming," as Deleuze and Guattari write in *A Thousand Plateaus,* functions through "a block of coexistence" (292), or a block of lines creating a zone of proximity where new systems can be formed. It is a zone where molar entities – subordinated to a certain structure or hierarchy of sameness and constrained in a field of territorialization – can be *de*-formed into molecules and particles that would produce a limbo of indiscernibility, where one does not have to conform to a model nor wander on a plane of consistency.

> A line of becoming is not defined by points that it connects, or by points that compose it; on the contrary, it passes *between* points, it comes up through the middle, it runs perpendicular to the points first perceived, transversally to the localizable relation to distant or contiguous points. A point is always a point of origin. But a line of becoming has neither beginning nor end, departure nor arrival, origin nor destination [...] A line of becoming has only a middle. The middle is not an average; it is fast motion, it is the absolute speed of movement. A becoming is always in the middle; one can only get it by the middle. A becoming is neither one nor two, nor the relation of the two; it is the in-between, the border or line of flight or descent running perpendicular to both. (293)

To borrow an example of becoming in *A Thousand Plateaus*, in *Moby-Dick* Captain Ahab's obsessive hunting for the white whale is certainly not for commercial success, nor does he gain a reputation for his bravery and courage for challenging nature. Instead, he is attracted by its "anomalous" charms. As an anomaly, Moby-Dick is not simply an exceptional subject differentiating itself from a band or pack. It is a frontier, a borderline, a Lovecraftian "Outsider" which "arrives and passes at the edge," which is "linear yet multiple, 'teaming, seething, swelling, foaming, spreading like infectious diseases, this nameless horror'" (Deleuze and Guattari 245). Captain Ahab asks: "How can the prisoner reach outside except by thrusting through the wall? To me, the white whale is that wall, shoved near to me" (Melville 157). It is through his consistent pursuit of Moby-Dick that Captain Ahab realizes his own becoming, breaking the white wall and escaping from the prison, even if this costs his life. The anomalous Moby-Dick is by no means abnormal nor exceptional. It embodies a line of flight through which Captain Ahab, as *becoming-whale*, transcends a certain state of being.

Like Captain Ahab, *Light*'s Michael Kearney is also obsessed with the sea. It is on a seashore, from the patterns of the waves and the arrangement of the pebbles, that Kearney in his childhood realizes that the condition of things is not continuity or consistency, but intervals and fractality. And it is at this moment that he finds the Shrander, or that the Shrander finds him. Years later, as he is trying to run away from the Shrander once again, Kearney stands on a beach once again, and this time he has "a sense of things as endless": "[I]n this scheme the beach became a metaphor for some other *transitional site* or *boundary*, a beach at the edge of which lapped the whole universe" (Harrison, *Light* 247; emphasis added).

This boundary can be created through not only the Shrander but also other things that bind Kearney's fate to the Kefahuchi Tract – the fractals in Tate's monitor, the cat that jumps inside it and the strange dice he takes from the Shrander. In fact, the Kefahuchi Tract is not as borderless as it seems. Although it is considered "a singularity without an event horizon," although there is "no firm distinction" between the inside and the outside of the Saudade event site (Harrison, *Nova* 28), the real boundary of the Kefahuchi Tract exists neither spatially nor geographically. It exists through the process of becoming that requires us to see things not as molar subjects but as molecular collectivities or *haecceities* – that is, as events or instances of unique new possibility rather than reproductions of pre-existing patterns of being (see Sauvagnargues 25–8). These events emphasize the diversity and heterogeneity of the world and the significance of affirming and celebrating the individual and the particular. Molar subjects, for Deleuze and Guattari, are defined through the linear or binary logic that distinguishes the Self and the Other as in Liu's and Clarke's novels, while the molecule embodies the potentiality of transcending such a binary logic and formulating a rhizomic plane based on becoming. The "haecceity," first coined by followers of Duns Scotus to indicate a person's or object's thisness, is further developed by Deleuze and Guattari in line with their critique of metaphysics and their focus on difference and inconsistency. A haecceity is a kind of "coming-together," a temporary moment of becoming. For Deleuze and Guattari, a haecceity has "neither beginning nor end, origin nor destination; it is always in the middle. It is not made of points, only of lines. It is a rhizome" (Deleuze and Guattari 263).

In other words, haecceities are all molecular, rhizomic, indicating a way of resisting the homogenizing and standardizing forces of modern society that seek to reduce everything to a common denominator. They are "a mode of individuation differentiated from that of a person, subject, thing or substance" defined by the molar line in the striated space, consisting entirely of "relations of movement and rest between molecules or particles, capacities to affect and be affected" (Deleuze and Guattari 261). This is the key to the limbo, to the Kefahuchi Tract or the event site, to the place that defies certainty, subjectivity, the Cogito, to the plane of immanence where there are only becomings, subject-*less* individuations and molecular collectivities.

I will now elaborate on three examples of haecceity in the Kefahuchi Tract trilogy, and one of them is constituted by Michael Kearney and the Shrander's dice. Kearney takes a few dice from the Shrander accidentally in his childhood, spending the rest of his life suffering from (or enjoying) his "terror and ecstasy" of the unreadable symbols on the dice and the unpredictable pattern after their throws: "For twenty years they had been his secret conundrum, part of the centralising puzzle of his life" (Harrison, *Light* 296, 125). The dice guide him, teach him, confuse him, convince him of "an obscure link between mathematics and prophecy" (Botting 229), and between the certainty of numbers and the uncertainty of probability. They lead him to his rendezvous with the Shrander and eventually with the Kefahuchi Tract.

Vic Serotonin and the daughter-code also constitute a haecceity in *Nova Swing*. He smuggles the daughter-code from inside the deterritorialized Saudade event site, along with the sense of *the multiple* connoted in its proliferation by "contagion, epidemics, battlefields, and catastrophes" (Deleuze and Guattari 241). It is a code of mutation and deformation, the "worst" thing people such as Vic have ever brought out of the site. For humans on Saudade, "a daughter code would change shape on you. It wasn't alive, it wasn't technology either: no one knew what it did, no one knew what it was for" (Harrison, *Nova* 60). It brings an epidemic in Saudade; it looks "like a catastrophe" (168). They build quarantine hulks high above the earth in Saudade's orbit for those who are infected and became non-people such as Paulie DeRaad, who is "by now more of a notion than a person you could actually describe" (229). They are deformed into the *body without organs*, freed from all the molar, binary structures in their previous world and sent on a journey to form a new species: "[I]f there *is* a new species," says Renoko, who is probably a robot made by the Shrander, "perhaps it's up there in those quarantine hulks" (Harrison, *Empty* 36; emphasis in original).

Anna Waterman and her summerhouse constitute another haecceity in *Empty Space*. The summerhouse is a place of oblivion, a storage space for the stuff she has collected throughout her psychotic and paranoid life.

"Everything that was wrong stemmed from the summerhouse" (Harrison, *Empty* 279), from all the ordinary objects that contained extraordinary forces and magics:

> Christmas tree decorations. A Hornby trainset still in its box. A cannon. Coloured plastic crockery too small for a picnic, too large for a toy [...] joke liquorice, "X-Ray Specs," handcuffs you couldn't take off [...] a japanned box in which you placed a billiard ball you would never find again [...] was the cup with a reflected face in the bottom that turned out not to be your own. (292–3)

It is in this environment that Anna falls into the future, becoming the transformative, woman-shaped creature Pearl in the Pearlent Labyrinth, a space "constructed with such exquisite fractality that the term 'centre' could only ever be a distraction" (142). Like those merging with the daughter-code in Saudade, she too is deterritorialized into a body without organs, an embodiment of the Kefahuchi Tract itself. In this way, she breaks the "white wall" that constrains Captain Ahab. She blends with the limbo beyond the comprehension of all creatures *with organs* in the universe. The essence of the Kefahuchi Tract is not for us to *understand*; it is a plane of immanence where we *become*, through the haecceities, through molecules, through Kearney's becoming-dice, Vic's becoming-daughter-code, Anna's becoming-summerhouse, as well as other becomings I do not have the space to elaborate here: Seria's becoming-posthuman (Jarvis 179), Chianese's becoming-fish-tank, the unnamed cyborg Assistant's becoming-Pearlent. Their familiar reality is cracking, the molar systems deconstructed, the Cognito undermined, the One replaced by the rhizome, and the formation of centre and hierarchy transgressed under the eerie light from the Kefahuchi Tract, a frontier towards the anomalous, towards the uncoded, towards the point of no return, through the line of flight.

Past the Point of No Return

Apparently, the title "Past the Point of No Return" is inspired by *The Phantom of the Opera* (1986). In Act II, towards the climax before the interval, there comes the famous duet between the Phantom and Christine:

> Past the point of no return
> The final threshold
> What warm, unspoken secrets will we learn
> Beyond the point of no return?
> [...]
> Past the point of no return
> The final threshold
> The bridge is crossed, so stand and watch it burn
> We've passed the point of no return

Of course, the line "past the point of no return" indicates the Phantom's obsessive love towards Christine, an affection without blessings. For the Phantom, this love is a way of escape, to run away from his miserable childhood and the humiliation caused by his deformed face. He tries to win this love from Christine, to go beyond the threshold, beyond the point of no return. Here in fact, "the *point* of no return" is not a point. It is a Deleuzian *line*, through which the Phantom could deterritorialize himself from his sufferings while pursuing love.

Then, what about the Kefahuchi Tract? What are Harrison's characters running from? What "unspoken secret" can we learn from the process of becoming and "wall-breaking" in these novels? Like all other writers of the British SF Boom, Harrison's works are also endowed with profound political connotations. A commonly recognized example of this is *Signs of Life* (1997), which Mark Bould considers "the most brilliant satire on the Britain of Thatcher-Major-Blair" ("Old, Mean" 330). It is deeply rooted in our reality, telling a story of "*personal* fulfilment and neoliberal *self*-fashioning in a Petri dish of biotechnology, marketing and capital, all unleashed by financial (and ethical) deregulation" (Botting 230; emphasis added). Despite the narrative strand set in the 2400s, the Kefahuchi Trilogy is solidly anchored in what happens in its contemporary strand.

Coerced by the Thatcherite governance of marketization and privatization, especially in higher education and research, Kearney and Tate's project is very much dependent on funding from Meadows Venture Capital. When Kearney confronts their sponsor Gordon Meadows, he is told: "[no] money [...] no research. We need fresh capital. And a move like [selling Kearney's project to a merchant bank] – as long as we thought it was good for the science – would expand our opportunities, not limit them" (Harrison, *Light* 130). And of course, by "opportunities" Gordon does not indicate potential scientific findings. What he means is to produce "a pure, weightless bubble: boost capitalisation, float, talk the stock up, and profit-take a stage or two before the product was due onstream" (129). In a similar manner, their research suite, an annexe of Imperial College, is also "orphaned recently into the care of free market economies" (106).

Four hundred years later around the Kefahuchi Tract, the same panorama of capitalist realism is still the foundation of human society. In the face of the ancient yet far more advanced technology left by previous adventurers, that is, the "ghost train" made of "alien vehicles that hung nose to tail in a long cometary orbit," human beings are more inclined to extract and exploit its economic values. "They mined those ships like any other kind of resource. Nobody knew what they did, or how they got here, or how to work them; so they cut them up and melted them down, and sold them via a subcontractor to some corporate [...] It made a local economy" (100). This is a cowboy economy – humans come not to discover, but to destroy. They wage wars against the aliens they find in this part of universe, regarding them as potential competitors splitting the profit they are about to earn. They think they are the centre, the point of origin of an arborescent discourse. They resort to the Self, to anthropocentrism, to a kind of certainty out of uncertainty, out of "an insecurity magnificent in scope, metaphysical in nature" (139), in the same way as the Dark Forest takes shape.

Likewise, Saudade in *Nova Swing* is also a place of conflict and market competition fuelled by capital. Genetically modified gladiators fight for money, and that is their "trade," their way of life. They live in "one-shot cultivars," cloned bodies able to sustain only one single fight, and after that they have to go to the "tailors" to fix the damage or to be copied into another cultivar. They can have infinite bodies in this way, but they belong to none. Essentially their mind is detached from their biological beings, becoming a set of numerical codes or algorithms for whom everything is judged based on mathematical calculations. This, again, chimes with how Michael Kearney views the Kefahuchi Tract before embracing it through constituting a haecceity, the *becoming-dice*. As he sees it on the news, he says to his ex-wife Anna, who comments on how beautiful it looks:

> It doesn't look like that [...] It doesn't look like anything. It's just data from some X-ray telescope. Just some numbers, massaged to make an image. Look around [...] That's all anything is. Nothing but statistics [...] Something called decoherence holds the world into place the way we see it: but people like Brian Tate [and himself] are going to find maths that will go round the end of that. Any day now we'll just go round decoherence on the back of the maths, and all this [images of the Kefahuchi Tract] will mean as much to us as it does to a photon. (92)

Such a sense of capitalist realism and self-centredness of competition and calculation in nature is what Harrison wishes to challenge through his creation of the Kefahuchi Tract and the Saudade event site, and what his characters strive to escape from throughout the trilogy. Under the unfathomable light from this singularity without an event horizon, immersed in a discourse of transition and mobility, the old industrial quarter in Saudade where a Kefahuchi fragment lands shatters like the night sky in the eyes of Luo Ji in *The Dark Forest*. Its structures – "the warren of factories, warehouses, docks and ship canals which at that time connected Saudade to the ocean" (Harrison, *Nova* 158) – become fluid, melting into the air: "Commerce had ended instantly, but its characteristic architecture remained [...] a maze of empty buildings with collapsing corrugated roofs and broken drainpipes, their iron window frames bashed in and emptied of glass" (158).

But these are not ruins. They are all different kinds of haecceities, things that are always in the process of becoming and shaping, each of which "in a different style of mediation," would "[generate] a brief norm, [while] reframing everything else" (164). "It [is] like a *parody* of the original function of the original place" (163; emphasis added), but it is not the "blank parody" that Fredric Jameson has criticized in the cultural logic of the late capitalism (Jameson, *Postmodernism* 17). It is not *blank* at all, but rather colourful, allowing for a line of flight that could lead us to a place without all the economic/financial bubbles and the ontology of competition that marks reality outside the reach of the Kefahuchi Tract.

In the final instalment *Empty Space*, Harrison adds something more about the economic context of contemporary London based on what he learned from the Financial Crisis of 2007–8. After Anna's death from a stroke, her daughter Marnie recalls the general social environment when her mother was still alive, a scene that appears opposite to the heyday of the Thatcherite market that Kearney experienced several decades ago in fictional time:

> Outside Wyndlesham [the village where Anna was living, twenty-five miles south-west of central London], stagflation wrote itself over everything like graffiti. Peak oil had come and gone. No one knew how to blow the next bubble. The financial sector, stunned by the discovery that money had been as postmodernised as everything else, passively allowed the state to clip its wings. Bankers seeking explanations read Baudrillard forty years too late [...] Adults were forced to find new ways of viewing the idea of success; children were having to mature earlier. (Harrison, *Empty* 296)

It seems that after this economic recession, people have changed a little. On the landscape of "empty industrial estates and abandoned parking structures" (297) which Marnie sees when she travels home by train, people propose a post-recession reform called "the New Economics" that calls for a discourse more based on cooperation, mutual association and social investment where banking is no longer the rule, and where Marnie is brought security.

As indicated in the lyrics of *The Phantom of the Opera*, the point of no return is the final threshold, the point where the bridge can be burned down, where all previous understandings, previous structures, previous history, politics, economy and society can all be put into question. With the Dark Forest and the Kefahuchi Tract, Liu Cixin and Harrison have elaborated completely different ways of responding to the sense of uncertainty in the face of the point of no return. The *Three-Body* trilogy is more like a declaration of war, prioritizing market competition, through its hunter metaphor, among all economized human capital as the only way of survival in a post-socialist China, a social Darwinian manifesto. In this way, it creates a rather different sense of sf realism, a term most famously attributed to Chen Qiufan who claims that sf is "the greatest realism at the present time [that] provides a window for imagination through its open realism, to delineate a reality no mainstream literature has written about" (Ren 55). This is also how Liu Cixin talks about the "narcissism" of sf, by which he is allowed to subvert and expand the concepts of mainstream literature (Liu, "Beyond" 24), and to design thought experiments like the Dark Forest as a response to politics, culture and history.

Harrison, however, creates a Deleuzo-Guattarian sense of transition and escape. Contrary to Liu Cixin's obsession with the engulfment of the Other by an omnipotent Self, the Kefahuchi Tract defies the binary structure of the Self-Other dichotomy. It defies the One, the point of origin and the tree system, envisioning a plane of immanence of multiplicity. It indicates a special way for us to interrogate the capitalist realism of contemporary London, where Kearney lost his research project to the market, where the left has not recovered its political influences ever since its defeat in the mid-1980s and where the legacies of Margaret Thatcher are still enshrined by policy makers today. In the end, compared to the market boom of the *Three-Body* industry, to the hunting ecstasy it reflects upon, I prefer the Deleuzian line of flight that welcomes and embraces the alternatives. I stand with Ed Chianese in this case, who achieves his deterritorialization in the last few pages of *Light* by flying straight into the Tract, somehow returning to us again in *Empty Space*. Literally appearing in a deformed body with no organs at all, he says: "I came to free the people" (Harrison, *Empty* 253). But the people who can be truly freed are not those who are fond of wars, unlike the humans around the Kefahuchi Tract, nor are they the Dark Forest hunters, who see only enemies.

Marching with Ed towards the final threshold, towards the point of no return, are those contained in hulks, the quarantine compartments to hold those who have been infected with the daughter-code and become haecceities. "There were hundreds of millions of them" (286), and they are the true future.

EPILOGUE

A Confession of Breach

> But if you breach, even if it's not your fault, for more than the shortest time ... you can't come back from that [...] None of us were born [in Breach]. We were all once in one place or the other. All of us breached once.
>
> – China Miéville, in *The City & The City*

Breaching the Boundary and Seeing the Booms

So, this is how we conclude the tale of The Boom & The Boom, a tale that constructs a zone of "Breach" where the British and the Chinese SF Boom may finally converge. In fact, the booms have been here all along, just below the radar of each other, like the twin cities of Besźel and Ul Qoma in China Miéville's *The City & The City*. There is an area-in-between, a limbo known as Breach beyond the horizon of both Besźel and Ul Qoma. Although people from both cities are trained only to see what they are supposed to see and to unsee what belong to the other side of reality, there are always those who breach the invisible barrier. Sometimes these breaches are committed intentionally for criminal purposes or out of people's growing dissatisfaction with the twin-city division, but more often they are inadvertently committed through hazard avoidance such as self-protection from fire or car accidents.

In either way, however, all breaches need to be taken care of. Orders of unseeing must be reinstated, and holes in the barrier require diligent repair. Maintaining the segregated autonomy of the two cities and the invisibility of *the other* appears more important than enforcing the local laws. This responsibility falls upon a mysterious organization that claims superiority over both governments, identifying itself as Breach. For the residents of Besźel and Ul Qoma, the avatars of Breach seem like elusive ghosts. They come from nowhere, take the breachers away, and vanish into obscurity once again. They are therefore considered a kind of secret police in a quasi-Orwellian fashion, a symbol of unspeakable terror.

But as *The City & The City* unfolds, we discover that the fate awaiting breachers is not necessarily torturous punishment or compulsory re-education. For some chosen ones, such as Inspector Tyador Borlú, it represents an invitation to cross the point of no return – a chance for rebirth or reincarnation. Once breached, the border is gone forever. "You'll never unsee again" (Miéville, *City* 371). The breachers become part of the Breach. They transcend the invisible barrier and live in both cities in an "unseen" state, but in so doing they also relinquish their original homes, becoming vagabonds just like Luoying who travels between Earth and Mars in Hao Jingfang's *Vagabonds.* They may walk across both Beszél and Ul Qoma, but they reside in neither.

Meanwhile, breaching the boundary also initiates a Deleuzian line of flight, enabling the breachers to break free "from its socially articulated, disciplined, semioticized, and subjectified state [...] to become disarticulated, dismantled, and deterritorialized, and hence able to be reconstituted in new ways" (Best and Kellner 90–1). They have breached all pre-settled structures that resist the potential of change, transition and transgression. As Borlú articulates in the final page of *The City & The City*: "Inspector Tyador Borlú is gone. I sign off Tye, avatar of Breach [...] We are all philosophers here where I am, and we debate among many other things the question of where it is that we live. On that issue I am a liberal. I live in the interstice yes, but I live in both the city and the city" (Miéville, *City* 373).

In this sense, I too have breached. I have seen both the Boom and the Boom that used to be parallel and invisible to each other, and since then, they are no longer separate. Their connections in historical and political-economic contexts, when examined in hindsight, begin to unveil themselves. This reminds me of Paul Kincaid's review of *The Cambridge History of Science Fiction* (2019) co-edited by Gerry Canavan and Eric Carl Link, a monumental anthology which he believes challenges the American-centric history of sf and re-writes it with a hope of amplifying the previously repressed voices from the "unseen" worlds – voices from China, South and South-eastern Asia, Eastern Europe, Middle East, Latin America and black Africa. "Such cultural differences give this sf a different feel from the Campbellian hard sf we are used to, but it is sf nonetheless" (Kincaid, "Is" 217), and they all respond in various ways to the socio-political condition in related countries, regions and nations at specific moments.

No matter how global or how planetary sf could have become, it is always anchored firmly and profoundly in the soil of particular places. And to truly understand a place, according to Yi-Fu Tuan, "requires long residence and deep involvement" that may result in collective experiences, emotions and memories (Tuan 164). This is why sf is in essence a historical and political genre, and thus should be read in line with history and politics. Despite the diverse array of sf writings disguised under the ostensible universality shaped largely by the American tradition, what is there is still there, waiting to be discovered and reinterpreted. "Once the will was there, it didn't really take long to start unearthing them" (Kincaid, "Is" 216).

World SF as Hyperobject

This rendezvous of the British and Chinese SF Boom is apparently long overdue. Emerging in a similar historical period and responding to an interconnected process of political-economic transition, they exist in a state of mutual invisibility for most of the time. To make sense of this rendezvous, Liu Cixin's Hugo Award in 2015 was seen as a pivotal moment. His bestseller *The Three-Body Problem* appeared as a manifesto of the Chinese Boom jumping right into the horizon of Anglo-American readers. Their surprise of witnessing the very first Hugo winner for Best Novel not originally written in English prompted English-speaking readers to truly realize what it means by the oft-cited phrase "sf is a global genre." In fact, sf is always a global genre. It is people – readers and scholars alike – who are confined in their limited horizons shaped by what is familiar to them, complying with the rules imposed by various boundaries. They must also breach the invisible wall before comprehending the convergence of the two booms and embrace what they have chosen, consciously or not, to unsee.

In many ways, I consider myself fortunate, because breaching the invisible boundary and having myself exiled into the limbo between the two Booms have allowed me to embark on another rewarding quest – one that probes into a larger conceptual entity commonly termed "world sf." On a cold winter morning in December 2017, I set out alone on a train journey from London's St Pancras to Canterbury, participating as a postgraduate student in my first academic conference, which aimed to commemorate the centenary of Arthur C. Clarke, titled "2017: A Clarke Odyssey," in this way paying homage to his classic novel *2001: A Space Odyssey*. The theme of my presentation, now seemingly outdated, had consumed all my intellectual energy at the time – a comparative case study of Liu Cixin and his sf mentor Arthur C. Clarke.

The conference was not large in scale, able to be squeezed into a single-day programme, and it was precisely this small group of people who eventually guided me to breach the boundary. After I elaborated at length on the "sense of wonder" and "sublime" in *The Dark Forest* and *Death's End*, someone in the audience approached me: "I've read the entire *Three-Body* trilogy. But compared to the last two volumes, I'd prefer the first one. Somehow, I feel *The Dark Forest* and *Death's End* seem to lack a lot of depth, so I couldn't really grasp the 'sense of wonder' and 'sublime' you just talked about." At that moment, I didn't realize what he meant by "lack of depth." I briefly explained the differences between the first volume *The Three-Body Problem* and its two sequels from the perspectives of translation and narratology, concluding the topic rather hastily.

It was not until much later that I truly understood the significance of this conversation. For a long time afterward, on numerous occasions in London, Liverpool, Leeds, Lancaster and Dublin, I heard similar questions and confusion. For Chinese readers, *The Three-Body Problem* is generally considered the prologue to the entire series. While all the excitement, twists, suspense and shock begin here, the greater impact of the trilogy lies in the dark laws of cosmology revealed in *The Dark Forest* and the apocalyptic MAD deterrence in *Death's End*. But why do British readers find the last two instalments lacking, with only the first being sufficiently interesting? In their eyes, what so-called "depth" is missing?

In October 2019 – two years after my trip to Canterbury – the London Science Fiction Research Community (LSFRC) annual conference, themed "Productive Futures," explored the inherent subversive and revolutionary aspects of sf writings from a political-economic perspective. During the event, I delved further into the cultural and literary significance of the middle volume *The Dark Forest*, emphasizing the reshaping of social subjects by the Chinese market economy over the past thirty years and the resulting shifts in power relations and cultural paradigms (which eventually became a major section in Chapter 5 of this book). During a coffee break, one of the panellists sought me out, sharing her ideas on the differences between *The Dark Forest* and its prequel. She noted that *The Three-Body Problem* felt more like a "Chinese" sf novel to her. What intrigued her the most was Liu Cixin's environmental descriptions of Radar Peak and the Greater Khingan Mountains, along with his references to Rachel Carson. These elements, in one way or another, were enlightening for her own research on contemporary Chinese history and politics. But to my surprise, the grand narratives in *The Dark Forest* and *Death's End* celebrated by Chinese readers were not something she would anticipate in her reading experience, only because they do not exhibit distinctive characteristics of "Chineseness."

At that moment, I came to realize that the reception of Chinese sf in the UK (and the rest of the world) might not solely be influenced by the quality of the original works and their English translation. It also depends on the subjectivity of British readers and the "fusion of horizons" between the text and the contemporary British social context (see Gadamer). From such a perspective of hermeneutics, the so-called "Chineseness" becomes one of the primary elements that British readers wish to see. In a way, Chineseness inherits the essence of the "Chinoiserie" that first emerged in the seventeenth-century France, when "Orientalism" was in vogue in Europe, heavily tinged with colonial undertones. The academic community showed a strong interest in literary works from the East, full of exotic charm. However, their starting point was not an acknowledgement of the intrinsic values of Asian literatures but rather viewing them as an "other" serving as a mirror in support of "the process of self-understanding," thereby participating in the political and cultural transition of Europe itself (Zhang L. 114).

Currently, the unprecedented attention of sf readers to works from non-English-speaking worlds is indeed a rarity in the entire history of British literature. Various concepts such as Afrofuturism, Sino-futurism, Latinx Futurism, Muslim Futurism, Indigenous Futurism and many other futurisms have become the most debated topics. At the 2022 Science Fiction Research Association (SFRA) annual conference themed "Futures from the Margins," Egyptian sf artist Ganzeer declared with great optimism and determination to highlight what was missing in mainstream sf studies: "Margins aren't at the fringes of a page; they are most of the page" (Lyu, "SFRA" 46). But at the same time, we also need to be vigilant: to what extent is the centre's focus on the margin about the margin *per se*? And how much of the expectation for the so-called "Chineseness" by British readers is genuinely about China?

Of course, I am not suggesting a wholesale rejection of the interpretations offered by British readers regarding *The Three-Body Problem* and other Chinese sf novels. After all, considering the "autonomy" of literary works, each reading represents a fusion of reader experience and the horizons of the text. There is no right and wrong in our comprehension of the text, as long as it aligns with the public rationality within the framework of hermeneutics. From a certain perspective, these interpretations from the English-speaking world even transcend the cultural and political context constituted in Chinese, enabling us to perceive issues and topics that are crucial but often overlooked among Chinese readers.

This said, however, the endorsement of Chineseness in the English-speaking world has indeed constructed a disciplinary discourse. It appears that only Chinese sf with a presumed foundation of Chineseness can be accepted by English readers, gaining attention in the market and academia, and therefore becoming part of the "world sf," which in turn influences the promotion and circulation of Chinese sf in the domestic market and defines what "good sf" looks like in the eyes of Chinese readers and authors. In this scenario, if Chinese sf were to diverge from the established cultural spectacle and writing paradigm associated with Chineseness, how can it establish a meaningful relationship with English readers? How can it truly integrate into the global landscape and be categorized as part of "world literature"?

As a response, the concept of "worlding" has been cited multiple times. In early 2020, the COVID-19 pandemic swept across the globe, sparing not even Harvard University, which was forced to suspend classes. David Damrosch returned to his home in Brooklyn, starting another global journey in a different sense. Beginning from June, he assumed the role of Phileas Fogg from Jules Verne's *Around the World in Eighty Days* (1873), updating on Harvard's website every day an article discussing a classic work of world literature. From Virginia Woolf in the UK to Italo Calvino in Italy, from Chinua Achebe in Nigeria to Rabindranath Tagore in India, from Eileen Chang in China to Yukio Mishima in Japan and finally to Margaret Atwood in Canada, these resounding names were once again interwoven here, forming a vast network known as "world literature," which aligns with his most well-known monograph *What is World Literature?* (2003). In fact, Damrosch's project of "Around the World with Eighty Books" itself can be considered a practice of world literature. From the first week of the journey, his articles have been simultaneously translated into various languages, including Arabic, Turkish, Romanian, German and, of course, Chinese (organized by Song Mingwei).

To some extent, this also shows the crucial role of "translation" in Damrosch's understanding of world literature. As he argues in *What is World Literature?*, world literature is not a fixed set of literary classics but rather a mode of reading, "an elliptical refraction of national literatures" that becomes enriched through translation (Damrosch 281). In this light, Chinese sf, benefitting from the current translation fervour, is gaining increasingly noticeable international influence. It appears to have truly become a part of the global literary scene, joining the diverse tapestry of sf from other countries and cultures. Together, they weave a grand narrative that can be aptly termed "world sf."

Since the 2010s, translators such as Ken Liu, Jin Xueni (Emily), Carlos Rojas, Andy Dudak, Joel Martinsen, Ni Xueting and others have tirelessly contributed with their excellent translation skills and selfless passion. They have shaped Chinese sf into the most dazzling growth point on the map of world sf. "Sino-futurism" has burst forth with vitality, and to a certain degree, the "worlding" of Chinese sf stays at the central position of the English-speaking world in the domain of sf. This has given rise to a "post-humanist" matrix of world sf based on differences, diversity and a rejection of universality and totality.

Therefore, the process of "worlding" seems to become an essential path for Chinese sf to join world sf. In 2017, after years in the making, *A New Literary History of Modern China* finally came into being. In this book, editor David Der-wei Wang borrows Martin Heidegger's concept of "being-in-the-world," considering it a key to writing the history of Chinese literature. Challenging the Cartesian dualism that divides the subject (consciousness) from the object (the external world), Heidegger believes our existence is not something separate from the world; instead, we are always already in the world, engaging with it in various ways. Similarly, *Dasein* does not exist as a detached subject observing the world from a distance, because the world serves the context in which *Dasein*'s existence may truly unfold. "Men alone, as mortals, by dwelling attain to the world as world. Only what conjoins itself out of world becomes a thing" (Heidegger 182). Following his Heideggerian arguments, Wang contends that the concept of worlding "may help us to understand Chinese literary modernity in the broader sense of *wen*, as a vehicle 'bringing the world home,' and, more importantly, as an agency that continuously opens up new configurations of the world" (Wang D. 14; emphasis in original).

From here, Song Mingwei steps further. In 2022, he contributed a chapter titled "The Worlding of Chinese Science Fiction" to the anthology *The Making of Chinese/Sinophone Literatures as World Literature*. Drawing from Damrosch, Song believes that the translation and overseas circulation of Chinese sf aim not only to construct and enrich "world sf" but also, to some extent, to engage in a process of self-reflection and correction for Chinese sf itself. In the unique publishing context with Chinese characteristics, certain works, due to touching on various sensitive issues, have been unable to reach readers in their most "authentic" form in Chinese. For instance, Liu Cixin's "China 2185," available to read in 1989 and seen as the beginning of the Chinese SF Boom, has never been officially published. Han Song's "My Country Does Not Dream," written in the early 2000s, only reached readers nearly twenty years later through the translation by Nathaniel Isaacson. In Bao Shu's "Songs of Ancient Earth," the music from a distant galaxy had to be changed from patriotic Chinese songs from the

Mao years to Soviet songs to pass the publisher's internal review. Similarly, Ken Liu's English translation of *The Three-Body Problem* restored the original narrative logic of the novel. The impact of the Cultural Revolution on Ye Wenjie is more pronounced, and the gender stereotypes in the original narrative are weakened and rewritten, "[making] the narrative more coherent and complete" (127). Without Ken Liu, *The Three-Body Problem*'s Hugo victory would simply be impossible.

However, since the publication of *What is World Literature?* in 2003, Damrosch's views have never been free from controversy and debate. The "elliptical refraction" between national literatures seems more like a Babel-like utopian vision but faces various challenges in practice. Although Damrosch's initial aim is to break away from English-centrism and rediscover the connection between literatures in minority languages and the "world" in general, readers in the English-speaking world are often unfamiliar with non-English literary works. Without English as an intermediary, the "worlding" of these local literatures is undoubtedly very difficult, which inevitably involves factors beyond literature itself. For popular cultural forms like sf, such intermediaries can even play a decisive role – only works accepted by readers can become bestsellers, and only works accepted by English readers can become bestsellers worldwide. This is what Istvan Csicsery-Ronay, Jr. means by "the language bottleneck and the politics of translation" (482) in his 2012 article in *SFS* "What Do We Mean When We Say 'Global Science Fiction'?"

In October 2020, the Dutch translation of *The Three-Body Problem* was published, marking the twenty-fifth language version of the novel. If there were indeed a category referred to as "world sf" or "global sf," *The Three-Body Problem* would definitely deserve a place on the list. However, what if it hadn't won the Hugo Award in 2015? What if the "Puppygate" incident of that year hadn't generated such a strong reaction? If *The Three-Body Problem* hadn't dominated the English market, would it still have had the opportunity to be translated into other languages? Are there alternative ways to comprehend "world sf" or even "world literature" itself?

Standing in the limbo between the Boom and the Boom, I find myself pondering whether sf has ever been truly global in the sense we commonly understand. According to Damrosch, world literature is in fact a *constructed* concept, a "cognitive-aesthetic artifact" or a "cognitive map" in Csicsery-Ronay, Jr.'s words, which is always "mutating and even passing away at the moment the map is drawn" ("What" 488). In other words, while national literatures enter the realm of the "world" through translation, every single work translated into another language holds the potential to influence and reshape the landscape of so-called "world literature." Consequently, national or local literature always draws inspiration from a world literature that has already changed, feeding back into its own cultural context, much like Heidegger's perception of the relationship between *Dasein* and the world. As Csicsery-Ronay, Jr. quotes Vilashini Cooppan:

> Any map presents the global as a local utterance, for any attempt to represent "the world" inevitably bespeaks the mapmaker's own placement. To change a map, then, is to change not only what we look at, but also the very place and premises from which we look. It is to encounter not just the strangeness of the world, but our own selves made strange. (Cooppan 27)

From this perspective, Damrosch's "elliptical refraction" seems limited only to the national literatures that can be *seen* – those endorsed or recognized by certain authorities before translated – while the rest remain invisible, left in the dark, awaiting the light that may never illuminate them. However, darkness does not imply emptiness. Beyond the horizon of world literature authorized by translation, this *unseen* world might have cradled a kind of literary vitality in its most extraordinary forms, offering profound responses and critiques to the dominating "totality."

This, eventually, brings us to "hyperobject." In 2013, drawing on Quentin Meillassoux's speculative realism and Graham Harman's object-oriented ontology, Timothy Morton published one of his most influential works *Hyperobjects: Philosophy and Ecology after the End of the World*. In his terminology, a hyperobject refers to an absolute being that is massively distributed in time and space, surpassing our normal perceptual and cognitive capacities. It is "non-local," implying that their entirety cannot be grasped at any specific location or moment; it is also "viscous," often associated with ordinary yet complex and interconnected phenomena present "right here in my social and experiential space" (Morton 27). Climate, for Morton, is considered a quintessential hyperobject. Everything visible to the naked eye – from rising sea levels and animal extinctions to frequent floods and even a fallen leaf nearby – appears as one of the numerous tentacles extending from the same entity. Some tentacles have reached us, becoming illuminated by an observing subject; others, however, are "withdrawn" from our world, forcing upon us a strange world where the subject is absent – a world "without us" (94). With the concept of hyperobject, our way of perceiving the world undergoes a profound transformation. "Intersubjectivity" is no longer effective; instead, "interobjectivity" takes its place. In this vast world of darkness, the interaction, fusion, change and becoming among objects are more intense, fascinating and productive than one can ever imagine.

Can we see "world sf" also as a kind of hyperobject? Or is "world sf" itself a manifestation of "world literature" as a hyperobject at a particular moment? From this perspective, all the attempts to perceive, categorize and conceptualize "world sf" might prove futile, since hyperobjects tend to withdraw from the horizon of subjects, consistently obscuring themselves. In fact, it is through its "local" experiences that a "national sf" becomes able to get close to the hyperobject behind "world sf." This does not necessarily require the mediation of a subject (such as English and the Anglo-American market), as objects do not need endorsement or validation from any authority. What is expected then the discovery of the specificity-rooted locality within the rift of totality.

This prompts us to consider different questions – where does the novel take place? What cultural traditions and political contexts inspire the novel from that specific place? Can we gain knowledge about that place *per se* through reading a piece of sf? Here in this tale of the Boom and the Boom, what insights can we derive about post-socialist China from novels by the Boom writers such as Liu Cixin, Han Song and Hao Jingfang? And, considering the British Boom as a political divergence from the globalized and neoliberalized "Empire" (see Hardt and Negri *Empire*) commonly associated with the US, what lessons can we learn about post-Thatcher UK from those listed in Andrew M. Butler's "(Partial) Census" ("Thirteen" 374–93)?

Local Lessons: Silent Clamour or Sense of Doubleness?

In *Scar* (2002), sequel to *Perdido Street Station*, China Miéville portrays a young sailor named Shekel. Born in New Crobuzon, Shekel is deprived of education and remains illiterate because of poverty. But when he arrives at the floating city of Armada, drifting on the Swollen Ocean like a Deleuzian nomad (Lyu, "Library" 47–53), all his previous social ties are deconstructed, shackles broken, sins forgiven, providing him with a fresh start and an opportunity to learn reading and writing. He feels "ravenous for the unprecedented sensation of meaning coming up at him from the page, from behind the letters like an escape" (Miéville, *Scar* 177–8). All of a sudden, he finds himself surrounded by words – "signs visible on the commercial street beyond the windows, signs throughout the library and across the city [...] and he knew that there was no way he would ever be deaf to all those words again." He is thrilled by this "silent clamour" (178), knowing that this newfound world of words, once seen, has now become an integral part of his being, making it impossible for him to *unsee* again.

This holds true for the British SF Boom as well. For most of the time, the Boom remained omnipresent but unnoticed, maintaining relative silence within the literary and cultural domains. The first spark of the Boom can be traced back to the melancholy of left-wing intellectuals in the 1980s, aligning with the anti-Thatcherism sentiments prevalent in mainstream literature at the time (see W. Brown, "Resisting" 19–27). Hiding behind the mainstream, British sf thrived quietly, nourishing themselves on the epochal shifts when individual men and women are left responsible for themselves, and when market competition has redefined social subjects. It was precisely due to this "silence" that British sf managed to escape assimilation into the mainstream during the mainstreaming process of British popular culture in the 1990s, marked by the Cool Britannia movement. It retained its political criticality, single-handedly sketching out the utopian alternatives that became increasingly hard to imagine in the context of capitalist realism.

At the turn of the millennium, the hidden clamour within this silence was finally set free. In the late summer of 2000, Andrew M. Butler, in *Vector*, explored the sf boom of the previous decade in the UK, stating,

> With writers like Miéville, MacLeod, [John] Meaney and many more, sf in Britain at the end of the century seems to be revolutionary: clearly in a tradition, but still finding new ways to tell new (and old) stories. Could this be another Golden Age? Or am I being just too utopian? ("View" 3)

Clearly, it was not merely Butler's utopian thinking. The following summer, the University of Liverpool organized an important conference themed "2001: A Celebration of British SF," in this way celebrating Arthur C. Clarke's *2001: A Space Odyssey* when the year 2001 was finally no longer in the future, with keynote speeches from prominent authors such as Stephen Baxter, Gwyneth Jones and Ken MacLeod (Mendlesohn, "Call" 381). Through these intellectual collisions, scholars finally recognized the British SF Boom that had been underestimated for too long. Similar to the world of words unveiled to Shekel in *The Scar*, British sf was not the elephant in the room anymore; it became an unmistakable left-wing trend that people could never ignore again. The Boom, therefore, provides a utopian *process* not an *end*, always self-changing, always in transition and always in conversation with the historical and political-economic discourses in which it is rooted, exploring the new possibilities of post-Thatcherism, post-Blairism, postcapitalism and even post-postcapitalism.

On the other side of the world, in a similar vein, the Chinese SF Boom should also be interpreted with historical and political-economic awareness, but the historical rupture it responds to appears more dramatic. Unlike the British Boom, which is able to inherit New Wave legacies from the writers of an older generation who continued their writing careers during the Boom, the Chinese Boom rose from ashes. No one was left from the older generation, all of them victimized during the politically endorsed campaign against "spiritual pollution" in late 1983. Since then, there was a void, a kind of collective aphasia within the sf community because the thaw-era writers had all turned their interests away from writing sf. They were all disappointed, discouraged and, above all, afraid of another round of political persecution.

The reasons behind this aphasia are complicated, but one of the most undeniable is the troubled relationship between the thaw-era Chinese sf and the elitist discourse of the new enlightenment formed after the Cultural Revolution, where intellectuals, students and reform-minded politicians "undertook a broad cultural reformation designed to liberate the Chinese from 'self-incurred immaturity'" (Tu 103) and to embrace the scientific values underpinning the Four Modernizations project. In a 1987 article published in *People's Daily*, Ye Yonglie shared his conversation in December 1981 with Han Suyin, who wrote in both English and French on modern China. She told Ye: "[W]hen I met Deng Xiaoping in 1977, I suggested to him that China should promote sf [...] which is a matter of future and of national development [...] I think that sf's influence on our children is enormous. It can be used to cultivate their interests in science" (Ye 8).

"Interests in science" – this was the prevailing perception of sf among Chinese intellectual elites in the late 1970s and early 1980s, including scientists and science writers who distained sf for descriptions of "pseudo-science," the authors of serious literature who saw sf as "unserious," and the authors of children's literature who only used sf for educational purposes and science popularization. Despite the brief renaissance of Chinese sf during this period, the intellectual field was still ill-prepared to accept it as a political genre. Tong Enzheng and Ye Yonglie, emphasizing the fictional rather than the scientific aspects of sf, soon found themselves targeted with political accusations in a "top-down" atmosphere where "a writer must stand on the high ground of history and bear responsibility to the people" (Li H., *Chinese* 8). While Li Hua contends in her 2021 book that "thaw-era PRC SF actually functioned as a type of government-backed literature," seeing writers as "in-house advocates of a key component of the central government's Four Modernizations agenda" (Li H., *Chinese* 173; emphasis added), I believe the otherwise: Chinese sf during the thaw-era never gained support from the state. What the government backed is a particular kind of sf writing – the kind responding positively to their appeal for technological progresses and enlightenment values. And once the political atmosphere turned against it, it went silent.

Therefore, the emergence of the Chinese SF Boom in the early 1990s is itself a historical rupture, a shift made possible by a broader socio-cultural transition that dismantled the "top-down" intellectual elitism. As the intellectual liberal consensus foundered as a result of the Tiananmen incident in 1989, another component of this consensus, economic transformation, was firmly retained and even strengthened. Any question or confusion of local governments about market reforms were laid to rest by Deng's "southern tour" to special economic zones where he appreciated China's economic development and clarified the necessity to expand these reforms nationwide.

From then on, the market has become the new normal. The new-enlightenment cultural manifestation during the 1980s gradually gave its way to a rising cultural industry, an inevitable consequence of commercialization and marketization. In this way, "pure literature," which once marginalized Chinese sf by denying its literary legitimacy, found itself disciplined by commercial principles. Publishers, too, underwent denationalization in this process. No longer beneficiaries of government public expenditure, many had to sustain themselves through the market. To thrive in the market, they needed to *sell* rather than *deliver* books to the public, whose preferences often differed from those of the intellectual elite. As Jason McGrath points out:

> The critical and scholarly elite were forced into the realization that the free market reforms they had endorsed as part of the overall project of enlightenment and modernization had the unfortunate effect of bringing the most visible cultural expressions down to the level of the common consumer, who seemed to value entertainment and sensory stimulation over enlightenment. (McGrath 27)

Such a transition sparked a fervent debate in the mid-1990s about the loss of the "humanist spirit" (*renwen jingshen*). A group of intellectuals expressed a sense of enlightenment melancholia in response to the surge of popular culture, which they deemed vulgar, self-indulgent and consumerist. However, who won the debate, if there ever was a winner, was hardly important. The momentum of China's marketization and the resulting historical rupture were not dictated by the intellectual elite. Their roles as mentors or advisors to the public came to an end as the "top-down" enlightenment intellectual field gave way to a "bottom-up" discourse, empowering the public with a stronger voice and creating a new political-economic environment in which Chinese sf may flourish once again.

Of course, China's conversion to a market economy is also criticized in many ways by a group of leftist advocates known as the Chinese "New Left." They remind us of the intrinsic problems of capitalist market:

> We must not allow a few financial groups to monopolize the common resources in the world, to set monopoly prices in employment and the market, and to enslave us and produce an antimarket financial crisis in which the rich do not buy for they owe too much, and most people cannot afford to buy for lack of money. We must strive for power for the working class, small and middle enterprises, and peasants. (qtd. in Xu Y. 7)

These warnings against a capitalist-realist future are frequently revisited by the writers of the Chinese Boom, most famously in Liu Cixin's "The Wages of Humanity" ("Shanyang Renlei," 2005), Chen Qiufan's *Waste Tide* (2013) and Hao Jingfang's "Folding Beijing" (2014), among many others. But whereas the British SF Boom aims to build a political stronghold for the left, the Chinese SF Boom has a subtler relation with the market. It shares a kinship with China's economic turn, and to some degree, it even becomes schizophrenic due to a dilemma between denouncing the dystopian capitalist future and eschewing the traumatic revolutionary past, between providing an alternative to the Capitalocene made of fragmental, ahistorical pastiches and avoiding the grand narrative established upon the "top-down" elitism.

For Song Mingwei, the Chinese SF Boom, or what he calls the "new wave" of Chinese sf, gives rise to a new mode of literariness – a poetics of the invisible. He argues that contemporary Chinese sf "points to realms beyond what we can ordinarily perceive, allows for the representations of fears and dreams, and challenges moral conventions and political doctrines" (Song, *Fear* 15). In essence, I agree with this. But in the meantime, as Chinese sf overcomes the fear of seeing and explores the invisible domains of Chinese society and politics, it also indicates a sense of doubleness. Inherently sown and grown in a marketized and denationalized context in the first place, the Chinese Boom holds an ambiguous and hesitant attitude towards China's post-socialist transition that empowers the mass public, on the one hand, and on the other hand also allows for market competition, economization and individualization. Old and new, past and future, nostalgia and prospect, reality and potentiality converge into one. Very often, sf works prompt us to broaden our perspectives, compelling us to explore the interplay between humans and other forms of being from a "global" standpoint. But nevertheless, sf is also grounded in the sense of historicity, woven into specific locales, contextualizing its narratives firmly within localized experiences. It is through this approach, by engaging with the hyperobjects withdrawn from us, that Chinese sf can transcend the ideological implications inherent in "world SF," attaining a state of "being in the world."

No Boom Today, or More Booms to Come?

By all means, Chinese sf is already "in the world." As Niall Harrison highlights "A trickle of Chinese SF has become a healthy and continuous flow, with the volume of new stories, collections and novels probably exceeding the ability of most readers to keep up with it" (N. Harrison 69). Over the past decade, there has been a boom of translating the Boom, making a huge corpus of Chinese sf texts available in English.

A comprehensive translation of Liu Cixin's works, including his *Three-Body* trilogy (2006–10/2014–16), *Ball Lightning* (2004/2017), *Supernova Era* (2003/2019), *Of Ants and Dinosaurs* (2004/2020), and collections such as *The Wandering Earth* (2013) and *Hold Up the Sky* (2020), can be found basically in every sf bookstore in the UK. Additionally, there are translations of *Pathological* (2009/2016) by Wang Jinkang, *Waste Tide* (2013/2019) by Chen Qiufan, *Vagabonds* (2011–12/2020) by Hao Jingfang, and the *Hospital* trilogy (2016–18/2023–5) by Han Song. Numerous novelettes and short stories have been collected in anthologies like *Invisible Planets* (2016) and *Broken Stars* (2019), both edited by Ken Liu, along with *The Reincarnated Giant* (2017) by Song Mingwei, *A Primer to Han Song* (2020) by Eric J. Guignard, *A Summer Beyond Your Reach* (2021) featuring Xia Jia, *AI 2041* (2021) co-authored by Chen Qiufan and Kai-Fu Lee, *Sinopticon* (2021) edited by Ni Xueting, *The Way Spring Arrives and*

Other Stories (2022) by Yu Chen and Wang Kanyu (Regina), and *New Voices in Chinese Science Fiction* (2022) by Neil Clarke, Xia Jia and Wang Kanyu (Regina). While there may be some overlap in the contents of these anthologies, it is important to note the presence of Chinese sf in magazines, particularly those maintaining close collaborations with SF agencies in China – *Clarkesworld* working with Storycom and *Future Science Fiction Digest* with Future Affairs Administration.

At the same time, the once dominant presence of American sf in the Chinese market, as identified by Jiang Qian (123), is undergoing a gradual transformation. The landscape is evolving, with an increasing number of novels and short stories from the British SF Boom becoming accessible to Chinese readers through translation. Notably, five *Culture* novels by Iain M. Banks – *The Player of Games* (2012), *Use of Weapons* (2014), *Consider Phlebas* (2021), *Inversions* (2023) and *Look to Windward* (2023) – have been made available in Chinese, with others in the making. The *Bas-Lag* trilogy by China Miéville, with *Perdido Street Station* and *The Scar* translated in 2013 and *Iron Council* in 2019, has garnered significant readership. Authors like Neil Gaiman, Stephen Baxter, Alastair Reynolds, Ian McDonald, Susanna Clarke, Charles Stross and Christopher Priest are gaining popularity due to the continuous publication of their works since the 2000s, accelerating in the 2010s.

In spite of this boom of translation, however, British sf is still very much underestimated. Some of the most influential works and writers of the British SF Boom are still untranslated, and thus unheard of, including M. John Harrison, Ken MacLeod, Gwyneth Jones, to name a few. James Lovegrove is luckier as he is known for his later IP writings, but his earlier works – those demonstrating the Boom spirit of the 1990s and early 2000s – have not attracted any attention so far.

As the invisible boundary separating the two sf Booms is finally breached, they seem to have entered the late stage of their life cycle. Like all forms of literary and artistic movements throughout our history, the booms emerge, have their days and then fade away or blend into something else. And more often than not, their programmed decline starts before we can notice it, before they reach their peak, and an early sign of this is the fact that people begin to talk about the booms, rather than just experience them. As I just mentioned, the 2001 conference "A Celebration of British SF" held at the University of Liverpool set the tone that the British SF Boom was indeed off and running. The special issues of *SFS* (November 2003) and *Foundation* (Spring 2005) provided a larger room for discussion on an academic and theoretical level, consolidating what used to be a vague impression that a boom was coming. This was a time when the Boom really got attention. But as Andrew M. Butler reminds us that even during its heyday, worried voices "are already beginning to mutter" (Butler, "Thirteen" 389). Paul Kincaid responds to Mark Bould's 2002 article "Bould on the Boom" by demonstrating that the pool of British publishers

> is growing smaller, and looking at the current economic climate, I suspect that advances will be falling, if they haven't fallen already [...] I may well be wrong – I certainly hope I am – but in my moments of typically British pessimism I do wonder whether we have the infrastructure to support the renaissance we seem to be engendering. (Kincaid, "Golden" 531)

Apparently, Kincaid's pessimism reflects more than just his British "can't do spirit." Like the boom itself, the end of the boom is also not a "mass delusion" (Butler, "Thirteen" 374). In a later version of his 2003 *SFS* article reprinted in an Australian fanzine *Steam Engine Time* in 2005, Butler adds a note to extend his discussion about the Boom's end by linking it to David Pringle's retirement as the editor of *Interzone* in 2004, who was in this position as a co-founder since 1982 and witnessed a whole new generation of the Boom writers. "Pringle's importance within British science fiction," as Butler claims, "and the emergence of the Boom, is unique – he is not the only begetter of it, but he did more than most to allow it to come forward" (25n2). During a threaded online discussion coordinated by Niall Harrison in 2010 on the *Vector* website, Kincaid made it clear that the British SF Boom "definitely feels like something in the past," echoing other people's ideas.[1] The contributors of this thread noticed multiple symptoms that may diagnose what lies behind the Boom's decline, mostly

1 This discussion is generally entitled "No Boom Today?" running from the 6th to 15th October 2010, with twenty-three comments from twelve contributors: <https://vector-bsfa.com/2010/10/06/no-boom-today/>.

that the Boom novels are "parodying themselves rather than being continually incentive" (Paul Kincaid), that recent publications have shifted "away from British settings" (Niall Harrison), and that "the emergence of new, high-profile authors slowed or stopped" (Evan). They all agree that the Boom has ended somewhere in the mid-2000s (though the exact date is a challenge to pinpoint, just like the date for its beginning), leaving its highlight – the all-British Hugo shortlist in 2005 – as the last of its glories.

The Chinese SF Boom, too, has already become a much-debated topic. While the *SFS* special issue on Chinese SF in 2013 served as a conceptual mapping of the historical field of Chinese sf since the 1900s, Song Mingwei's 2015 article in *China Perspectives* firmly implanted the term "Chinese New Wave" into the minds of both readers and critics. Fuelled by the Hugo victories of *The Three-Body Problem* in 2015 and "Folding Beijing" in 2016, Chinese SF appears to have entered an unprecedented golden age. The sf industry experienced an explosive growth, accumulating an outcome of 65.87 billion *renminbi* (about 7.4 billion GBP) in 2019 (R. K. Wang 62). New commercial sf agencies are being established consecutively, all dedicated to building new publishing platforms – both in print and online – for emerging writers. Numerous sf works are adapted into other forms of cultural production including film, animation, comics, audio books and *jubensha* (murder mystery games). Hot money is injected into dozens of sf competitions, where the winners will become the targets for future investments. International communication and interaction are accelerating to a degree that Chengdu – the home city of the veteran magazine *Science Fiction World* – felt confident enough to host its own Worldcon in 2023, first time in China.[2]

2 However, the Chengdu Worldcon is hardly a success. Serious concerns were raised over the transparency in the Hugo voting process, where several potential nominees (such as Rebecca F. Kuang, Xiran Jay Zhao, Paul Weimer, among others) were ruled ineligible without proper explanation (according to leaked email messages, it appears to be US-based administrators unilaterally deciding that these works might cause political offence). The ballot was published much later than usual, whereas further scrutiny has been levelled towards possible inconsistencies or anomalies in the statistics themselves. As the result of this ballot controversy, some

Chinese sf, throughout its history, has never wielded more influence. It appears to no longer be a marginalized, second-class genre, as an increasing number of sf works are being published in mainstream magazines, particularly in *Harvest* (*Shouhuo*), *Flower City* (*Huacheng*), *Mountain Flowers* (*Shanhua*) and *Petrel* (*Haiyan*). In March 2022, a new committee of the China Writers Association (CWA) – the Committee of Science Fiction – was established, leading to another historical stage of Chinese sf. "Mark this day," Wu Yan made the call in his WeChat Moments, "Chines sf writers now have their own committee. They can march towards a new era."

How could we even imagine a decline of Chinese sf in the face of such a prosperity? The party has just started, has it not? However, like Kincaid, I also have a concern to utter right during the heyday – a worried voice – which is perhaps out of the British sense of pessimism I have developed as a doctoral student in London. The market prosperity of Chinese sf shares a similar mathematical model with house prices, and once it is pushed to somewhere far beyond its intrinsic value, the bubble is bound to burst. Since the early 1990s, Chinese sf writers – a rather small group – have tried their best to carve out a space in a unique yet turbulent cultural discourse. While the new enlightenment grand narrative, to some extent, steps back from the mass public empowered by expanding private sectors, it still exists at the state level, signalling the state's imperatives for scientific innovation and education. To align with these imperatives, Chinese sf needs to persuade the state of its educational potential for science popularization – a field that, in practice, has been largely detached from sf writings. Additionally, it also needs to cultivate a passionate fandom among teenagers and young adults – a new generation of readers more likely to embrace this genre.

Back then, sf was not money-making. It was a time when sf was written for sf's sake. The publication of sf followed a healthy and productive cycle: new writers would initially emerge in the pages of magazines,

---

Hugo winners of 2023, including Adrian Tchaikovsky and Samantha Mills, have denounced their awards; proposals to decouple the Hugos from Worldcon will be raised and discussed in the business meeting during the 2024 Glasgow Worldcon. A detailed report on the Chengdu scandal, written by Chris M. Barkley and Jason Sanford, can be found at File 770: <https://file770.com/the-2023-hugo-awards-a-report-on-censorship-and-exclusion/>.

primarily in *Science Fiction World*. Subsequently, they would evolve to handle novels and garner a reputation based on their prior works that had already attracted widespread attention. This process was time-consuming, taking years, but after 2015 when money came into this field, people are not patient anymore. A substantial number of sf writing competitions, sponsored by various investors and commercial agencies, are currently underway. They offer nice prizes, but also harsh requirements for copyright. They want products, not works. They wish to create sf stars with many award titles so they can do business, but most of them do not really care for the literary and cultural values of the works *per se*. There is a large corpus of sf works published in China every day, but people are still talking about the names that have been known for more than ten or even twenty years.

Meanwhile, the capital's inclination towards sf has a thin premise. During the latter half of the 2010s, the grand narrative of the state, which had retreated to the background since the 1990s, has become increasingly influential again in the cultural governance in China in tandem with a wave of nationalism among the public. Popular culture products that diverge from this "top-down" grand narrative have once again come under stringent state censorship and supervision, particularly fantasy, queer and other forms of sub-culture. Sf, somehow, is below the radar, as it is still labelled at the state level as a subgenre of science writing and children's literature that functions to enlighten people with a larger horizon of futuristic imagination.

This imagination, however, has now been largely appropriated for domestic nationalist projects, represented by the 2019 film *The Wandering Earth* (dir. Guo Fan) adapted from Liu Cixin's short story and its 2023 sequel. As Song Mingwei observes, "the SF narrative of humans braving grave dangers in *The Wandering Earth* merges with the mainstream theme that advocates for China's rise and participation in global affairs" (*Fear* 307). The potential of Chinese sf for envisioning political transgression and historical rupture, however, has not been properly noticed by the state *yet*. This makes sf one of the few forms of popular culture that may continue to grow, one of the few places where cultural investments may still be rewarded. But how long will this last? How long does it take before the state finds out the truth of sf? What will happen if they do – another campaign against spiritual pollutions? What will be left if money runs away? As the literary legitimacy of Chinese sf has been officially recognized with the establishment of the sf committee at CWA, will sf be put under greater scrutiny by the state? Will it be "mainstreamed"? I really hope this is me over-thinking.

Breaching the boundary between the British and Chinese SF Boom provides us with a unique stance for political-economic inquiries, as reading them together reveals how the two countries react to the historical transitions since the 1980s and the 1990s. It helps us understand that although sf can be perceived as a kind of planetary literature or "hyperobject" indeed, it is anchored deeply in the ground on which writers and readers stand, demonstrating a sense of place and locality muffled by the globality shaped according to the Anglo-American values. Each nation on this planet has their own way of writing sf, each with a different sf history. Over the recent years, we have already heard the voices from the margins. These voices tell us that "world sf" is never a monologic concept. Instead, it is dialogic, indicating a Bakhtinian polyphony that consists of a "plurality of independent and unmerged voices and consciousnesses" (Bakhtin, *Problems* 6), a plurality of numerous booms. In the past we did not know much about other booms, but now we know they are there, and once we are willing to look at them – to quote from Kincaid again – it does not "really take long to start unearthing them" (Kincaid, "Is" 216). By then, perhaps we could feel what David Bowman feels in front of the stargate in *2001: A Space Odyssey*: "[…] it goes on for ever – and – oh my God – *it's full of stars*!" (Clarke, *2001* 216; emphasis in original).

Bibliography

Adams, Ian. *Ideology and Politics in Britain Today*. Manchester: Manchester University Press, 1998.

Adorno, Theodor W. *Negative Dialectics*. Trans. E. B. Ashton. London: Routledge, 1973 [1966].

Aldiss, Brian. "Introduction." In *Space Opera: An Anthology of Way-Back-When Futures*. Ed. Brian Aldiss. Garden City: Doubleday, 1974. ix–xiii.

Alter, Alexandra. "World Collider." *The New York Times Magazine* (8 December 2019): 33L.

Andolfatto, Lorenzo. "Han Song's 'A Guide to Hunting Beautiful Women' and the Restricted Horizon of 'Chinese SF.'" *Science Fiction Studies* 49, no. 1 (2022): 81–99.

Arnold, John H., and Andy Wood. "Nothing Is Written: Politics, Ideology and the Burden of History in the Fall Revolution Quartet." In *The True Knowledge of Ken MacLeod*. Ed. Andrew M. Butler and Farah Mendlesohn. Reading: The Science Fiction Foundation, 2003. 29–46.

Ashley, Mike. *Science Fiction Rebels: The Story of the Science-Fiction Magazines from 1981 to 1990*. Liverpool: Liverpool University Press, 2016.

Bakhtin, Mikhail Mikhaĭlovich. *Problems of Dostoevsky's Poetics*. Ed. and Trans. Caryl Emerson. Minneapolis: University of Minnesota Press, 1984.

——. *The Dialogic Imagination: Four Essays*. Ed. Michael Holquist. Trans. Caryl Emerson and Michael Holquist. Austin: University of Texas Press, 1981.

Bakunin, Mikhail. *God and the State*. New York: Dover, 1970.

Ballard, J. G. "Which Way to Inner Space?" *New Worlds* 40, no. 2–3 (1962): 116–18.

Banks, Iain M. "A Few Notes on the Culture." *rec.arts.sf.written* (1994) <http://www.vavatch.co.uk/books/banks/cultnote.htm>, accessed 16 January 2024.

——. *Consider Phlebas*. London: Macmillan, 1987.

——. "Preface." In *The Wasp Factory*. London: Abacus, 2013. ix–xi.

——. *The Player of Games*. 1988. London: Orbit, 2012.

——. *The State of the Arts*. London: Orbit, 1991.

——. *Use of Weapons*. New York: Bantam Books, 1990.

Barton, Dominic, Yougang Chen, and Amy Jin. "Mapping China's Middle Class." *McKinsey Quarterly* (2013). <https://www.mckinsey.com/industries/retail/our-insights/mapping-chinas-middle-class#> accessed 16 January 2024.

Baudrillard, Jean. *Simulacra and Simulation*. Trans. Sheila Faria Glaser. Ann Arbor: University of Michigan Press, 1994 [1981].

Bauman, Zygmunt. *Modernity and the Holocaust*. Cambridge: Polity Press, 1989.

——. *The Individualized Society*. Cambridge: Polity Press, 2001.

——. *Wasted Lives: Modernity and Its Outcasts*. Cambridge: Polity Press, 2004.

BBC News. "Tony Blair: 'My job was to build on some Thatcher policies'" (8 April 2013). <https://www.bbc.co.uk/news/av/uk-politics-22073434/tony-blair-my-job-was-to-build-on-some-thatcher-policies> accessed 18 April 2020.

Beckett, Andy. *When the Lights Went Out: Britain in the Seventies*. London: Faber and Faber, 2009.

Benjamin, Walter. *The Arcades Project*. Trans. Howard Eiland and Kevin McLaughlin. Cambridge, MA: Harvard University Press, 1999 [1982].

Benn, Tony. *More Time for Politics: Dairies 2001–2007*. London: Arrow Books, 2008.

Bentley, Nick. "Rewriting National Identities in 1990s British Fiction." In *The 1990s: A Decade of Contemporary British Fiction*. Ed. Nick Hubble et al. London: Bloomsbury Academic, 2015. 67–94.

Berman, Marshall. *All That Is Solid Melts into Air: The Experience of Modernity*. New York: Simon & Schuster, 1982.

Best, Steven. "The Commodification of Reality and the Reality of Commodification: Baudrillard, Debord, and Postmodern Theory." In *Baudrillard: A Critical Reader*. Ed. Douglas Kellner. Oxford: Blackwell, 1994. 41–67.

Best, Steven, and Doulas Kellner. *Postmodern Theory: Critical Interrogations*. London: MacMillan, 1991.

Blackmore, Leigh. "'Undoing the Mechanisms': Genre Expectation, Subversion and Anti-consolation in the Kefahuchi Tract Novels of M. John Harrison." *Studies in the Fantastic* 2 (2008): 21–47.

Bloch, Ernest. *The Principle of Hope, Volume One*. 1954. Trans. Neville Plaice, Stephen Plaice and Paul Knight. Cambridge: The MIT Press, 1995.

Botting, Fred. "Flutter, Fracture and Froth: Event, Object and Act of Metaphor in M. John Harrison." In *M. John Harrison: Critical Essays*. Ed. Rhys Williams and Mark Bould. Canterbury: Gylphi, 2019. 229–47.

Bould, Mark. "Bould on the Boom." *Science Fiction Studies* 29, no. 2 (2002): 307–10.

——. "Old, Mean and Misanthropic: An Interview with M. John Harrison." In *Parietal Games: Critical Writings by and on M. John Harrison*. Ed. Mark Bould and Michelle Reid. London: The Science Fiction Foundation, 2005. 326–41.

——. *The Anthropocene Unconscious: Climate, Catastrophe, Culture*. London: Verso, 2021.

——. "What Kind of Monster Are You." *Science Fiction Studies* 30, no. 3 (2003): 394–416.

Bould, Mark, and Andrew M. Butler. Eds. "Voices on the Boom." *Science Fiction Studies* 30, no. 3 (2003): 483–91.

Bowlby, Rachel. *Carried Away: The Invention of Modern Shopping*. New York: Columbia University Press, 2001.

Braidotti, Rosi. "A Theoretical Framework for the Critical Posthumanities." *Theory, Culture & Society* 36, no. 6 (2019): 31–61.

Brodie, Bernard. *Strategy in the Missile Age*. Princeton: Princeton University Press, 2015.

Brødsgaard, Kjeld Erik. "Institutional Reform and the *Bianzhi* System." *The China Quarterly* 170 (2002): 361–86.

Brooke, Stephen. "Living in 'New Times': Historicizing 1980s Britain." *History Compass* 12, no. 1 (2014): 20–32.

Brown, James. "Not Losing the Plot: Politics, Guilt and Storytelling in Banks and MacLeod." In *The True Knowledge of Ken MacLeod*. Ed. Andrew M. Butler and Farah Mendlesohn. Reading: The Science Fiction Foundation, 2003. 55–75.

Brown, Roger, and Helen Carasso. *Everything for Sale?: The Marketisation of UK Higher Education*. London: Routledge, 2013.

Brown, Wendy. "Resisting Left Melancholy." *Boundary 2* 26, no. 3 (1999): 19–27.

——. *Undoing the Demos: Neoliberalism's Stealth Revolution*. New York: Zone Books, 2015.

Burton, Dawn, et al. "Making a Market: The UK Retail Financial Services Industry and the Rise of the Complex Sub-prime Credit Market." *Competition & Change* 8, no. 1 (2004): 3–25.

Butler, Andrew M. "Beyond Consolation: An Interview with China Miéville." *Vector* 233 (2002): 4–7.

——. "Introduction: The True Knowledge?" In *The True Knowledge of Ken MacLeod*. Ed. Andrew M. Butler and Farah Mendlesohn. Reading: The Science Fiction Foundation, 2003. vii–xiii.

——. "The View from the Revolution." *Vector* 213 (2000): 3.

——. "Thirteen Ways of Looking at the British Boom." *Science Fiction Studies* 30, no. 3 (2003): 374–93.

——. "Thirteen Ways of Looking at the British Boom." *Steam Engine Time* 4 (2005): 15–26.

Butler, Andrew M., and Farah Mendlesohn. Eds. *The True Knowledge of Ken MacLeod*. Reading: Science Fiction Foundation, 2003.

Cai Xiang. "Daotong, xuetong yu zhengtong" (《道统、学统与政统》, "Orthodox, Heritage and Politics"). *Dushu* 6 (1994): 46–55.

Çalışkan, Koray, and Michel Callon. "Economization, Part 1: Shifting Attention from the Economy towards Processes of Economization." *Economy and Society* 38, no. 3 (2009): 369–98.

Callaghan, James. *Time and Chance*. London: Collins, 1987.
Callow, Jr, Christos, and Anna McFarlane. Eds. *Adam Roberts: Critical Essays*. Canterbury: Gylphi, 2016.
Campbell, John. *Margaret Thatcher. Volume 2: The Iron Lady*. London: Jonathan Cape, 2003.
Campsie, Alexandre. "'Socialism will never be the same again': Reimagining British Left-Wing Ideas for the 'New Times.'" *Contemporary British History* 31, no. 2 (2017): 166–88.
Canavan, Gerry. "New Paradigms, after 2001." In *Science Fiction: A Literary History*. Ed. Roger Luckhurst. London: The British Library, 2017. 208–34.
Cao Xuenan. "The Multiple Bodies of *The Three-Body Problem*." *Extrapolation* 60, no.2 (2019): 183–200.
Caroti, Simone. *The Culture Series of Iain M. Banks: A Critical Introduction*. Jefferson: McFarland, 2015.
Carr, Terry. "Letter"." *Interzone* 7 (1984): 37.
Chan, Jenny, and Mark Selden. "The Labour Politics of China's Rural Migrant Workers." *Globalizations* 14, no. 2 (2017): 259–71.
Chen, Qiufan. *Waste Tide*. Trans. Ken Liu. London: Head Zeus, 2019 [2013].
——. "Why Did I Write a Science Fiction Novel about E-Waste?" *Vector* 293 (2021). <https://vector-bsfa.com/2021/03/10/chen-qiufan-why-did-i-write-a-science-fiction-novel-about-e-waste/> accessed 16 January 2024.
Chen Qiufan, and Ken Liu. "The Torn Generation: Chinese Science Fiction in a Culture in Transition." Tor.com. (2014). <https://www.tor.com/2014/05/15/the-torn-generation-chinese-science-fiction-in-a-culture-in-transition/> accessed 16 January 2024.
Chia, Aleena. "Welcome to Me-Mart: The Politics of User-Generated Content in Personal Blogs." *American Behavioral Scientist* 56, no. 4 (2012): 421–38.
China Internet Network Information Center. *The 47th China Statistical Report on Internet Development* (2021). <http://www.cac.gov.cn/2021–02/03/c_1613923423079314.htm> 1 May 2021.
Christie, Thomas. *Notional Identities: Ideology, Genre and National Identity in Scotland in Scottish Fiction since the 1970s*. Newcastle: Cambridge Scholars Press, 2013.
Clarke, Arthur C. "Clarke's Third Law on UFO's." *Science* 159, no. 3812 (1968): 255.
——. *2001: A Space Odyssey*. London: Orbit, 1998 [1968].
——. *3001: The Final Odyssey*. London: Voyager, 1997.
Clarke, Peter. *Hope and Glory: Britain 1900–2000*, 2nd edn. London: Penguin, 2004.
Clute, John. "Harrison, M. John." *The Encyclopaedia of Science Fiction* (2021). <http://www.sf-encyclopedia.com/entry/harrison_m_john> accessed 1 January 2024.

——. "Science Fiction from 1980 to the Present." In *The Cambridge Companion to Science Fiction*. Ed. Edward James and Farah Mendlesohn. Cambridge: Cambridge University Press, 2003. 64–78.

Cobley, Michael. "Eye to Eye: An Interview with Iain Banks." *Science Fiction Eye* 2, no. 1 (1990): 22–32.

Colebrook, Martyn, and Katharine Cox. Eds. *The Transgressive Iain Banks: Essays on a Writer Beyond Borders*. Jefferson: McFarland, 2013.

Collins, Michael. *Money and Banking in the UK: A History*. New York: Routledge, 2012.

Conn, Virginia. "Photographesomenonic Sinofuturism(s)." *SFRA Review* 50, no. 2–3 (2020): 79–85.

Conservative Party. *General Election Manifesto*. London: Conservative Party, 1979. <https://www.margaretthatcher.org/document/110858> accessed 16 January 2024.

——. *General Election Manifesto*. London: Conservative Party, 1992. <http://www.conservativemanifesto.com/1992/1992-conservative-manifesto.shtml#wealth> accessed 16 January 2024.

Cooppan, Vilashini. "World Literature and Global Theory: Comparative Literature for the New Millennium." *Symploke* 9, no. 1–2 (2001): 15–43.

Coutts, Ken, Andrew Glynn, and Bob Rowthorne. "Structural Change under New Labour." *Cambridge Journal of Economics* 31 (2017): 845–61.

Cross, Rich. "British Anarchism in the Era of Thatcherism." In *Against the Grain: The British Far Left from 1956*. Ed. Evan Smith and Matthew Worley. Manchester: Manchester University Press, 2014. 133–52.

Csicsery-Ronay, Istvan, Jr. "Editorial Introduction: The British SF Boom." *Science Fiction Studies* 30, no. 3 (2003): 353–54.

——. "The SF of Theory: Baudrillard and Haraway." *Science Fiction Studies* 18, no. 3 (1991): 387–404.

——. "What Do We Mean When We Say 'Global Science Fiction'? Reflections on a New Nexus." *Science Fiction Studies* 39, no. 3 (2012): 478–93.

Damrosch, David. *What is World Literature?* Princeton: Princeton University Press, 2003.

Davis, William. "The New Neoliberalism." *New Left Review* 101 (2016): 121–34.

Debord, Guy. *The Society of Spectacle*. Trans. Ken Knabb. London: Rebel Press, 2004 [1967].

Deleuze, Gilles, and Félix Guattari. *A Thousand Plateaus: Capitalism and Schizophrenia*. Trans. Brian Massumi. Minneapolis: University of Minnesota Press, 1987 [1980].

Delman, Jørgen, and Yin Xiaoqing. "Individualization and the Political Agency of Private Business People in China." In *iChina: The Rise of the Individual in*

Modern Chinese Society. Ed. Mette Halskov Hansen and Rune Svarverud. Copenhagen: NIAS Press, 2010. 94–131.
Deng Xiaoping. *Deng Xiaoping wenxuan Vol. 3* (《邓小平文选》第三卷; *Selected Works of Deng Xiaoping Vol. 3*). Beijing: Zhonggong zhongyang dangxiao chubanshe, 1993.
Dougherty, Stephen. "Liu Cixin, Arthur C. Clarke, and 'Repositioning.'" *Science Fiction Studies* 46, no. 1 (2019): 39–62.
Du Bois, W. E. B. *The Souls of Black Folk*. Ed. Brent Hayes Edwards. Oxford: Oxford University Press, 2007 [1903].
Duggan, Robert. "Iain M. Banks, Postmodernism and the Gulf War." *Extrapolation* 48, no. 3 (2007): 558–77.
Edwards, Caroline, and Tony Venezia. Eds. *China Miéville: Critical Essay*. Canterbury: Gylphi, 2015.
——. "Unintroduction: China Miéville's Weird Universe." In *China Miéville: Critical Essay*. Ed. Caroline Edwards and Tony Venezia. Canterbury: Gylphi, 2015. 1–38.
Engels, Friedrich. "Outlines of a Critique of Political Economy." In *Karl Marx/ Friedrich Engels Collected Works*, vol.3. London: Lawrence & Wishart, 1975. 418–43.
English, James F. *The Economy of Prestige: Prize, Awards and the Circulation of Cultural Value*. Cambridge: Harvard University Press, 2005.
Erney, Hans-Georg. "Ecological Science Fiction with Chinese Characteristics: *The Three-Body Problem*." *MOSF Journal of Science Fiction* 5, no. 1 (2021): 80–92.
Evans, Stephen. "Thatcher and the Victorians: A Suitable Case for Comparison?" *History* 268 (1997): 601–20.
Fanon, Frantz. *Black Skin, White Masks*. Trans. Charles Lam Markmann. London: Pluto Press, 1986 [1952].
Feher, Michel. "Self-Appreciation; or, the Aspirations of Human Capital." *Public Culture* 21, no. 1 (2009): 21–41.
Fei Dao. "Science Fiction: Embarrassing No More." In *Broken Stars: Contemporary Chinese Science Fiction in Translation*. Ed. Ken Liu. London: Head of Zeus, 2019. 473–9.
Fekete, John. "'The Dispossessed' and 'Triton': Act and System in Utopian Science Fiction." *Science Fiction Studies* 6, no. 2 (1979): 129–43.
Finlayson, Alan. *Making Sense of New Labour*. London: Lawrence and Wishart, 2003.
——. "Tony Blair and the Jargon of Modernisation." *Soundings* 10 (1998): 11–27.
Fisher, Mark. *Capitalist Realism: Is There No Alternative?* Winchester: Zero Books, 2009.
——. *Postcapitalist Desire: The Final Lectures*. London: Repeater, 2021.

Fitting, Peter. "Utopia, Dystopia, and Science Fiction." In *The Cambridge Companion to Utopian Literature*. Ed. Gregory Claeys. Cambridge: Cambridge University Press, 2010. 135–53.

Fitzgerald, Charles Patrick. *Mao Tsetung and China*. London: Hodder & Stoughton, 1976.

Foucault, Michel. "Of Other Spaces." Trans. Jay Miskowiec. *Diacritics* 16, no. 1 (1986): 22–7.

——. *The Birth of Biopolitics: Lectures at the Collège de France 1978–1979*. Trans. Graham Burchell. Ed. Michel Senellart. New York: Palgrave Macmillan, 2008.

Freedman, Carl. *Art and Idea in the Novels of China Miéville*. Canterbury: Gylphi, 2015.

——. "Science Fiction and Critical Theory." In *Science Fiction Criticism: An Anthology of Essential Writings*. Ed. Rob Latham. London: Bloomsbury Academic, 2018. 225–45.

——. "Science Fiction and Utopia: A Historico-Philosophical Overview." In *Learning from Other Worlds: Estrangement, Cognition, and the Politics of Science Fiction and Utopia*. Ed. Patrick Parrinder. Liverpool: Liverpool University Press, 2000. 72–97.

Frenkel, Stephen J., and Yu Chongxin. "Chinese Migrants' Work Experience and City Identification: Challenging the Underclass Thesis." *Human Relations* 68, no. 2 (2015): 261–85.

Fukuyama, Francis. "The End of History?" *The National Interest* 16 (1989): 3–18.

Fulcher, James. "A New Stage in the Development of Capitalist Society." *Sociology Review* 1, no. 2 (1991): 2–5.

Gadamer, Hans-Georg. *Truth and Method*. Trans. Joel Weinsheimer and Donald G. Marshall London: Bloomsbury, 2013 [1960].

Garnaut, Ross. "40 Years of Chinese Economic Reform and Development and the Challenge of 50." In *China's 40 Years of Reform and Development: 1978–2018*. Ed. Ross Garnaut, Song Ligang and Fang Cai. Acton, ACT: ANU Press, 2018. 29–52.

Garnaut, Ross, Ligang Song, and Yang Yao. "Impact and Significance of State-Owned Enterprise Restructuring in China." *The China Journal* 55 (2006): 35–63.

Gąsiorek, Andrzej. "'Refugees from Time': History, Death and the Fight from Reality in Contemporary Writing." In *British Fiction of the 1990s*. Ed. Nick Bentley. London: Routledge, 2005. 42–56.

Gevers, Nick. "Cities Near, Cities Far: An Interview with China Miéville." *Infinity Plus* (2003). <http://www.infinityplus.co.uk/nonfiction/intchina2.htm> accessed 16 January 2024.

Gifford, Chris. *The Making of Eurosceptic Britain*. Aldershot: Ashgate, 2008.

Gilmour, Ian. *Dancing with Dogma: Britain under Thatcherism*. London: Simon & Schuster, 1992.

Gilroy, Paul. *After Empire: Melancholia or Convivial Culture*. London: Routledge, 2004.
——. *The Black Atlantic: Modernity and Double Consciousness*. London: Verso, 1993.
Gittings, John. *The Changing Face of China: From Mao to Market*. Oxford: Oxford University Press, 2006.
Gordon, Joan. "Hybridity, Heterotopia, and Mateship in China Miéville's Perdido Street Station." *Science Fiction Studies* 30, no. 3 (2003): 456–76.
Gordon, Joan, and China Miéville. "Revelling in Genre: An Interview with China Miéville." *Science Fiction Studies* 30, no. 3 (2003): 355–73.
Gottlieb, Erika. *Dystopian Fiction East and West: Universe of Terror and Trial*. London: McGill-Queen's University Press, 2001.
Greenland, Colin. "'Use of Weapons' by Iain M. Banks (Book Review)." *Foundation* 50 (1990): 90–4.
Guattari, Félix. *Chaosmosis: An Ethico-Aesthetic Paradigm*. Trans. Paul Bains and Julian Pefanis. Bloomington: Indiana University Press, 1992.
Haigron, David. "'Caring' John Major: Portrait of a Thatcherite as a One-Nation Tory." *Observatoire de la Société Britannique* 7 (2009): 177–96.
Hall, Stuart. "Old and New Identities, Old and New Ethnicities." In *Culture, Globalisation, and the World System*. Ed. Anthony D. King. Basingstoke: Macmillan, 1991. 41–68.
——. "Thatcher's Lessons." *Marxist Today* (March 1988): 20–7.
——. "The Centrality of Culture: Notes on the Cultural Revolutions of Our Time." In *Media and Cultural Regulation*. Ed. Kenneth Thompson. London: Sage, 1997. 208–38.
——. "The Great Moving Right Show." *Marxist Today* (January 1979): 14–21.
——. *The Hard Road to Renewal: Thatcherism and the Crisis of the Left*. London: Verso, 1988.
——. "The Meaning of New Times." In *New Times: The Changing Face of Politics in the 1990s*. Ed. Stuart Hall and Martin Jacques. London: Lawrence and Wishart, 1989. 116–38.
Hall, Stuart, and Martin Jacques. "Introduction." In *New Times: The Changing Face of Politics in the 1990s*. Ed. Stuart Hall and Martin Jacques. London: Lawrence and Wishart, 1989. 11–20.
Hames, Scott. "The New Scottish Renaissance." In *The Oxford History of the Novel in English: Volume 7: British and Irish Fiction Since 1940*. Ed. Peter Boxall and Bryan Cheyette. Oxford: Oxford University Press, 2016. 495–512.
Han Song. "Chinese Science Fiction: A Response to Modernization." *Science Fiction Studies* 40, no. 1 (2013): 15–21.
——. *Huoxing zhaoyao meiguo* (《火星照耀美国》, *Red Star over America*). Nanjing: Jiangsu fenghuang wenyi chubanshe, 2018.

——. *Xiangxiangli xuanyan* (《想象力宣言》, *Manifesto of Imagination*). Chengdu: Sichuan renmin chubanshe, 2000.

Hao Jingfang. Acceptance Speech for Hugo Awards (Best Novelette). The 74th World Science Fiction Convention (MidAmeriCon II), Kansas City, Missouri. 2016. <https://www.youtube.com/watch?v=SKNuFDRnmEI> accessed 11 December 2020.

——. *Vagabond*. Trans. Ken Liu. London: Head of Zeus, 2020 [2011–12].

Hardt, Michael, and Antonio Negri. *Commonwealth*. Cambridge, MA: Harvard University Press, 2009.

——. *Empire*. Cambridge, MA: Harvard University Press, 2000.

Harrison, M. John. "A Literature of Comfort." In *Parietal Games: Critical Writings by and on M. John Harrison*. Ed. Mark Bould and Michelle Reid. London: The Science Fiction Foundation, 2005 [1971]. 166–72.

——. *Empty Space: A Haunting*. London: Gollancz, 2012.

——. *Light*. London: Gollancz, 2002.

——. *Nova Swing*. London: Gollancz, 2006.

——. "The Profession of Science Fiction." *Foundation* 46 (1989): 5–13.

Harrison, Niall. "Accelerated History: Chinese Short Science Fiction in the Twenty-First Century." *Vector* 293 (2021): 69–81.

Harvey, David. *A Brief History of Neoliberalism*. Oxford: Oxford University Press, 2005.

——. "Cosmopolitanism and the Banality of Geographical Evils." *Public Culture* 12, no. 2 (2000): 529–64.

Healey, Cara Michelle. "Estranging Realism in Chinese Science Fiction: Hybridity and Environmentalism in Chen Qiufan's *The Waste Tide*." *Modern Chinese Literature and Culture* 29, no. 2 (2017): 1–33.

Heartsweet. "Thomas Wade: Things You Should Know." 2010. <https://book.douban.com/review/4500238/>accessed 6 July 2021.

Heidegger, Martin. *Poetry, Language, Thought*. New York: Harper Perennial, 2001.

Hetherington, Kevin. *The Badlands of Modernity: Heterotopia and Social Ordering*. London: Routledge, 1997.

Higham, Nick. "Cabinet Papers Reveal 'Secret Coal Pits Closure Plan.'" *BBC News*, 3 January 2014. <https://www.bbc.co.uk/news/uk-25549596> accessed 2 May 2022.

Horton, Emily. "Literary History of the Decade: The Bomb, Kidnappings and Yuppies: British Fiction in the 1980s." In *The 1980s: A Decade of Contemporary British Fiction*. Ed. Emily Horton, Philip Tew and Leigh Wilson. London: Bloomsbury Academic, 2014. 21–50.

Hubble, Nick. "Fictions of Escape: SFF and Class." *Vector* 294 (2021): 2–14.

Hubble, Nick, et al. eds. *The Science Fiction of Iain M. Banks*. Canterbury: Gylphi, 2018.

Huss, Mikael. "Hesitant Journey to the West: SF's Changing Fortunes in Mainland China." *Science Fiction Studies* 27, no. 1 (2000): 92–104.

Isaacson, Nathaniel. *Celestial Empire: The Emergence of Chinese Science Fiction*. Middletown: Wesleyan University Press, 2017.

Jacobs, Alan. "The Ambiguous Utopia of Iain M. Banks." *The New Atlantis* 25 (2009): 45–58.

Jameson, Fredric. *Archaeologies of the Future: The Desire Called Utopia and Other Science Fiction*. London: Verso, 2005.

——. *Postmodernism, or, The Cultural Logic of Late Capitalism*. London: Verso, 1991.

Jarvis, Timothy. "'Sparks in Everything' or 'A Tearful Overnight Understanding': Posthuman Becoming in the Empty Space Trilogy." In *M. John Harrison: Critical Studies*. Ed. Rhys Williams and Mark Bould. Canterbury: Gylphi, 2019. 175–91.

Ji Jianxun, and Zheng Sikuang. "Xingshi, yiyi yu jiegoushi yuyan: Liu Cixin <Santi> 'Hei'an senlin' faze xintan" (形式、意义与结构式寓言——刘慈欣《三体》"黑暗森林"法则新探, "Form, Meaning and Structural Allegory: New Thoughts on Liu Cixin's 'Dark Forest' Principles"). *Modern Chinese Culture and Literature* 1 (2017): 258–69.

Jiang Qian. "Translation and the Development of Science Fiction in Twentieth-Century China." *Science Fiction Studies* 40, no. 1 (2013): 116–32.

Kelly, Stuart. "Iain Banks: The Final Interview." *The Guardian*, 15 June 2013. <https://www.theguardian.com/books/2013/jun/15/iain-banks-the-final-interview> accessed 2 March 2022.

Kempson, Elaine, and Claire Whyley. *Kept Out or Opted Out? Understanding and Combating Financial Exclusion*. Bristol: The Policy Press, 1999.

Kincaid, Paul. *Iain M. Banks*. Urbana: University of Illinois Press, 2017.

——. "Jetsam on the Terminal Beach: M. John Harrison's 'Empty Space.'" *Los Angeles Review of Books*, 21 May 2013. <https://lareviewofbooks.org/article/jetsam-on-the-terminal-beach-m-john-harrisons-empty-space/> accessed 23 July 2021.

——. "Is This Who We Are?: Review of *The Cambridge History of Science Fiction*." *Extrapolation* 61, no. 1–2 (2020): 215–20.

——. "The Golden Age Is Now." *Science Fiction Studies* 29, no. 3 (2002): 530–1.

Kinkley, Jeffery C. *Visions of Dystopia in China's New Historical Novels*. New York: Columbia University Press, 2015.

Kong Shuyu. *Consuming Literature: Best Sellers and the Commercialisation of Literary Production in Contemporary China*. Stanford: Stanford University Press, 2005.

Kulbicki, Michal. "Iain M. Banks, Ernst Bloch and Utopian Interventions." *Colloquy: Text Theory Critique* 17 (2009): 34–43.

Kumar, Krishan. "The Ends of Utopia." *New Literary History* 41, no. 3 (2010): 549–69.

Labour Party. *General Election Manifesto*. London: Labour Party. 1997. <http://www.labour-party.org.uk/manifestos/1997/1997-labour-manifesto.shtml> accessed 18 April 2020.

——. *Rule Book 2019*. London: Labour Party, 2019. <https://labour.org.uk/wp-content/uploads/2019/04/Rule-Book-2019.pdf> accessed 18 April 2020.

Lash, Scott, and John Urry. *The End of Organized Capitalism*. Cambridge: Polity, 1987.

Lawrence, Jon, and Florence Sutcliffe-Braithwaite. "Margaret Thatcher and the Decline of Class Politics." In *Making Thatcher's Britain*. Ed. Ben Jackson and Robert Saunders. Cambridge: Cambridge University Press, 2012. 132–47.

Lawson, Nigel. *The View from No. 11: Memoirs of a Tory Radical*. London: Bantam Press, 1992.

Le Guin, Ursula. *The Dispossessed*. London: Victor Gollancz, 2002 [1971].

——. "The Ones Who Walk Away from Omelas." In *The Wind's Twelve Quarters*. Toronto: Bantam Books, 1975 [1973]. 251–9.

Leadbeater, Charles. "Power to the Person." *Marxism Today* (October 1988): 14–20.

Leese, Daniel. "A Single Spark: Origins and Spread of the Little Red Book in China." In *Mao's Little Red Book: A Global History*. Ed. Alexander C. Cook. Cambridge: Cambridge University Press, 2014. 23–42.

Li Guangyi. "Eerie Parables and Prophecies: An Analysis of Han Song's Science Fiction." Trans. Nathaniel Isaacson. *Chinese Literature Today* 7, no. 1 (2018): 28–32.

Li Hua. *Chinese Science Fiction during the Post-Mao Cultural Thaw*. Toronto: University of Toronto Press, 2021.

——. "Spaceship Earth and Technological Utopianism: Liu Cixin's Ecological Science Fiction." *Tamkang Review* 47, no. 2 (2017): 17–32.

——. "The Environment, Humankind, and Slow Violence in Chinese Science Fiction." *Communication and the Public* 3, no. 4 (2018): 270–82.

——. "Twenty-First Century Chinese Science Fiction on the Rise: Anti-authoritarianism and Dreams of Freedom." In *The Cambridge History of Science Fiction*. Ed. Gerry Canavan and Eric Carl Link. Cambridge: Cambridge University Press, 2019. 647–63.

Liu Cixin. "Beyond Narcissism: What Science Fiction Can Offer Literature." *Science Fiction Studies* 40, no. 1 (2013): 22–32.

——. *Death's End*. Trans. Ken Liu. London: Head of Zeus, 2016 [2010].

——. "Remarks by Imagination Awardee Cixin Liu." The Clarke Foundation (2018). <http://www.clarkefoundation.org/wp-content/uploads/2018/11/Liu-Cixin-Speech.pdf.> accessed 2 July 2021.

——. *The Dark Forest*. Trans. Joel Martinsen. New York: Tor, 2015 [2008].

——. *The Three-Body Problem*. Trans. Ken Liu. New York: Tor, 2014 [2006].

——. "The Worst of All Possible Universes and the Best of All Possible Earths: *Three Body* and Chinese Science Fiction." *Tor.com.* (2014). Trans. Ken Liu. <https://www.tor.com/2014/05/07/the-worst-of-all-possible-universes-and-the-best-of-all-possible-earths-three-body-and-chinese-science-fiction> accessed 5 July 2021.

Locke, John. *Two Treaties of Government and a Letter Concerning Toleration.* Ed. by Ian Shapiro. New Haven: Yale University Press, 2003.

Long Yi. *Diqiu sheng* (《地球省》, *Earth Province*). Beijing: Renmin wenxue chubanshe, 2018.

——. "Zhenzheng de kongju laizi women zishen" (《真正的恐惧来自我们自身》; "The True Terror Comes from Ourselves"). *Wen yi bao* 18 March 2018.

Lovegrove, James. *Days.* London: Phoenix House, 1997.

Lu Jie. "Multiple Time-Spaces: Dialogical Representation of the Global City in Chinese New Urban and Rural-Migrant Films." *Prism: Theory and Modern Chinese Literature* 19, no. 1 (2022): 6–27.

Luckhurst, Roger. "Cultural Governance, New Labour, and the British SF Boom." *Science Fiction Studies* 30, no. 3 (2003): 417–35.

——. *Science Fiction: Cultural History of Literature.* London: Polity, 2005.

——. "The Contemporary London Gothic and the Limits of the 'Spectral Turn.'" *Textual Practice* 16, no. 3 (2002): 527–46.

Lyu Guangzhao. "Capitalist Monster and Bottled Passengers: Political Stakes of Embodiment in The Reincarnated Giant and The Last Subway." *SFRA Review* 50, no. 2–3 (2020): 124–32.

——. "Dark Forest or Grand Central: Self and Other in Liu Cixin and Arthur C. Clarke." In *Rendezvous with Clarke: Centenary Essays.* Ed. Andrew M. Butler and Paul March-Russell. Canterbury: Gylphi, 2023. 175–91.

——. "Divide in Time and Space: Social Stratification in Wei Ma's 'Formerly Slow' and Hao Jingfang's 'Folding Beijing.'" *Vector* 294 (2021): 33–40.

——. "SFRA Conference Report: Futures from the Margins (Oslo, 2022, Co-hosted by CoFutures)." [illegible] ([illegible]): [illegible].

Ma Chen (Mia). "Waste Workers in Waste Tide: Ecoambiguity, Failure, and Emotional Propaganda." *The Bochum Yearbook of East Asian Studies* 42 (2019): 67–80.

MacLeod, Ken. "Phlebas Reconsidered." In *The True Knowledge of Ken MacLeod.* Ed. Andrew M. Butler and Farah Mendlesohn. Reading: The Science Fiction Foundation, 2003. 1–3.

——. "Politics and Science Fiction." In *The Cambridge Companion to Science Fiction.* Ed. Edward James and Farah Mendlesohn. Cambridge: Cambridge University Press, 2003. 230–40.

——. *The Cassini Division.* London: Orbit, 1998.

——. *The Stone Canal.* London: Orbit, 1996.
——. *The Star Fraction.* London: Legend Books, 1995.
Malmgren, Carl D. "Self and Other in SF: Alien Encounters." *Science Fiction Studies* 20, no. 1 (1993): 15–33.
——. "Towards a Definition of Science Fantasy." *Science Fiction Studies* 15, no. 3 (1988): 259–81.
Mannheim, Karl. *Ideology and Utopia: An Introduction to the Sociology of Knowledge.* London: Routledge & Kegan Paul, 1954.
Marx, Karl. *Capital: A Critique of Political Economy*, vol. 1. Trans. Ben Fowkes. London: Penguin Books, 1976 [1867].
——. *Karl Marx/Friedrich Engels Collected Works*, vol. 3. London: Lawrence & Wishart, 1975.
Massumi, Brian. "Deleuze." In *A Companion to Continental Philosophy.* Ed. Simon Critchley and William R. Schroeder. London: Blackwell Publishers, 1998. 559–73.
——. "Translator's Foreword: Pleasures of Philosophy." In *A Thousand Plateaus: Capitalism and Schizophrenia.* Minneapolis: University of Minnesota Press, 1987. ix–xv.
Mathews, Richard. *Fantasy: The Liberation of Imagination.* London: Routledge, 2002.
May, Todd. *The Political Philosophy of Poststructuralist Anarchism.* University Park, PA: The Pennsylvania State University Press, 1994.
Mbembe, Achille. "Necropolitics." Trans. Libby Meintjes. *Public Culture* 15, no. 1 (2003): 11–40.
McGrath, Jason. *Postsocialist Modernity: Chinese Cinema, Literature, and Criticism in the Market Age.* Stanford: Stanford University Press, 2008.
McRae, John R. *The Northern School and the Formation of Early Ch'an Buddhism.* Honolulu: University of Hawaii Press, 1986.
McRobbie, Angela. "Looking Back at New Times and Its Critics." In *Stuart Hall: Critical Dialogues in Cultural Studies.* Ed. David Morley and Kuan-Hsing Chen. London: Routledge, 1996. 238–61.
Melamed, Jodi. "Racial Capitalism." *Critical Ethnic Studies* 1, no. 1 (2015), 76–85.
Melville, Herman. *Moby-Dick.* Ed. Charles Child Walcutt. London: Bantam Books, 1987 [1857].
Mendlesohn, Farah. "Call for Papers: 2001 – A Celebration of British SF." *Science Fiction Studies* 27, no. 2 (2000): 381–2.
——. "Impermanent Revolution: The Anarchic Utopias of Ken MacLeod." In *The True Knowledge of Ken MacLeod.* Ed. Andrew M. Butler and Farah Mendlesohn. Reading: The Science Fiction Foundation, 2003. 16–28.

Miéville, China. "Afterword: Cognition as Ideology: A Dialectic of SF Theory." In *Red Planets: Marxism and Science Fiction*. Ed. Mark Bould and China Miéville. London: Pluto Press, 2009. 231–48.

——. *Iron Council*. New York: Random House, 2004.

——. *King Rat*. London: Pan Books, 2011 [1998].

——. *Perdido Street Station*. London: Pan Macmillan, 2000.

——. *Scar*. London: Pan Books, 2011 [2003].

——. "Symposium: Marxism and Fantasy. Editorial Introduction." *Historical Materialism* 10, no. 4 (2002): 39–49.

——. *The City & The City*. 2009. London: Picador, 2018.

Miller, Faren. "Consider Phlebas." *Locus* 316 (1987): 13–15.

Miller, Daniel. "Consumption as the Vanguard of History: A Polemic by Way of an Introduction." *Acknowledging Consumption: A Review of New Studies*. Ed. Daniel Miller. London: Routledge, 1995. 1–52.

Miller, Gavin. "Iain (M.) Banks: Utopia, Nationalism and the Posthuman." In *The Edinburgh Companion to Contemporary Scottish Literature*. Ed. Berthold Schoene. Edinburgh: Edinburgh University Press, 2007. 202–9.

Milne, Seumas. *The Enemy Within: The Secret War against the Miners*. London: Verso, 2004.

Mitchell, Chris. "Iain Banks: Whit and Excession: Getting Used to Being God." *Spike Magazine* (1996). <https://spikemagazine.com/0996bank/> accessed 5 August 2020.

Moore, John. "Miracle Stalker: Personal and Social Transformation in Arkady and Boris Strugatsky's Roadside Picnic." *Foundation* 71 (1997): 63–76.

Moore, Owens. "A Fanonian Perspective on Double Consciousness." *Journal of Black Studies* 35, no. 6 (2005): 751–62.

Moore, Suzanne. "The Cultural Revolution." *Marxism Today* (Nov/Dec 1998): 17–21.

Moran, Thomas. "The Perverse Utopianism of Willed Human Extinction: Writing Extinction in Liu Cixin's *The Three-Body Problem*." In *Ethical Futures and Global Science Fiction*. Ed. Zachary Kendal et al. Cham, Switzerland: Palgrave Macmillan, 2020. 119–40.

Morgan, Kenneth O. "The Twentieth Century (1914–2000)." In *The Oxford History of Britain: Revised Edition*. Ed. Kenneth O. Morgan. Oxford: Oxford University Press, 2010. 582–676.

Morgan, Oliver and Nick Mathiason. "Public Private Discord: Taxpayers Will Foot the Bill If the City Has Got Its Sums Wrong on PFI." *Guardian* (6 October 2002) <https://www.theguardian.com/business/2002/oct/06/publicservices.publicservices> accessed 23 August 2024.

Mort, Frank. "The Politics of Consumption." In *New Times: The Changing Face of Politics in the 1990s*. Ed. Stuart Hall and Martin Jacques. London: Lawrence and Wishart, 1989. 160–72.

Morton, Timothy. *Hyperobjects: Philosophy and Ecology after the End of the World*. Minneapolis: University of Minnesota Press, 2013.

Moylan, Tom. *Demand the Impossible: Science Fiction and the Utopian Imagination*. Ed. Raffaella Baccolini. Oxford: Peter Lang, 2014 [1986].

——. *Scraps of the Untainted Sky: Science Fiction, Utopia, Dystopia*. Oxford: Westview Press, 2000.

Murphy, Rachel. "Introduction." In *Labour Migration and Social Development in China*. Ed. Rachel Murphy. London: Routledge, 2009. 1–15.

Murray, Robin. "Fordism and Post-Fordism." In *New Times: Changing Face of Politics in the 1990s*. Ed. Stuart Hall and Martin Jacques. London: Lawrence and Wishart, 1989. 38–53.

Nairn, Tom "Break-Up: Twenty-Five Years On." In *Scotland in Theory: Reflections on Culture and Literature*. Ed. Eleanor Bell and Gavin Miller. Amsterdam: Rudopi, 2004. 17–34.

——. "The Twilight of the British State." *New Left Review* 101–2 (1977): 3–61.

National Bureau of Statistics. *Report of the Seventh Census*. Beijing, 11 May 2021. <http://www.gov.cn/guoqing/2021–05/13/content_5606149.htm> accessed 23 November 2021.

National Coal Board. "Orders of the Day." London, 23 November 1981. <https://api.parliament.uk/historic-hansard/commons/1981/nov/23/national-coal-board> accessed 15 April 2020.

Newton, Scott. *The Reinvention of Britain 1960–2016: A Political and Economic History*. London: Routledge, 2018.

Newton, Scott and Dilwyn Porter. *Modernization Frustrated: The Politics of Industrial Decline in Britain since 1900*. London: Unwin Hyman, 1988.

Ngok, Kinglun. "Migrant Labor, Urban Exclusion and Social Harmony in China." *Journal of Poverty and Social Justice* 20, no. 3 (2012): 247–60.

Nielsen, Ingrid, and Russell Smyth. "Towards a Harmonious Society: Challenges for China in the Pursuit of Social-Protection-as-Social-Justice." In *Migration and Social Protection in China*. Ed. Ingrid Nielsen and Russell Smyth. Singapore: World Scientific, 2008. 247–56.

Nozick, Robert. *Anarchy, State and Utopia*. Oxford: Blackwell, 1974.

O'Connell, Huge Charles. "The Boom's Near Future: Postnational Ill-Fantasy, or Literature under the Sign of Crisis." *CR: The New Centennial Review* 13, no. 2 (2013): 67–100.

——. "The British Science Fiction Boom: Tracking the Currents of the Future between Postimperialism, Postnationalism, and Globalization: Editorial Introduction." *CR: The New Centennial Review* 13, no. 2 (2013): 1–12.

O'Connor, Robert. *A Miéville Bestiary: Monsters as Commentary of the Hybridity of Real and Conceptual Landscapes in the Work of China Miéville*. The University of Leeds and York St John University, PhD Thesis, 2020.

Ong, Aihwa. *Neoliberalism as Exception: Mutations in Citizenship and Sovereignty*. Durham: Duke University Press, 2006.

Ong, Aihwa, and Zhang Li. 2008. "Introduction: Privatizing China; Powers of the Self, Socialism from Afar." In *Privatizing China: Socialism from Afar*. Ed. Zhang Li and Ong Aihwa. Ithaca: Cornell University Press, 2008. 1–20.

Peach, Ceri. "Slippery Segregation: Discovering or Manufacturing Ghettos?" *Journal of Ethnic and Migration Studies* 35, no. 9 (2009): 1381–95.

Pearson, Wendy Gay. "Ursula K[Roeber] Le Guin (1929—)." In *Fifty Key Figures in Science Fiction*. Ed. Mark Bould et al. London: Routledge, 2009. 136–41.

Perri 6. "Governing by Cultures." In *Life after Politics: New Thinking for the Twenty-First Century*. Ed. Geoff Mulgan. London: Fontana, 1997. 260–82.

Phillips, Trevor. "After 7/7: Sleepwalking to Segregation." Address delivered at the Manchester Council for Community Relations, Manchester, 22 September 2005.

Pohl, Frederik. "Foreword: Science Fiction and China." In *Science Fiction from China*. Ed. Dingbo Wu and Patrick D. Murphy. London: Praeger, 1989. i–ix.

Pollert, Anna. "Dismantling Flexibility." *Capital and Class* 12, no. 1 (1988): 42–72.

Poulsen, Michael. "The 'new geography' of Ethnicity in Britain?" In *Conference Paper Delivered at the Annual Conference of the Institute of British Geographers and the Royal Geographical Society*, London, 31 August 2005.

Pun, Ngai. "Discursive Dyslexia and the Articulation of Class: A Theoretical Perspective on China's Young Female Migrant Workers (*Dagongmei*)." In *Mapping China: Peasants, Migrant Workers and Informal Labour*. Ed. Chongqing Wu. Leiden: Brill, 2016. 80–102.

Pun, Ngai, et al. "The Class Formation: Control of Capital and Collective Resistance of Chinese Construction Workers." In *Mapping China: Peasants, Migrant Workers and Informal Labour*. Ed. Chongqing Wu. Leiden: Brill, 2016. 103–41.

Red Pine. Ed. *The Zen Teaching of Bodhidharma: A Bilingual Edition*. New York: North Point Press, 1989.

Reitan, Earl A. *The Thatcher Revolution: Margaret Thatcher, John Major, Tony Blair, and the Transformation of Modern Britain, 1979–2001*. Oxford: Rowman and Littlefield Publishers, 2003.

Ren Dongmei. "Interpreting *Folding Beijing* through the Prism of Science Fiction Realism." Trans. Xu Chenmei. *Chinese Literature Today* 7, no. 1 (2018): 54–7.

Richards, Thomas. *The Commodity of Victorian England: Advertising and Spectacle, 1851–1914*. Stanford: Stanford University Press, 1990.
Riddell, Peter. "The Conservatives after 1992." *The Political Quarterly* 63, no. 4 (1992): 422–31.
Ritzer, George. "Prosumer Capitalism." *The Sociological Quarterly* 56, no. 3 (2015): 413–45.
——. *The McDonaldization of Society: Into the Digital Age*, 9th edn. Thousand Oaks: Sage Publishing, 2018.
Ritzer, George, and Nathan Jurgenson. "Production, Consumption, Prosumption: The Nature of Capitalism in the Age of the Digital 'Prosumer.'" *Journal of Consumer Culture* 10, no. 1 (2010): 13–36.
Rose, Mark. *Alien Encounters: Anatomy of Science Fiction*. Cambridge: Harvard University Press, 1981.
Ross, Andrew. *Strange Weather: Culture, Science and Technology in the Age of Limits*. New York: Verso, 1991.
Rothbard, Murray. *Making Economic Sense*. Auburn, AL: Ludwig von Mises Institute, 1995.
Ruane, Sally. "Access to Data and NHS Privatisation: Reducing Public Accountability." In *Date in Society: Challenging Statistics in an Age of Globalisation*. Ed. Jeff Evans, Sally Ruane and Humphrey Southall. Bristol: Bristol University Press, 2019. 171–82.
Ruppert, Peter. *Reader in a Strange Land: The Activity of Reading Literary Utopias*. Athens: University of Georgia Press, 1986.
Rundle, James. "Interview: Iain M. Banks." *SciFiNow* (2010). <https://www.scifinow.co.uk/news/interview-iain-m-banks/> accessed 5 August 2020.
Samuel, Raphael. "Mrs Thatcher's Return to Victorian Values." *Proceedings of the British Academy* 78 (1992): 9–29.
Sardar, Ziauddin. *Breaking the Monolith: Essays, Articles and Columns on Islam, India, Terror and Other Things That Annoy Me*. Gurgaon: ImprintOne, 2008.
Sargent, Lyman Tower. "The Three Faces of Utopianism Revisited." *Utopian Studies* 5, no. 1 (1994): 1–37.
Sauvagnargues, Anne. *Artmachines: Deleuze, Guattari, Simondon*. Trans. Suzanne Verderber and Eugene W. Holland. Edinburgh: Edinburgh University Press, 2016.
Sawyer, Tom. "Space Opera." In *The Routledge Companion to Science Fiction*. Ed. Mark Bould et al. London: Routledge, 2009. 505–9.
Schelling, Thomas C. *Arms and Influence*. New Haven: Yale University Press, 1966.
Scholz, Christina. "Quantum fiction! – M. John Harrison's Empty Space Trilogy and Weird Theory." *Textual Practice* 31, no. 6 (2017): 1149–63.

Segal, Lynne. "Theoretical Afflictions: Poor Rich White Folks Play the Blues." *New Formations* 50, no. 1 (2003): 142–56.

Seldon, Anthony. "Consensus: A Debate Too Long?" *Parliamentary Affairs* 47, no. 4 (1994): 501–14.

Shanghai Duke Book Co., Ltd. *IPO Prospectus (Updated)*. China Securities Regulatory Commission (2021). <http://www.csrc.gov.cn/pub/newsite/fxjgb/cybzczl/zcsqwj/202009/P020210608679737185635.pdf> accessed 5 July 202.

Shaviro, Steven. "Capitalist Monsters." *Historical Materialism* 10, no. 4 (2002): 281–90.

——. *Connected, or What It Means to Live in the Network Society*. Minneapolis: University of Minnesota Press, 2003.

Shi Tong. "Kehuan zuopin zhongde jingshen wuran ye ying qingli" (《科幻作品中的精神污染也应清理》; "The Spiritual Pollution in SF should also be Eliminated"). *People's Daily*, 5 November 1983. <http://www.laoziliao.net/rmrb/1983-11-05-3#641728> accessed 2 May 2022.

Simmel, Georg. *The Philosophy of Money*, 3rd Enlarged edn. Ed. David Frisby. London: Routledge, 2004.

Sivanandan, Ambalavaner. "All That Melts into Air Is Solid: The Hokum of New Times." *Race and Class* 31, no. 3 (1989): 1–30.

Sleeboom-Faulkner, Margaret. *The Chinese Academy of Social Sciences (CASS): Shaping the Reforms, Academia and China (1977–2003)*. Leiden: Brill, 2007.

Sloterdijk, Peter. *In the World Interior of Capital: For a Philosophical Theory of Globalisation*. Trans. Wieland Hoban. Cambridge: Polity Press, 2013.

Snow, Edgar. *Red Star over China: The Classic Account of the Birth of Chinese Communism*. New York: Grove, 1968.

Solinger, Dorothy J. "The Creation of a New Underclass in China and Its Implications." *Environment & Urbanization* 18, no. 1 (2006): 177–93.

Song Ligang. "State and Non-state Enterprises in China's Economic Transition." In *Routledge Handbook of the Chinese Economy*. Ed. Gregory C. Chow and Dwight H. Perkins. New York: Routledge, 2015. 182–207.

——. "State-Owned Enterprise Reform in China: Past, Present and Prospects." In *China's 40 Years of Reform and Development: 1978–2018*. Ed. Ross Garnaut, Ligang Song and Cai Fang. Acton, ACT: ANU Press, 2018. 345–74.

Song Mingwei. "After 1989: The New Wave of Chinese Science Fiction." *China Perspectives* 101, no. 1 (2015): 7–13.

——. *Fear of Seeing: A Poetics of Chinese Science Fiction*. New York: Columbia University Press, 2023.

——. "Liu Cixin's Three-Body Trilogy: Between the Sublime Cosmos and the Micro Era." In *Lingua Cosmica: Science Fiction from around the World*. Ed. Dale Knickerbocker. Champaign: University of Illinois Press, 2018. 107–28.

——. "Representations of the Invisible: Chinese Science Fiction in the Twenty-First Century." In *The Oxford Handbook for Modern Chinese Literatures*. Ed. Carlos Rojas and Andrea Bachner. Oxford: Oxford University Press, 2016. 546–65.

——. "The Worlding of Chinese Science Fiction: A Global Genre and Its Negotiations as World Literature." In *The Making of Chinese-Sinophone Literatures as World Literature*. Ed. Kuei-fen Chiu and Yingjin Zhang. Hong Kong: HKU Press, 2022. 122–41.

——. "Variations on Utopia in Contemporary Chinese Science Fiction." *Science Fiction Studies* 40, no. 1 (2013): 86–102.

Standing, Guy. "The Precariat: From Denizens to Citizens?" *Polity* 44, no. 4 (2012): 588–608.

Stanish, Deborah. "Interview: Hao Jingfang." *Uncanny Magazine*, January to February 2015. <http://uncannymagazine.com/article/interview-hao-jingfang/> accessed 11 December 2020.

Struck, Bernhard, et al. "Introduction: Space and Scale in Transnational History." *The International History Review* 33, no. 4 (2011): 573–84.

Sun Mengtian. "Alien Encounters in Liu Cixin's *The Three Body Trilogy* and Arthur C. Clarke's *Childhood's End*." *Frontiers of Literary Studies in China* 12, no. 4 (2018): 610–44.

——. "Imagining Globalization in Paolo Bacigalupi's *The Windup Girl* and Chen Qiufan's *The Waste Tide*." *Science Fiction Studies* 46, no. 2 (2019): 289–306.

Suvin, Darko. *Metamorphoses of Science Fiction: On the Poetics and History of a Literary Genre*. New Haven: Yale University Press, 1979.

Tao, Ran. "Hukou Reform and Social Security for Migrant Workers in China." In *Labour Migration and Social Development in Contemporary China*. Ed. Rachel Murphy. London: Routledge, 2010. 73–95.

Tapscott, Don, and Anthony D. Williams. *Wikinomics: How Mass Collaboration Changes Everything*. New York: Portfolio, 2006.

Tatsumi, Takayuki. "Japanese and Asian Science Fiction." In *A Companion to Science Fiction*. Ed. David Seed. Oxford: Blackwell Publishing, 2005. 323–36.

Tew, Philip et al. "Critical Introduction: Recovering the 1990s." In *The 1990s: A Decade of Contemporary British Fiction*. Ed. Nick Hubble et al. London: Bloomsbury Academic, 2015. 1–34.

Thatcher, Margaret. "Interview for Woman's Own ('no such thing as society')." Interview, No. 10 Downing Street, 23rd September 1987. <https://www.margaretthatcher.org/document/106689> accessed 6 May 2020.

——. "Speech to 1922 Committee ('the enemy within')." Speech delivered to House of Commons, London, 14 July 1984. <https://www.margaretthatcher.org/document/105563> accessed 15 April 2020.

——. "Speech to Conservative Central Council." Speech delivered at Pavilion Gardens, Buxton, 19 March 1988. <https://www.margaretthatcher.org/document/107200> accessed 28 December 2021.

——. *The Downing Street Years*. London: Harper Collins, 1993.

Thompson, David. *England in the Twentieth Century, 1914–63*. Baltimore: Penguin Books, 1965.

Three-Body Community. "The Watcher of Human Civilization: A Brief Discussion on Zhang Beihai in the *Three Body* trilogy." 2017. <https://www.acfun.cn/a/ac3451472?from=video> accessed 6 July 2021.

Tidar, Lavie. "Science Fiction, Globalization, and the People's Republic of China." *Foundation* 89 (2003): 93–99.

Tomlinson, Jim. "Tale of a Death Exaggerated: How Keynesian Policies Survived the 1970s." *Contemporary British History* 21, no. 4 (2007): 429–48.

Tong, Enzheng. "Tantan wo dui kexue wenyi de renshi" (《谈谈我对科学文艺的认识》, "On My Understandings of Science Art and Literature"). *Renmin wenxue* 6 (1979): 110.

Tsu, Jing. *Failure, Nationalism, and Literature: The Making of Modern Chinese Identity, 1895–1937*. Stanford: Stanford University Press, 2005.

Tu Hang. "Anticipatory Utopia and Redemptive Utopia in Postrevolutionary China." In *Utopia and Utopianism in the Contemporary Chinese Context: Texts, Ideas, Spaces*. Ed. David Der-wei Wang, Angela Ki Che Leung and Zhang Yinde. Hong Kong: Hong Kong University Press, 2020. 99–114.

Tuan Yi-Fu. "Place: An Experiential Perspective." *Geographical Review* 65, no. 2 (1975): 151–65.

Urry, John. "The End of Organised Capitalism." In *New Times: The Changing Face of Politics in the 1990s*. Ed. Stuart Hall and Martin Jacques. London: Lawrence and Wishart, 1989. 94–103.

van Elteren, Mel. "U.S. Cultural Imperialism Today: Only a Chimera?" *SAIS Review* 23, no. 2 (2003): 169–88.

van Schaik, Sam. *The Spirit of Zen*. New Haven: Yale University Press, 2019.

Vertovec, Steven. "Super-diversity and Its Implications." *Ethnic and Racial Studies* 30, no. 6 (2007): 1024–54.

Vinen, Richard. *Thatcher's Britain: The Politics and Social Upheavals of the 1980s*. London: Pocket Books, 2009.

Vint, Sherryl. *Bodies of Tomorrow: Technology, Subjectivity, Science Fiction*. Toronto: University of Toronto Press, 2013.

——. "Cultural Imperialism and the Ends of Empire: Iain M. Banks's 'Look to Windward.'" *Journal of the Fantastic in the Arts* 18, no. 1 (2007): 83–98.

——. "From the New Wave into the Twenty-First Century." In *Science Fiction: A Literary History*. Ed. Roger Luckhurst. London: British Library, 2017. 181–208.

Walder, Andrew. "Organized Dependency and Cultures of Authority in Chinese Industry." *Journal of Asian Studies* 43, no. 1 (1983): 51–76.

Wang Ban. "Conclusion: In the Beginning Is the Word: Popular Democracy and Mao's Little Red Book." In *Mao's Little Red Book: A Global History*. Ed. Alexander C. Cook. Cambridge: Cambridge University Press, 2014. 266–77.

Wang, David Der-wei. "Introduction: Worlding Literary China." *A New Literary History of Modern China*. Ed. David Der-wei Wang. Cambridge, MA: Harvard University Press, 2017. 1–28.

Wang Hui. *China's New Order: Society, Politics, and Economy in Transition*. Ed. Theodore Huters. Cambridge: Harvard University Press, 2003.

Wang Meng. "Renwen jingshen wenti ougan" (《人文精神问题偶感》, "Random Thoughts on Questions Concerning Humanistic Spirit"). *Renwen jingshen xunsilu* (《人文精神寻思录》, *In Search of Humanist Spirit*). Shanghai: Wenhui chubanshe, 1996. 106–19.

Wang Wenhua. *Qian Xuesen shilu* (《钱学森实录》, *Chronology of Qian Xuesen*). Chengdu: Sichuan wenyi chubanshe, 2001.

Wang Xiaoming. "Kuangye shang de feixu: Wenxue he renwen jingshen de weiji" (《旷野上的废墟——文学和人文精神的危机》, "Ruins in the Wilderness: The Crisis of Literature and Humanist Spirit"). *Shanghai wenxue* 6 (1993): 63–70.

Wang Yao. *Weilai de zuobiao: Quanqiuhua shidai de zhongguo kehuan lunji* (《未来的坐标：全球化时代的中国科幻论集》, *Coordinate of Future: Chinese Science Fiction in the Time of Globalisation*). Shanghai: Shanghai wenyi chubanshe, 2019.

Wasserstrom, Jeffrey N. *China in the 21st Century: What Everyone Needs to Know*. Oxford: Oxford University Press, 2010.

Wegner, Phillip E. "Ken MacLeod's Permanent Revolution: Utopian Possible Worlds, History and the *Augenblick* in the *Fall Revolution* Quartet." In *Red Planet: Marxism and Science Fiction*. Ed. Mark Bould and China Miéville. London: Pluto Press, 2009. 137–55.

Wessendorf, Susanne. "'Being Open, But Sometimes Closed': Conviviality in a Super-diverse London Neighbourhood." *European Journal of Cultural Studies* 17, no. 4 (2014): 392–405.

White, Jerry. *London in the Twentieth Century: A City and Its People*. London: Penguin, 2001.

Williams, Rhys, and Mark Bould. Eds. *M. John Harrison: Critical Essays*. Canterbury: Gylphi, 2019.

Winter, Jerome. "'Moments in the Fall': Neoliberal Globalism and Utopian Anarcho-Socialist Desire in Ken MacLeod's Fall Revolution Quartet and Iain M. Banks's Culture Series." *Extrapolation* 55, no. 3 (2014): 323–48.

——. *Science Fiction, New Space Opera, and Neoliberal Globalism: Nostalgia for Infinity*. Cardiff: University of Wales Press, 2016.
——. "Turbulent Years Ahead: An Interview with Ken MacLeod." *Los Angeles Review of Books*, 24 February 2014. <https://lareviewofbooks.org/article/turbulent-years-ahead-interview-ken-macleod/> accessed 5 August 2020.
Wood, Robert. "'Extravagant Secular Swarming': Space and Subjectivity in China Miéville's *Perdido Street Station*." *Critique: Studies in Contemporary Fiction* 59, no. 1 (2018): 75–89.
Wright, Richard, et al. "Reconsidering Both Diversity and Segregation: A Reply to Poulsen, Johnston and Forrest, and to Peach." *Journal of Ethnic and Migration Studies* 37, no. 1 (2011): 167–76.
Wu Dingbo. "Looking Backward: An Introduction to Chinese Science Fiction." In *Science Fiction from China*. Ed. Wu Dingbo and Patrick D. Murphy. London: Praeger, 1989. xi–xli.
Wu Yan. Ed. *20 shiji zhongguo kehuan xiaoshuo shi* (《20世纪中国科幻小说史》, *The History of 20th Century Chinese Science Fiction*). Beijing: Peking University Press, 2022.
Wu Yan et al. "A Very Brief History of Chinese Science Fiction." *Chinese Literature Today* 7, no. 1 (2018): 44–53.
Xiong, Christine. "Rethinking the Cyborg in Chen Qiufan's *Waste Tide*." *Foundation* 139 (2021): 75–89.
Xu Jilin. "Contradictions within Enlightenment Ideas." In *Culture and Social Transformations in Reform Era China*. Ed. Cao Tianyu, Zhong Xueping and Liao Kebin. Leiden: Brill, 2010, 197–234.
Xu Youyu. "The Debates between Liberalism and the New Left in China Since the 1990s." *Contemporary Chinese Thought* 34, no. 3 (2003): 6–17.
Yan Feng. "Chuangshi yu mieji: Liu Cixin de yuzhou shixue" (《创世与灭寂——刘慈欣的宇宙诗学》, "Genesis and Apocalypse: the Cosmic Poetics of Liu Cixin"). *Nanfang wentan* 5 (2011): 73–7.
——. "Ping Liu Cixin, Jiang Xiaoyuan duitan" (《评刘慈欣、江晓原对谈》"Comments on the Conversation between Liu Cixin and Jiang Xiaoyuan"). *Xinmin weekly* 45 (2007). <https://web.archive.org/web/20210517223111/https://shc2000.sjtu.edu.cn/0711/chaisbs.htm> accessed 23 August 2024.
Yan Yunxiang. "Introduction: Conflicting Images of the Individual and Contested Process of Individualization." In *iChina: The Rise of the Individual in Modern Chinese Society*. Ed. Mette Halskov Hansen and Rune Svarverud. Copenhagen: NIAS Press, 2010. 1–38.
Ye Yonglie. "Han Suyin guanhuai 'Hui guniang'" (《韩素音关怀"灰姑娘"》, "Han Suyin's Consideration of 'Cinderella'"). *People's Daily*, 11 December 1987.

Zhang Haitao. "20 shiji 80 niandai zhongguo de xinqimeng yundong ji qi zhongduan de wenxue houguo" (《20世纪80年代中国的新启蒙运动及其中断的文学后果》, "China's New Enlightenment in the 1980s and the Literary Consequence of its Interruption"). *Social Scientist* 145 (2009): 30–3.

Zhang Longxi. "The Myth of the Other: China in the Eyes of the West." *Critical Inquiry* 15, no. 1 (1988): 108–31.

Zhang Xudong. *Postsocialism and Cultural Politics: China in the Last Decade of the Twentieth Century.* Durham: Duke University Press, 2008.

Zhang Yiwu. "Xinzhuangtai de jueqi" (《"新状态"的崛起》, "The Emergence of 'the New State of Affairs': New Possibilities for Chinese Fiction"). *Zhongshan* 92 (1994): 115–17.

Zhang Zhizhong. "Renwen Jingshen er bian" (《人文精神二辩》, "Second Debate of Humanist Spirit"). *Renwen Jingshen xunsilu* (《人文精神寻思录》, *In Search of Humanist Spirit*). Shanghai: Wenhui chubanshe, 1996. 172–80.

Zhou Yang. "Guanyu makesi zhuyi de jigelLilun wenti de tantao" (《关于马克思主义的几个理论问题的探讨》, "On some Theoretical Notions about Marxism"). *People's Daily*, 16 March 1983. <http://www.laoziliao.net/rmrb/1983-03-16-4#620743> accessed 2 May 2022.

Žižek, Slavoj. "Have Michael Hardt and Antonio Negri Rewritten the *Communist Manifesto* for the Twenty-First Century?" *Rethinking Marxism* 13, no. 3–4 (2001): 190–98.

——. *The Universal Exception: Selected Writing,* vol. 2. London: Continuum, 2006.

Index

WORLD SCIENCE FICTION STUDIES

SERIES EDITORS:

Professor Sonja Fritzsche, Michigan State University
Professor Gerry Canavan, Marquette University

World Science Fiction Studies understands science fiction to be an inherently global phenomenon. Proposals are invited for monographs and edited collections that celebrate the tremendous reach of a genre that continues to be interpreted and transformed by a variety of cultures and linguistic communities around the world. The series embraces this global vision of the genre but also supports the articulation of each community's unique approach to the challenges of science, technology and society. The series encourages the use of contemporary theoretical approaches (e.g. postcolonialism, posthumanism, feminisms, ecocriticism) as well as engagement with positionalities understood through critical race and ethnicity studies, gender studies, queer theory, disability studies, class analysis, and beyond. Interdisciplinary work and research on any media (e.g. print, film, television, visual arts, video games, new media) is welcome. The language of the series is English.

Iva Polak
Futuristic Worlds in Australian Aboriginal Fiction
2017. ISBN 978-1-78707-200-8

Anindita Banerjee and Sonja Fritzsche (eds)
Science Fiction Circuits of the South and East
2018. ISBN 978-1-78707-593-1

Lyu Guangzhao
The Boom & The Boom: Historical Rupture and Political Economy in Contemporary British and Chinese Science Fiction
2024. ISBN 978-1-80374-232-8

www.ingramcontent.com/pod-product-compliance
Ingram Content Group UK Ltd.
Pitfield, Milton Keynes, MK11 3LW, UK
UKHW020127290926
15471UKWH00003B/330

9 781803 742328